Kansas City and How It Grew, 1822–2011

KANSAS CITY
and How It Grew, 1822–2011

JAMES R. SHORTRIDGE

 UNIVERSITY PRESS OF KANSAS

© 2012 by the University Press of Kansas

Published by the University Press of Kansas (Lawrence, Kansas
66045), which was organized by the Kansas Board of Regents and
is operated and funded by Emporia State University, Fort Hays
State University, Kansas State University, Pittsburg State University,
the University of Kansas, and Wichita State University

Library of Congress Cataloging-in-Publication Data

Shortridge, James R., 1944–
  Kansas City and how it grew, 1822–2011 / James R. Shortridge.
    p. cm.
  Includes bibliographical references and index.
  ISBN 978-0-7006-1882-8 (cloth : acid-free paper) 1. Kansas City
(Mo.)—History. 2. Kansas City (Mo.)—Maps. I. Title.
  F474.K257S54 2012
  977.8'411—dc23
                              2012024108

British Library Cataloguing-in-Publication Data is available.

Printed in the United States of America

10 9 8 7 6 5 4 3

The paper used in this publication is recycled and contains 10 percent postconsumer waste. It is acid free and meets the minimum
requirements of the American National Standard for Permanence
of Paper for Printed Library Materials Z39.48–1992.

For Barbara,
who told me to write about home

Contents

Illustrations

Drawings and Photographs

Preface

Geographers write about places. This simple definition goes back millennia, but professionals in the field now regularly set it aside to pursue fashionable social theory. Social theory certainly is worthy of study, and its application has improved our understanding of place itself. I worry, though, that over-theorization has diverted us too much from our central task. When I travel, I look for books that will help me understand the city or region I will be visiting. The choices usually are either a detailed political history that nearly ignores the local landscape or a coffee-table book of photographs that provides beauty without understanding. I view such situations as geographers' abdication of their responsibility. This book is an attempt to turn the tide.

My research began eight years ago when I completed *Cities on the Plains*, a history of the urban system in Kansas. Although that Plains volume was comparative in tone, all the cities I was studying operated in the shadow of Greater Kansas City. Thoughts about the growth and function of this urban center gradually came to intrigue me. Then, subconsciously, they began to fuse with aspects of personal and family experience that I never had considered seriously before. I was born in Kansas City. More important, I grew up 30 miles southeast of there and now have lived 30 miles to the west for over four decades. For better or worse, Kansas City was the standard on which I judged all cities.

The personal connection actually is stronger than this. Samuel Shortridge, my direct paternal ancestor, migrated from Kentucky to rural Independence in 1839. One of his sons-in-law served as sheriff of Jackson County in the 1840s and 1850s, and another freighted on the Santa Fe Trail. More recently, my grandfather and father both graduated from the Kansas City College of Pharmacy; a great-uncle ran a drayage business in the West Bottoms; an uncle drove a Manor Bread route in Wyandotte County; and my mother worked as an executive secretary for Trans World Airlines. Today, one of my daughters lives in Leawood, and her children form the eighth generation of Shortridges in the area. As I have visited with them and watched the city make its way east to my old hometown of Pleasant Hill and west to my current home in Lawrence, I realized that its aura envelops me still. I wanted to know Kansas City better.

Any writer owes debts to many people. My biggest is perhaps to the anonymous compilers at the Union Historical Company, whose 1881 *History of Jackson County, Missouri,* contains a wealth of data on the early city. The more recent scholars A. Theodore Brown, Charles N. Glaab, Kevin F. Gotham, Susan D. Greenbaum, Sherry L. Schirmer, William H. Wilson, and William S. Worley have made my task much easier. So have five of my students who wrote theses on Kansas City subjects: Nathan W. Brinson on the Wyandotte County revival, Jennifer A. Claybrook on exurban Piper, Thomas Hornbeck on the expansion of Catholic churches, Joseph T. Manzo on Strawberry Hill, and Jason M. Woods on the jazz district. For recent decades, reporters at the *Kansas City Star* have been invaluable. The list here is long, but the works of Arthur S. Brisbane, Kevin Collison, Monroe Dodd (another former student), Lynn Horsley, Jeffrey Spivak, and Mark Wiebe stand out.

Conversation and map browsing also have helped me to understand the city. For the former, my primary debts are to my family, especially Robert and Barbara Shortridge and Amy Shortridge McCarthy. For the latter, the Kansas City (Missouri) Public Library and the Western Historical Manuscript Collection at the University of Missouri–Kansas City were invaluable. I especially made use of the library's digital collection of historical Sanborn Fire Insurance maps. Maps constitute an important part of this book as well, clarifying and enhancing my text. Darin Grauberger and Lauren James of the Cartographic Service at the University of Kansas were mainstays here, creating quality finished products from my pencil sketches.

Finally, I want to acknowledge the broader-based support of Barbara Shortridge, my companion for forty-five years, and the University of Kansas, my employer for forty-one. Barbara inspired the project and critically edited the entire manuscript. Sabbatical leave from the university allowed a first, deep immersion into the writing process in 2008. A Higuchi-Endowment Association Award helped fund the costs of indexing, map production, and photograph acquisition.

1 Introduction

Descriptions of Kansas City invariably concentrate on a small set of landscapes and images. An extensive boulevard system punctuated by statuary and fountains comes quickly to mind. So do barbecue and Chiefs football. When local people consider residential splendor, their vision is Mission Hills and adjacent Ward Parkway. When they hear the phrase *Kansas City, Kansas,* they focus on industrial parks and working-class homes. The list is varied but well defined—Union Station as a monument to past glories, Lee's Summit and Overland Park as demonstrations of middle-class success, and Prospect Avenue as a corridor of African American poverty. At another scale, nearly everybody identifies the metropolitan area as the heart of America.

The practice of linking cities with stereotypic sites and themes is commonplace and easily understood. Residents and outsiders alike need generalizations if they are to make sense of a complex world. The process is as true for Kabul, Kiev, Knoxville, and Kyoto as it is for Kansas City. My concern in this book is not the existence of such imagery. Instead, I ask how this particular set of symbols and landscape identifications emerged for Kansas City.

People sometimes assume that a city's icons are inevitable and enduring. They are not. Consider, for example, how Kansas City residents of a century ago viewed their community. Their judgments included almost nothing about fountains or football, Mission Hills or Lee's Summit. Instead, they felt deeply about places now on our mental peripheries: the West Bottoms (or Central Industrial District) that straddles the state line near the mouth of the Kansas River; the city market

area squeezed between Interstate 70 and the Missouri River; and Minnesota Avenue in downtown Kansas City, Kansas. These three locations were then the economic core for the entire metropolitan region. The West Bottoms housed Kansas City's signature meatpacking industry and the union railroad depot; the market area featured an elaborate city hall and Minnesota Avenue a series of busy department stores.

What caused some urban districts to sprout mansions and others slums? Why has almost no part of the city maintained a single role for all or even most of its urban existence? These are basic questions I want to address. They are part of a larger quest to explain how Kansas City has come to look and function the way it does and to be perceived the way it is.

This book examines Kansas City's changing geography in straightforward, chronological fashion. Within this framework, I look at local responses to the universal economic pressures that mold urban structure. I also explore circumstances that are specific to this community. Among the former issues are reorientations inherent in changing the transportation focus from rivers to railroads and then again from railroads to superhighways and international airports. Other obvious themes in this vein are the parallel processes of suburbanization and the restructuring of older areas.

Conditions that make Kansas City unique include regional economics and time of settlement. With no minerals of consequence in the area, the city obviously could not become a major steel center. In contrast, proximity to Great Plains ranches and farms fostered early and sustained success for meatpackers and flour millers. Centrality within the country has similarly aided wholesaling activity. Kansas City's first economic boom, in the 1870s and 1880s, came after the German immigration to the United States had passed its crest. The community's ethnic population therefore has tended more toward later-arriving Croatians and Italians plus African Americans who moved north after Reconstruction and Mexicans who followed the Santa Fe railroad northeast to jobs in that company's switching yards and repair shops. Timing also was critical to the city having an extensive boulevard and park system. Enthusiasm for parks was high nationwide circa 1900, but Kansas City leaders supported their construction with special enthusiasm as part of an effort to transform the community's image beyond that of cow town.

Within the economic restrictions of their time, individual entrepreneurs made decisions that also have contributed greatly to city form and image. Without the period of selective law enforcement under political boss Thomas Pendergast, Kansas City would not enjoy its legacy of jazz. Without the gift of Thomas Swope's namesake park in 1896, upscale residential expansion likely would have gone east instead of south. And without J. C. Nichols, Johnson County suburbs would surely have developed in a far less spectacular manner. Failed ideas are important, too, as reminders of what might have been. Financier Willard Winner, to cite one example, envisioned major developments for Independence and what is now North Kansas City before going broke in the city's economic depression of the 1890s. A plan from the 1910s called for construction of a new city hall and other major civic buildings near the just-completed Union Station at the intersection of Main and Twenty-second streets. Had this municipal complex been erected, it likely would have drawn the central business district south to its vicinity. In turn, J. C. Nichols might have reconsidered construction of his Country Club Plaza only 3 miles away on Forty-seventh Street, and other domino effects would have followed. The more a person studies the past, in fact, the less the urban form of Kansas City (or anywhere else) seems even slightly preordained.

Finally, anybody who spends time in Kansas City learns that basic physical geography and political geography are critical elements in how the community looks and functions. Think about topography, for instance. The town's site at the junction of the Kansas and Missouri rivers was essential to early economic success, but the valleys of these rivers (aligned as a letter Y lying on its left side) have divided the modern metropolitan area into three natural regions. The largest includes the original townsite and extends south from the two

streams. A nearly equivalent land area stretches north of the Missouri River, and a much smaller wedge lies between the two streams. Bridges connect these districts, of course, but they do so imperfectly, and therefore, isolation is inevitable. Isolation, in turn, leads to differences in culture and development. Physical division actually is more than tripartite. Tributary valleys subdivide each of the major territories, and the two big rivers have produced extensive bottomlands on their inside bends, several hundred feet lower than the surrounding bluffs.

To its varied physical landscape, Kansas City also adds a state boundary that bisects the community along a section of the Missouri River and then south from the Kansas River junction. Seemingly innocuous in comparison to the obvious influence of landforms, this political border arguably has affected local urban geography even more. Thus, Euro-American settlers occupied the Missouri section a generation before they did the Kansas one, and some of these Missourians then created Kansas City, Kansas, as a site for heavy industry and immigrant workers that would be near (but not too near) their own upscale residences. More recently, this sociopolitical situation has reversed itself. Kansas suburbs in Johnson County now provide a convenient haven for affluent area citizens who do not care to confront issues of racial segregation in the larger Missouri city. By tending to focus attention only on one side of this political border or the other, local historians have missed much of the contrast across it. Kansas City is best understood as a complete metropolitan unit.

The Land at the River's Bend

Builders of a new housing subdivision would never want their acreage bisected by a state line or major river valley. Such features would be obvious diseconomies, sources of increased costs and inconvenience for future residents. One might assume that a similar logic of avoidance applied 150 or 200 years ago to city founders on the midwestern frontier. The case of Indianapolis at the virtual center of its state would support this thinking. So would Columbus (Ohio), Des Moines (Iowa), Lansing (Michigan), Madison (Wisconsin), and Springfield (Illinois). But these six are exceptional cities, conceived to be political centers without major economic activity. Creators of industrial metropolises followed a different line of reasoning. They wanted sites along major waterways because of transportation advantages. Legislators often identified these same rivers and lakes as convenient political boundaries, but such decisions annoyed entrepreneurs only slightly.

Actually, location at a political border could sometimes be a plus. During a city's early years, for example, the land to the west might still be a frontier with restrictions on settlement. Local businesspeople could therefore enrich themselves by developing a transportation and trade network throughout this region that was focused on themselves. Such connections could ensure business success far into the future.

The look of Kansas City begins with its rocks, a series of limestones and shales that accumulated some 300 million years ago on the floor of an oceanic basin. The shales, formed from muds that washed into this ocean, are soft and easily eroded. Limestones, in contrast, come from shells of various marine animals and are relatively hard. If these alternating layers had been unmodified since their origin, we would experience perfectly flat terrain in Mid-America. A particular limestone or shale would blanket the entire surface, with the others buried beneath it. Reality is not this simple. Although the rock layers appear horizontal to the eye, they actually tilt slightly. This distortion, minor but important, was caused when a bubble of magma intruded beneath what is now the Ozarks. This bubble pushed overlying rocks upward into the shape of a broad dome. Then, as erosion took place over subsequent geologic eras, younger rocks at and near the top of the dome were gradually washed away. The process has left today's surface rocks, when mapped, arranged in a pattern of concentric circles. Older rocks appear at the center, younger ones at the edge. Kansas City lies on the northwestern flank of this gigantic dartboard.

Rock layers in the metropolitan area dip to the northwest at the rate of about 10 feet per mile. A particular formation exposed at the surface near Lone Jack at the southeastern edge of the metropolitan area would therefore be buried 500 feet deep at Lansing in the northwest. Increasingly, younger rocks outcrop as one travels in this same southeast-to-northwest

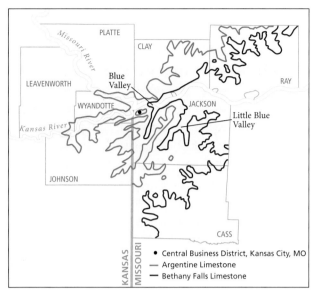

Map 1. Outcrop Bands of the Bethany Falls and Argentine Limestones. Compiled from multiple sources.

direction, arranged like a deck of cards spread across a table (diagram 1). This means that the local landscape displays many distinct rock formations. Two of these hold special visual and economic significance. The older is a 20-foot-thick limestone known as Bethany Falls, which forms a prominent, ragged escarpment across eastern Jackson County and is exposed farther west in the valleys of the Little Blue and Blue rivers (map 1). Its bluffs along these latter streams contribute greatly to the beauty of Swope Park and Longview Lake. Historically, the solid upper surface of the Bethany Falls constituted Kansas City's original wharf. Some 8 feet of debris now cover this quay at the foot of Main Street, but a sharp-eyed explorer can still find a section of it just west of Delaware Street.[1]

The city's second major limestone formation is called the Argentine. Resting some 140 feet above the level of the Bethany Falls and averaging 28 feet in thickness itself, Argentine bluffs are prominent throughout the older sections of both Kansas Cities. This rock underlies the downtown skyscrapers. It also forms the spectacular escarpments one sees at Quality Hill and along Cliff Drive; delineates the "ridge" in Blue Ridge Boulevard; and creates the varied terrain of Penn Valley, Wyandotte County Lake, and Shawnee Mission parks. The city's landmark Liberty Memorial stands upon Argentine limestone.

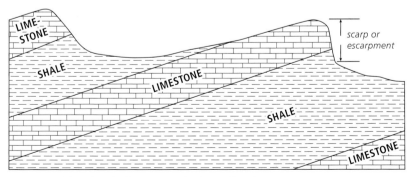

Diagram 1. Typical Rock Alignment in the Kansas City Area.

3

Both the Bethany Falls and the Argentine limestones have long furnished most of the gravel used in the area. More recently, they have become important for underground storage and manufacturing. At about twenty-five sites, some 3,000 people now work in commercial spaces carved into these bedrocks. The area encompasses over 16 million square feet. Kansas City is far and away the leader in such development, with at least 15 percent of the community's total warehouse capacity in this form. Park University in Platte County utilizes remodeled quarries in the Argentine stone for its library and computer laboratories, Brunson Instrument Company takes advantage of a vibration-free environment within the Bethany Falls for its manufacturing, and several huge storage companies use the space for food and other commodities.[2]

Conversions of mines into warehouses began about 1960. The two limestones themselves are thick, nearly flat, and overlain by waterproof shale. Their outcrops also are accessible to the city's existing railroad and highway system, especially in the valleys of the Kansas, Missouri, and Blue rivers. The advantages of underground operations are many, including major savings in rent (the space essentially is a by-product of mining), insurance (reduced danger of theft, fire, and tornadoes), and utilities (the temperature is naturally about 55 degrees). Air pumps for ventilation are the only significant added cost.

As soon as Kansas City's limestones and shales were tilted and uplifted, erosion began to modify their shape. Streams are important in this process, but some of the most striking changes are associated with glaciation. Four times over the last million years, gigantic ice sheets have been in or near this region, altering drainage patterns and other aspects of the landscape. Close observers of the Missouri River, for instance, notice that this valley is much wider downstream from Kansas City than it is above. The reason is that before glaciation, the downstream portion was an extension of the Kansas River basin, whereas the upstream part was either nonexistent or just a small tributary to the Kansas. Advancing ice apparently shifted the path of the preglacial Platte River far to the southwest, cutting what now is the channel of the Missouri River south from Omaha, Nebraska. Its new junction point with the Kansas River, of course, is today's Kansas City.[3]

Because of the glacial modification to its channel, the Missouri River changes direction abruptly in western Missouri. What is predominately a south-flowing stream in Iowa and Nebraska becomes an east-flowing one the rest of the way to St. Louis. Nineteenth-century eyes saw tremendous economic potential in this geometry. Trade goods bound for western and southwestern destinations in the United States could ascend the river to this great bend and then be transferred to wagons or other means of overland transportation. The bend, in other words, was destined to become an emporium. Army officials had grasped this implication in 1827 when they established Fort Leavenworth as the principal supply station for their western operations. City builders soon wanted to do the same. A typical account from a Kansas City newspaper in 1863 called this "elbow" region "the natural shipping point and trading center of a region of country as large as all New England, New York and Pennsylvania combined," a place destined to be "one of the best business centers upon the continent."[4]

A second, more localized example of an ice sheet forcing drainage to the south occurred on the preglacial Kansas River. Blockage near that stream's present-day mouth impounded waters until they overflowed the valley near today's Twenty-third Street Viaduct. The breach dumped a wall of water into Turkey Creek, a small tributary of the Missouri that flowed parallel with the main stream until joining it farther east between Kansas City and Independence (map 2). Glacial meltwater widened this lower portion of Turkey Creek to a half mile. Then, when the original blockage ended, the Kansas River resumed its former course, and Turkey Creek shortened its path by flowing straight north into the Kansas River through the glacial breach. These events left an abandoned channel 6.5 miles long that angles north and east through the big limestone beds. One end (now partially occupied by the diminutive OK Creek) is the modern intersection of Southwest Boulevard and Twenty-fifth Street. The other is near the old ARMCO Steel plant on Independence Avenue.

The importance of a lowland corridor through the heart of Kansas City, Missouri, might not be apparent to a generation of Americans raised to travel on interstate highways. But nineteenth-century railroad people quickly saw the promise. The Turkey Creek passageway combined with lowlands along the Kansas River to the west, the Missouri to the north, and the Blue to the east to make downtown Kansas City a commercial island that railroads could link efficiently to the outside world. People compared the situation favorably with New York's Manhattan Island and its great access to ships. When railroad and civic leaders relocated their major railroad depot to this old channel in 1914, Kansas City experienced some of its headiest commercial successes.

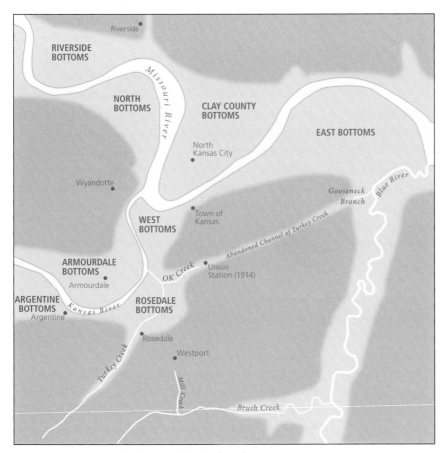

Map 2. River Bottoms, Bluff Lines, and Upland Surfaces.

Kansas River—the Armourdale Bottoms along the Union Pacific Railroad; the Argentine Bottoms along the Santa Fe tracks; and the Turkey Creek (or Rosedale) Bottoms near the Missouri, Kansas and Texas and the St. Louis and San Francisco railroads. Industrialization came later to the remaining, more isolated lowlands, much of it through initiatives sponsored by railroads. The Burlington company helped to create a new mercantile community called North Kansas City on the Clay County Bottoms in 1912. Union Pacific officials did much the same thing for eastern Wyandotte County in the early 1930s, transforming the North Bottoms into the highly praised Fairfax Industrial District.

The more that businesspeople located their railroads and factories in Kansas City's valleys, the more these strips became prominent regional boundaries within the community. The concentration of warehouses and smokestacks in the wide Clay County Bottoms, for example, discouraged construction of suburban housing for decades on the northern uplands now occupied by Gladstone and its neighboring communities. Similarly, the company town of North Kansas City on these same bottoms has always looked and felt quite different from the more heterogeneous Kansas City across the river to the south. Parallel partitions exist in Kansas. Argentine, Armourdale, and Rosedale on the bottoms were each separate towns originally, united by their industrial characters but divided by rivers. People in each also felt themselves distinct from residents of the older upland community founded as Wyandotte. Consolidating these independent cities into a single Kansas City, Kansas, was not an easy task. The job began in 1886 and was theoretically completed in 1922, but residents still see themselves as inhabiting separate social worlds.

Within the older Kansas City, Missouri, distinctiveness for the industrialized East Bottoms and West Bottoms has always been obvious. So has the effective barrier formed by the Blue River between the first city of Jackson County—Independence—and its upstart competitor to the west. Three smaller

City entrepreneurs saw river valleys with potential for industry as well as transportation. They liked the accessibility of sites along the Blue River but focused primary attention on what they called "big bottoms." These are graceful crescents of land that have formed inside the bends of the Kansas and Missouri rivers. The streams deposit silt there where the current is slack. Considered from the perspective of centuries rather than years, any given bottomland is temporary and prone to regular flooding as its river shifts the channel back and forth across the valley. Businesspeople in the nineteenth century largely ignored these sobering facts. They preferred to think instead about the large factories they could erect next to the railroads and to believe that a system of levees would protect their investment.

For the men who founded Kansas City in 1850, the two most important bottoms lay adjacent to their wharves at the river's edge. These they pragmatically named East Bottoms and West Bottoms (map 2). Then, as railroads made the state of Kansas the city's most lucrative trade area, industrial priorities trended in that same direction. The West Bottoms developed first, followed by three lowlands farther upstream on the valleys became important as the city expanded to the south. First, the abandoned channel of Turkey Creek came to separate the city's business district to the north from its principal residential zone to the south. Later, a parallel valley called Brush Creek near Forty-seventh Street did much the same between middle-class and upper-class housing. The positioning of the Country Club Plaza shopping center there accentuates this demarcation. Finally, the upper portion of Turkey Creek that leads southwest from the city became a popular route for railroads and highways. Interstate 35 follows this valley today. In all these ways, the significance of the old river lines as cultural divides remains strong on the modern landscape. The exact nature of this differentiation has changed greatly over the decades, to be sure, but the boundaries themselves would be familiar to any resident past or present.

Connections between modern Kansas City and the great ice sheets of the distant past do not end with the river system. The glaciers indirectly added new soil deposits to parts of the upland. This fact sounds insignificant but is not. As area streams carried away glacial meltwater, their channels became clogged with silts and clays. Winds picked up some of this debris and carried it to adjacent bluffs, where it routinely accumulated to heights of 40 feet and occasionally to 100 feet

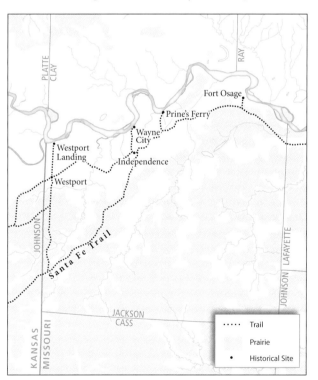

Map 3. *Presettlement Prairie and Early Trails. Modified from a map in Walter A. Schroeder, "The Presettlement Prairie in the Kansas City Region,"* Missouri Prairie Journal *7 (December 1985): 4.*

or more. These impressive totals are restricted to the immediate vicinity of the streams, however, and are greater along the Missouri River than along the Kansas.[5]

Wind-deposited soils are able to stand high in vertical cliffs without collapsing, and the ones in Kansas City have a distinctive, yellow-brown color. Yet what caught the attention of early town planners was their location. People fully realized the trade potential for a new city at the river junction, but they were frustrated at the possibilities for placement. A successful site needed to be above the floodplain, but the only upland available was capped by the highest of these nearly vertical bluffs, rising 120 feet. Goods could be unloaded from riverboats easily at this point, but moving heavily laden wagons over palisades that stood within a block of the water was another matter indeed. In fact, these cliffs were forbidding enough to delay Kansas City's founding for at least twenty years and to produce several rival communities. Thus, Independence arose to the east, Parkville to the northwest, and Westport to the south. Another important but nearly forgotten segment of Kansas City history concerns the cutting of roads through these bluffs and then, gradually, their complete removal down to bedrock. Employment for these tasks attracted many Irish immigrants to the community.[6]

A final element of physical geography with significant but underappreciated influence on local urban development is natural vegetation, specifically the location of presettlement prairies. Every pioneer group used native grasslands, but this resource was especially critical in western Missouri because of the area's vital overland trade with Santa Fe, Colorado, and other parts of the West. Such business required thousands of oxen, mules, and horses, and these animals spent considerable time in local pastures recovering from trips, waiting for new groups to gather, and simply wintering over.

We know that rangeland was scarce in the southern portion of Clay and Platte counties from reports of land surveyors during the 1820s and 1830s. The same was true for northwestern Jackson County south to the vicinity of what is now Fifty-third Street (map 3). Grass predominated elsewhere, however, particularly in the eastern and southern sections of this county. The key prairie for early traders formed a peninsula atop the divide between the Blue and Little Blue rivers. This grass helped entrepreneurs at Independence (near the prairie's northern end) to control the Santa Fe trade from the late 1820s to the middle 1830s.[7]

A second wedge of prairie, this one west of the Blue River and extending on to the aptly named Prairie Village and

Overland Park of today, gave the founders of Westport, Missouri, confidence that they might steal the Santa Fe business from Independence. Their chance came when farmers began to plow the grasses along the traditional route and freighters began to eye untapped prairie to the west. This change required a new Westport Landing on the Missouri River, of course, and also a pathway south from Westport to the pastures. This route is today's Wornall Road. To retain their lucrative business as long as possible, the larger traders also purchased big tracts of grass ahead of the farmers. One investor was Alexander Majors, whose 1856 house still stands at 8145 State Line Road. Another was David Waldo, whose name is applied to the modern neighborhood centered at Seventy-fifth Street and Wornall.

Political Lines

Visitors to St. Louis or Cincinnati are not surprised to find these metropolitan areas split by a state line. Both cities straddle major rivers, and such streams are traditional political divides. Kansas City is different. Newcomers are amazed that much of the Kansas-Missouri boundary is marked not by sandbars or channel buoys but by the pleasant State Line Road. Why, they wonder, would this urban area be bifurcated politically when the situation easily could have been avoided?

The boundary question is key because this line's presence has long frustrated needed development. Modern planners, for instance, have bemoaned the difficulties of building support for a regionwide performing arts center or a new stadium for the Chiefs or Royals. If such a structure were to be placed on the Missouri side of the border, should Kansas residents share in the costs? How easy might it be to implement a bistate tax initiative? How often would such a measure pass? Petty jealousies arising from such concerns occasionally prompt calls from newspaper columnists to move the entire urban area into one state or the other.[8]

The location of Missouri's western border was decided through diplomatic compromise. A location 24 miles east of the current position seemed most logical during the territorial years, a placement that (if implemented) would have allowed Kansas City to develop within a single political jurisdiction. This original demarcation was created in 1808 just after federal officials established Fort Osage on the Missouri River bluffs near the current village of Sibley. The fort lay beyond the zone of Euro-American settlement and was planned as the primary trading center for the Osage Nation. Osage

entrepreneurs appreciated the new facility, and as a show of good faith, they ceded their ancestral lands east of the fort along a line drawn straight south to the Arkansas River. Territory west of that limit, however (including most of present-day Jackson County), would remain in Osage hands.

The treaty terms of 1808 still held true in 1817 when Missourians first petitioned for admission to the Union. Their western border was to be this Osage line, including an extension to the north. Members of Congress had no objection to the boundary, but they rejected the whole initiative as premature. Local people tried again the next year. This time, the proposal stretched borders in three directions, with the western limit set some 60 miles into present-day Kansas. Again, the future Kansas City would have been unified politically, but also again, federal officials opposed the idea. Their argument now was that a territory so large would be hard to administer. A compromise then led to a third and successful petition in 1820. The new border on the west, a line running north and south from the midpoint of the Kansas River at its mouth, still produced a state with more acreage than any other save Virginia. The Osage reluctantly moved farther south and west, and territorial delegate John Scott said that the new Missouri was "as large as I was able to obtain."[9]

Although the position of Missouri's boundary lines remained constant for sixteen years after 1820, agitation grew for expansion to the northwest. Settlers focused on what they called the Platte Country, a wedge of fertile land east of the Missouri River and west of the existing state line. When these lobbyists finally forced another Indian expulsion and then an annexation to Missouri in 1836, politics for the future Kansas City became somewhat simplified. The northern third of the state now extended west to the Missouri River.

During the 1830s and 1840s, when the local economy centered on overland trade with Santa Fe merchants and the Indian nations that had been relocated to what is now eastern Kansas, few residents saw the boundary line as a problem. This all changed in the 1850s. A combination of land hunger, gold strikes in the West, and dreams of a transcontinental railroad quickly prompted the transformation of Kansas from permanent Indian territory to incipient state. Members of the growing business community in Kansas City saw that their economic future lay with this new country, and they began to fear adverse consequences of being politically apart from it. The result was four separate and quite serious attempts between 1855 and 1879 to move the city politically from Missouri into Kansas.[10]

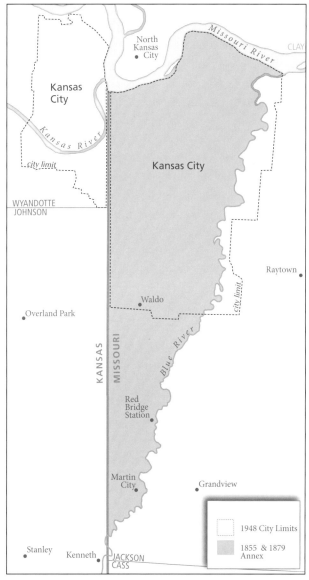

Map 4. Area Proposed for Annexation to Kansas, 1855 and 1879. The city limits shown for Kansas City, Kansas, and Kansas City, Missouri, are those of 1948.

then south-southwest along this tributary stream to where it intersects the current border in southernmost Jackson County (map 4). The venture still needed approval from Congress, but this action was seen as routine. Proslavery forces there were strong, and Senator David Atchison of Missouri was a leader. An emissary sent from Westport to Washington failed to take the needed action, however (some say because of a sudden love affair), and the plan collapsed. By the time local people could resubmit the initiative, politics had changed. Neither the Free State people who were gaining control in Kansas nor Missouri state legislators now saw benefit in a boundary adjustment.

Three additional attempts to append the Missouri portion of Kansas City to Kansas occurred in the 1870s. All were prompted by commercial issues, and all enjoyed widespread support throughout Kansas and Kansas City, Missouri. But state bureaucrats in Jefferson City could see no reason to forfeit the tax dollars generated by this growing city, and so they smothered each plan in turn. In 1873, the Kansas legislature offered funds for an outright purchase of the city plus an extra mile in each direction. Three years later, Kansans had Representative John R. Goodin introduce federal legislation to move the entire state border between the Missouri River and Arkansas 3 miles to the east. Again, support was small.

The last attempt at annexation, in the winter of 1878–1879, came from Kansas City businesspeople. Starting with an editorial assertion that "the only obstacle to the material progress of Kansas City is the state line," Mayor George M. Shelley assembled a special delegation that petitioned the legislatures of both states. The delegates' argument for annexation along the same Blue River boundary as in 1855 was summarized nicely by the *Kansas City Times*: "Kansas City, Mo., is the legitimate outgrowth of the state of Kansas. In everything but a line on the map she is essentially a city of Kansas. There is scarcely any difference of opinion in Kansas City on this question." The lobbyists found success in Topeka, where legislators not only approved the resolution in January but also appointed a special senate-house commission to negotiate with their counterparts in Jefferson City. Missouri solons, predictably, were much less enthused and let the initiative die. Vested state-level interests thereby overcame the otherwise laudable goals and considerable advantages of metropolitan unity.[11]

If the political lens is turned on counties rather than states, Kansas City's history is like that of other large commercial centers in having to cope with multiple jurisdictions. Five

The impetus for the first initiative was actually Civil War politics more than trade. Members of the initial Kansas territorial legislature held proslavery sentiments and realized that annexation of the similarly minded population in and around Westport would help their cause. Westport people agreed and began an impressive lobbying campaign led by newspaperman Robert T. Van Horn. He convinced the Missouri legislators that the loss of 60 or so square miles of their state was a price worth paying to ensure that neighboring Kansas would enter the Union with a true Southern constitution. The state boundary would be relocated to follow the Missouri River east to the mouth of the Blue (just west of Independence) and counties are principally involved, three in Missouri and two in Kansas. When these units were first established, the region's two large rivers were obvious sites for boundaries. The original pattern remains in Missouri—Jackson County south of the Missouri River and Clay County to the north. West of Clay lies Platte County, part of the state's annexation to the northwest in 1836. Life in Parkville, Platte City, and other communities there functioned largely independent of the larger urban center until 1972, when the Kansas City International Airport opened in their midst.

In Kansas, the initial county geometry of 1855 was rear-ranged early on to accommodate city growth. The Kansas River originally separated Leavenworth County on the north and Johnson County on the south. As urban development began near the mouth of this stream, however, promoters urged that a new political unit be established. Wyandotte County was the result, created from territory taken from both parent units in January 1859. The Kansas River now united rather than divided the businesses that would become Kansas City, Kansas. Not until the 1950s would suburbanization extend far enough south to reach the redesigned Johnson County.[12]

2 River Towns and Trailheads, 1822–1860

The direct ancestor of Kansas City, a community that called itself the Town of Kansas, was officially organized in 1850. This date is later than one might expect. Missouri legislators had created the local Jackson County a quarter century earlier; Independence, the courthouse site, was founded predictably in 1827 and nearby Westport in 1833. Why not Kansas City? Even St. Joseph, 80 miles farther up the Missouri River, is twelve years older than the modern metropolis. Such a delay for a townsite that was later acclaimed one of the best in the country clearly suggests that people evaluated urban potential differently in the early nineteenth century than we do today.

The rise and relative prosperities of early Kansas City and its neighboring communities are directly related to several changes in regional business opportunities. When Independence was established, overland trade with Santa Fe and the rest of the West was not yet large and steamboats did not ply the Missouri River with any regularity. Nor had the government moved 10,000 eastern Indians to a supposedly permanent homeland that adjoined Missouri's western border. As these three new realities materialized, local people saw a potential for profit. Older towns began to assume additional roles, and entrepreneurs platted newer communities at well-considered sites. Independence, for example, was founded at a convenient point for conducting local politics, but it soon became an outfitting post for traders as well. Westport's creators wanted a location on the state line primarily to take advantage of marketing opportunities with the new Indian migrants. Kansas City represented a third stage of development,

as the West began to grow and as businesspeople perceived greater possibilities for river and overland transportation. Many of the city's founders, in fact, were former residents of Independence and Westport. This chapter explores the changing aspirations and fortunes of these communities.

Urban development in the Kansas City area had several beginnings. French traders were the first Europeans to settle there. They established a small fur depot called Fort de Cavagnial just north of present-day Leavenworth in 1744 and maintained it until 1763, when their king ceded the entire region to Spain. Following the Louisiana Purchase, Americans invested in a similar venture between 1808 and 1822. Their Fort Osage, some 25 miles east of today's city center, held a government monopoly on the local fur trade.[1]

The first Euro-American settlement within today's metropolitan boundaries came in 1822. St. Louis people sought to take over the fur business recently abandoned at Fort Osage and so sent François Chouteau and his wife, Berenice, west. This young couple established a trading post on the north bank of the Missouri River at what we now call Randolph Bluffs, a half mile west of the modern (and aptly named) Chouteau Bridge. The Chouteaus had no interest in city building. But because they were well connected financially and politically (the city of St. Louis had been founded by François's grandfather and his uncle, and Berenice's father served as the first lieutenant governor of Illinois), the Chouteau enclave was stable and attracted a growing cluster of people. At least thirty-five were there from the outset.[2]

Chouteau selected his site for easy contact with the Kansa

people, the area's primary trappers. His business necessitated a river location for efficient storage and transportation, but he would have preferred to be on the south bank so that customers and agents could have ascended the Kansas River valley without having to cross the Missouri. West of Fort Osage, however, the river's south bank was Indian territory and settlement was illegal. The Randolph site, adjacent to a traditional river crossing, was the next best option. After Chouteau had been in business for four years, a flood in April 1826 destroyed all of his structures. He rebuilt almost immediately but not at the same site. In addition to seeking slightly higher ground that had escaped the previous flood, he also crossed to the river's south side onto land that the Osage Nation had ceded the previous year. His new outpost, arguably Kansas City's birthplace, lay about seven blocks east of today's city market at what is now the foot of Harrison and Gillis streets.[3]

The Chouteau holding covered several hundred acres. In addition to being a river landing and warehouse, it also was a working farm with cattle, horses, and hogs. No photograph or sketch of the couple's home exists, but it has been described as a spacious, double-pen log structure with two wings. The position of two Indian trails probably explains why the outpost was not closer to the state line. One of these routes extended south from the ford at Randolph Bluffs toward the main Osage villages and ascended to the upland about 1 mile east of the Chouteau wharf. The other, an east-west path running from Fort Osage to the Kansa settlements, crossed the first trail about 2 miles south of the river, near the current intersection of Linwood Boulevard and Prospect Avenue.[4]

By the early 1830s, Chouteau's landing was the center of a French-speaking community of at least a hundred people. Many—perhaps most—of these individuals had been involved in the fur trade, a business that was beginning to ebb at the time. Some were of pure French descent; others were French and Indian blends. All farmed for their primary livelihood, but most hunted and fished as well. Although a few of their farms extended as far east as the Chouteau homestead, most were located on what we now call the West Bottoms near the mouth of the Kansas River. Bearing the name French Bottoms then, this was productive farming land that settlers had laid out in long strips leading away from the main streams.[5]

Life in the community at Kawsmouth was said to be sociable, with regular dances during the winters. No commercial ambitions are known to have existed beyond a single grocery store started in 1838 and possibly a tavern. François

Chouteau served as an informal banker at his warehouse. At least two brickmasons were in residence by 1840, but people generally were self-sufficient. Wags from St. Louis had nicknamed the settlement Nouveau Vide Poche, a reference to a neighborhood in that older community that was so poor it had nothing to trade (*vide poche* meaning "empty pocket").[6]

If left in place, the informal settlement on the French Bottoms would certainly have been the direct progenitor of Kansas City. No accurate survey of its size exists, but it had grown large enough by 1833 to merit a missionary priest from the St. Louis Diocese. This man, Father Benedict Le Roux, purchased 40 acres in 1835 on the blufftop later known as Quality Hill. He promptly deeded the bishop 10 of these near what is now the corner of Pennsylvania and Eleventh streets. As a log church rose on this site later that year, the community made its first move away from the river. Symbolically, perhaps, this church (St. Francis Regis) and a few nearby homes were the only buildings in the community to survive a natural disaster in 1844. On June 16, a flood thought by many to be the largest ever to occur locally destroyed all the lowland farms plus Chouteau's wharf and warehouse. François was not around to witness the event, having died six years earlier, but his financial backers decided not to rebuild. Most of the settlers moved on as well, many to St. Louis and Ste. Genevieve, leaving the Kawsmouth waterfront open to other developers. The French Bottoms were reported to be completely reforested by 1855.[7]

Independence

Nearly simultaneous with the establishment of the French community adjacent to Chouteau's warehouse, Missouri state legislators began to organize the same general area into Jackson County. A treaty with the Osage Nation in 1825 secured the land title. Two years later, the solons appointed three commissioners to select a courthouse location. By law, this was to be near the middle of the county. These men were honest and explored diligently, but after judging the county's southern half to be "useless" prairie, they decided to modify their charge. The new town, they reasoned, should be central within the wooded, northern sector (map 3). Their upland site, called Independence, was well supplied with springs. It also lay astride the same Indian trail west from Fort Osage that likely influenced Chouteau's site selection the year before. The Missouri River flowed 4 miles to the north.[8]

The practice of locating county seats away from major streams was standard for the time. Big rivers almost always defined county edges, not cores, and centrality within these political units was important to rural taxpayers with their slow, horse-drawn buggies. People also associated swampy bottomlands with fevers and other disease. Liberty and Richmond, the seats of slightly older counties immediately to the north of Jackson, both were positioned inland. So were Columbia, Fulton, Keytesville, and other key government centers downstream on the Missouri.

The site selection for Independence was an obvious compromise between true centrality (a spot about equidistant from today's Blue Springs, Independence, and Raytown) and a riverine setting at or near the modern Sugar Creek. Had the three commissioners of 1827 opted for either of these alternatives, the urban history of the region would have been quite different. An Independence at the midpoint position within Jackson County would have been too remote from the Missouri River ever to have assumed a significant role in the Santa Fe trade. In this scenario, wagon masters and other entrepreneurs by 1830 almost certainly would have made deals with Chouteau to secure a share of his wharf and warehouse space. In turn, this alliance would have speeded development at the site of what is now Kansas City and allowed this community to achieve regional dominance sooner. But had Independence been platted on the river at the Sugar Creek site, it is entirely possible that merchants there could have retained control of overland trade without serious competition. Railroad builders then would have seen this community as their logical terminus, and the only Kansas City to emerge might well have been the one in Kansas. Instead, of course, the reality for Independence and the rest of the metropolitan area is more complicated.

By all accounts, Independence grew slowly during its first five years of existence. The community had a log courthouse but only a few hundred people and little in the way of commerce. The distinguished writer Washington Irving, who visited there in September 1832, praised the fertility of the surrounding land but judged the town itself still to be "a straggling little frontier village." This situation was a product of isolation. Both the Kansa and the Osage peoples had vacated the immediate area, and what was left of the declining fur trade was centered on Chouteau's warehouse, not the county seat. A few stores supplied local farmers, but Irving's traveling partner, Charles Latrobe, observed that "a little beyond this point, all carriage roads cease."[9]

Isolation changed to centrality rather abruptly in western Missouri. The establishment of Fort Leavenworth in 1827

initiated the process. Because this post was to be the supply point for all army operations in the West, it required regular shipments from St. Louis. Such demand greatly increased traffic on the Missouri River. It also prompted the replacement of keelboats by modern, steam-driven vessels. Entrepreneurs in the central Missouri towns of Franklin and Boonville quickly noticed this change. They had been developing an overland freight business with Mexicans in Santa Fe and realized that, by transporting goods farther upstream, they could shave several days off their journeys. They sought a new depot at a south-bank location (so as to avoid fording the stream) and identified Lexington, a town 60 miles west of Boonville, as one possibility. Independence was another. Obviously, its position slightly away from the river was a handicap, but freighters liked that it was 30 miles closer than Lexington to the Rio Grande.[10]

The trade outlook for Independence first brightened in 1829. That year, the army sent troops from Fort Leavenworth to accompany the Santa Fe traders. The two groups selected a central point just southwest of Independence for rendezvous and while there discovered three local assets. Quality grassland for the drovers' livestock existed just south of the community (map 3), a good river landing could be developed at an existing ferry site 6 miles to the northeast, and an experienced mercantile firm had just established a branch store in town. Independence's chances for future growth also were enhanced when investors in the 1829 expedition made profits several times greater than ever before (goods worth a total of $24,000 returned $240,000).[11]

Independence became the principal outfitting point for Santa Fe traders in 1832. Its citizens had done little to promote this status, but they certainly enjoyed the experience. Somewhat ironically, the biggest beneficiaries early on were James and Robert Aull of nearby Lexington, Missouri. Owning stores not only in their hometown but also in Independence, Liberty, and Richmond, these brothers could handle the growing needs of the freighters. Between 100 and 160 Independence men made trips to Mexico each year in the 1830s, the group netting up to $200,000 annually. The community soon became home to numerous wainwrights, harness makers, and blacksmiths. Residents also began to experience a society more diverse than they had ever imagined. According to one account from the period: "Mexicans, Californians and strangers from every state in the union find their way thither. Among such a motley multitude, there is much of human nature to be seen."[12]

Independence reached its pinnacle as a regional urban focus about 1844. The local population was still small—742—but the previous year had seen Santa Fe trade valued in excess of $450,000. This volume provided more than enough business for the seven wagon firms and twelve general merchandise stores now in town. Merchants also reported significant commerce with Indian traders, the army at Fort Leavenworth, and smaller communities throughout Jackson County and neighboring Van Buren County (the latter renamed Cass in 1849). One measure of the city's status can still be seen on maps of Pleasant Hill and Harrisonville, towns 22 and 33 miles, respectively, to the south. Both have principal north-south streets named Independence.[13]

Along with its overland trade, Independence in the early 1840s acquired a second ingredient necessary for growth—a good promoter. This man was William Gilpin, a graduate of West Point who had gained political influence through friendships with Senator Thomas Hart Benton of St. Louis and the explorer John C. Frémont. He lived in Independence until the Civil War and wrote persuasively. Gilpin's passion was a destiny he foresaw for the United States to become as powerful in the Pacific basin as it was in the Atlantic. He promoted transcontinental telegraph lines and railroads and always saw his adopted hometown as the logical beginning point for westward expansion.[14]

In a detailed statement in 1853, Gilpin described not only how Independence had acquired its current status but also how it "seems to possess the commanding geographical locality to retain it." He began with a description of the elbow region of the Missouri River and its advantages for controlling overland trade to the south and west. The key for the particular site of Independence, however, was "a prairie crest, level and smooth" that divided the waters of the Missouri and Arkansas river systems and was "the great natural road of communication, both of travel and commerce." One might have expected access to this routeway from the Missouri River to be difficult, but Gilpin assured readers it was not. By "throwing off a finger between the two little streams called the Blues, [the upland] traverses Jackson county, and reaching the south bank of the Missouri, flattening out, becomes spacious and level, and at its contact with the river forms the site of Independence."[15]

Gilpin made a good case. But he neglected to mention several problems at Independence and penned an outright lie when he claimed that the prairie south of his city was "the most westwardly in the State, and the last one below the Kan-sas [River]." Everybody connected with the Santa Fe trade knew that Jackson County's grasslands actually extended west to the state border and then north nearly to the competitor town of Westport (map 3). This physical reality soon produced a threat to Independence's commercial hegemony, and it meant that city merchants would have to work hard to retain their trade. They tried, especially in the late 1840s, but a combination of petty jealousies and natural conditions doomed their efforts by about 1855.[16]

The jealousy issue first pitted the town against its river landing at Prine's Ferry, 6 miles to the northeast. When an entrepreneur developed a successful flour mill near this wharf, Independence people feared the rise of a rival community. City leaders therefore shunned cooperative improvements to the anchorage and its access route and put their money instead into a new, slightly closer landing directly to their north. This creation, Wayne City, was an inferior site. The same jealousies as at the older Blue Mills–Prine's Ferry location also hindered its development. A good illustration is the story of the Independence and Missouri River Railroad. Providing the first tracks west of the Mississippi River, this project would seem to have been praiseworthy. It cost $32,000, ran 3.5 miles to Wayne City, and featured mule-drawn cars. The problem was timing. Independence people delayed its construction until 1848, after most of the overland trade had already gone elsewhere. The rail company collapsed financially within three years.[17]

Road and grass conditions south from Independence were a second challenge to city leaders. The prairie in this area was lush in 1827, but it occupied a strip only a few thousand yards wide for the first 20 or so miles of the trail toward Santa Fe (map 3). This geography hampered wagon masters. The route became rutted and muddy, the grass overgrazed. Then, as farmers started to file claims in the region, conditions worsened even more. A final road problem for Independence people was the Blue River. This stream, which marked the western flank of the prairie finger, was small enough to be forded easily under normal circumstances, but high water could cause major delays for wagons, and people complained about the situation regularly. A new, more westerly landing on the Missouri River that could bypass the Blue looked ever more appealing.[18]

Residents today like to refer to Independence as the Queen City, a shortened form of Queen City of the Trails. The name of an annual festival, Santa-Cali-Gon Days, supplies the trail names: Santa Fe, California, and Oregon. Independence's claims to glory in this regard are only partially true. The first wave of settlers bound for Oregon in 1838 did indeed rendezvous in the city, but the business of supplying emigrants never rivaled that of the traders from Santa Fe. Since the best route to Oregon, California, and Utah followed the Platte River of Nebraska, it made sense for travelers to continue on steamboats farther upstream than Independence. When the Platte Purchase expanded Missouri to the northwest in 1836, the new town of St. Joseph soon claimed most of this business.[19]

By combining small pieces of the Oregon and California traffic with a decent local trade and remnants of the Santa Fe business, Independence actually grew faster in the late 1840s than it had during its initial commercial expansion. The community counted some 1,600 residents at this time and claimed to be the state's second-largest city. Still, even as citizens sent out circulars to entice gold seekers to purchase supplies locally, they realized that their time of glory was almost past. After a period of transition during the early 1850s, writers began to describe a new ambience. A commentator from Westport in 1859, for instance, said that Independence was "one of the handsomest towns we ever saw. As a place for pleasant residence she has no superior." His sentiment was echoed by a St. Louis man who praised the town as a refined escape "from the whirlpool of commercial life." These words, not entirely welcomed by a proud citizenry, nevertheless proved applicable for the remainder of the nineteenth century and most of the twentieth.[20]

Westport

Logistical problems for the Santa Fe business at Independence meant opportunities for others. Westport people were the first to take advantage. After a few traders grazed their stock in the area during the late 1830s while ordering supplies from Independence, local entrepreneurs became outfitters themselves. They controlled half of this commerce by 1846 and nearly all of it three years later. Their success was ironic because Westport, like Independence, was several miles from the Missouri River and therefore similarly dependent on a separate landing site. Westport also was like Independence in that neither town was founded with the Mexican trade in mind.

To understand Westport, one must first know about developments just west of the Missouri state line during the 1820s. This land, the future eastern portion of Kansas, was occupied by the Kansa and Osage nations before 1825. Its status then changed abruptly. William Clark, the former explorer and later superintendent of Indian affairs at St. Louis, convinced these peoples to sell most of their land to the government. The government's purchase was part of a larger plan. Since at least 1817, federal officials had wanted to relocate Indians from the eastern United States. The goal, in theory, was simultaneously to create more room for white settlement and to provide havens where Native Americans could acculturate to modern life. Many missionaries supported this latter concept, including Isaac McCoy, a Baptist from Michigan. McCoy visited the Kansas River area in 1828 along with representatives of the Potawatomi and Ottawa nations. Everybody liked what they saw, and McCoy decided to join the migrants and set up a mission.[21]

Between the late 1820s and the middle 1840s, some 10,000 Indians from the region north of the Ohio River resettled in what is now Kansas. Among them were approximately 1,600 Delawares and Wyandots immediately north of the Kansas River and 1,250 Shawnees just to the south. McCoy chose to serve the latter group and so relocated his family in 1831. His mission overlooked Turkey Creek in the northernmost part of today's Johnson County, about 2 miles from Missouri.[22]

The presence of a sizable Native American community on the Missouri border meant trading opportunities. These immigrant peoples had developed sophisticated tastes for manufactured goods in their former homes, and now, as part of their agreements to resettle, they received annual cash payments from the federal government. Estimates for these annuities vary between $300,000 and $500,000, sums more than adequate to attract a new wave of store owners to compete with François Chouteau and other longtime operators. Westport was the outgrowth of one of these stores.[23]

The settlement at Westport succeeded for several reasons. Its principal founder, John Calvin McCoy, was the missionary's son and therefore enjoyed political connections. McCoy also found a good location. He wanted to be close to the Shawnee villages and his father's mission, of course, but legally, he had to stay on the Missouri side of the state line. He also needed access to Independence, the region's principal supply depot. These conditions were satisfied at an upland site 4 miles south of the Missouri River and 1 mile from Indian territory. The old Osage pathway that linked Independence with the Kansas River valley passed that way, and a number of "excellent springs" lay just to the south at the head of Mill Creek (maps 2 and 3).[24]

McCoy built a two-story, double-pen log store in 1833. Two years later, he acquired adjacent land, surveyed nine square blocks, and officially filed his plat with state officials. The importance of Independence to McCoy is suggested by the plat's orientation. Instead of following cardinal directions, his main street ran (and still runs) from the northeast to the southwest. It was a replication of the Indian trail, of course, and followed the divide between O.K. and Brush creeks. Crossing the Blue River near today's Blue Valley Park at Twenty-seventh Street and Topping Avenue, the trace reappears on modern maps of Independence bearing the name Westport Road. This street is the oldest in both communities and thus in Greater Kansas City.

Trade with the Shawnees and other immigrant Indians was extremely profitable. McCoy raised the capital he needed through a partnership with two men from Independence, but all three worried about their supply line. Its 26-mile length was not ideal, and the ford across the Blue was steeply banked and often impassable. An alternative depot site was available, of course, directly north of Westport. Its development would save many miles and avoid the Blue River, but only a crude trail laid out by earlier French settlers ran in that direction. Negotiating a way through bluffs that stood up to 120 feet tall and only yards from any potential wharf along the Missouri River was no small problem either.[25]

Although McCoy and his partners obtained most of their store goods from Independence, they experimented with the shorter route as early as 1834. That year, they instructed a steamship captain to unload their order from St. Louis at, in McCoy's words, "the nearest accessible point of the river." This point was a forested ledge near the foot of today's Grand Avenue. McCoy recalled that he made his way along the French trace with three teams of oxen and then cut a path through a brush-filled break in the bluffs to reach his supplies. This route, gradually improved throughout the late 1830s, was fundamental to the growth of Westport. It ran nearly arrow straight, following what is now Broadway north to a crossing of OK Creek in Penn Valley Park. There, it angled a few blocks east before continuing north along today's Main Street. At about Ninth Street, it bent to the northwest along a small depression near Delaware Street. Then, at Sixth, it turned eastward again, following this same ravine to Grand Avenue and the final descent to the wharf.[26]

Westport during the 1840s and 1850s was a boisterous, self-confident community. The economy was diversified, and the landing site on the Missouri River proved workable despite its formidable bluffs and some losses incurred during the big flood of 1844. The Shawnee trade was a constant, and

business grew with communities to the Shawnees' south, including the Miami, Ottawa, Potawatomi, and Sauk and Fox nations. Of the Missouri cities with good mercantile connections, Westport was the closest to all these peoples. Indians who personally went to town provided a distinctive air to the city. Lewis Garrard, a visitor in 1846, was impressed with their physical variety, their "handsome ponies," and their "fanciful dresses." He added, though, that most of the Indians were "debased by liquor," and he chided unprincipled traders for exploiting this illegal market.[27]

Westport outfitters originally saw the Santa Fe trade as a nice complement to their Indian business. The supplies for both groups were much the same. The overland business soon became the more significant, however, especially after a majority of wagon masters began to base themselves in Santa Fe rather than Missouri. Traveling in from the south, these people preferred to buy in Westport instead of Independence because this option shaved four days off their round-trip. All drovers, regardless of origin, praised the area's extensive grasslands that began just a mile and a half south of town (map 3). When the commercial needs of a growing number of farmers and small towns in southern Jackson County plus a series of emigrant groups bound for California and Oregon are added to this total demand, it is little wonder that Westport attracted the attention of outside observers. Outfitting houses lined the streets for over four blocks, including one owned by Albert G. Boone, a grandson of Daniel. Visiting journalists also were impressed with the vast assemblage of tents and wagons that seasonally materialized on the adjacent prairie. To one reporter's eye, the scene resembled "the camp of a great army." In 1857, at the peak of this activity, the permanent population in Westport Township reached about 2,000.[28]

The Town of Kansas

Whereas the early histories of Independence and Westport are straightforward in date and purpose, the beginnings of their eventual rival, the Town of Kansas, are blurred. It is possible to assign almost any year between 1838 and 1853 as the date of its origin. Similarly, it is unclear whether members of the original town company saw their site as a potential metropolis or as little more than an isolated landing and ferry point.

Urban activity at what is now Kansas City began with the estate of Gabriel Prudhomme, one of the residents of the French community at Kawsmouth. Prudhomme had purchased 257 acres from the government in 1831. It was an intriguing tract with over a mile of frontage along the Missouri

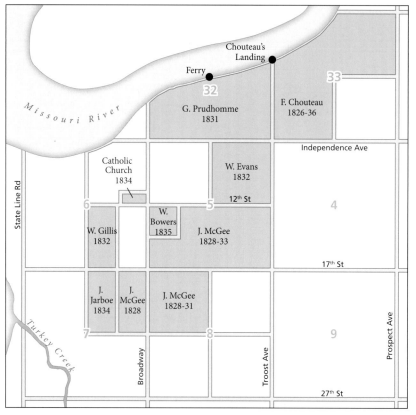

Map 5. *Selected Early Land Entries in Northwestern Jackson County. Data from Union Historical Company,* The History of Jackson County, Missouri *(Kansas City, Mo.: Birdsall, Williams, 1881), pp. 380–381, and Dorothy B. Marra,* Cher Oncle, Cher Papa: The Letters of François and Berenice Chouteau *(Kansas City, Mo.: Western Historical Manuscript Collection–Kansas City, 2001), p. 150.*

company of fourteen men bid a more realistic $4,220.[30]

The November sale proved nearly as faithless as the one in July. The buyers represented several power groups within the county, particularly one from Independence and another from Westport. Historian A. Theodore Brown has suggested that this coalition may have been assembled to spread the potential for profit widely and thereby to forestall legal challenge to the sale. This issue proved moot, however, when the effects of a national financial panic in 1837 reached the frontier. The buyers, later described by McCoy (one of their members) as "a few good men with no capital," could not raise the $4,220 payment. Consequently, they could not offer good title to prospective buyers of their lots. Lawsuits followed, and the debt was not cleared until 1843. Positive actions from this period are few. Company members erected a small log warehouse and named their community Kansas in honor of the nearby river. More important to investors was an increase in ferry traffic caused by the annexation of the Platte region to Missouri. The southern tip of this new acreage lay just 3 miles to the north.[31]

River and extension southward to the blufftops. The modern boundaries are Independence Avenue on the south, Broadway on the west, and Troost Avenue on the east (map 5). Prudhomme died a few months after gaining title. The land passed to his widow and remained largely undeveloped for the next seven years. An exception was a ferry established by Pierre Roy, another French settler, which utilized an outcropping of Bethany Falls limestone near the foot of what is now Grand Avenue. This was the same ledge where John Calvin McCoy picked up supplies for his Westport store in 1834.[29]

In 1838, as the oldest Prudhomme child came of age and requested her share of the estate, the county court authorized a public sale. Advertisements for this event, to be held on July 7, stressed the possibilities for a new townsite, but the property sold for the unexpectedly low price of $1,800. The reason was fraud. After a confession from James H. McGee, the man who had served as auctioneer and who already owned over 500 acres in northwestern Jackson County, the court voided the deed (map 5). At a second sale date in November, a town

Money remained tight in western Missouri until at least 1845. As a result, the prospects for town booming were poor. Perhaps four stores existed in the new settlement in 1843, but all were small. Theirs was a "truck and dicker" trade with the local French community, neighboring Indians, and rivermen. It featured gunpowder, tobacco, coffee, and alcohol. Only one person, William M. Chick, had sufficient financial resources to erect a warehouse and so engage in larger-scale mercantilism. His site, where the town's new Main Street met the levee, stood several feet higher than the principal landing point three blocks to the east.[32]

The slow pace of development between 1838 and 1843 proved to be a blessing the following summer. On June 13, heavy, persistent rains upstream on the Kansas River produced a great surge of floodwater. This water piled into a Missouri River that itself was several feet over its banks. The West Bottoms filled rapidly to a depth of 20 feet, and the torrent then passed unabated into the Missouri's main channel. Three days later, when water levels began to drop, people realized that the entire French community at Kawsmouth had disappeared. So had the warehouse and farm of Berenice Chouteau and an adjacent, rival mercantile building that had just been erected by the brothers William G. and George W. Ewing. The town of Kansas was similarly devastated. Floodwaters took all the small stores, the ferry, and the company's storage building. Chick's warehouse was the only business to survive.[33]

Two years after the flood, as money became more available, the town company reconstituted itself. The fourteen original shares were now held by only seven men, most with strong connections to Westport. The major exception was Robert Campbell, a wealthy businessman from St. Louis who had sensed the potential of this landing in earlier years when he had worked as a fur trader. Campbell helped to stabilize a venture that had been seriously underfunded.[34]

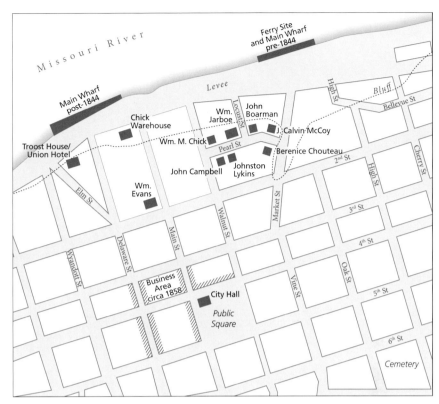

Map 6. Town of Kansas, circa 1850. Bluff location from old photographs and from Walter Edward McCourt, assisted by M. Albertson and J. W. Bennett, The Geology of Jackson County, 2nd ser., vol. 14 (Rolla: Missouri Bureau of Geology and Mines, 1917). House and business sites primarily from William L. Campbell, "Fashionable Pearl Street," Annals of Kansas City 1 (1921–1924): 109–113; Washington H. Chick, "A Journey to Missouri," Annals of Kansas City 1 (1921–1924): 96–103; and Chick, "The Vicissitudes of Pioneer Life," Annals of Kansas City 1 (1921–1924): 207–218.

John Calvin McCoy, who now owned two shares of the town company as well as the local ferry across the Missouri, resurveyed the town early in 1846 (map 6). This effort was followed by a successful auction, with lots on the levee going for as much as $341. By that fall, the community claimed 300 residents, and it had 400 more in 1848. A business inventory included "eight or ten stores, several blacksmith shops, a gunsmith's shop, wagon maker's shops, [and] three hotels."[35]

Kansas in the late 1840s was neither a boomtown nor a bust; its advantages and disadvantages as a site lay in close balance. Like Westport, its location was ideal for trade with local Indians. Two of McCoy's street names—Delaware and Wyandott—identify the targeted groups, who lived just north of the Kansas River. Yet investors saw the city's greatest asset as its solid limestone landing, beautifully positioned within the elbow region of the Missouri River. Travelers from there overland to the south and west could avoid fords on both the Blue and Kansas rivers. This potential had tempted the

largest Santa Fe trader—Bent, St. Vrain and Company—to unload supplies at the ferry site in 1845. Carting these goods to Westport was not easy, however. The bluffs just behind the levee—40 to 100 feet high and often a morass of mud—were the new town's great handicap.[36]

Evidence of the bluffs is nearly invisible on McCoy's survey, but they extended across the entire city (map 6). Abutting the river westward from Wyandotte Street, the cliffs angled slightly away from the water toward the east, creating several blocks of low, flat land. Then, just beyond Market Street, the escarpment turned back toward the river. Not by chance, the eastern and western edges of the small cove below the bluffs corresponded with the limits of the townsite. Company members owned the upland surface farther in each direction, but they judged such acreage as distinctly less valuable.

The bluffs influenced nearly every aspect of the Kansas cityscape. The precise grid of streets that McCoy laid out parallel with the river, for example, would be more dream than

Figure 1. Gilliss House Hotel and the Levee, circa 1867. Built in 1849 as Troost House, this sixty-room inn between Wyandotte and Delaware streets was the city's finest commercial building for a decade. A bell in its cupola announced meals. When people began to move away from the levee, the building devolved into a brothel and then a pickle factory. Workers demolished it in 1909. (Courtesy Missouri Valley Special Collections, Kansas City Public Library)

reality for over a decade. Delaware, Main, and most of the other routes at right angles to the river actually existed in two separate, disconnected sections. One set of stubs extended from the levee to the bluffs; another traversed the upland. Market Street, notable on the plat for its unusual orientation, was the exception to this rule. As its name suggests, Market was a principal business route that led south from the ferry station. Its path traced the west flank of the only sizable breach in the cliff face and therefore offered the easiest way to move between the upland and lowland surfaces. The site for the ferry had been selected with this route in mind, and McCoy himself had followed the ravine when he picked up supplies for his Westport store in 1834. Although Market Street was essential to the development of the city, people routinely complained about its steep grade, clinging mud, and "precipitous banks." Still, minus the slope, the stream, and even the name, the street has managed to endure. When city officials began to excavate road cuts through the bluffs in 1857, they made Market Street a priority. Then, in the 1860s, they changed its name to Grand Avenue.[37]

If an observer envisions a right triangle with the veering Market Street and the levee as two of its sides, it is easy to understand McCoy's plan for the rest of his new community. The remaining leg of this triangle, intersecting Market Street atop the bluffs, would be a good place for another concentration of businesses. He logically named this corridor Main Street and converted its junction with Market Street into a public square. This square also persists to the present, now constituting the southwestern quarter of the city market.

The interior of McCoy's basic triangle was a challenge to develop because of the bluffs. Utilizing the access route of Market Street, McCoy laid out a road running west along the crest of this ridge. This short lane, called Pearl Street, featured superb vistas and easy access to stores and the wharf. It immediately became the residential choice for the town's most distinguished people. McCoy himself built there, as did warehouse owner William Chick. So did John Campbell (the nephew and representative of the city's major financial backer, Robert Campbell of St. Louis) as well as the local grande dame, Berenice Chouteau, who had been forced from her longtime farm by the flood of 1844.[38]

The few contemporary descriptions of Kansas that survive from the 1840s and early 1850s emphasize the town's topography. Francis Parkman in 1846 observed only that Chick's log house "stands upon a high hill," but Lewis Garrard bluntly asserted that the town's "mud bluff banks destroy the pleasing effects" he saw elsewhere in the West. McCoy's memoirs confirm that this latter view was common, especially among writers from rival communities. "Adding insult to injury," he noted, these people went so far as to apply "the low humiliating sobriquet of 'Gully Town.'"[39]

Charles Spalding, who wrote the first promotional book for the city in 1857, felt he had to address the issue of the bluffs directly. Admitting that they were a problem that "will require a large outlay of money," he insisted that the investment would be made soon and would silence all skeptics. Although the hills were high, he argued, they reached back only "about seven blocks" and were composed of soil, not rock. When removed, a nearly level upland surface would stretch to Westport and beyond. This process, he concluded, would furnish employment "for hundreds of laborers" and create "the most healthy and beautiful city in the Union."[40]

From the perspective of the twenty-first century, it is hard to imagine that the communities of Kansas and Westport

Figure 2. "The Grade" in Kansas City, 1857. The only path inland from the levee in the 1840s and 1850s followed an angling ravine through loess bluffs. This "grade," 15 to 20 feet deep and often muddy, was gradually transformed into today's Grand Avenue. Alfred R. Waud's line drawing was published in Albert D. Richardson's Beyond the Mississippi *in 1867.*

would not be intense rivals throughout the 1850s. Yet there is little evidence that a competition existed. Perhaps learning from the reluctance of Independence people to promote the Wayne City landing, business leaders in Westport took the lead in developing Kansas. They moved goods, money, and themselves back and forth on a regular basis, and the Santa Fe trade anchored both economies. In a classic case of symbiosis, one site had the wharf but no pasturage and the other stood inland, adjacent to a vast prairie.

Two illustrations of the cooperative spirit survive to the present. One is Union Cemetery, established in 1857 on 49 acres midway between the two towns. Contrary to some popular opinion, the name Union refers to this joint civic venture and not to the war that came a few years later.[41] The other example is Grand Avenue. The northern section of this route served as the commercial lifeline between Westport and its landing, and therefore, it was laid out wider than other streets and given a better surface. This extra width has been maintained, along with the street's reputation as a good address for major institutions such as the *Kansas City Star* newspaper and the Federal Reserve Bank.

The City of Kansas

Following a period of transition between 1849 and 1853, the small group of men who controlled investment in both Westport and Kansas decided to focus efforts on the river city. Their logic, as always, was practical. Partly, it stemmed from a conviction born of experimentation that Kansas could overcome its major physical limitation. They envisioned first a series of cuts through the disruptive bluffs and then complete excavation, leaving a townsite nearly perfect in site and situation. McCoy, James McGee, Robert and John Campbell, and several other local investors bought into this thinking, including former Indian trader William Gilliss and former missionaries Johnston Lykins and Nathan Scarritt. More important, perhaps, so did several capitalists from outside the state. One of these, Hiram Northrup of New York, created the town's largest store, with $3,500 in merchandise. Another, Kersey Coates of Philadelphia, invested heavily in local real estate on behalf of a Pennsylvania syndicate. The town's transition in self-image from haphazard landing site to promising community is also suggested by two successful petitions: to the county in 1850 to formally organize the "Town of Kansas" and to the state in 1853 to charter the "City of Kansas."[42]

The new City of Kansas (immediately shortened to Kansas City by nearly everybody) contained fewer than 500 residents in 1855, but it expanded rapidly to 3,224 in 1857 and to 7,180 in 1859. Much as McCoy and his fellow promoters would have liked to claim otherwise, this boom had little to do with their salesmanship. Instead, they were simply taking advantage of a bigger political event—the abrupt transition in 1853 and 1854 of the land just to their west from permanent Indian territory to the incipient state of Kansas. This move, which uprooted 10,000 Native Americans and destroyed part of the traditional economies of both Westport and Kansas City, was orchestrated in the boardrooms of New York and Washington, D.C. Powerful business and political leaders

there had railroads on their minds, in particular a transcontinental line that would link Chicago and/or St. Louis with the new American populations in California, Oregon, and other western sites.

For St. Louis people to have a chance to control the new way west, a pathway would have to be cleared. This effort would mean wholesale Indian removal, of course, and a loss of the Indian trade to Kansas City. Looking beyond these immediate problems, however, western Missourians soon recognized alternative business opportunities on a scale unimagined in the past. For instance, cities there likely would become stops on any railroad running west from St. Louis. This area also was the obvious gateway for settlers moving into the new Kansas Territory. Warehouse owners who supplied Santa Fe now began to dream about doubling or tripling their business with sales to stores about to sprout by the hundreds across the central plains.[43]

As several thousand new people moved to Kansas City in the middle 1850s, the community acquired a larger physical footprint and a more complex social geography. Robert T. Van Horn, editor of the city's first newspaper, provided a retrospective on this change in 1859. When he viewed the town initially in October 1855, the wharf as reestablished after the flood of 1844 had been restricted to a single block between the Union Hotel and Chick's warehouse and the street system was "a common country road" that ran beneath the bluff and "into the ravine below Market Street." Just before Van Horn's arrival, workers had extended this lone street west along the river into the West Bottoms. The cut through the bluffs was narrow, just wide enough for a wagon.[44]

Plans for more extensive trenching through the bluffs so that Main and its parallel streets could be more than stubs were bolstered by the success of the cut along the levee but frustrated by a lack of money. Crowded conditions forced action early in 1857, however, and city leaders issued several major contracts for the following two summers. These agreements authorized five north-south excavations: Main and Delaware streets flanking the busy wharf; Market Street three blocks to the east; and Broadway, a new road just west of the original town plat. By this selection and the ignoring of cuts for Walnut, Locust, High, and Cherry streets, officials clearly favored the west side of town with its wharf and close access to the new markets of Kansas Territory. Excavation contracts went out slightly later for Second, Third, Fourth, and Fifth streets, completing the grid nearly as McCoy had envisioned it but leaving the interiors of the blocks elevated 10 to 40

Figure 3. Excavation on Walnut Street, 1868, Looking North from Third. Bluff removal behind the levee was essential for city growth. This barrier was dirt, not stone, but stood 40 feet high and extended south about six blocks. The process, begun in 1857, continued for at least fifteen years. Note that the trench for intersecting Second Street is even deeper than that for Walnut. (Courtesy Missouri Valley Special Collections, Kansas City Public Library)

feet above passing wagons. A sculptor would have called the scene alto-relieveo, but for residents on the hilltops, it was something to endure rather than appreciate. People accepted long staircases to their isolated aeries only because they saw this condition as transitional to an even bigger round of earth removal. Journalist Albert Richardson, who visited in 1857, saw "much stir and vitality" in the town but also a certain chaos as "carts and horses wallowed in the mud of these deep excavations; and the houses stood trembling on the verge as if in fear of tumbling over."[45]

The new road cuts freed the city from its bluff imprisonment. Because the crest of the escarpment stood at about Second Street, cuts were deepest there and the possibilities for building least desirable. People therefore saw two immediate possibilities for business location. They could either remain along the thin line of the wharf or skip two or three blocks south to where the elevation gap between block and road levels was more manageable. Entrepreneurs not directly dependent on the river preferred the latter option. Their stores and offices sprang up along the through streets of Delaware and

Main between Third and Fifth. A decision in 1856 to locate the first city hall on the public square led to a clustering of government buildings in that vicinity. Landscape evidence of this early expansion no longer exists along Main Street and the square, but a few of the old storefronts remain in the 300 and 400 blocks of Delaware.

With conditions on the levee so crowded by 1857 that it was "impossible to keep open a passageway through the immense piles of freight," it is not surprising that the city's residential sector joined the business community in its move away from the river. But instead of migrating several blocks, housing advanced much farther, which can be seen by a look at changing political boundaries. After a period of little

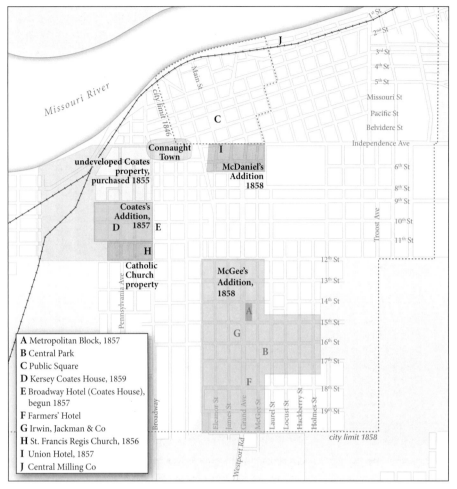

Map 7. *City of Kansas, circa 1860. Data primarily from Union Historical Company,* The History of Jackson County, Missouri *(Kansas City, Mo.: Birdsall, Williams, 1881).*

and-range survey system (map 5). These boundaries, like those elsewhere across the Midwest, became sites for a network of rural roads spaced 1 mile apart. Then, as Kansas City expanded, it seemed logical to upgrade these existing pathways into city streets. In fact, the early presence of such roads on the urbanizing landscape meant that they often became major thoroughfares. Certainly, this was true for the three that bordered the original city—Broadway on the west, Independence Avenue on the south, and Troost Avenue on the east.[47]

Although the city limits of 1858 suggest that the community extended farther east and west than it did north and south, this was not true of actual development. Lack of appropriate passageways through the bluffs inhibited access to eastern and southeastern acreage, and a recession of the Bethany Falls limestone away from the river in the West Bottoms curtailed wharf development there.

expansion between 1846 and 1855, officials approved two additions to the original town in 1856 and an amazing seventeen in 1857. These additions spread building lots south more than 2 miles from the river and forced a corresponding extension of city services. Optimistic new corporate limits, adopted in February 1858, stretched west to the state line, south to Twenty-second Street, and east to Troost and Lydia avenues (map 7).[46]

An eightfold enlargement of the city's physical size during the late 1850s quickly produced social distinctions among neighborhoods. It also provided opportunity for a literal reorientation. Surveyors for the new additions aligned their street grids to match cardinal directions instead of the river. This change, apparently made without controversy, was a practical matter. The original town property as purchased from the Prudhomme estate in 1838 had been bounded by cardinal lines as part of the government's standard township-

Land south and southwest of the original town offered more possibilities. This land was easily accessible via the Broadway, Delaware, Main, and Market street cuts; it already contained a settlement focus with the French Catholic church of St. Francis Regis on Broadway between Eleventh and Twelfth; and it provided nearly level building lots all the way south to the valley of OK Creek near Twentieth Street. Most important, perhaps, the land also lay along the two principal overland routes that connected Kansas City with the broader world.

Trails south to Westport and west to Indian villages along the Kansas River both existed long before any formal townsite at Kawsmouth. The actual location of these routes was somewhat variable during the 1840s and early 1850s, though, as wagon drivers and others would detour slightly to avoid ruts or find better grass. Land developers saw this route flexibility as a way to add value to their properties. If they platted their subdivisions with skill and cultivated the proper political connections, they might be able to rechannel these potential business arteries.

Social Patterns of 1860

The most successful manipulators of land and roads were Kersey Coates and Elijah Milton "Milt" McGee. McGee, whose father, James, had accumulated 1,000 acres of local property before his death in 1840, became the city's biggest developer. In 1856, just as laborers were preparing to make the first road cuts through the bluffs, he subdivided 160 acres that stretched from Twelfth to Twentieth streets and from Main to Holmes (map 7). Then, with a winning combination of personal flamboyance and capital investment, he promoted this area's 1,326 building lots to the town's younger merchants and artisans. More than 100 homes were erected there during the initial building season, and people soon began to see the place as nearly separate from the rest of the city. Among eighteen other new property developments at this time, McGee's alone commanded the simple title of "The Addition."[48]

McGee identified with the upwardly mobile middle class. Although a Southerner himself with proslavery views, he recruited broadly, including many German families. About a third of his buyers were wealthy enough to erect brick homes, several of them concentrated around the 5-acre Central Park he had laid out southeast of McGee and Sixteenth streets. The addition's success derived more from commercial accessibility than from suburban amenities, however. The road from Kansas City to Westport bisected the property, and McGee had recognized its possibilities as a business center immediately. Ambitiously, he named this muddy path Grand Avenue and argued successfully that its improvement was essential to city growth. A turnpike company was organized in 1857, and by 1860, the surface had been macadamized and the width expanded to an impressive 100 feet.[49]

Grand Avenue served three distinct purposes in the late 1850s. Certainly, it was Kansas City's first commuter route. It also retained its earlier role as gateway to Westport and the world beyond. McGee persuaded the firm of Irwin, Jackman

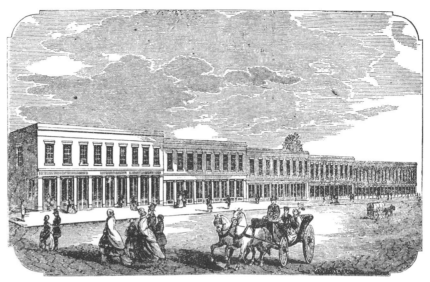

Figure 4. Metropolitan Block, between Fourteenth and Fifteenth streets on Grand, circa 1858. Elijah Milton McGee promoted southward expansion of the city in 1856 by subdividing 160 acres between Twelfth and Twentieth streets, Main to Holmes. He widened the connector road from the levee to create Grand Avenue and encouraged shops by erecting the Metropolitan Block in 1857. This early mall accommodated eighteen businesses in six connected brick buildings and was successful from the start. Vanduzee and Barton's line drawing was published in Charles C. Spalding's Annals of the City of Kansas *in 1858.*

and Company (the city's most prominent overland freighter and outfitter) to relocate to the west side of the 1500 block. He also catered to long-distance travelers personally by converting his house at the southeast corner of Eighteenth Street into the city's second major hotel. Grand Avenue's third purpose looked to the future. Foreseeing and encouraging a movement of the entire urban core to the south, McGee in 1857 created the Metropolitan Block along the east side of the street between Fourteenth and Fifteenth. This $60,000 development, set within a cornfield, was essentially a suburban mall—six solid brick buildings, each two stories tall and with shared sidewalls. The resulting eighteen business sites (three per building) filled quickly and included two groceries, a variety store, an attorney's office, and the studio of artist George Caleb Bingham.[50]

As early as 1857, outside commentators began to label the new southern development as "the best part" of the city. McGee's influence on this perceptual shift is hard to overstate. Consider the streets, for example. Writers were comparing his Grand Avenue to New York's Broadway and Philadelphia's Chestnut Street at a time when Kansas City's official Main Street contained few businesses south of the 400 block. Like most developers, McGee named all the streets in his addition. Typically, such coinages proved to be ephemeral, giving

23

way to the older names of the original city as urban patterns coalesced. Some of Mc-Gee's names shared this fate, including the conversion of Eleanor and James streets (his parents' names) to Main and Walnut, respectively. Yet several of his names live on, demonstrating the political power of the new south side of town. Most noticeably, Grand Avenue triumphed over Market and Vine streets (map 6). Locust did the same over High, as did Holmes over Williams. McGee Street survives as well, although it does not extend north as far as the original city limit.[51]

As Milt McGee worked to provide a residential haven for middle-class Kansas City, Kersey Coates was doing the same for the community's elite. The strategies of the two men were much the same. Both favored southern locations in close proximity to major thoroughfares. Both also chose to live within their respective developments and to add accoutrements with special appeal to the targeted social group.

Coates, a wealthy attorney from Pennsylvania, arrived in Kansas Territory in 1854. Although an abolitionist and agent for a Philadelphia emigrant aid company, he was most interested in business investments and decided that Kansas City offered the region's best prospects. He became a leading promoter of railroads, department stores, and banks, but he was most involved with real estate. A key purchase, made in 1855, comprised 110 acres acquired from Berenice Chouteau (map 7). This land extended south and west from the corner of Independence Avenue and Broadway, straddling the line of the bluffs. Coates kept the portion that was in the West Bottoms for future industrial development (the city's first union depot would be erected there in 1878) but platted 32 upland acres as Coates's Addition. From Broadway on the east to the bluffs on the west and from Ninth to Eleventh streets, this neighborhood exuded sophistication. People soon nicknamed it Quality Hill.[52]

Coates set the tone for his addition by paving all the roads

Figure 5. Coates House Hotel, circa 1880. To complement his fashionable Quality Hill residential area, developer Kersey Coates built the city's finest hotel at the corner of Tenth and Broadway. Started in 1857 and completed in 1868, its five stories of rooms featured gas lamps and steam heat. Note the horse trolley line along Broadway. Banta and Brazel's line drawing was published in the Union Historical Company's History of Jackson County, Missouri, *in 1881.*

and permitting only brick construction. He named the principal north-south street Pennsylvania after his home state and, in 1859, built a two-story Italianate home there at the corner of Tenth Street. People with the social and economic standing of Kersey Coates were not numerous in Kansas City during those years, but the two blocks of Pennsylvania between Ninth and Eleventh gradually filled with Victorian turrets and filigree porches.[53]

Broadway, two blocks east of Pennsylvania Street, was Coates's primary business focus. This route arguably possessed even more potential for development than Grand Avenue. Both roads connected Kansas City with the Santa Fe Trail and settlements along the Kansas River, but the Broadway route bypassed Westport and was 6 miles shorter overall. Local entrepreneurs championed this newer linkage as early as 1855 and constructed a bridge across Turkey Creek near what is now the intersection of Twenty-fifth and Fairmount streets. The route went south on Broadway to about Twenty-third Street and then angled west-southwest across the creek and along the divide between this stream and the Kansas River.[54]

To increase traffic past his addition, Coates decided to build a showplace inn, one grand enough to rival any in St. Louis. His Broadway Hotel (later known as the Coates House) occupied a footprint 100 feet long and 148 feet deep at the southeast corner of Tenth Street. With a French-inspired mansard roof atop its five stories and gas lamps and steam heat within, it was the most praised building in town.[55]

The three-year speculative surge that had increased Kansas City's population from a few hundred residents to an impressive 7,180 ended in 1859. The supply of eastern money needed to finance railroads dried up following a financial panic in 1857, and increasing hostility toward the slavery issue in Kansas prompted many citizens to move elsewhere. Census officials counted only 4,418 residents in 1860, a number not much higher than the 3,164 in nearby Independence.[56]

If census data are mapped with the aid of locations from a city directory, basic patterns emerge for this community in transition. First, it is clear that the recent street excavations through the bluffs had been successful. The public square between Fourth and Fifth streets has replaced the levee as the city core, and a built-up area between Broadway and Grand

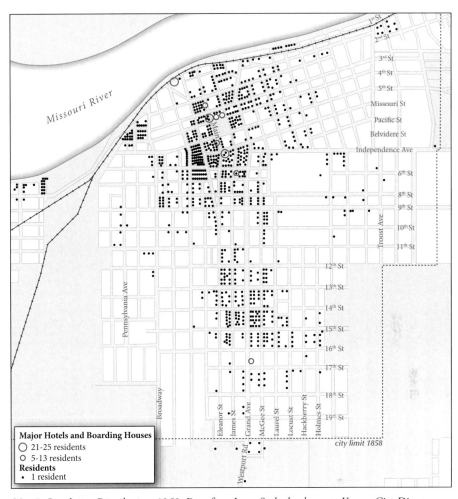

Map 8. *Population Distribution, 1860. Data from James Sutherland, comp.,* Kansas City Directory and Business Mirror for 1860–61 *(Indianapolis, Ind.: James Sutherland, 1860).*

Avenue now stretches south to Ninth Street (map 8). Low-lying areas in the East Bottoms and West Bottoms, in contrast, have attracted few residents. Of the twenty subdivisions added to the city through 1857, only four had significant populations in 1860. Three of these, because they adjoin the original town on the south or west, are easily understood. The fourth, McGee's Addition, stands large and isolated as a powerful testament to salesmanship. Owner decisions to hold properties produce noticeable gaps in the pattern east of Broadway downtown and north of Coates's Addition.[57]

Small communities almost by definition have low degrees of residential segregation. Beyond the physical isolation of larger homes atop the bluffs from smaller ones beneath, Kansas City fit this description before 1855. In contrast, growth would bring a permanent switch to the other end of the continuum by the middle 1870s. Conditions in 1860

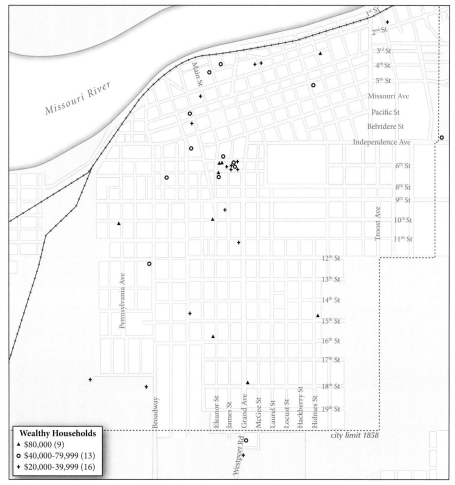

Map 9. Wealthy Households, 1860. Data from Hattie E. Poppino, Census of 1860: Population Schedules for Jackson County, Missouri *(Kansas City, Mo.: H. E. Poppino, 1964), and from James Sutherland, comp.,* Kansas City Directory and Business Mirror for 1860–61 *(Indianapolis, Ind.: James Sutherland, 1860).*

were midway through the process. One can see tendencies for groups to cluster but not clear patterns.

The social geography of Kansas City logically begins with its wealthiest citizens (map 9). Only two of the thirty-eight people worth $20,000 or more continued to reside on Pearl Street, the town's first elite location. Both of these individuals—William J. Jarboe and Jesse Riddlesbarger—owned businesses on the nearby levee. Similarly, Quality Hill and Independence Avenue, two locations that within a decade would recapture the aura of early Pearl Street, contained only one large house apiece in 1860. Kersey Coates initiated Quality Hill, of course, but attorney and land developer Henry B. Bouton preferred the Independence road.

In the interim between the heyday of Pearl Street and the flourishing of Quality Hill, the wealthy temporarily favored

housing near the intersections of Sixth Street with Main and Walnut. Joseph S. Chick, a son of Kansas City's original merchant, built a home there, as did banker Hiram M. Northrup. Three of the new plutocrats lived in the Union Hotel at the southeast corner of Sixth and Main, and three others were nearby at a boardinghouse owned by John S. Campbell. The Union, a $9,000 brick building, had been erected in 1857 by Thompson McDaniel as the centerpiece for his namesake city addition (map 7). Before completion of the Broadway Hotel in 1868, it offered the best lodging in town.[58]

The dispersed pattern of the elite in 1860 was duplicated by at least three other social groups. The city's small African American population of 190, almost all enslaved at the time, lived near their owners (map 10). The symbols on their map, in fact, correlate with the homes of many wealthy citizens. Amelia Evans, a sister of Milt McGee who lived on the eastern edge of his addition, owned twelve slaves. Thompson McDaniel at the Union Hotel owned nine.

More surprising than African Americans in their wide-ranging distributions are immigrants from Germany and from New England and other "Yankee" states. These peoples each constituted about 12 percent of the city population and saw themselves as culturally distinct from the predominant Virginians and Kentuckians. Yet neither group felt unwelcome enough in the new city to cleave only to themselves. The explanation probably has to do with their relatively high incomes; their job skills; and in the case of the Germans, their familiarity with Missouri society. German natives were 50,000 strong in St. Louis at this time, and many of their kin sought opportunities in the newer city up the river. Much the same was true for Yankees. In a young and prosperous community, people with money always are tolerated and usually are welcomed. Mapping confirms this with patterns nearly identical to the population as a whole.[59]

Irish immigrants were the major exception to the fluid social geography of early Kansas City. They were an unexpected people as well, at least in the large numbers that located there. Despite having little money and few previous connections with the state, 1,271 Irish resided in Jackson County in 1860, where they constituted at least 15 percent of the city's population. Even more mysterious, they almost all emigrated from the northwestern province of Connaught.[60]

The explanation for the large and focused Irish presence relates to a single man—Father Bernard Donnelly. Donnelly, a native of County Cavan adjacent to Connaught, arrived in Kansas City in 1846 as the first resident priest. Eager to increase the number of parishioners, he saw opportunity in the city's need to excavate roads through its high bluffs. He offered

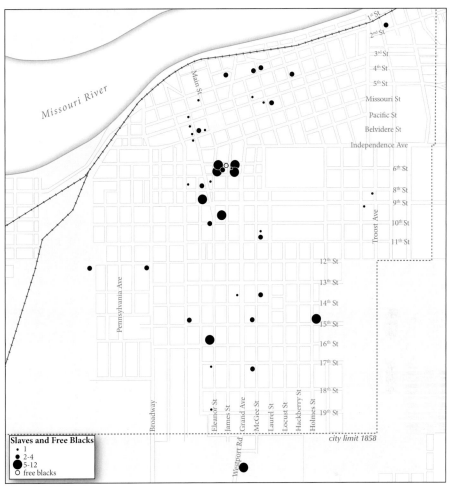

Map 10. Slaves and Free Blacks, 1860. Data from Hattie E. Poppino, Census of 1860: Population Schedules for Jackson County, Missouri *(Kansas City, Mo.: H. E. Poppino, 1964), and from James Sutherland, comp.,* Kansas City Directory and Business Mirror for 1860–61 *(Indianapolis, Ind.: James Sutherland, 1860).*

to recruit the laborers needed, and when city officials accepted his offer, he began a successful campaign. In letters to Irish newspapers in Boston and New York, he offered free passage to Kansas City for 300 men, plus better wages than those offered in eastern cities. Two restrictions applied: the laborers had to abstain from liquor, and (in the name of unity) they had to be Connaught born.[61]

Donnelly's results greatly exceeded expectations. Early arrivals such as Peter Soden became major contractors for sewers and wells in addition to roads. Others became bricklayers, stonemasons, and retail tradesmen. Donnelly himself stayed closely involved, opening a brickyard and a lime kiln on the church property at the top of Quality Hill. The residential distribution for 1860 demonstrates these successes (map 11). Locations in the new McGee's Addition are partial testimony;

so are large homes in the original town owned by merchant Joseph Shannon and real estate developer John Campbell.[62]

Still, the overall housing pattern for the Irish does not match that of the city as a whole. As mostly poor laborers, their concentration north and east of the public square suggests that this part of the original town was dominated by small houses and apartments. Father Donnelly recognized the group's presence there by renting a building at the corner of Second and Cherry to serve as a temporary church. Three other clusterings also can be related to economics. The Irish along the levee at Williams Street (now Holmes) worked at the nearby Central Flouring Mill. Those pioneering in the West Bottoms were adjacent to two sawmills. Boardinghouses along and near Sixth Street west from Delaware accommodated the largest numbers of the new workers. This area, called

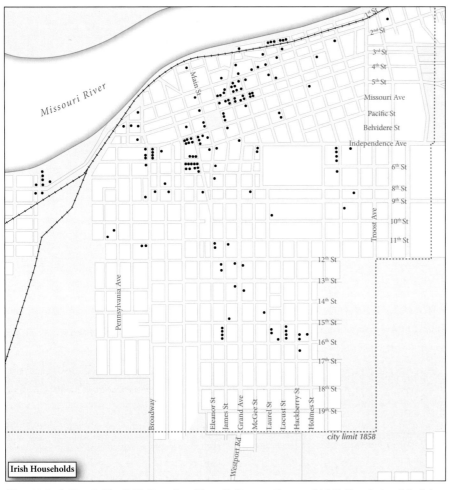

Map 11. Irish Households, 1860. Data from Hattie E. Poppino, Census of 1860: Population Schedules for Jackson County, Missouri *(Kansas City, Mo.: H. E. Poppino, 1964), and from James Sutherland, comp.,* Kansas City Directory and Business Mirror for 1860–61 *(Indianapolis, Ind.: James Sutherland, 1860).*

Connaught Town, was where Father Donnelly had housed his first recruits in temporary buildings.[63]

The social separateness of the local Irish is perhaps best illustrated by a story about Andrew Reeder, the first territorial governor of Kansas. In 1856, after being forced from office by a series of actions that had angered Missourians, he found himself in danger at a hotel on the Kansas City levee. He was able to escape openly and undetected, however, by adopting a brogue and dressing as "an Irish paddy." Nobody notices the hired help.[64]

3 The Rise of a Metropolis, 1867–1889

The opening of Kansas Territory in 1854 initiated a slow-building but long-term economic boom that transformed Kansas City from a frontier outpost into a major city. As settlers trekked to new farms and towns, Kersey Coates and other leaders dreamed of and then implemented a system of radiating railroad lines and big wholesale houses to serve the emerging prairie hinterland. This chapter explores the effects of such growth on the city itself, particularly on the function and culture of its many neighborhoods and adjoining towns. The emphasis on railroads instead of the river, for instance, meant new locations for existing business and industry as well as several completely new economic endeavors. These modifications, in turn, affected the residential choices of elite citizens, new immigrants, and everybody in between.

A Precarious Decade

In studying the history of Kansas City, it sometimes seems that the town's early success was inevitable. From the perspective of the twenty-first century, one achievement appears to follow another in dizzying fashion. This view is largely correct for the twenty-year period starting about 1867. Companies had made the decision to focus railroads on the city by that date, and their action produced the subsequent boom. Our selective memory often overlooks the ten years before 1867, however, when new rival communities and political turmoil placed the city's metropolitan dreams in serious jeopardy. The opening of Kansas Territory, for example, initially threatened nearly as much local business as it created, especially overland freighting and Indian trade. Citizens worried that such losses

might convince moneyed railroad people to construct their lines through other locations on the western frontier.

Securing the terminus of the Pacific Railroad of Missouri, a line already under construction west from St. Louis, was a major goal. This connection would improve access to eastern markets and capital, and a continuation on to the west could tap the goldfields of Colorado and California. Outside observers expected Kansas City to be part of this transportation artery, but local leaders took nothing for granted. Because the route had started out south of the Missouri River and state legislators had promised a terminus somewhere in Jackson County, people worried little about competition from Liberty, Parkville, and other area north-bank communities. They also saw no threat from Independence. Even if the railroad were to pass through that older community, Independence's location directly east of Kansas City would mean an easy and inevitable extension on to their city. Westport, a second old rival, prompted more concern. Its upland site would be easier for rail builders to reach than Kansas City's valley, and St. Louis people were already on record as favoring an upland route, since they had diverted their tracks away from the river at Jefferson City toward Sedalia and Warrensburg.[1]

Besides the possibility of renewed competition from Westport, Kansas City people in 1854 also faced urban ambitions to their west. Kansas Territory was a speculator's paradise. On one scale, this included Leavenworth, a new community 30 miles up the Missouri River and adjacent to the military supply depot at Fort Leavenworth. Development closer to home was a more immediate concern. The Wyandot Indians, an acculturated and educated people, already had a village on the bluff overlooking Kansas City's West Bottoms. Several nearby sites along the Kansas River and Turkey Creek also looked promising.

Business leaders in Kansas City handled the threats to their immediate regional authority in classic fashion. Using the advantages of political and monetary clout that their city's size provided, they methodically outmaneuvered smaller Missouri communities and assumed financial control of the key new townsite in adjacent Kansas. The threat in Westport proved easiest to counter. The economy there was narrowly based on trade with area Indians and Santa Fe merchants. Once Kansas Territory opened in 1854, these businesses declined rapidly. When most store owners decided to relocate rather than endure slow decline, their ability to lobby for the railroad evaporated. The coup de grâce came in 1859 when a fire destroyed thirteen blocks of the business core on Christmas Day. People in the surrounding cluster of houses had little choice but to gradually fall into the commercial orbit of an expanding Kansas City.[2]

When Westport people opted not to challenge Kansas City for the Pacific Railroad, observers expected a quick completion of the line. This was not to be the case. Railroad officials did not officially designate Kansas City as the terminus until 1858, and they did not complete their tracks until 1865. These delays occurred despite the best efforts of Kansas City leaders, providing a humbling demonstration of how forces beyond the city could determine its fate. First, financial backing from St. Louis for the line proved to be only marginally adequate and attempts to infuse eastern money were stopped by an economic panic in 1857. At the same time, political and military turmoil enveloped adjacent Kansas. The city's economy went from incipient boom to severe depression in less than a year.[3]

When representatives in Congress opened Kansas Territory, they expected neighboring Missouri to guide its development toward an eventual entrance into the Union as a slave state. This scenario sat well with Kansas City business leaders, for they, with few exceptions, were Southern born and solid supporters of the Democratic Party. Problems began to surface in 1856, however, when the number of Northern abolitionists in the new territory grew large enough to threaten this assumption. As Free State people gained a clear majority the next year, regional violence seemed likely. What were Kansas City residents to do in this situation: embrace the new reality in Kansas, fight against it, or try to maintain a studied neu-

trality? When several people supported the first of these possibilities by selling the town's principal hotel (Troost House) to the New England Emigrant Aid Company for use as a way station for new settlers, many residents reacted angrily. Among them was Milt McGee, who pointedly rechristened his Farmer's Hotel on Grand Avenue as The Southern. Other people intercepted steamboats that carried Northern immigrants. In this way, the city quickly became a tinderbox.[4]

Whereas the residents of Independence and Westport made no secret of their Southern sympathies during the 1856–1865 period, their kin in Kansas City attempted neutrality. This decision, which has been well studied by historians, was not easy to make or maintain. It alienated the city from its partisan trade areas on both sides of the state border and caused outside investors such as the Philadelphia syndicate represented by Kersey Coates to withdraw their capital. To keep the peace, business leaders invited in troops from Fort Leavenworth, who created a makeshift Camp Union inside the foundation of the unfinished Broadway Hotel at the corner of Tenth and Broadway. The garrison did its job but added military-civilian tension to the mix.[5]

At war's end in 1865, it was not easy to judge whether the strategy of noninvolvement had been a success. Most of the urban infrastructure remained intact, but surrounding Jackson County was thoroughly looted and burned. Approximately half of the city's prewar residents remained, some 3,000 strong, but their confidence in the future was shaken. Particularly worrisome for business leaders was the city's position relative to upstart Leavenworth. That newer community now had over twice the population of Kansas City, and being in Free State Kansas, residents there figured to gain political favor from the victorious Republican Party that controlled the national government.

When Kansas City people assessed their economic prospects, they found solace in a combination of railroads, potential financial and political aid from St. Louis, and open industrial sites in the West Bottoms and adjacent lowlands. All these assets were interconnected. Once the terminus of the Pacific Railroad of Missouri had been guaranteed to Kansas City, for example, the railroad's St. Louis backers necessarily became supporters of Kansas City aspirations. They reasoned that any wealth destined for Kansas City via the new tracks and their extensions to the west ultimately would pass down the line to St. Louis. A tremendous asset in this regard already was in place—congressional legislation to construct the nation's first transcontinental railroad.

The Pacific Railroad Act of 1862 authorized a single track through the Rocky Mountains in Wyoming plus a series of branch lines to link with the existing transportation network in the Midwest. One such route would cross Iowa to Chicago, but St. Louis people demanded and received another to follow the valley of the Kansas River. Leavenworth leaders campaigned hard to base this second route at their city, but more powerful men in St. Louis insisted that new construction begin just across the border from their own direct rail connection in Kansas City.[6]

Even as wartime atrocities were dominating local life, the railroad legislation of 1862 must surely have lifted spirits in Kansas City and adjacent Wyandotte County. A critical test came when the railroad's construction company requested separate bond issues from rival Wyandotte and Leavenworth counties. Each passed such a measure, but only the Wyandotte aid came without restrictions. This response, it is believed, solidified the resolve of Union Pacific officials to build directly up the Kansas River valley instead of deviating through Leavenworth. It was a victory for Kansas City, of course, and also for a newer, partner community just across the river to the west.[7]

The place that was to become Kansas City, Kansas, had its beginnings on the high bluffs that overlook the junction of the Kansas and Missouri rivers. This was and is an impressive site, but no urban promoters appeared there during the hectic first three years of Kansas settlement. This delay occurred because the property's owners, several hundred Wyandot Indians, wanted to control development for themselves. Quite sophisticated in business matters, they worked first to attain American citizenship and its accompanying rights to property. With this goal realized in 1855, they began to consider investment possibilities. The best offer paired three Wyandot landowners—Silas Armstrong, Isaiah Walker, and Joel Walker—with ten men from Lawrence and Kansas City to create a town company.[8]

The new community, called Wyandott on the original plat but spelled Wyandotte by most residents, was founded in March 1857 (maps 12 and 13). Its boundaries were irregular initially, matching the holdings of Armstrong and the two Walkers, but focus was provided by four wide avenues (Kansas, Minnesota, Nebraska, and Washington) that extended west from a levee on the Missouri River. Early businesses concentrated on the eastern blocks of Nebraska and Washington avenues, but border raids and political tension during the early years limited progress. Wyandotte's residents,

numbering 400 after the first year and 1,259 in 1859, were necessarily pragmatic and united in their efforts to promote growth. The vote in 1863 to help the builders of the Union Pacific reflected this stance.[9]

Construction work for the new railroad transformed Wyandotte in the fall of 1863. Newspapers advertised for a thousand laborers at premium wages, and company officials selected this site for their headquarters and machine shops. Wyandotte was nicely situated for these roles, especially since the railroad's charter required a path north of the Kansas River. The route began at the state line in the West Bottoms, as stipulated. It then crossed the Kansas River about a mile above its mouth and followed the northern edge of that river's lowland on a path nearly due west.[10]

With the advantages of hindsight, it is easy to identify 1863 as the critical year for metropolitan aspirations in Kansas City. The railroad route guaranteed local entrepreneurs a spot on a major, east-west traffic flow in the country as well as an important interchange between river and rail transportation. It also opened to development both the West Bottoms and its twin lowland across the bridge (map 2). Yet people at the time did not celebrate. For one thing, the critical Pacific Railroad from St. Louis had been completed only to Sedalia (still 95 miles from Kansas City), and Southern sympathizers made it a regular practice to harass building crews and destroy track. For another, units of the regular Union and Confederate armies were both active in the area, culminating with the bloody battle of Westport in October 1864. Trade was at a near standstill.

The Boom Begins

Solid transportation infrastructure began to pay dividends for Kansas City in the late 1860s. As the Civil War officially ended, guerrilla actions declined sharply and citizens reoccupied rural Jackson County. A key date was September 21, 1865, when the Pacific Railroad finally completed trackage into the city. Its route followed the lowland along the Missouri River from Independence to a new depot at the foot of Grand Avenue. From there, the line extended on to the West Bottoms, where a second depot, State Line Station, marked its junction with the Union Pacific (map 14). The railroad men also platted a new town 12 miles south of Independence where their route crossed the stream divide between the Little Blue River and Big Creek. This community, appropriately called Lee's Summit, was nicely positioned to attract rural trade from the county's southern half.[11]

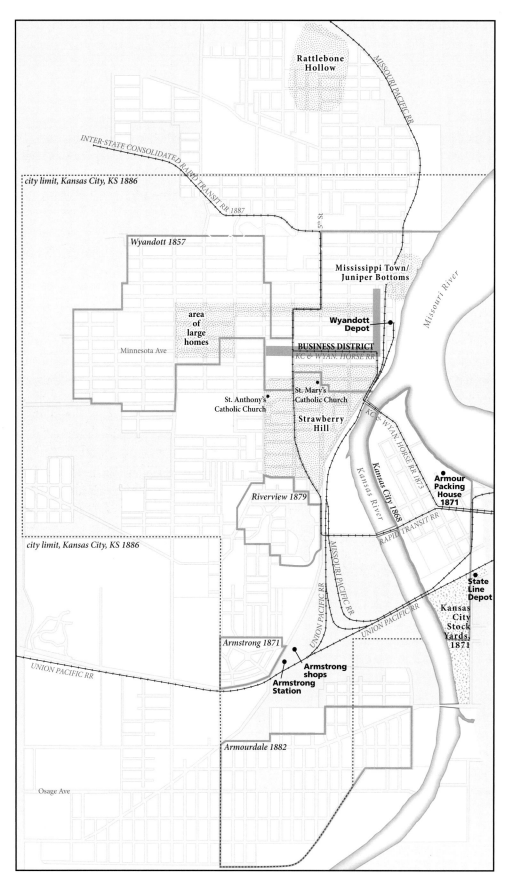

Rattlebone
Hollow

MISSOURI PACIFIC RR

INTER-STATE CONSOLIDATED RAPID TRANSIT RR 1887

city limit, Kansas City, KS 1886

5th St

Wyandott 1857

Mississippi Town/
Juniper Bottoms

Missouri River

area
of
large
homes

Wyandott
Depot

Minnesota Ave

BUSINESS DISTRICT
KC & WYAN. HORSE RR

St. Anthony's
Catholic Church

St. Mary's
Catholic Church

Strawberry
Hill

KC & WYAN. HORSE RR 1873

Kansas River 1868

Riverview 1879

Armour
Packing
House
1871

RAPID TRANSIT RR

city limit, Kansas City, KS 1886

MISSOURI PACIFIC RR

State
Line
Depot

UNION PACIFIC RR

Kansas
City
Stock
Yards,
1871

Armstrong 1871

Armstrong shops

UNION PACIFIC RR

Armstrong
Station

Armourdale 1882

Osage Ave

Map 12. Kansas City, Kansas,
and Its Constituent Communities, 1889. Modified from
Insurance Maps of Kansas
City, Kansas *(New York:
Sanborn Map and Publishing,
1889), with additional data
from Union Historical
Company,* The History of
Jackson County, Missouri
*(Kansas City, Mo.: Birdsall,
Williams, 1881), pp. 668–
712; William G. Cutler, ed.,*
History of the State of Kansas,
*vol. 2 (Chicago: A. D. Andreas,
1883), pp. 1226–1254; and
other sources.*

Map 13 (facing page).
Wyandotte, 1869. A
portion of "Bird's Eye View
of Wyandotte, Wyandotte
County, Kansas," drawn by
Albert Ruger. (Courtesy of
Library of Congress, Prints
and Photographs Division)

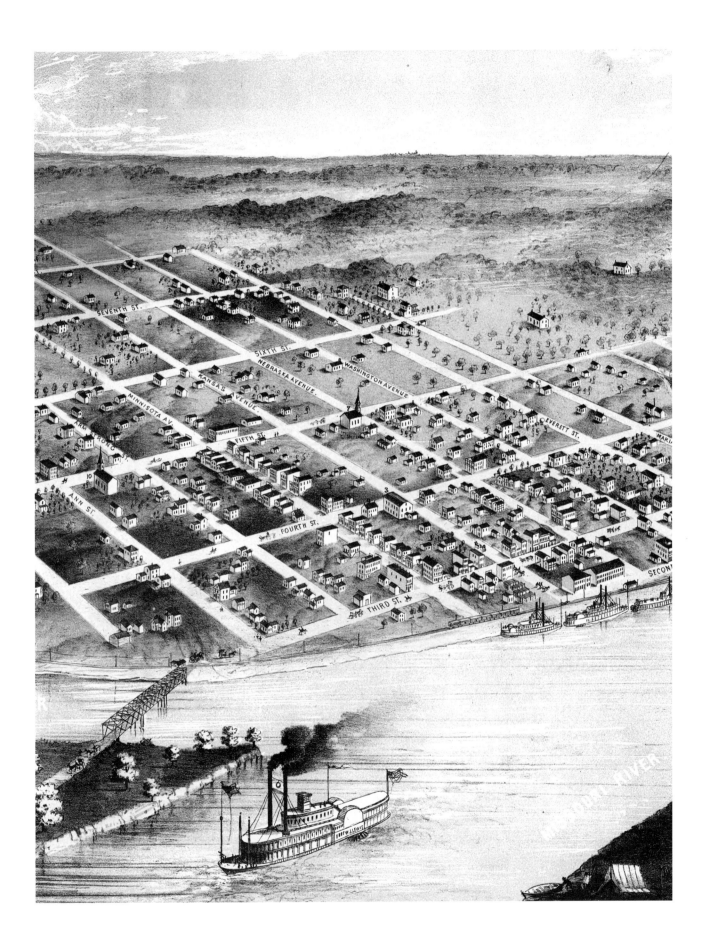

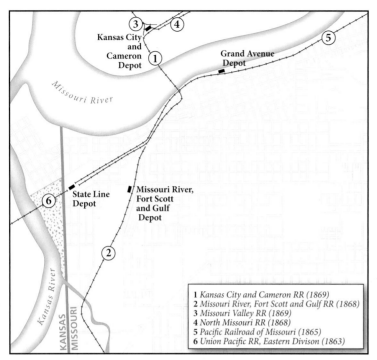

Map 14. Railroads, 1870. Data primarily from Charles N. Glaab, Kansas City and the Railroads: Community Policy in the Growth of a Regional Metropolis *(Madison: State Historical Society of Wisconsin, 1962).*

Business leaders in Kansas City saw their two railroads as a springboard to greatness. United by the adversity of the recent past and accustomed to thinking large by decades of trade with Santa Fe, they advocated action rather than complacency. Success, they reasoned, lay in making Kansas City a true junction point, with tracks going in many directions. A route south to ports on the Gulf of Mexico would be logical in this regard. So would one north that could connect directly with Chicago.

Several charters and land surveys for north-south railroads existed even before workers on the Pacific line had laid their final pieces of steel. Originally, these ideas were as much stunts as true plans, inducements to convince St. Louis people that they should select Kansas City as their railroad terminus before others beat them to it. Once the St. Louis connection was secure, Chicago became the next priority. This city on Lake Michigan was growing rapidly. On paper, the route also looked easy to complete. Chicago already was linked to northern Missouri via the Hannibal and St. Joseph Railroad, which had been in operation since 1859. Only 54 miles of new track to the town of Cameron could connect Kansas City with this route and therefore with Chicago. The one obstacle was a bridge across the powerful Missouri River.[12]

Kansas City's boosters long have touted the Cameron

Branch Railroad and the construction of what became known as the Hannibal Bridge as the community's finest hour. They note that these creations led directly to a world-famous stockyard and meat-packing industry and, in turn, to a general growth from small town to major city. In the process, the community quickly eclipsed its railroad rivals of Atchison, Leavenworth, and St. Joseph. All these things are true, and local leaders of the time deserve credit for maintaining a united front and working hard. But just as was the case with the decision of Union Pacific people to go to Wyandotte, the real power behind the bridge, the stockyard, and the vanquishing of rival towns came from outside investors. The only difference was that Boston now replaced St. Louis as the source.

The Boston financial alliance sprang from the ownership of the Hannibal and St. Joseph Railroad. This company was part of the larger Chicago, Burlington and Quincy rail system controlled by John Murray Forbes. Forbes and his fellow New England investors concentrated primarily on a route across Iowa that could be part of the transcontinental system to California. The Hannibal and St. Joseph, however, provided an opportunity to exploit another great realm. By acceding to the Kansas City plea for a branch route south from Cameron, the Burlington system would have access not only to Kansas via the new Union Pacific line, but also to the country farther south and west with a new track of its own.[13]

The company man who pushed for and eventually sold the Cameron concept was James F. Joy, president of the Hannibal and St. Joseph. In turn, Joy was motivated by the salesmanship of Charles E. Kearney, Theodore S. Case, and other Kansas City people. These men, through a corporation called the West Kansas Land Company, owned the core of the West Bottoms. This vast area had major industrial potential via the new railroads to the east and west, but it was still nearly vacant. Kearney and Case sold Joy enough company shares so that he himself could direct the company and, through it, the future of the entire West Bottoms. It was brilliant strategy.

With Joy on board, the biggest remaining obstacle was the bridge. Here, too, Kansas City people helped themselves. The hero this time was Robert T. Van Horn, a newspaper editor who had been elected to the U.S. Congress. In 1866, he obtained federal authorization for this bridge plus a land grant to extend the Cameron line south to the Gulf of Mexico.

Although Kansas City's bridge was not completed until 1869, an approval of funds by the Boston investors in November 1866 essentially sealed the deal. It was then that local people and outsiders alike realized the community would become the gateway between the country's urban Northeast and the rich resources of the greater Southwest. As investors arrived by the hundreds, the city not only boomed, but also began to reconfigure its internal geography.

In retrospect, the only unusual thing about Kansas City's new prosperity was that the industries that would capitalize most on the new railroad nexus—cattle marketing and meat-packing—caught local boosters off guard. In 1867 and 1868, Joy and his Kansas City partners concentrated on bridge construction and funding for an extension of their Cameron route south toward Texas. In so doing, they ignored the immediate economic potential of the Union Pacific, a railroad they did not control.

As the Union Pacific had built across Kansas in the late

Figure 6. Hannibal Bridge, 1868, Looking Northwest from near Third and Wyandotte. A symbol of Kansas City's growth, this bridge linked the Union Pacific Railroad that ran across Kansas with Chicago and other eastern cities. Engineer Octave Chanute began construction in 1867 and finished on July 3, 1869. The design included seven piers of local limestone and a pivoting center section to allow passage of river barges. The bridge endured until 1917. (Courtesy Missouri Valley Special Collections, Kansas City Public Library)

1860s, most talk about it revolved around transcontinental connections and Colorado gold. It took an outsider from Illinois, Joseph C. McCoy, to glimpse more immediate profits in the shipping of rangeland cattle. McCoy positioned himself as a middleman in Abilene, Kansas, buying animals from drovers and selling them to the railroad. The 18,000 head he sent east in 1867 got people's attention. When this number ballooned to 53,000 in 1868, investors rethought their priorities.[14]

Two financiers guided the scope and form of the new cattle trade in Kansas City and, through this, the entire social and economic pattern of the emerging metropolis. Philip D.

35

Figure 7. Kansas Stock Yards, 1874. The city's signature stockyard industry began in 1871 as a cooperative venture by local railroad companies and grew large in 1876 with the backing of Boston financier Charles F. Adams. By 1878, it covered a hundred acres of the West Bottoms and handled over 200,000 head of cattle annually. Henry Worrall's line drawing was published in Joseph G. McCoy's Historic Sketches of the Cattle Trade of the West and Southwest *in 1874.*

Armour and Charles F. Adams, Jr., were their names. They came from different backgrounds—the former a self-made man who had pioneered the packing business in Chicago and the latter a Harvard-educated grandson of President John Quincy Adams—but both made big investments beginning in 1871. That year, Adams cofounded the city's first major stockyard, located just south of the Pacific's main line in the West Bottoms. Its 13.5-acre site lay mostly in Kansas and was adjacent to the Kansas River for easy disposal of manure and other waste. Armour's big investment that year—a new packing plant that expanded his business from Chicago to Kansas City—was carefully coordinated with the emerging stockyard. His was the first substantial slaughterhouse in the area and one of the most modern to exist anywhere. Its presence was a demonstration that Kansas City could indeed become a premier cattle market, and it led to a series of ex-

pansions at the stockyard and the attraction of other packing companies.[15]

The choices of initial locations for the stockyard and the Armour plant within the urban area were vital because these decisions affected far more than just other packers. In a domino effect, they also influenced sites for later warehouse operators, retail businesspeople, and even residential developers. Philip Armour's choice was a 15-acre tract a half mile north of the stockyard. Like its kindred business, it also lay in the Kansas portion of the West Bottoms and adjacent to a river (the Missouri) for easy disposal of waste. Neither Adams nor Armour ever explained their selections of slightly more remote Kansas over Missouri, but the locations made good business sense. Both were on a small thumb of bottomland that extends west from the state line between the Kansas and Missouri rivers (map 12). Kansas City, Kansas, as this place had been incorporated in 1868, spanned less than a half mile east to west and only a mile north and south along the state line. Besides offering proximity to railroads for shipment and rivers for refuse, this town's newness and its slight removal from the commercial center in Missouri meant that acreage was inexpensive and available in large parcels. The combination was exactly what Adams and Armour needed.[16]

The economic boom promised by the juxtaposition of railroads, stockyard, and meatpackers started strong but then stagnated for several years beginning in 1873. The causes were almost all external to the city, but they were enough to limit the local population growth to only a thousand from 1873 to 1877. A national business panic started the process, drying up investment dollars. Then came two years of grasshopper plagues across the Great Plains. Additional problems were specific to the packing industry—a railroad rate discrimination that favored older, eastern livestock centers over newer, western ones and an inability of the Armour plant to expand beef output much beyond salted and canned products. The much larger market for fresh, dressed beef in eastern cities was closed to western packers since there was no means to refrigerate the product for the long haul across the country. Such technology did not materialize until the early 1880s.[17]

The stagnation of 1873–1877 typically has been interpreted as a minor interruption during an otherwise prolonged period of growth between 1869 and 1890. This view is correct, but it overlooks a central aspect of these anomalous years that heavily influenced the city's future. Such a "pause" in the action gave Armour and Adams valuable time to consider their next investments. Neither man lived in the area, but both saw its future as bright and therefore appointed resident aides to inspect local potentials and recommend sites for purchase. The results, especially for Adams, were spectacular. He later wrote that "all the money I have made has been in dealing in real estate in Kanzas [sic] City."[18]

Philip Armour sent two of his brothers to oversee the family's Kansas City operations. Simeon headed the packing-house, and Andrew, in 1878, created the Armour Brothers Banking Company at Fifth and Delaware downtown. Both businesses thrived. Andrew's venture is ancestral to today's Commerce Bank, and the packing company capped a steady expansion with the 1892 construction of the largest dressed-beef plant in the world. With over 3,000 jobs available, the opening of this facility was said by a contemporary observer to be "probably the greatest event in the history of Kansas City."[19]

Charles Adams, who had considerable money of his own, controlled even more capital through an association with Nathaniel Thayer, a prominent Boston banker. With Thayer's blessing, he purchased a controlling interest in the Kansas City Stock Yards in 1875, quadrupled its acreage between the Kansas River and the state line, and began to scout out additional real estate. To oversee these enterprises, he hired

another Boston man, Charles F. Morse. Morse was already successful in his own right as general superintendent of the Atchison, Topeka and Santa Fe Railway, but Adams offered him a chance to mold an entire metropolitan area. Morse moved from Topeka to Kansas City early in 1879.[20]

Morse's first recommendation was wildly successful. The industrial potential of the West Bottoms was obvious to everybody, but many warehouses already operated there and prices had risen quickly after 1878 when railroad owners chose that site for the city's first union depot. Morse observed that property of similar character lay just across the Kansas River to the west, adjacent to Adams's stockyard. This, too, was bottomland and abutted the Union Pacific tracks, but it was still being farmed and could be purchased for $150 to $300 per acre instead of the $1,000 common for the West Bottoms. Adams approved acquisition plans early in 1879, and within months, his investment company owned 1,000 compact acres. Next came construction of a bridge across the Kaw to the stockyard and the platting of a new community that combined residential lots with large industrial sites. Adams allowed his name to be used for one street, but he called the new town Armourdale to honor his business ally and to make his purpose clear (map 12).[21]

Although the Armour family elected to keep their plant at its original location, Armourdale otherwise developed exactly as Adams and Morse envisioned. Their offer of free plant sites at the river's edge attracted several new packers, including the large Swift and Company and the predecessors of both Cudahy and Wilson, the remaining two of the country's "big four" packers of the early twentieth century. These companies were joined by three other sizable enterprises that used cattle by-products as their raw materials: soap companies ancestral to today's Colgate-Palmolive and Procter and Gamble and a fertilizer plant owned by Adams and his associates. It was a tightly focused community that epitomized heavy industry in Kansas City. Armourdale also provided nearly a 600 percent return on investment to Adams and his partners.[22]

An Industrial Core

The Kansas state census of 1885 revealed that the Adams-Armour vision was well on its way to maturity. Adams completed expansion of his stockyard with acreage north of the Union Pacific tracks for easier access to the Armour plant and a new brick headquarters building with 350 offices at the corner of Sixteenth Street and State Line Road. Armour, too, was prospering, as his company and four smaller ones reported a

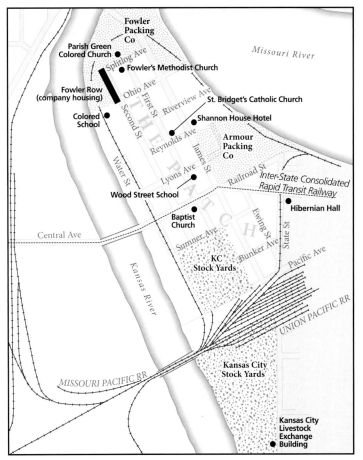

Map 15. The Original Kansas City, Kansas, 1889. Data primarily from Insurance Maps of Kansas City, Kansas *(New York: Sanborn Map and Publishing, 1889).*

by 341 from Ireland and 243 from Germany. The Irish component is obvious on a map via the Shannon House hotel on James Street, the Hibernian Hall on Central, and St. Bridget's Catholic Church on First. The census reported no African Americans in the city, but this omission contradicts evidence to the contrary, including the presence of both the Parish Green Colored Church on Splitlog Avenue and a segregated school on Second Street near Ohio.[24]

Armourdale was similar in purpose to Kansas City, but it was newer and still developing in the 1880s (map 16). The town was planned for industry from the start, and a residential core along Osage Avenue was encircled by industrial sites near the railroad and the Kansas River. As late as 1889, only the eastern half of the area was fully occupied. Adams's own fertilizer operation, the Kansas Desiccating and Refining Company, commanded a prime block, but two large packinghouses built in 1887—Swift and Kingan—were the town's pride (map 17). Both faced Railroad Street at its intersection with Kansas Avenue. They conveniently adjoined an 1886 expansion of the stockyard company.[25]

Armourdale's population was only 1,582 in 1885, but it more than doubled over the next three years as new packers bolstered Wyandotte County employment in this industry alone to 4,265. Irish, German, and other immigrants constituted 14 percent of the 1885 population, and again, census takers seriously underreported African Americans. With a separate school present as early as 1882, the town obviously contained more than the two black residents announced in the census. Kansas Avenue west from

total of 2,285 employees. Kansas City, Kansas, the nucleus of this activity, was virtually a company town (map 15). The Union Pacific tracks crossed its center, and numerous spurs extended south into the stockyard and north to the plants of Armour and George Fowler and Son.[23]

Most workers at the plants lived nearby in a series of boardinghouses, tenements, and small single-family homes. Collectively known as The Patch, many of these dwellings were company owned, including Fowler Row on Second Street between Splitlog and Ohio. Small shops lined James Street and Central Avenue; public buildings clustered along First Street. Of the 3,802 people who lived there in 1885, a quarter were foreign born, led

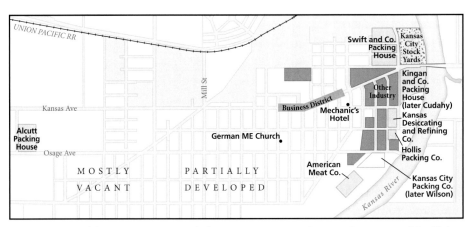

Map 16. Armourdale, 1889. Data primarily from Insurance Maps of Kansas City, Kansas *(New York: Sanborn Map and Publishing, 1889).*

the plants was lined with retail shops. Hotels and tenements clustered between First and Third streets, with single-family homes beyond.[26]

The industrial core of the 1880s actually extended beyond the cluster of packinghouses east to the Missouri side of the West Bottoms and west to another lowland slightly upstream in the Kansas River valley. This latter development was initiated by officials of the Atchison, Topeka and Santa Fe Railway. As the company grew, these men decided, in 1875, that Kansas City offered better potential as an eastern terminal than did Atchison, their original choice. They therefore laid track along the south bank of the Kaw and found an ideal site for their yards at the river's bend just west from Armourdale (map 2). Buying 128 acres there, the firm erected extensive shops and switching facilities that employed nearly 600 people by 1882.[27]

Simultaneous with construction of the rail yard, entrepreneur William N. Ewing arrived to inspect the developing bottomland. Ewing was a friend of Charles F. Morse from the days when both had worked for the Santa Fe in Topeka. More recently, he had opened a gold and silver smelter in Colorado, but capital and labor shortages there limited his productivity. Morse proposed a relocation. Kansas City now had good rail connections to both mines and markets; a decent labor pool; and, best of all, solid financial assistance from the ubiquitous Charles Adams. It was an easy sell.[28]

Ewing's reborn enterprise, the Kansas City Smelting and Refining Company, opened in 1880 to immediate success. It employed 250 men by 1882, processing not only silver and gold ores from Colorado but also lead and zinc from the relatively close Joplin area. To accommodate the influx of workers, railroad officials partnered with a local man in 1880–1881 to create a new town adjacent to both big employers. They called it Argentine, from the Latin word for silver, in honor of the smelter (map 18). By 1885, this blue-collar community had a population mix nearly identical to Armourdale's. A quarter of its 1,412 residents were German, Irish, and others who were foreign born; another ninth were African American.[29]

As Kansas City's railroad connections to the rest of the nation progressed quickly from modest to outstanding, many other entrepreneurs joined the packers and the smelter owners in seeking sites for new plants and warehouses. Elevator operators hoped to create a grain market on the same scale

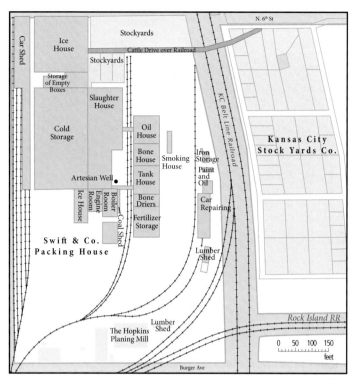

Map 17. *Swift and Company Packing House, 1889. Modified from pl. 35 of* Insurance Maps of Kansas City, Kansas *(New York: Sanborn Map and Publishing, 1889).*

as the market that was developing for cattle. Other people saw profit in supplying new towns and farms across the Great Plains with everything from agricultural machinery to furniture and canned goods.

The new businesspeople concentrated their operations in the northern and eastern sections of the West Bottoms. This area was close to the city's commercial center, of course, and to the freight depots of the Missouri Pacific, the Hannibal and St. Joseph, and several newer railroads. Not coincidentally, most of these locations also were on property developed by the West Kansas Land Company. Headed originally by a group of local businesspeople, this enterprise had passed to the control of railroad tycoon James Joy as part of the critical deal brokered to construct the Hannibal Bridge. Joy, like Adams and Armour, saw great potential in this bottomland. Although he himself remained focused on railroad construction, including a route south toward the Gulf of Mexico, his promise of good shipping rates to Chicago was at least partly responsible for Joseph McCoy bringing his cattle business to Kansas City. Joy's Hannibal and St. Joseph Railroad also was the prime underwriter for the local stockyard before Adams entered the scene. Selling tracts of West Kansas land at discount to attract key industries was less spectacular but even

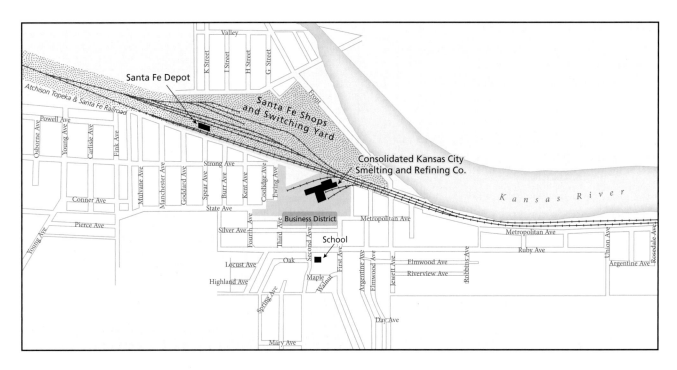

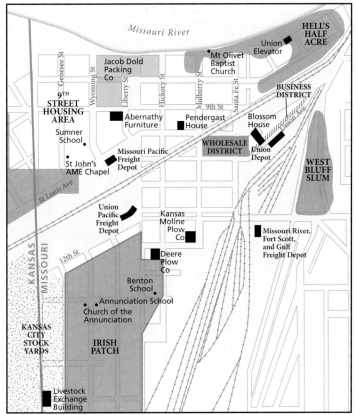

Map 18 (above). Argentine, 1889. Data primarily from
Insurance Maps of Kansas City, Kansas *(New York: Sanborn
Map and Publishing, 1889).*

*Map 19 (left). The West Bottoms (Missouri portion), circa
1884. Data primarily from Union Historical Company,* The
History of Jackson County, Missouri *(Kansas City, Mo.:
Birdsall, Williams, 1881), and from* Insurance Maps of
Kansas City, Missouri *(New York: Sanborn-Perris Map, 1895).*

Because Joy did not control all the land, the West
Bottoms was not planned as precisely as Armourdale.
Railroad location was key to its internal geography
(maps 14 and 19). All routes from the east and north
entered the area via a narrow corridor between the
downtown levee and the bluffs. Once in the bottom,
the tracks separated. The Missouri Pacific bisected the
district along a west-southwest angle, whereas Joy's
newer Missouri River, Fort Scott and Gulf line ran
almost due south, hugging the base of the bluffs below
the mansions on Quality Hill.

The single best site lay where the railroads forked.
Here, on what became Union Avenue, Joy erected a
small wooden passenger station in 1872. He cleverly
offered its use to competing companies, and as busi-
ness increased, city officials selected this location for their first
consolidated terminal. The new $225,000 Union Depot was
elegant—a French Empire design executed in brick with a
four-story tower. When it opened in 1878, Kansas City's first

more lucrative for Joy and his local agent, Octave Chanute.
In fact, they deserve almost as much recognition for spurring
local industrialization as the Boston patrician Charles Adams
and the Chicago packer Philip Armour.[30]

Figure 8. Union Depot, 1880. Located in the West Bottoms where rail lines diverged to the south and west, the city's first consolidated railroad station occupied a lot only 50 feet wide. James A. McGonigle completed the building in 1878 using Romanesque windows and a mansard roof. Another architect enlarged it just after this photograph was taken and made the roofline more complex. (Courtesy Missouri Valley Special Collections, Kansas City Public Library)

passenger station at the foot of Grand Avenue became obsolete. The new structure and its attendant freight depots also anchored subsequent development. The north side of Union Avenue, for example, quickly filled with hotels, saloons, and other businesses catering to travelers. Directly opposite the depot stood the five-story Blossom House, and a more modest (but soon to be famous) hotel/saloon called Pendergast House arose two blocks west at 1328 St. Louis Avenue. The corridor's atmosphere, especially at night, was that of a midway—busy, loud, and more than a little sordid.[31]

Wholesalers, whose trade required constant use of rail transportation, clustered just west of the depot between the Missouri Pacific and the Fort Scott lines. Their brick buildings soon dominated land use in a compact, three-block area south from St. Louis Avenue to Eleventh Street and west to Mulberry (map 19). Just beyond these jobbers (and to a degree interspersed with them) stood a ring of factories. By the late 1880s, this zone extended south to Joy Street and west to Liberty and was dominated by the John Deere and the Kansas Moline plow companies on Thirteenth Street. North of the Missouri Pacific tracks, between Wyoming and Santa Fe streets, lay a second manufacturing district. Diversity was the rule there. The Jacob Dold Packing Company was the biggest employer, but Abernathy Furniture sat just across Ninth Street from Dold, and several grain elevators stood farther to the east.

Considering the Kansas and Missouri portions of the West

Figure 9. West Bottoms, 1876, Looking West from Twelfth Street. Although industry filled the lowland north of Tenth Street by the middle 1870s, the southern section remained largely empty. Tracks of the Missouri River, Fort Scott and Gulf Railroad follow the base of the bluff with shops of the Hannibal and St. Joseph line just beyond. An expanding stockyard and various rail yards would soon force worker housing to other sites. (Courtesy Missouri Valley Special Collections, Kansas City Public Library)

Bottoms as a unit, a visitor in about 1890 would have seen not only distinctly partitioned industrial clusters but also three residential areas occupying the interstices. All of these areas housed working-class people, many in shanties and tenements. As in Armourdale and Argentine, Irish and German immigrants were common. So were African Americans.

The smallest, poorest, and most distinctive housing enclave was called Hell's Half Acre (map 19). This was a triangle of land, seemingly well situated in the northeast corner of the bottoms. Its location north of the Missouri Pacific tracks isolated it from the new depot, however, and from the main

routes that connected the station with downtown businesses. Construction workers for the Hannibal Bridge in the late 1860s found this site convenient for camping, and it grew in ramshackle fashion from there. African Americans were present from the start, and their numbers grew in 1880 with the addition of several dozen refugee families from Texas and Mississippi. This population was large enough to erect a Baptist church (Mount Olivet) on the levee just east of Mulberry Street but did not constitute a local majority. Instead, the African Americans formed just one part of a largely transient, unskilled group who had found first jobs nearby as laborers and porters, prostitutes and con men.[32]

The two other residential areas in the bottoms represented a step up the economic ladder. Although still described by upper-class visitors as "unattractive in a high degree" and as "a singular hotchpotch of bad hotels . . . sleazy inns, [and] dilapidated homes of Irish laborers," photographs suggest better conditions.[33] Houses, though small, appear neatly

constructed and sometimes accented with fenced and flow-ered yards. One district, conveniently positioned between the packing plants of Dold and Armour, evolved around the intersection of Genesee and Ninth streets. Houses stretched north to the river and south to St. Louis Avenue; Ninth Street contained retail shops. Other neighborhood foci for African American residents included Sumner School on Wyoming Street and St. John's AME Chapel on Genesee.

Directly south across the Missouri Pacific tracks stood the third residential neighborhood. It was similar in appearance and ethnic composition but relied on different employers for support. Here, the Kansas City Stock Yards company was king. Having constructed its headquarters building on the state line at Sixteenth Street in 1876, the company expanded one block into Missouri in 1886 and another in 1893 (map 19). Genesee Street, its new eastern limit, was one of the busiest places in the city with "clouds of dust . . . [from] the bel-lowing and plunging herds in transit" and hundreds of people

Figure 10. Genesee Street, 1881, Looking South from Ninth Street. Although this photograph was occasioned by an April flood, it also shows a typical working-class neighborhood. In this neighborhood, located only a block west of the Dold Packing Company and a block north of railroad freight yards, local jobs were plentiful and the popula-tion ethnically diverse. Ninth Street provided retailers and a streetcar line. Note the narrow, 25-foot lots. (Courtesy Missouri Valley Special Collections, Kansas City Public Library)

"buzzing about from sunrise to sunset." A series of hotels, saloons, and general retail shops lined Genesee to serve this clientele, and houses extended from there east to the railroad tracks and northeast to the manufacturing district. As the largest of the three residential areas, this was the site for the West Bottoms's first public school (Benton) in 1870 and its first Catholic church (Annunciation) in 1872.[34]

Beyond Argentine, Armourdale, and the West Bottoms, Greater Kansas City contains four other large lowlands, all of which featured at least some railroad service by the 1870s. The list includes the Rosedale Bottoms along Turkey Creek to the southwest and three others abutting the Missouri River: the East Bottoms and North Bottoms on its south bank and the Clay County Bottoms on its north (map 2). The latter two attracted virtually no industry throughout the nineteenth century, however, and the others only a little. Such nondevelopment stemmed from a slightly inferior location, an absence of influential owner-promoters, and the availability of space in earlier-platted districts.

The Rosedale area, physically connected to the West Bottoms and as accessible to Union Depot as was Armourdale, actually experienced a short-lived economic boom at an early date. James Joy built his railroad to the Gulf of Mexico through this valley in 1868 but attempted no site promotion because he had made earlier financial commitments to the West Kansas Company closer to downtown. But in 1875, entrepreneur A. B. Stone decided this was the place to relocate a large roller mill from Decatur, Illinois. Stone manufactured iron rails for trains and wanted better accessibility to the railroad frontier. When an exploratory shaft next to the new hamlet of Rosedale found coal for his furnaces, prosperity followed. The mill and associated mine and ironworks employed 600 men by 1881, a third of Rosedale's population. Stone could not adjust when railroad companies abruptly changed to steel tracks, however, and his operations closed in 1883. Rosedale people were forced to become commuters.[35]

The East Bottoms was the second site of modest industrialization. This land was relatively remote from the city's railroad nexus but adjacent to the central business district and easily accessible via Jackson County's first railroad, the Missouri Pacific. Development was slow primarily because the principal investor for this railroad, Robert Campbell of St. Louis, elected to speculate on downtown real estate instead of land in the bottoms. A map from 1896 shows four small grain elevators in the area and four yards selling coal, bricks, and/or lumber but only a single large factory. This exception, the Ferdinand Heim Brewing Company, manufactured the city's most popular beer. Its owners had moved to the corner of Chestnut and Guinotte avenues in 1885 to escape cramped quarters downtown.[36]

An Expanded Downtown

Kansas City's business district was never geographically stable throughout the nineteenth century. It focused initially on the levee, of course, but extremely limited space below the bluffs forced town founders to place their public square several blocks south of the river and some hundred feet higher in elevation. By the time of the Civil War, when excavation

work to cut paths through the bluffs for Delaware, Main, and other streets was complete, most retailers and government officials had moved their stores and offices nearer the square (map 6).

The face of downtown changed faster still in the 1870s and 1880s. Railroads were the primary force. Their role as catalyst for extraordinary growth is well known. Less obvious but still profound was their influence on road patterns and business locations. The process began in 1865 when city officials allowed the Pacific Railroad of Missouri to lay tracks along the levee. This provided a downtown depot, but the right-of-way occupied the only existing overland route into the West Bottoms.

Access to the big lowland did not loom as critical in 1865, but it became so rapidly after 1869. James Joy and his Hannibal and St. Joseph company knew that manufacturers and jobbers would migrate toward whatever spot they selected for their Chicago-linked line to join with the Pacific railroad. Bridging the Missouri River near the existing Grand Avenue station downtown might seem to have been a logical choice, but Joy actually wanted to cross directly into the West Bottoms. That way, the incipient industrial district of his West Kansas Land Company could control subsequent developments. As it happened, the need for solid footings forced the bridge site east to the edge of downtown, but this slight detour was inconsequential from the company's perspective (map 14).[37] The transportation nexus developed on West Kansas property just as expected. Such success was mixed news for the city's business community, however. The same bridge and track locations that created the central railroad depot now severely limited pedestrian and wagon entry to it.

The new railroad junction was some nine blocks south of the downtown levee and eleven blocks west. By itself, this distance was cause for concern, but topography made the problem worse. Because railroad tracks now filled the lowland channel between these end points completely, any trip required a trek up and down the 100-foot riverside bluffs. The first solution involved carving a roadway into the side of the escarpment, angling southwest from Fourth, Fifth, and Sixth streets to the new depot. With retaining walls above and below, this Bluff Street was picturesque but dangerous. Heavily laden freight wagons were the biggest problem, making

Map 20 (facing page). Downtown Kansas City, Missouri, 1878. A portion of "Bird's Eye View of Kansas City," drawn by Albert Ruger. (Courtesy of Missouri Valley Special Collections, Kansas City Public Library)

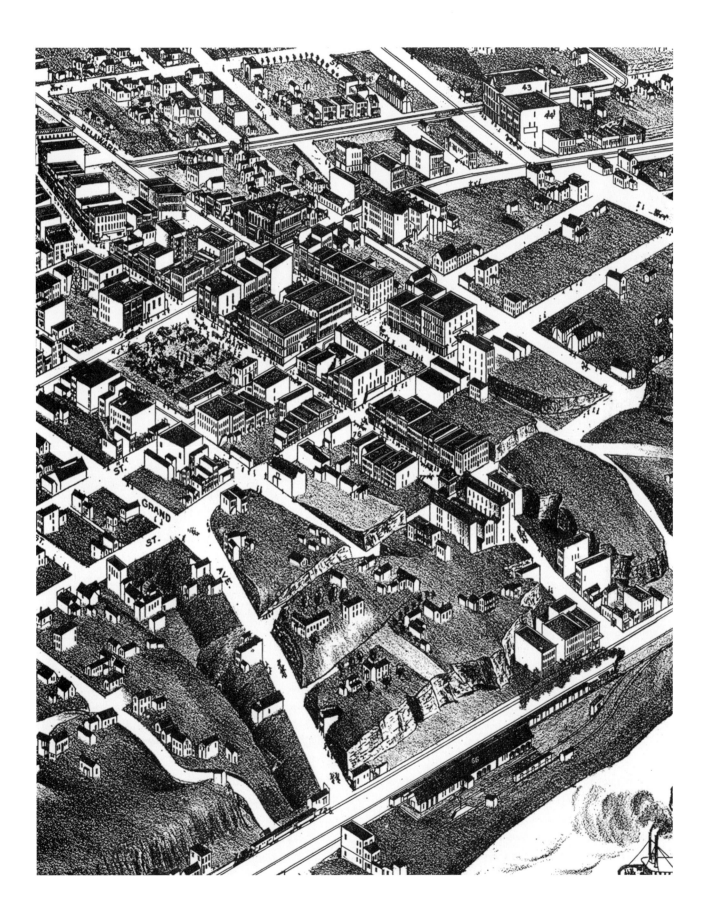

Figure 11. Main Street, 1868, Looking North from Missouri Avenue. The arrival of the Pacific Railroad from St. Louis and construction of the Hannibal Bridge in 1867 meant the end of business activity on the levee and a boom on Main Street. The mix of wooden and brick buildings in this view indicates a period of transition, but stone gutters suggest the expectation of a bright future. Third Street crosses at the top of the hill; the gap in the middle right marks an edge of the market square. (Courtesy Missouri Valley Special Collections, Kansas City Public Library)

the route "almost impassable" in wet weather. To reduce such traffic, city officials pleaded with their railroad counterparts to move all cargo operations from the bottoms to the Pacific's station at Grand Avenue. This notion was rejected, but some relief came in 1870 when the town council appropriated funds to pave Bluff and its feeder streets.[38]

In 1873, transportation to the railroad junction advanced another step as the Jackson County Horse Railroad Company began regular service along the Bluff Street route. This arrangement still evoked criticism, but increased passenger movement along Fourth and Fifth streets encouraged busi-nesspeople to move operations there from the levee. In so doing, they not only shortened their distance to the West Bottoms depot but also contributed to a new, repositioned commercial center.[39]

The core of downtown Kansas City by the middle 1870s had become a rectangle bounded by Third and Fifth streets, Walnut and Wyandotte (map 20). Businesses extended south along Main Street almost to Eighth, and the corner of Tenth and Broadway formed an outlier where entrepreneur Kersey Coates owned property and had erected the city's best hotel and theater in the late 1860s. Market Square, with its small city hall dating back to 1856, anchored this new downtown symbolically. Also present were the city's two other first-class hotels (the Pacific House and the Union, both constructed in the late 1850s) and Frank's Hall, the principal theater before the Coates Opera House was opened. The legitimacy of this emerging urban center was confirmed in 1877. That year, officials at the city's commodities market, the Board of Trade, moved from offices in the West Bottoms to a newly constructed building at 502 Delaware. Brick, three-stories tall, and designed in high Victorian style by architect Asa Cross, this structure epitomized Kansas City's new commercial power.[40]

As businesses near Fifth and Main prospered, those north of Third Street declined. Some were physically destroyed when the Pacific railroad and then the Chicago and Alton ran parallel sets of tracks along the narrow levee. The persistence of the old bluffs was another problem. An 1878 drawing of this area shows Delaware, Main, Walnut, and Second streets all still deeply entrenched and their enclosed blocks correspondingly elevated (map 20). The dirt could have been removed, of course, but its retention is evidence of the relative attraction of business sites farther south. In an atmosphere of street canyons and railroad infringements, a slum developed. Whorehouses and saloons were common and the mood raucous. A young medical student described the scene there one night as "demon laughter, yells, screams, obscenity, profanity, ribaldry, drunken half and wholly naked women, pimps, gamblers, cutthroats etc. (your imagination please)."[41]

Most of the neighborhood depravity was on the west side. Shanties and cheap boardinghouses predominated near the Hannibal Bridge, and a block to the east, brothels lined Wyandotte Street. Of these, the most famous operated openly from 1871 until 1921 in the mansion home of Annie Chambers at the northwest corner of Third Street. Land values increased farther east, primarily because of the presence of the Jackson County Courthouse at the northeast corner of Second and Main. This building officially was subsidiary to another courthouse in Independence, but it was impressive nonetheless—five stories tall with French Empire styling and a large clock tower. The location of such a grand civic structure on Second Street might have made sense in 1850 or 1860, but this courthouse was completed in 1872, after similar public offices had all moved south. The anomaly is explained by a business deal. A luxury hotel had been planned for this site in the 1860s, but its funding was compromised midway through construction. Investors then offered the partially completed structure to the county at a price too good to refuse.[42]

As the local economy flourished in the early 1880s, problems of poor connections between the Union Depot in the bottoms and the commercial center at Fifth and Main increased. People searched for innovative solutions and found

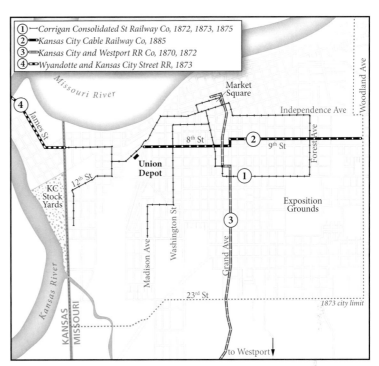

Map 21. Streetcar Lines, 1885. Data from Monroe Dodd, A Splendid Ride: The Streetcars of Kansas City: 1870–1957 *(Kansas City, Mo.: Kansas City Star Books, 2002).*

one sooner than expected in the person of Robert Gillham, a young engineer who had arrived in town in 1878. Gillham immediately saw the steep bluffs as a challenge appropriate for his professional skills. In fact, he proposed a plan to city officials within three months of his arrival.[43]

Taking a cue from a recent implementation in San Francisco, Gillham thought a system of cable cars could conquer the bluff. These would operate upon a steel–and-wood trestle erected at a breathtaking 18.5 percent gradient and extending from the depot eastward to Ninth Street at the top of the bluff. Upon this framework, two cars powered by a single, steam-driven cable would be counterbalanced on separate tracks. As one would ascend to the city, the other would return to the depot.[44]

Ninth Street as an exit point for the trestle made sense from several perspectives. Since it lay directly east of Union Depot, the arrangement was efficient. This route also endeared Gillham to the influential Kersey Coates, for Ninth Street marked the northern edge of Coates's Quality Hill residential development and was only a block from his hotel and theater at Tenth and Broadway (map 7). Coates became Gillham's first major ally. Finally, Ninth Street was far enough south to avoid direct competition with another east-west trolley that ran along Independence Avenue from Grand to Troost (map 21).[45]

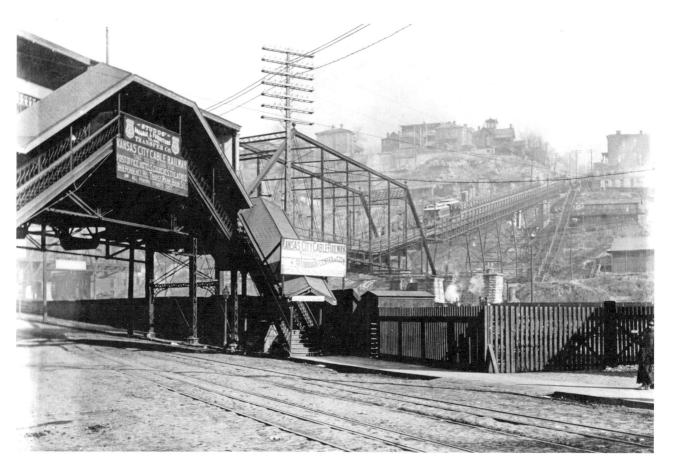

Figure 12. The Ninth Street Incline, 1895. Cable cars provided an innovative way to move people between Union Depot in the West Bottoms and the main downtown area atop the bluffs. Engineer Robert Gillham's design counterbalanced an ascending car with a descending one and was widely hailed at its unveiling in 1885. The Ninth Street route also strongly encouraged a southward migration of the city's business center. Newer, competing cable systems on Eighth and Twelfth streets led to closure of this pioneer trestle in 1904. (Courtesy Missouri Valley Special Collections, Kansas City Public Library)

Although most local residents favored Gillham's proposal, he faced opposition from a rival trolley operator as well as other people with financial interests in the older part of town. These naysayers feared what indeed came to pass—that with a depot-connected cable railway, Ninth Street would become the new commercial center of Kansas City. Negative comparisons of the trestle design to a coal chute and arguments that Ninth Street was too narrow to accommodate tracks delayed construction for several years. This interruption served Gillham better than his detractors, however, because it gave him time to raise more money. A revised plan extended the cable system all the way to Woodland Avenue at the eastern edge of the city.[46]

The Kansas City Cable Railway opened its 2-mile run on June 15, 1885, with high praise. Everybody acknowledged its significance in binding the community together economically. More unexpected, the new machinery also became "the most interesting—certainly the most exciting—feature of the city." As visitor Charles Warner described the cars: "They climb such steeps, they plunge down such grades, they penetrate and whiz through such crowded, lively thoroughfares . . . that the rider is in a perpetual exhilaration. I know no other locomotion more exciting and agreeable."[47]

Warner's description of the new cable railway conveyed an enthusiasm that applied to the city as a whole, for the 1880s decade was a time of unprecedented growth. The success of railroads and the packing industry inspired dreams for other businesspeople, and seemingly everybody speculated in real estate. The annual value of property transfers, for instance, rose from a relatively steady $2 million throughout most of the 1870s to $5 million in 1880 and $39 million in 1886. Commercial architecture was a vital aspect of this boom, and the positioning of new buildings reveals another southward migration of the downtown core.[48]

The change, clearly encouraged by the cable railway, began in 1884 with the construction of a large federal building to

Figure 13. New York Life Insurance Building, 1896, Looking North along Baltimore from Tenth Street. Standing ten stories tall, the graceful New York Life Building was the city's largest at its completion in 1890. It also symbolized the repositioning of the business district to Ninth Street. Note the abrupt transition from commercial to residential land use evident in this view and the continuing presence of loess bluffs. The building with its signature bronze eagle still stands. (Courtesy Missouri Valley Special Collections, Kansas City Public Library)

house the local post office, customhouse, and federal court. With a prominent clock tower and substantial Renaissance styling, its location at 911 Walnut served as a beacon for other white-collar entrepreneurs. Two of their most prominent structures still line Ninth Street today—the New England Building at the northeast corner of Wyandotte Street and the New York Life Building a block east at Baltimore. Both echo the design of the federal building, and when they were completed in 1888 and 1890, respectively, they gave form to the new commercial heart of the city.[49]

The business community of the late 1880s was considerably larger than it had ever been before. Its core extended from Fifth to Eleventh streets and from Wyandotte three blocks east to Walnut. This area incorporated the older city center at Fifth and Main and extended southwest nearly to the now venerable Coates House hotel. Its greater dimension north and south was a reflection of transportation. Although connections to the river via Main Street and Grand Avenue remained important, ones to the railroads and industry of the West Bottoms had become more so. In fact, two new trams were added at this time. The first—employing a 786-foot

tunnel through the bluffs at the west end of Eighth Street— was another project of the ubiquitous Robert Gillham.[50]

Gillham's tunnel had three goals: to increase the total capacity for moving people to and from the depot, to provide a lower-gradient alternative to his earlier line, and to access the existing downtown area more directly. It succeeded on all fronts. Workers dug through the bluff in the summer of 1887, and by fall, passengers were ascending to Washington Street at a gentle 8 percent rise and then continuing east on an elevated line into the city core. Property values along the route immediately increased, and both Seventh and Eighth streets joined Ninth as sites for new investment.[51]

The most prominent construction associated with the

tunnel occurred in 1888—a new home for the rapidly growing Board of Trade and a hotel grand enough to fit the city's
growing aspirations. Both attracted national attention. The
former, located a block north of the New England Building
at 210 West Eighth, was one of the finest creations of the
Chicago architects Burnham and Root. Utilizing a heavy,
terra-cotta design arranged in an H pattern, the Board of
Trade building featured a beautiful arched entrance and an
immense trading room on the fifth floor. Inside and out, its
seven stories radiated a sense of corporate power. Three blocks
to the east, Burnham and Root created a second Kansas City
landmark. For the Midland Hotel, they echoed the height
and Romanesque styling of the Board of Trade but designed a
more ornate interior. The building occupied the entire block
between Seventh and Eighth, Walnut and Grand, but focused
inward on a towering spiral staircase with marble steps. Luxurious appointments abounded, including a basement swim-
ming pool, and the Midland reigned as the city's finest inn
for a decade and a half. It hosted every president from Grover
Cleveland through William Howard Taft.[52]

A third cable railway from the West Bottoms stretched the
urban core even farther in 1888. This route, from Twelfth
Street down a viaduct to the Kansas City Stock Yards, was
built somewhat ahead of demand. The reason, though, was
obvious. Charles F. Adams, the principal owner of the stockyard, also headed a syndicate that had purchased the city's
major trolley system in 1886.[53]

Real estate development on and near Twelfth Street was
not as immediate as it was slightly farther north, but it was
still substantial. Two beneficiaries were the Cathedral of the
Immaculate Conception and St. Teresa's Academy between
Pennsylvania and Broadway, the site of Father Donnelly's
original Catholic church. Another was the Coates House on
Broadway. To better compete with the new Midland Hotel,
the Coates people constructed an addition at the Eleventh
Street corner in 1886–1887, and two years later, they rebuilt the original structure to match. The biggest investment,
however, and the best indicator that Kansas City's southward
movement would continue, came from the community's
leading department store. Having outgrown a building on
Seventh Street, the principals at Bullene, Moore, Emery and
Company plus newer partners Joseph T. Bird and William B.
Thayer constructed a retail palace in 1889. Using the standard Romanesque architecture of the time, their building
stretched from Walnut to Grand along Eleventh Street and
stood five stories tall. Over time, this Emery, Bird, Thayer

store helped Eleventh Street to become the city's shopping
hub. People dubbed the two blocks between Grand and Main
as Petticoat Lane.[54]

In looking back, it is easy to misjudge the significance that
residents of the time accorded the new commercial developments along Ninth, Tenth, and Eleventh streets. Entrepreneurs definitely saw these places as their future, but they also
expected the older business district near Market Square to
remain vital. *Expansion* was their byword, not *replacement*.
Several investments on the northern side of town attested to
this belief, including another grand hotel and two major government buildings.

The hotel, called the Centropolis, was constructed in 1880
at the northwest corner of Fifth and Grand. With additions,
it offered 141 rooms and was the first in the city to install
electric lighting. The Centropolis was convenient to the many
stores along Main and Walnut streets, and so it prospered.
Two newer neighborhood buildings helped its cause. The
first, a replacement for a small city hall that had served for
thirty-five years, was erected in 1891 at 411 Main. Its six-
story design was dark and undistinguished, but the offices
brought traffic to this part of the city. A year later and three
blocks to the east came a new courthouse. This unexpected
development was made necessary after a tornado destroyed
the existing building on Second Street in 1886. Officials selected the new site, an entire block southeast of the intersection of Fifth and Oak, because it was vacant and relatively inexpensive. Nobody praised the Romanesque design, but like
the city hall, it kept neighborhood employment high.[55]

Elite Neighborhoods

As Kansas City's business fortune expanded rapidly in the
1870s and 1880s, it created growing numbers of wealthy
merchants and professional people who desired fine Victorian homes. The locations selected for these mansions reveal
values of the time and set the tone for the rest of the city's
residential geography. After all, middle-class people always
have wanted to live near the rich, while the poor make do
with whatever sites are left over.

Pearl Street, the city's first elite address as described in
chapter 2 (map 6), was no longer viable after about 1870.
Once it had crowned the bluff and overlooked a busy levee,
but it became nearly inaccessible when workers entrenched
surrounding streets. Then, as the bluff itself was hauled away,
Pearl Street literally disappeared.

Quality Hill was the most obvious site for the new mer-

chant princes' homes. Kersey Coates had platted this addition in 1857 specifically for an elite clientele, and two years later, he built his own mansion there at the corner of Tenth and Pennsylvania (map 7). His construction of a premier hotel and opera house nearby on Broadway added to the site's cachet, as did magnificent blufftop views north to the Missouri River and west to the Kaw. The physical setting, in fact, was reminiscent of Pearl Street.

Quality Hill developed exactly as Coates had expected, in that it attracted residents much like himself. Charles F. Morse, the manager of the Adams investments in Kansas City, built there in 1880, as did Simeon Armour's son Kirkland in 1884. Simeon lived only a block away at 1216 Broadway. The area did not charm all the city's elite, however. Indeed, its presence repelled as many as it attracted. The reason went back to the Hannibal Bridge and the abundant opportunities for economic growth it had engendered. Money for development at this scale was concentrated in the northeastern states, and as Yankee entrepreneurs migrated to western Missouri, they did not always mix easily with the resident upland Southerners. Business needs produced the cooperation required to build factories and roads, but such cooperation had its limits. So-

Figure 14. Residence of Kersey and Sarah Coates, Southwest Corner of Tenth and Pennsylvania, 1868. Coates, the city's first major financier, promoted banks, railroads, and an elite residential area called Quality Hill. He permitted only brick homes in this ten-block area between Broadway and the bluffs, Ninth and Eleventh streets. The Coates's own residence, built in 1859, featured verandas on the east and north where they could watch the growing city. To attract others to Quality Hill, they paved the streets and lined them with trees. (Courtesy Missouri Valley Special Collections, Kansas City Public Library)

cially, according to witnesses from the time, North and South stayed apart throughout the nineteenth century. As one man remembered, "a Mason and Dixon line divided the city" along Main Street, and "Quality Hill became the mecca for those who fought under Grant, Sherman, and Sheridan."[56]

The moneyed people who shunned Quality Hill built their mansions in two different neighborhoods. Neither was a planned development, but each grew instead by accretion around a single large estate. The earlier and more expansive of the two agglomerations began a mile east of downtown, where Independence Avenue was transformed into a showcase for towered and turreted houses. Development extended from Highland Avenue three-quarters of a mile to Gladstone Boulevard. It continued north on Gladstone to the edge of

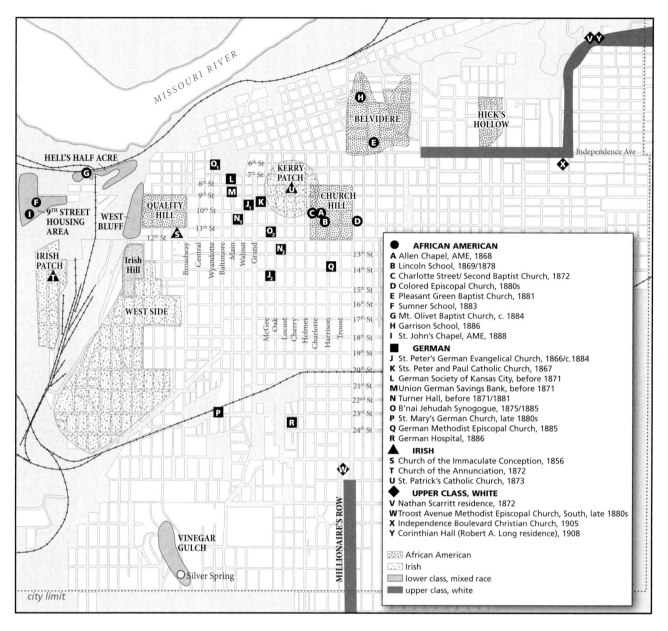

Map 22. Neighborhoods in Kansas City, Missouri, circa 1886. Compiled from multiple sources.

the Missouri River bluffs and then east another half mile along Norledge Avenue (map 22).

The Independence-Gladstone neighborhood grew from the chance purchase in 1862 of a 100-acre farm by a teacher named Nathan Scarritt. Scarritt became wealthy in the 1870s through real estate he owned near Eighth and Grand downtown, and so he decided to replace the farm's log cabin with a luxurious, twelve-room house. His setting, on what is today called Scarritt's Point at the intersection of Walrond and Norledge, included beautiful overlooks to the north and west. By itself, this property probably would have attracted other

wealthy builders to the area, but Scarritt added appeal by giving land along Norledge and Gladstone to his nine children for their own estates and by deeding the bluffland to the city for a park.[57]

Most of the mansions along Independence Avenue were constructed in the 1880s. Like their contemporaries on Quality Hill, they were stone and brick creations, rich in stained glass, and set two or three to the block. Wide verandas, jutting bays, and conical towers completed the scene. Residents also matched the Coates group in prestige. The local list included bankers David T. Beals and Churchill White; merchant-manufacturers Jemuel Gates, Robert Keith, and Jacob Loose; trolley engineer Robert Gillham; and most famously August

Meyer and Robert A. Long. Meyer, a native of St. Louis, had moved to the area to run the large smelting company that had helped to create the Argentine community in 1880. In the 1890s, as head of a movement to create a citywide system of parks and boulevards, he made sure to include his home territory, the Gladstone neighborhood. Long, a lumber baron, lived in a large house at the corner of Independence Avenue and Bellefontaine until he built an even more palatial one just to the north in 1911. This seventy-room structure, Corinthian Hall at 3218 Gladstone, is now a city museum. Long also is largely responsible for a second surviving element of this patrician landscape—the Independence Boulevard Christian Church at the southwest corner with Gladstone. Greek Revival in design with a circular, domed sanctuary that seats more than a thousand people, the building is impressive. The denomination's roots in Kentucky and Tennessee also are significant, reflecting the origins of most Independence Avenue residents and providing obvious contrast with the New England Unitarians and Pennsylvania Quakers on Quality Hill.[58]

The third elite housing neighborhood of the 1880s lined six blocks of Troost Avenue at the city's southern edge (map 22). The inadvertent instigator in this case was James Porter, a slaveholding minister from Tennessee whose farm once spread between Twenty-third and Thirty-first streets and from Locust to The Paseo. Porter died in 1851, but the acreage remained intact until 1880. Then, a chance purchase of a large lot at 2700 Troost by William A. Wilson initiated a trend. By the end of the decade, the blocks between Twenty-sixth and Thirty-second streets had become known as Millionaire's Row. Although small, this enclave competed on equal terms with any in the city. A recent governor of Missouri, Thomas T. Crittenden, lived there. So did banker William T. Kemper; department store owner George B. Peck; and Robert Gillham's business partner, William J. Smith. As was the case with Independence Avenue, Yankees stayed away from this area. The neighborhood's signature church, Troost Avenue Methodist Episcopal, South, reflected the faith of Reverend Porter.[59]

Slums and Racial Enclaves

The growth of Kansas City during the 1880s was truly spectacular. Office buildings and fancy homes went up fast, and by the last half of that decade, over 4,000 structures were erected annually. As the population increased from some 55,000 residents in 1880 to over 132,000 by 1890,

Kansas City became a metropolis. Officials in 1885 moved the city limit east a mile from Woodland Avenue to Cleveland and south the same distance from Twenty-third Street to Thirty-first. Such growth also allowed and even encouraged greater social and economic segregation. Bankers and doctors sought scenic locales for their palaces. The city's poor looked for places where they could escape inflated prices and get to work easily.[60]

In the absence of detailed income data, the best available surrogates for assessing poverty levels may be the African American and foreign-born populations. These peoples represented 15 and 17 percent, respectively, of all residents in 1880. Ten years later, after the economic boom, their total numbers were much higher but their percentages slightly lower—10 and 16 percent, respectively. Countering modern stereotypes, maps for both groups reveal a fairly even distribution at the ward level (map 23). This depiction of an unsegregated city is partly true. No zoning laws existed at the time, and consequently, cheap tenements could be and were erected next to mansions. The rich decried such proximity, of course, but it was necessary in a way. If no trolley was near,

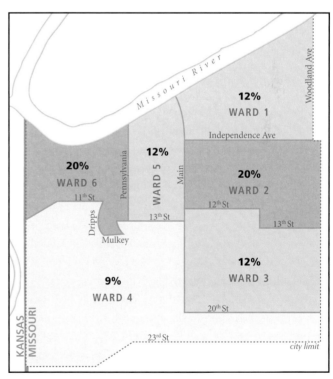

Map 23. African American Population in Kansas City, Missouri, 1880. Census data compiled by Dwayne R. Martin, "The Hidden Community: The Black Community of Kansas City, Missouri, during the 1870s and 1880s" (master's thesis, Department of History, University of Missouri–Kansas City, 1982), p. 14.

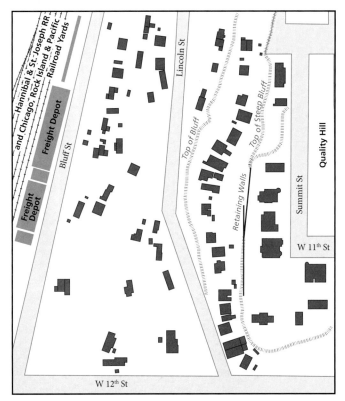

Map 24. The West Bluff Slum, 1895. Modified from pl. 21 of Insurance Maps of Kansas City, Missouri *(New York: Sanborn-Perris Map, 1895).*

servants had to live within walking distance of their employers' estates.[61]

Still, the coarse grid of a ward-level map hides many clusters of disadvantaged residents. Several such sites have already been noted in Argentine, Armourdale, the West Bottoms, and parts of the original downtown, where poor and working-class people dominated local life. The city of Wyandotte contained similar enclaves at this time, as did the rest of Kansas City, Missouri, beyond the bottoms. Although some of these areas could be strongly associated with one ethnic group or another, most were mixed in that sense. Poverty alone united the residents.

The cultural core of Kansas City's black community in the 1880s was Church Hill. This neighborhood, just east of downtown, was approximately bounded by Eighth and Twelfth streets, Holmes and Troost (map 22). Not coincidently, these streets also defined Perry Place, an 1857 addition financed by Kersey Coates and his Quaker associates from Philadelphia. Coates essentially created this community by selling exclusively to African Americans until 1870 and providing lots for churches and a school. Out of this came three critical institutions: the Allen Chapel, AME church

(1868) and the Charlotte Street (or Second) Baptist church (1872), located across from one another on Tenth Street, and Lincoln School (1869) at Eleventh and Campbell. Church Hill housed approximately 15 percent of the city's black population, and the neighborhood itself was about the same percentage black. Race aside, the place was lower middle class in tone, with many residents working as domestics in McGee's Addition to the south or in the Independence Avenue mansions to the northeast.[62]

Church Hill Baptists had money enough to establish a mission church in the Hell's Half Acre section of the West Bottoms about 1880. The Hill's social amenities and relative status also attracted poorer blacks to two nearby neighborhoods. Just north of Independence Avenue and east of Troost, where the Missouri River's bluffline is breached by a series of ravines, speculators erected cheap houses at places known as Belvidere and Hick's Hollow (map 22). As these structures deteriorated, the percentage of African American residents rose, reaching about 40 percent by 1890. Reports suggest that conditions, although bad, nevertheless represented a step up from Hell's Half Acre. A trolley along Independence Avenue allowed easy access to jobs, and by the 1880s, Belvidere's black population had its own church (Pleasant Green Baptist) and school (Garrison).[63]

Somewhat fewer Irish-born people than African Americans lived in Kansas City in 1870 (2,869 versus 3,764). This differential grew over the next twenty years, but if second-generation residents are added to the foreign-born count, the Irish total actually exceeded that of blacks and represented some 20 percent of the city's population during the 1880s. It was a diverse group. Although writers maintained the old stereotype of laborers and servants, the city's police and fire departments had become "essentially Irish organizations" by this time. Joseph B. Shannon was kingmaker for the local Democratic Party, and both Patrick Shannon and Robert H. Hunt had served as mayor.[64]

Irish residential clusterings in the 1880s were tied to church and job (map 22). The biggest neighborhood, with some 1,200 families, lay in the West Bottoms. Its center was just east of the stockyard, where Annunciation Parish had been created in 1872 and a church and school erected a decade later. Even though other groups lived in this area as well, people called it the Irish Patch. Newer immigrants and those unable to hold regular jobs gravitated to one of three slums. The oldest, Hell's Half Acre on the levee, was small. People then began to build shacks on steep hillsides. One area, sepa-

Figure 15. Annunciation Hall, 1405 Wyoming Street, circa 1890. This modest building was built in 1872 as the Church of the Annunciation of the Blessed Virgin to serve a largely Irish community in the West Bottoms. Eight years later, workers moved it across the street and constructed a larger brick church. The new church and the old hall served 5,000 parishioners in the 1880s, but this number dropped precipitously as industries expanded into the residential area. Missing clapboards suggest the decline. (Courtesy Missouri Valley Special Collections, Kansas City Public Library)

rating Quality Hill from the stockyard district, was known as the West Bluff (map 24). Another, a mile and a half south, was an extension of the same escarpment where OK Creek had cut the deep ravine today occupied by Penn Valley Park (map 2). Squatters especially favored an area near Thirtieth and Broadway where a good spring flowed. This was Vinegar Gulch.[65]

Because the "dirty looking hovels" of West Bluff provided "a most unfortunate introduction" to the city for passengers at the nearby Union Depot, this neighborhood was subject to intense public scorn. Irish Americans were not overly concerned, however, because most of their families were moving to better locations. Many gravitated toward Eighth and Cherry streets, where a new Catholic church, St. Patrick's, had opened in 1873. Similar in income level to adjacent Church Hill and convenient to downtown jobs, this area became known as the Kerry Patch.[66]

The most popular destination for upwardly mobile Irish was Kansas City's West Side. This pleasant, bluffside neigh-borhood south of the Twelfth Street viaduct and west of Broadway was close to the West Bottoms for easy access to jobs and to friends who remained in The Patch. It was also adjacent to Immaculate Conception Church, the original but newly renamed Catholic parish in the city that soon would be designated a cathedral. Families with the most money sought property near this church and, not coincidentally, the adjoining estates of Quality Hill. Their new neighborhood around Thirteenth and Madison soon was dubbed Irish Hill. To the south, kinfolk purchased more modest homes across forty or

Figure 16. West Bluff Shanties, 1892, Looking Southeast from Union Avenue. Of the city's several slums, the most visible occupied the bluffs between Quality Hill and Union Depot. Every visitor saw it as they ascended the Ninth Street Incline; so did nabobs living atop the escarpment. Lincoln Street, in the center of the photograph, provided access to the area. Freight houses for the Rock Island and the Hannibal and St. Joseph railroads occupy the foreground, and the Twelfth Street cable railway is on the right. (Courtesy Missouri Valley Special Collections, Kansas City Public Library)

so blocks down to OK Creek and the strip of retail shops along Southwest Boulevard.[67]

German immigrants were the only other ethnic group regularly identified by contemporary writers. With numbers of 1,884 in 1870, 2,209 in 1880, and 6,109 in 1890, they constituted about 5 percent of the city's population. If second-generation residents are added, this German American total rises to a significant 15 percent by the end of the period. Kansas City Germans were a mixed lot in terms of religion but solidly middle class in income and attitude. A plot of their cultural institutions, in fact, can be used to trace the main corridor of urban expansion in the 1870s and 1880s (map 22).[68]

An 1871 visitor to Kansas City reported several German businesses in the old levee district, but these locations were atypical for the time. As early as 1858, for example, "German mechanics, industrious artisans, and family grocery dealers"

constituted "a good portion" of the large McGee's Addition south of Twelfth Street and east of Baltimore (map 7). Milt McGee had developed this property for middle-income people such as the German entrepreneurs partly because it occupied a "middle" geographic position as well. West of Broadway sat the Quality Hill mansions; the working-class neighborhoods of Kerry Patch and Church Hill lay north and east of Twelfth and Locust (map 22).[69]

In the early 1870s, local Germans clustered their institutions within a central, north-south corridor focused on Main Street from Seventh to Tenth. Fifteen years later, this pattern had shifted to the east some five blocks and to the south three times that distance. Some of this change represents expansion, some relocation. The movement of B'nai Jehudah Synagogue, the German Evangelical church, and Turner Hall all document the increasing commercialization of Main and adjacent streets south to Eleventh. The sites of the new St. Mary's Church and German Hospital (to be renamed Research during World War I) suggest how rapidly people expanded to the south.

Wyandotte, Independence, and Harlem

It is not surprising that the same railroad lines that enabled Kansas City to grow rapidly in the 1870s and 1880s had similar effects on adjoining communities. Argentine;

Armourdale; the original Kansas City, Kansas; and Rosedale are cases in point. More intriguing, perhaps, are the experiences of three other towns that, despite having many of these same railroads, grew only modestly. Wyandotte and Independence, the original towns in their respective counties, occupied upland sites similar to Kansas City itself. These areas were too remote to function as suburbs and were snubbed by factory owners, who preferred the convenience of West Bottoms locations; consequently, their residents competed as best they could for a share of local trade. A third neighbor, Harlem, sat directly across the Missouri River from the big city. The Hannibal Bridge reduced isolation on this north bank, but it also removed any chance for independent retail growth.

Of the three slow-growing communities, Wyandotte was the most complex. Its founders saw potential greater than for any other town near the river junction, and this belief was reinforced by solid Free State credentials during the Civil War and the acquisition of the railroad shops and headquarters for the Union Pacific, Eastern Division. Residents also promoted the area whenever possible, touting "fine elevated situations for residences" and in 1875 hosting a "mass convention" where senators and governors spoke glowingly of this spot ordained by nature to be "the commercial metropolis of the State."[70]

All tactics to outmaneuver the combined efforts of Charles Adams, Kersey Coates, and James Joy proved futile, of course. One problem was that the railroad's main line actually bypassed Wyandotte, running a mile to the south (map 12). This reality soon prompted Union Pacific officials to relocate their headquarters and shops away from the levee. In 1871, they purchased farmland from Silas Armstrong and platted a new town named in his honor. Supervisors tended to stay on in the older community, but most of the 370 workers moved south to modern company houses. As a result, Wyandotte's population stagnated at about 3,000 for most of this decade.[71]

As meatpackers began to favor the Kansas City area in the late 1870s, Wyandotte leaders expected big growth. Instead, the population figures rose only modestly, to 6,149 in 1880 and about 14,700 in 1890. This time, the culprits were the developers of Armourdale and Kansas City, Kansas, who laid out residential areas practically adjacent to the new packinghouses. Wyandotte was able to compete to a degree via a horse-drawn trolley. Established in 1873, this trolley ran past the Armour and Fowler plants and, after bridging the Kaw, entered the city at its southeastern corner.[72]

The trolley spurred construction of working-class houses south of Armstrong Street and east of Seventh, an area called Strawberry Hill. Lots were small but free from floods, and they proved especially popular with German and Irish Catholics. These people were attracted by the chance neighborhood presence (since 1866) of St. Mary's Church at the corner of Fifth and Ann. As new homes spread to the south and west, the St. Mary's congregation grew to some 150 families. Germans were able to establish their own parish in 1885, which provided a second local landmark, St. Anthony's Church on Seventh Street between Barnett and Tauromee. Several hundred African Americans gave the area additional diversity. Most had come as refugees from Missouri during the war years.[73]

Ironically, the biggest single boost to Wyandotte's population came independent of any promotion. Starting in the spring of 1879 and continuing for eighteen months, some 20,000 African American refugees from the abuses of Reconstruction in Louisiana, Mississippi, and Texas arrived at the wharf and depot. Hearing rumors of free land in Kansas, these so-called Exodusters were nearly penniless. Local officials were sympathetic but soon were overwhelmed, until state-level programs helped with resettlement. When the crisis had passed in 1885, the city's black population had quadrupled to 3,301, with another 552 residing in rural Quindaro Township a few miles to the northwest. The Wyandotte Exodusters clustered in two spots along the bluffs of the Missouri River (map 12). The larger, at the mouth of Jersey Creek, was referred to interchangeably as Mississippi Town, Juniper, and Juniper Bottoms. Half a mile upstream, another collection of shacks made up Rattlebone Hollow.[74]

By the early 1880s, as visitors were beginning to call Wyandotte "the Brooklyn of Kansas City," town leaders made another attempt at promotion and self-definition. Part of the problem, they reasoned, was the existence of a unified political entity on the Missouri side versus a divided one in Kansas. What if the sizable population base of Wyandotte could somehow be combined with the industrial clout of Armourdale, Armstrong, and Kansas City, Kansas? They began to implement this dream modestly in 1881 by annexing unincorporated Riverview, a small suburb platted two years earlier by Samuel Simpson on the slopes just south of Strawberry Hill. People in the other three communities saw merit in the Wyandotte plan, particularly for the sale of industrial bonds through eastern brokers. They also had concerns. Union Pacific officials liked the self-government they

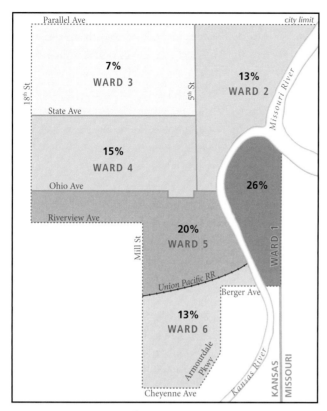

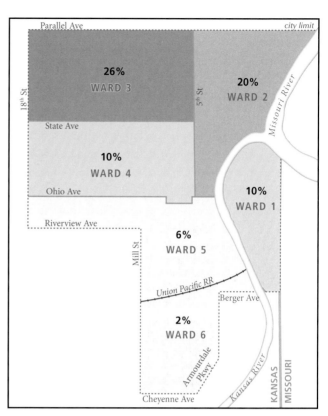

Map 25. Foreign-Born Population in Kansas City, Kansas, 1890. Data from U.S. Census.

Map 26. African American Population in Kansas City, Kansas, 1890. Data from U.S. Census.

enjoyed in their narrow-streeted company enclave, and residents of Armourdale and Kansas City, Kansas, worried that Wyandotte would steal tax dollars from their industries. The proposal likely would have collapsed had Wyandotte leaders not arranged legislation that allowed Governor John Martin to literally proclaim a merger. When he did so on March 6, 1886, the cheering in Wyandotte was muted by his choice of names. Bankers had lobbied successfully for the designation Kansas City over Wyandotte on the grounds that a known label would help bond sales.[75]

The new Kansas City, Kansas, with a huge meatpacking industry and some 21,229 citizens, was indeed a presence on the national scene. It was still Brooklyn to Kansas City, Missouri, however, in that all major hotels, banks, office buildings, and mansion districts remained east of the state line. On a more local scale, Wyandotte became the retail center for the consolidated city, with shops along Minnesota Avenue west to Seventh Street and on Third Street north to Oakland. Large homes of local professional people lined nearby Washington Avenue from Third to Tenth streets, with extensions south to Minnesota at the west end.[76]

Ward-level maps show a fairly even distribution of Ger-

man, Irish, and other foreign-born residents across the new community, with slight concentrations in old Kansas City and Armstrong, Wards One and Five, respectively (map 25). African Americans were scarce in Armourdale and Armstrong and most common in the Exoduster areas of Wards Two and Three (map 26). Connecting workers with jobs, the old horse trolley was replaced in 1887 by the Inter-State Consolidated Rapid Transit Railway. From the Armour plant, its cars crossed the Kaw into Riverview and then traveled north on Sixth and Fifth streets through the heart of Wyandotte.[77]

In comparison to the high expectations of Wyandotte people in the 1870s, the mood of residents 12 miles to the east in Independence was much more subdued. These individuals had strongly supported the Southern cause during the war. Then, over the next two decades, they seemed to accept that this allegiance somehow limited their participation in the railroad and industrial boom that followed. In 1870, retail trade and courthouse activity supported a population of 3,184 quite nicely, but ten years later, the situation was

Map 27 (facing page). Independence, 1868. A portion of "Bird's Eye View of Independence, Jackson County, Missouri," drawn by Albert Ruger. (Courtesy of Library of Congress, Prints and Photographs Division)

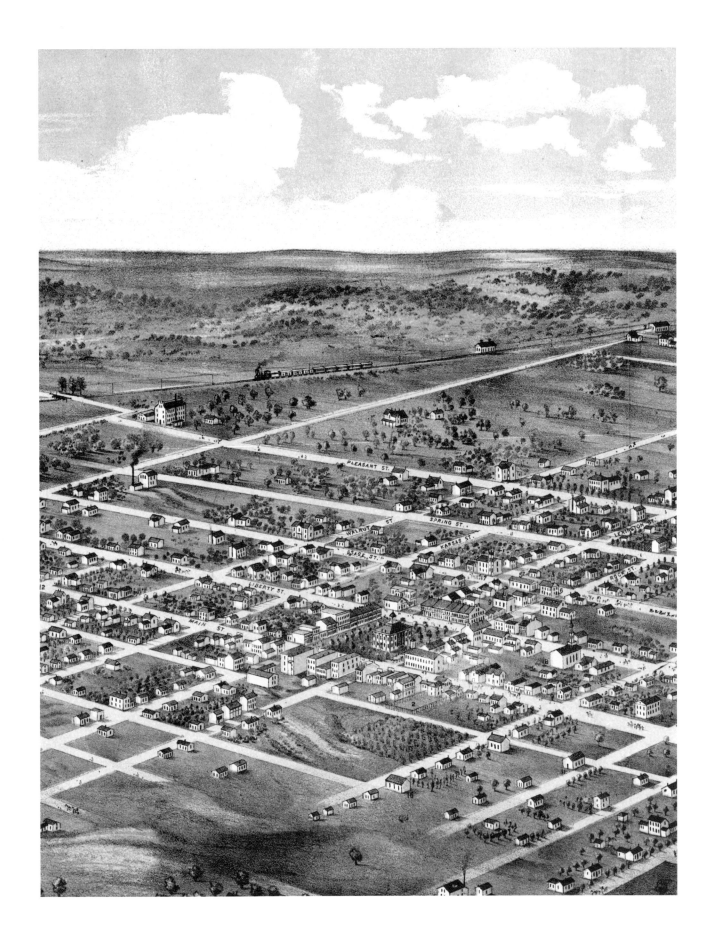

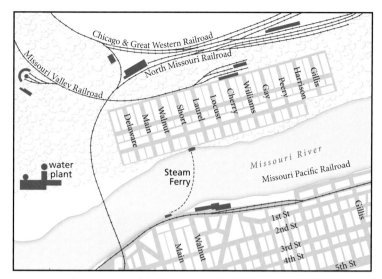

Map 28. Harlem, 1871. Modified from a portion of the map "Kansas City, Mo. and Wyandott Kas.," by G. A. Karwiese, a copy of which is in the Special Collections department of the Kansas City Public Library.

almost exactly the same. In fact, the headcount was 38 fewer (map 27). The *St. Louis Republican* in 1871 reported that although Independence was "a pleasant place, with a refined and hospitable society," it also lacked entrepreneurs and so operated "under the shadow of Kansas City."[78]

The first suggestion of a new role for Independence came in about 1880. Several local men, led by attorney Charles Crysler, promoted a grand, 7.5-mile boulevard that would connect with Independence Avenue in Kansas City. Obviously inspired by the mansions already beginning to rise in the Gladstone area, the dreamers extolled the beauty of the Blue River bluffs and foresaw a combination of estates, parks, and spas that would rival those of Paris. They raised $15,000 for the project but waited in vain for similar money from Kansas City.[79]

Crysler was six years too early. A real estate boom starting about 1883 pushed new houses and trolley lines outward in Kansas City at a pace that amazed even the developers. OK Creek on the south side proved no obstacle to expansion and, in the eyes of at least one dreamer, Willard E. Winner, neither did the Blue River to the east. Winner was an extremely ambitious investor who had subdivided some 2,000 acres on Kansas City's east side between 1883 and 1886. During 1886, his company purchased a nearly unbroken strip of 2,400 acres along Crysler's planned route, including 400 acres in the valley of Rock Creek that they reserved as a park. The next year saw completion of the long-anticipated boulevard

(Winner Road) plus a parallel Kansas City, Independence, and Park commuter railway and, of course, many choice residential lots. All went well for two years, with the new Washington Park becoming a popular weekend destination and western Independence a fashionable address.[80]

The real estate bubble burst in 1889, and Washington Park was converted into Mt. Washington Cemetery, but Winner's efforts ended the long dormancy of Independence. With mature trees and good shopping on the courthouse square, people began to promote the town as Kansas City's "royal suburb." The biggest of the new houses rose on North Delaware Street, four blocks west of the square. By 1890, the community had 6,380 residents, still a small number but double the total of the previous census.[81]

People in Kansas City's third close neighbor, Harlem, had only modest urban aspirations. Their location on the north levee of the Missouri River facing the Kansas City wharf was advantageous in some ways, but the surrounding lowland was prone to flooding. A ferry prompted development of the town. This service connected to Grand Avenue on the south bank and had operated since 1836. Seeing a demand for a hotel/restaurant when passenger traffic might be delayed for some reason, Kansas City newspaperman Robert T. Van Horn and others platted a townsite in 1857 (map 28). It was small in scale (only three blocks deep and thirteen long) and simply extended the familiar Kansas City street labels across the water, Delaware to Gillis. The town name honored the home of Van Horn's Dutch ancestors.[82]

Harlem at its peak contained a hotel, several saloons, a grocery, a school, and a post office. Many of its few hundred residents fished for a living; others were truck farmers. Both groups sold in Kansas City's Market Square. Construction of the Hannibal Bridge only five blocks west of the ferry port did little to alter local life. In 1887, however, the same Willard Winner who had awakened Independence seemed poised to do the same to Harlem. Seeing untapped industrial potential in the surrounding North Bottoms, his North Kansas City Improvement Company purchased 10,000 acres and made plans for a new bridge. Then, of course, came the collapse of the local real estate boom. By 1891, Winner was in bankruptcy and Harlem was still an unincorporated village.[83]

4 Maturity in a Railroad Mode, 1893–1933

Kansas City's population more than doubled on the Missouri side of the state line during the 1880s. On the Kansas side, it tripled. These gains, although spectacular, were not fully appreciated at the time because of frenzy over a recent collapse in the local real estate market. The next census, however, made things clear. With 132,716 residents, Kansas City, Missouri, was now the nation's twenty-fourth-largest urban center. If adjacent Kansans were added, the ranking became an even more impressive eighteenth.[1]

Local people swelled with pride as they considered the recently acquired status. Their new commercial club told anybody who would listen that Kansas City was now America's second-largest railroad center and livestock market (behind only Chicago) and number one in the sale of agricultural implements. Residents saw themselves as part of the nation's "youngest and most prosperous" metropolis, and they concocted a three-part story of hard work and self-promotion to account for the success. They first had overcome the muddy bluffs behind the levee. Next came maneuvering to acquire the Hannibal Bridge and, with it, railroads and packing companies. Their capstone was Robert Gillham's trolley system, an innovative scaling of the West Bluff to connect the town's commercial and industrial interests. Completely ignored, of course, was the role in all this of Charles Adams and other outside capitalists.[2]

Formal acknowledgment of a new place in the sun came in February 1900. The city had just erected a 20,000-seat convention hall at the corner of Twelfth and Wyandotte, and the Democratic National Committee selected it as the site for that summer's presidential convention. Expectations grew rapidly but then seemingly were dashed in April when the hall burned. Local leaders swallowed hard but vowed to rebuild. They raised $60,000 in four days and coordinated the completion of a new, fireproof hall just before the opening gavel in July. It was a triumph of "Kansas City spirit, Kansas City pluck and Kansas City money" that generated applause nationwide. Locally, it became still another chapter in the story of self-made greatness.[3]

"Kansas City Spirit," a convenient phrase to summarize the miracle of the convention hall, was the city's first widely accepted slogan. Its usage and relevance were reinforced in 1903. On May 30, heavy rains in Kansas produced the largest local flood since 1844. Over the next several days, water inundated Armourdale to a depth of 15 feet and necessitated evacuation of some 16,000 people. Two-thirds of Argentine was similarly affected, together with the stockyard, packinghouses, and residential neighborhoods of the West Bottoms. Union Depot, on slightly higher ground, had water 4 feet deep. With many bridges washed out and all public transportation and utilities for the bottomlands suspended, the potential for human disaster was great. Local relief efforts proved to be efficient and generous, however—the "Kansas City Spirit" in action. Even the rebuilt convention hall downtown was involved, providing sleeping quarters for a thousand people and meals for three times that number. Nearly all churches helped, too, and total donations exceeded $133,000.[4]

Would economic maturity and a heightened sense of self-esteem change the internal geography of Kansas City? One could make a theoretical argument either way. The newness of most buildings would suggest the status quo. Eleventh and Twelfth streets were just coming into their own as commercial settings, so why would business move elsewhere? Similarly, most of the mansions along Independence and Troost avenues were less than fifteen years old in 1900. Why would their owners want to relocate? Finally, the economic underpinnings of the city—railroads, packers, and wholesalers—all were prospering and had no need to change their current modes of operation.

The case for an altered local geography would have been harder for people of the time to foresee. Still, in those years before zoning laws, they would have known it was highly probable that slum housing or noisy businesses would someday be constructed near more stately homes and offices. The rich would then flee. Another issue concerned race. Would the city's unstated but reasonably open policy toward housing and business practices be maintained, or would segregation become the rule? Then, if segregation was the choice, what sites might emerge as black shopping districts, elite neighborhoods, and slums? Finally—and far more frequently anticipated—was the creation of art galleries, museums, parks, and universities. Such cultural centers would be logical additions to a new metropolis, but where exactly should they be built? And what impact might these decisions have on other urban development?

A City Beautiful

Looking back at the first third of the twentieth century, it is easy to see that, however unanticipated, the forces of change were stronger than those of stability. The central business districts of both Kansas Cities did remain largely as they were. So did the stockyard and the packers. Residential areas, however, completely reinvented themselves, with Quality Hill, Independence Avenue, and Troost all losing their elite status. Segregation also became a fact of life, redefining the city's east side and creating new housing developments to the south. Intermediate on the scale of change, the art institutions arrived as predicted, but they did not greatly affect urban development. Finally, three changes proved grander and more influential than anybody (save their creators) had imagined—a system of parks and boulevards, a replacement railroad depot necessitated after the big flood of 1903, and automobiles.

Ever since Kansas City had become a prominent business center after 1869, its visitors had been of two minds. They praised the hustle of the people but bemoaned the crudeness of the site and its buildings. Rose Kingsley wrote in 1871 that she could not imagine "a more unpleasant" place to spend time. Thirty-six years later, the publisher Henry Holt echoed the same sentiment, calling Kansas City "the busiest and smokiest workshop I had ever seen; but . . . a place not fit to live in. It has no Fifth Avenue or Beacon Street, and nothing corresponding to the neighborhoods of those streets." Frontier towns routinely received such rebukes, of course, but by the 1880s and 1890s, the city's boosters found them a great embarrassment.[5]

Fortunately for Kansas City, the concept of urban and landscape planning was gaining national momentum at the very time that local leaders realized its importance and possessed the financial resources to adopt it. Called the City Beautiful Movement, the idea traced its roots to the creation of New York's Central Park by Frederick Law Olmstead in 1851. Green spaces such as this, the logic went, would provide beauty and clean air, plus a rise in neighborhood land values. Other enthusiasts went further and argued that a system of parks with connecting boulevards could create de facto zoning districts that would effectively separate commerce from industry and mansions from hovels.[6]

Between 1893 and 1915, the Kansas City park board implemented a coordinated system of 2,050 park acres together with 26 miles of boulevards. The result was the most intricate and elegant demonstration of City Beautiful design in America, and words of high praise soon replaced the disparaging remarks of Kingsley and Holt. Local pride rose to a new pinnacle. Yet this achievement surprised many observers because it seemed out of character for the hard-nosed pragmatists who had guided Kansas City's fortunes up to that point. How did it happen?

Timing was a big factor. Adoption of City Beautiful principles in Baltimore, Boston, and other older cities was limited by expensive costs of land and opposition from groups with vested interests. Similarly, leaders in Denver, Los Angeles, and other urban centers newer than Kansas City either did not have the money or did not yet see the need for such extravagance. In contrast, when Kansas City voters were told that parks would increase land values and cost much less now than in the future, they were just the right "age" to go along. Beyond general timing, several local issues also pushed the Kansas City cause. The biggest, without doubt, was the ugliness so commonly reported by visitors and epitomized by the West Bluff shacks that loomed above Union Depot. Something had to be done about these.

If the conversion of the West Bluff from slum to park was a cause looking for a crusader, the perfect knight rode into town in the person of William Rockhill Nelson. Nelson was a newspaperman with money, an outsized personality, and a zeal for progressive ideas. He founded the *Kansas City Star* in 1880 and immediately set out to improve his adopted city. An editorial on May 19, 1881, was one of the first to make the case for park development, and he identified a young landscape architect named George E. Kessler as the right man for the job. Historians also add a third name to the list of park insiders—August R. Meyer, another relative newcomer who ran the large smelter that gave Argentine its name. Known as a good public speaker and master of backroom deals, Meyer happened to live near Nelson and came to share the publisher's ideas for improvement. Meyer's appointment to head the first park board in 1892 proved to be an inspired choice. The industrialist, in turn, hired Kessler to create a master landscape plan and then navigated a host of political and financial hazards to see it to completion.[7]

Kessler unveiled his ideas as a single, comprehensive program in 1893 (map 29). Although he stressed the importance of green spaces for relaxation and the potential for social engineering, the public was most impressed by his scale. Three large parks dominate the plan—the North and West bluffs (Kessler tastefully calls them terraces) and the ravine near the mouth of OK Creek (Penn Valley). These were predictable choices. The North Terrace project enhanced the city's most spectacular view and established goodwill with the business leaders whose homes lined nearby Gladstone and Independence boulevards. West Terrace and Penn Valley, in contrast, were essentially slum reclamations. The need for West Terrace was obvious to all, but Penn Valley's Vinegar Gulch was more remote and therefore hidden from most Kansas City eyes. It happened to lie along the daily commuting route William Rockhill Nelson took to his newspaper, however, and so received priority.[8]

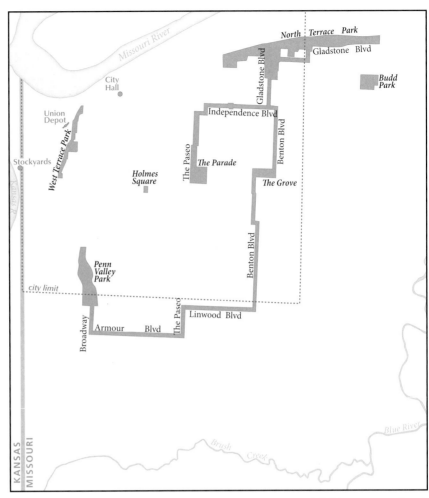

Map 29. Plan for the Park System in Kansas City, Missouri, 1893. Modified from a map in Board of Park Commissioners, Kansas City, Missouri, *Report of the Board of Park Commissioners for the Fiscal Year Ending April 19, 1915* (Kansas City, Mo.: Board of Park Commissioners, 1915).

Kessler originally had designed boulevards to connect all three parks. Opposition from business leaders scuttled a conversion of Eleventh Street to that purpose, but routes he initially termed South Boulevard and East Boulevard came to fruition as Armour/Linwood and Benton, respectively. Map 29 also shows the first phase of The Paseo, Kessler's showpiece boulevard. Bearing the Spanish name for promenade to echo the city's historical ties with Santa Fe, The Paseo was half a block wide. This width allowed room for a divided roadway and extensive landscape design. Separate blocks featured, in the words of one admirer, "fountains, a fine pergola in three flights, an imposing architectural terrace, a sunken garden, a small lake shrouded by water shrubbery and several warm stretches of lawn."[9]

As the crown jewel of the park system, The Paseo had to be centrally located. But its exact position was opportunistic. Just

Figure 17. West Terrace Park, 1921, Looking Northeast from Kersey Coates Drive. Plans to transform the West Bluff into a park began in 1893 but were delayed ten years by lawsuits. Landscape architect George Kessler then replaced the uppermost row of shacks with a curving parkway. Above this, he designed a series of limestone retaining walls, graceful stairways, and landings. Twin towers at the end of Tenth Street provide observation points. Construction of Interstate 35 in 1966 removed part of the park, but the towers and stairs remain. (Courtesy Missouri Valley Special Collections, Kansas City Public Library)

east of Lydia, between Ninth and Eighteenth streets, haphazard development had produced two north-south roads only a half block apart. These streets were lined with small, poorly built houses. Using the power of eminent domain to purchase this acreage, Kessler converted Grove and Flora avenues into the single, broad corridor he needed. No one seemed to notice the displaced, mostly black people.

The new park system received an unexpected boost in 1896 when an aging bachelor, Thomas H. Swope, donated a 1,334-acre tract to the city. It was beautifully wooded and in the valley of the Blue River but located 7 miles south of the business district and 4 miles beyond the city limit. Distance

notwithstanding, Kessler and other officials praised the land's potential, and some 18,000 people attended an elaborate dedication ceremony that summer. Although Swope Park remained largely undeveloped for several years, its influence on the city's evolving geography was immediate and profound.

Kansas City developers had debated the relative potentials of the community's east and south sides for at least fifteen years. Which locality would experience faster growth? Which one would attract the richer clientele? Willard Winner, the city's biggest speculator of the 1880s, had believed in the east side and so promoted what is today Winner Road as a link to Independence. The density of east-west trolley lines at the time also exceeded that of north-south ones. Although the south side had champions as well, including William Rockhill Nelson at his country estate near what is now Forty-fifth and Oak, Swope Park was the major catalyst for that direction.[10]

By 1909, a new map prepared by the park board revealed a skeleton of boulevards that stretched two times farther south than east (map 30). In this design, The Paseo assumes a more prominent role than in 1893, having been extended north

Figure 18. Sunken Garden on The Paseo, 1908, Looking North. In a city known for its parks and boulevards, The Paseo was the showpiece. George Kessler designed it to provide shifting landscape scenes for travelers along its divided lanes from Admiral Boulevard to Seventeenth Street. Fountains graced two intersections, and a high stone terrace (upper right in photograph) marked Twelfth Street. A large sunken garden filled the block south to Thirteenth Street. The New York Apartments building on the left was built in 1903. It and much of the sunken garden were sacrificed to urban renewal in the 1970s. (Courtesy Missouri Valley Special Collections, Kansas City Public Library)

to North Terrace Park and south to Forty-seventh Street. A new Swope Parkway then runs another 3.5 miles to the park. The march to the south is also evident near the state line. A connector from West Terrace Park to Penn Valley has been extended through old Westport to Brush Creek. Gillham Road, a third route inserted midway between Penn Valley and The Paseo, accentuates the trend, as does a pair of new southern parks. Both of these latter additions, Roanoke and Spring Valley, were donated by neighborhood groups and are evidence that the ongoing program of park development enjoyed popular support. Predicting the next stage of Kansas City's residential development would not require a Cassandra. The prime open land lay just south of Brush Creek and west of Swope Park. Areas east of The Paseo, many of which were developed too fast in the 1880s, would be hard pressed to compete. So would those in Kansas City, Kansas, which did not enjoy the magical overlay of green promenades.[11]

A Railroad Palace

The Gillham Road corridor shown on map 30, seemingly too close to other boulevards, was inserted by Kessler to serve a new urban landmark—Union Station. This railroad depot, still under construction at the 1909 date of the map, rivaled the park-and-boulevard system as an influence on overall urban development. Geographically, a station at Twenty-

65

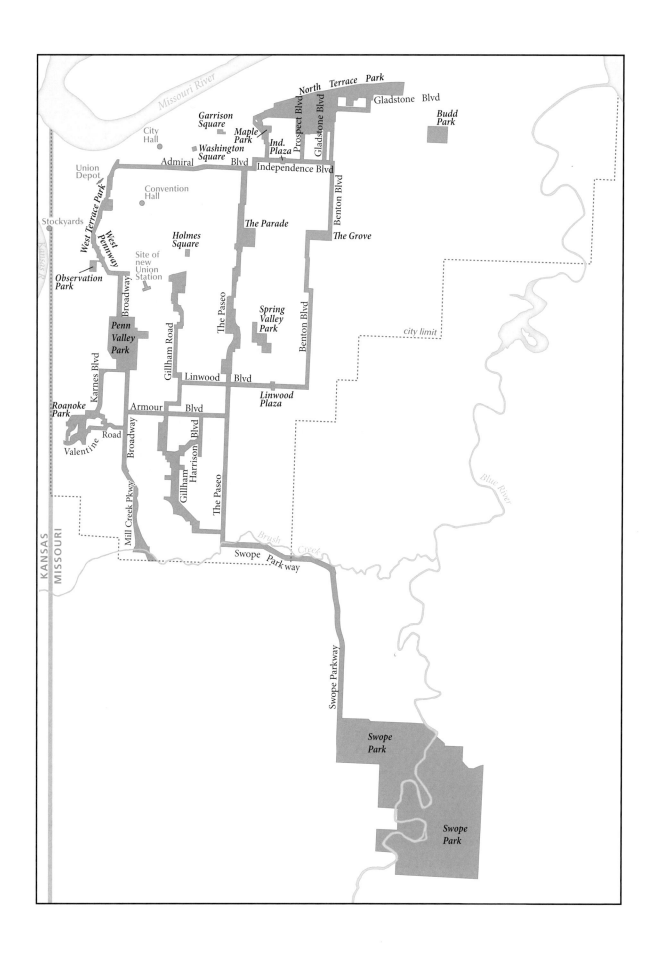

third and Main implied an almost complete reorientation of commercial activity from that associated with the old depot on Union Avenue in the West Bottoms. Aesthetically, the new station was designed on a physical and artistic scale unmatched outside of New York City. It was a part of Kessler's City Beautiful Movement as much as it was integral to changing patterns of transportation and industry. How it came about is a question fundamental to Kansas City's image and evolution.[12]

A railroad station in the West Bottoms had made sense in 1878 when Union Depot was constructed there. Grades were gentle and space abundant, and if local businesspeople were not overly happy to descend the steep bluff, that was no great concern to the rail executives who made the decision. Circumstances began to change in the 1880s. The city and its rail traffic both grew rapidly, and the station became crowded. Newspapers lobbied for relocation, but the railroad officials responded only with a modest expansion of the old building. Their site was too small to accommodate additional development, and construction elsewhere would have been expensive and disruptive. They talked—but with no sense of urgency.[13]

Three general locales for a possible new depot emerged from these talks. Most obvious was another site in the West Bottoms. This location would require only minimal construction of new tracks and thereby lower total costs. Consequently, a majority of the six railroad executives whose companies controlled the depot favored this idea. An alternative appeared in 1887 when Congress authorized a second local bridge across the Missouri River. Located near Cherry Street, five blocks east of Main, this construction would create a depot site convenient to downtown. Land there also was expected to be relatively inexpensive, since it was part of the underdeveloped East Bottoms (map 2). The ubiquitous Willard Winner saw this potential first. He purchased the tract and had the bridge partially completed by 1891. When he was forced into bankruptcy later that year, the property passed to other hands and then, about 1902, to a subsidiary of the Burlington railroad. This maneuver gave momentum to the site because Burlington was one of the conglomerates that jointly

Map 30 (facing page). The Park System in Kansas City, Missouri, 1909. Modified from a map in Board of Park Commissioners, Kansas City, Missouri, Report of the Board of Park Commissioners for the Fiscal Year Ending April 19, 1915 (Kansas City, Mo.: Board of Park Commissioners, 1915).

controlled the depot decision. The *Kansas City Star* and the city's commercial club both added endorsements.[14]

The third location proposed, where Main Street intersected OK Creek some fifteen blocks south of downtown, was relatively remote. Still, it possessed strong physical and political assets. Physically, as detailed in chapter 1, OK Creek occupies part of a channel cut originally by Turkey Creek during glacial times. This lowland trends east-northeast and emerges at the East Bottoms (map 2). Trackage along its course would have gentle grades all the way and could connect easily with existing lines in the West Bottoms.

The rail potential of OK Creek was recognized as early as 1878 by Charles F. Morse, the agent of financier Charles Francis Adams. Adams purchased acreage there just as he was doing simultaneously in Armourdale. Four years later, Morse himself became active in the area, promoting the Kansas City Belt Railway along the valley as a cooperative venture for all the major rail companies. This initiative proved premature, and he found no takers. Things changed in 1884. Morse's former employers at the Atchison, Topeka and Santa Fe Railway now envisioned OK Creek as part of a new, direct line to Chicago. Partnering with the Kansas City, Fort Scott and Gulf company (whose tracks ran through the adjacent Turkey Creek valley) and Adams's stockyard, they quickly constructed the beltway and demonstrated its advantages.[15]

Depot relocation was at a stalemate early in 1903. Burlington people obviously favored the northern site and Santa Fe partisans the southern one. Others vacillated but tended to lobby for the cheaper, third option of the West Bottoms. Most observers thought that this last view eventually would prevail, but then came the floodwaters of late May. The old depot closed for a week, and abruptly, the long-term options dropped to two.

The railroad executives finally seemed ready to decide in February 1905. Burlington officials had increased the attractiveness of their East Bottoms site by adding the giant Armour and Swift meatpacking companies as partners. Missouri Pacific and Wabash people strongly supported this solution, and the others acquiesced. All that remained was to reach agreement on a price. This seemingly simple matter proved otherwise. The men of the Burlington consortium demanded three times the appraised value for their land, the other railroad men balked, and the meeting adjourned in bitterness.[16]

Another year passed before a deal was completed. This time, the impetus came from Edward H. Harriman, a New

Figure 19. Union Station, 1915, Looking East from Pennsylvania Street. Kansas City's iconic railroad station is usually photographed from the south to reveal its grand facade. This view captures the working building, with sixteen tracks entering its train sheds beneath a long passenger waiting room. During the 1920s, a train would arrive every eight minutes. A viaduct for Broadway crosses the center of this scene, and the just-completed, curve-sided Coca-Cola Building (later Western Auto) appears in the left background. (Courtesy Missouri Valley Special Collections, Kansas City Public Library)

York mogul who had been a partner with the Burlington and who himself controlled both the Union Pacific and the Chicago and Alton railways. Abruptly ending his Burlington affiliation, Harriman began negotiations with Santa Fe people for a site at OK Creek. Spurned officials at the Burlington, Missouri Pacific, and Wabash companies refused to join his effort, but a union of six other railroads purchased a 36-acre tract. Then, surprisingly, they voted to erect not just a serviceable station but a "magnificent" one with a total budget of $20 million.[17]

Harriman was the primary force behind the station's form and generous budget. His agents assembled the block of land, and he personally approved the architect. The man who was chosen, Jarvis Hunt, was young and inexperienced but committed to classical design. He had witnessed the rebirth of

Imperial Rome's horizontal lines, symmetry, and understated grandeur at Chicago's Columbian Exposition in 1893, and he had applied the style on his own to a depot in Mexico, Missouri. This Mexico station happened to be on the Chicago and Alton Railroad, whose president was Harriman's agent in Kansas City. Later in life, Hunt recalled Harriman's single charge for the new depot: "Make a monument."[18]

Hunt's Union Station ended up costing $6.4 million exclusive of land, tracks, and other infrastructure. Construction took eight years. The final product, although not architecturally innovative, was certainly grand. Its main, south-facing facade stretched over two city blocks. A triple archway, 70 feet in height, led into a mammoth central lobby. This great hall, featuring marble and a 95-foot ceiling, was flanked by two wings, one primarily for baggage handling and the other for restaurants and shops. To the north, elevated over parallel lines of tracks, were the deep wooden benches of the passenger waiting room.[19]

Local residents were most impressed with Union Station's size. The railroad men had built it to serve a community of 2 million people. And since this figure was some six times larger than that of the two Kansas Cities combined in 1910, people saw the building as prophecy. Here, in solid marble and lime-

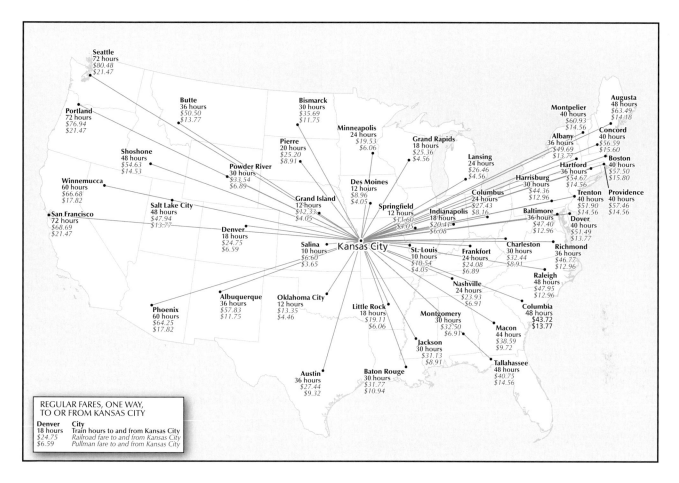

Seattle
72 hours
$80.48
$21.47

Portland
72 hours
$76.94
$21.47

Butte
36 hours
$50.50
$13.77

Bismarck
30 hours
$35.69
$11.75

Minneapolis
24 hours
$19.53
$6.06

Grand Rapids
18 hours
$25.36
$4.56

Montpelier
40 hours
$60.93
$14.56

Augusta
48 hours
$63.49
$14.18

Shoshone
48 hours
$54.63
$14.53

Pierre
20 hours
$25.20
$8.91

Powder River
30 hours
$33.54
$6.89

Lansing
24 hours
$26.46
$4.56

Albany
36 hours
$49.69
$13.77

Concord
40 hours
$56.59
$15.60

Winnemucca
60 hours
$66.68
$17.82

Des Moines
12 hours
$8.96
$4.05

Columbus
24 hours
$27.43

Harrisburg
30 hours
$44.36
$12.96

Hartford
36 hours
$54.67
$14.56

Boston
40 hours
$57.50
$15.80

San Francisco
72 hours
$68.69
$21.47

Salt Lake City
48 hours
$47.94
$13.77

Grand Island
12 hours
$12.33
$4.05

Springfield
12 hours
$11.60
$4.05

Indianapolis
18 hours
$20.41
$6.08

Baltimore
36 hours
$47.40
$12.96

Trenton
40 hours
$51.90
$14.56

Providence
40 hours
$57.46
$14.56

Dover
40 hours
$51.49
$13.77

Denver
18 hours
$24.75
$6.59

Salina
10 hours
$6.60
$3.65

Kansas City

St. Louis
10 hours
$10.54
$4.05

Frankfort
24 hours
$24.08
$6.89

Charleston
30 hours
$32.44
$8.91

Richmond
36 hours
$46.77
$12.96

Phoenix
60 hours
$64.25
$17.82

Albuquerque
36 hours
$57.83
$11.75

Oklahoma City
12 hours
$13.35
$4.46

Little Rock
18 hours
$19.11
$6.06

Nashville
24 hours
$23.93
$6.91

Montgomery
30 hours
$32.50
$6.91

Macon
44 hours
$38.59
$9.72

Raleigh
48 hours
$47.95
$12.96

Columbia
48 hours
$43.72
$13.77

Austin
36 hours
$27.44
$9.32

Baton Rouge
30 hours
$31.77
$10.94

Jackson
30 hours
$31.13
$8.91

Tallahassee
48 hours
$40.75
$14.56

REGULAR FARES, ONE WAY,
TO OR FROM KANSAS CITY

Denver   City
18 hours   Train hours to and from Kansas City
$24.75   Railroad fare to and from Kansas City
$6.59   Pullman fare to and from Kansas City

stone, was testimony that their future would be bright. Some 100,000 citizens attended the opening ceremony, and the depot's ongoing bustle became a mark of civic pride. Maps of the nation's railroad system converging at this site probably even inspired the city's most enduring slogan (map 31). In the same year as the station's opening, 1914, the local commercial club first promoted "The Heart of America" catchphrase.[20]

Once construction was under way at OK Creek, entrepreneurs began to consider the new station's implications for other businesses and activities. At the same time, Willard Winner, the Armour-Swift-Burlington (ASB) alliance, and others who almost had secured the depot for the East Bottoms must have pondered their loss. Consider first what a northern station might have meant. Certainly, the ASB people would have completed their namesake bridge across the Missouri River sooner than its actual 1911 date. More important, a station at the head of Cherry Street would have rejuvenated the city's original business district. The city hall on Market Square would again be centrally positioned, and new office construction likely would venture no farther south than Twelfth Street. Meanwhile, the East Bottoms surely

Map 31. The Heart of America, 1920. Modified from a promotional map produced about 1920 by the local chamber of commerce, a copy of which is in the Western Historical Manuscript Collection at the University of Missouri–Kansas City.

would boom, perhaps attracting many wholesale merchants. Their cramped sites near the old depot would no longer hold much allure.[21]

Implications of the actual OK Creek location were relatively hard to forecast. Its fifteen-block distance from downtown was awkward—too far for commercial expansion to fill in the gap and create an enlarged business district and yet too close to imagine a successful secondary or rival retail complex. Incorporation of the station into George Kessler's park system was one possibility. The existing Penn Valley Park lay only two and a half blocks to the southwest, and the railroad executives had already agreed to donate 8 acres just south of the station to the city. Joining the two parcels would be easy.[22]

Having public space just south of the station was a pragmatic decision. City officials insisted on it initially to prevent a recurrence of the saloons and other earthy businesses that lined Union Avenue across from the old depot. Physical

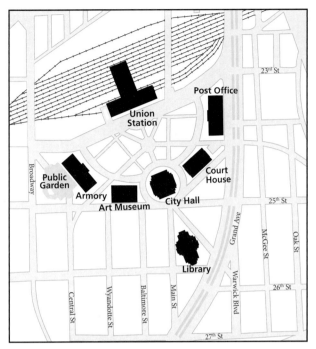

Map 32. Proposal for a Civic Center Adjacent to Union Station, 1910. Modified from a sketch prepared by Jarvis Hunt, the architect of Union Station, and reproduced in Jeffrey Spivak, Union Station: Kansas City *(Kansas City, Mo.: Kansas City Star Books, 1999), p. 31.*

geography was involved as well. The station faced south and up the valley slope instead of north across the lowland and toward downtown. This orientation angered business leaders but permitted an efficient, multiple-level building with trains able to pass beneath the waiting room on its downslope side and ground-level public access on the south. The elaborate entry would require a suitable counterpoint across the street, however. A park might work, but so could other ideas.[23]

Promoters of the City Beautiful Movement, whether in Kansas City or elsewhere, had always lobbied for projects beyond parks and boulevards. They welcomed Union Station into their fold, for instance, and were even more enthusiastic about grand civic centers. Such creations united on a single, formal plaza a series of architecturally linked buildings. A city hall might be central, perhaps, flanked by museums, a courthouse, libraries, and more. Architects were designing such plazas for Chicago, Cleveland, San Francisco, and other cities at the same time that Jarvis Hunt pondered his depot. It is little wonder that he, George Kessler, and others saw a similar civic complex as the perfect use for the open land south of the new station.[24]

A civic center made sense to many Kansas City people. They long had suffered from having visitors judge their com-

munity poorly because of the tawdriness of Union Depot's neighborhood. How wonderful it would be to turn that image on its head. As J. C. Nichols, one of the city's rising young developers, asked, "Don't you believe that the creation of a beautiful setting would do much to bring fresh capital here?" Other supporters noted that the city's existing public buildings were too scattered to promote synergy and that both city hall and the courthouse sat in the increasingly backwater part of town north of Sixth Street. Finally, in 1911, Mary McAfee Atkins bequeathed the city $300,000 to create an art museum. This, too, could be part of a new plaza.[25]

The first specific plan for a civic center appeared in 1907. George Kessler, after conferring with Hunt and others, suggested leveling the hillside from Broadway to Grand Avenue to create a platform. This foundation would extend south to Twenty-fifth Street. A monument at the intersection of Twenty-fifth and Main would be its focal point, from which short radials would lead to the various buildings. This vision fell victim to poor timing, for a national financial panic that year discouraged investors. With the return of prosperity in 1909, Jarvis Hunt offered two new plans. The first emphasized Main Street, widening it south of the station and lowering the grade. New buildings would line this corridor in a manner reminiscent of The Paseo. The second plan revisited the site of Kessler's design (map 32). Instead of a central monument, however, Hunt suggested a domed city hall. Flanking this around a semicircular drive would be a new post office, courthouse, art museum, and armory. Grand Avenue and Broadway would provide access.[26]

The Dispersal of Civic Buildings

Despite their strong support for an elaborate park-and-boulevard system and a stately Union Station, Kansas City people never built a civic center at OK Creek. Just why they did not remains somewhat mysterious. The location, midway between the local business and residential sectors, was ideal. Financing was available, and construction of the center likely would have guaranteed national acceptance of the city's cultural maturity and progressive character. Historians lay part of the blame on midwestern practicality. Why spend $250,000 to excavate a hillside when one could build elsewhere at much lower cost? A more significant reason, perhaps, was lack of leadership. August Meyer had died in 1905, and William Rockhill Nelson was ill. George Kessler, although still active, now lived in St. Louis.[27]

Lacking a champion, plans for the land across from the

station devolved for nearly a decade after 1910. After discarding the idea of a civic center, public opinion first favored an art gallery alone, then a large park, and then a more modest greenery of 40 acres. In 1919, however, a new cause arose. Lumberman Robert A. Long proposed that Kansas City use this hilltop to honor the sacrifices of the recent world war. A subscription drive easily raised $2 million, and New York architect Harold Van Buren Magonigle created a design that took full advantage of the elevation. Setting a central, 217-foot shaft atop a 100-foot base, he drew viewer eyes upward and so emphasized a hopeful future. When completed in 1926, this Liberty Memorial attracted praise internationally.[28]

Magonigle's work reopened discussion on new buildings for government and the arts. For example, philanthropist William Volker suggested to Robert Long's planning committee early on that a university might be a more appropriate and enduring way to honor war veterans. He was overruled, but the memorial design did include potential locations for a music hall and similar arts structures. These facilities could line a three-block mall planned as the formal entry to the tower from the south.[29]

Civic interest centered first on a university. Motivation came partly from a chamber of commerce survey that revealed Kansas City to be the largest American community without such an institution. The idea also promised both practical (professional schools) and cultural (fine arts) dividends. A special committee began to assess funding alternatives in 1922. Three years later, with plans about ready for release, two new proposals led to an even grander possibility.[30]

First, leaders of the Methodist Episcopal Church, South, offered to relocate their Central College for Women to the city from Lexington, Missouri. Then, almost immediately thereafter, a local widow donated 147 acres to the Methodist Episcopal Church, North, provided that planners would agree to use the site for a college. Bishop Ernest Waldorf was enthusiastic. He arranged a merger with the Central College group, obtained the endorsement of Kansas City's chamber of commerce, and set out to raise $5 million. A month later, in September 1925, the project was well under way. The site, bounded by Seventy-fifth and Seventy-ninth streets, State Line Road, and Belinder Avenue, was somewhat remote and still under lease to the Meadow Lake Country Club, but architects already were at work. Bishop Waldorf also had a name. Reflecting the state line location and local history, this new institution was to be Lincoln and Lee University, where "north met south and east met west."[31]

Plans for Lincoln and Lee slowed after 1926. Methodists beyond the immediate area proved reluctant to pledge money, and Kansas City people were diverted by news of a second major arts project. William Rockhill Nelson's estate had become available to the city in February 1926 upon the death of his only child. Under the terms of Nelson's will, the *Kansas City Star* was to be sold and the proceeds (estimated at $8 million) used to purchase art for a public gallery.[32]

Room for a new art museum certainly could have been found at the Lincoln and Lee campus, and the prospect likely would have helped with fund-raising. But instead, a better gallery site quickly emerged. Nelson had lived on a 200-acre tract near the intersection of Forty-fifth Street and Oak. When his heirs offered this site to the city for free, together with money to construct a suitable building, acceptance was easy. The land lay within the existing system of boulevards and in a neighborhood of quality homes (most of them constructed by Nelson).[33]

The question of the gallery moving to the university site was now reversed. The two institutions clearly would benefit from proximity, and the Nelson estate included undeveloped acreage a mile or so south of the planned gallery, on the other side of Brush Creek. The downside to the idea was a possible loss of Methodist support, including the land on State Line Road. Various compromises were floated—among them a name change to Lincoln and Lee, the University of Kansas City—but by 1930, the Methodists had backed out. Two major gifts allowed the city to push ahead. Methodist land donor Kate (Mrs. Charles B.) Hewitt sold her property but donated the proceeds to the city's new effort plus the operating rights to her late husband's private Kansas City Dental College. William Volker, a local man who had become wealthy manufacturing window shades and picture frames, was the other angel. He provided $100,000 for the purchase of 40 acres of Nelson's land to form a campus core. The new University of Kansas City and the William R. Nelson Gallery of Art both opened in 1933.[34]

Although the twinned setting of the gallery and the university did not fulfill Jarvis Hunt's vision of a complete civic center, it was nevertheless impressive. Large collections of East Asian ceramics and ongoing series of university lectures could help residents and visitors alike to believe that Kansas City was now sophisticated. The complex actually contained more than just its signature entities. Adjoining the Nelson on the northwest was a new Kansas City Art Institute, based in the former home of August Meyer. It, too, was created with pri-

Figure 20. *Municipal Auditorium, 1937, Looking Southwest from the Corner of Thirteenth and Wyandotte. With the passage of a major bond issue in 1931, Kansas City people gained a trio of new public buildings: a city hall, a county courthouse, and an auditorium. All are modernist structures with strong, symmetrical lines softened by Art Deco detail. Municipal Auditorium is especially appealing. It was one of the country's best convention and entertainment venues when it opened in 1935, and renovation keeps it relevant today. So does a location adjacent to major hotels and to the newer Bartle Convention Center. (Courtesy Missouri Valley Special Collections, Kansas City Public Library)*

vate money, most of it from grain merchant Howard Vander-slice and a developer's widow, Mary Elizabeth Epperson. To the south, just east of the university campus, arose a new hospital and a second school. Rockhurst College, opened by the Jesuits in 1917, was actually older than the other institutions. It was still quite small in the 1930s, however, not having had a building of its own until 1922. The hospital, Menorah, was far larger. It was built in 1931 by and for the local Jewish community, but it operated in nonsectarian fashion.[35]

Greater Kansas City in the 1920s was a prosperous place, growing in size to a half million people and enjoying favorable press coverage for its new park system, railroad station, and Liberty Memorial. The promise of the Nelson gallery and a university added to this stature. Feeling so buoyed, local officials were only moderately surprised when the Republican National Committee decided to hold its 1928 presidential nomination convention in the city. This selection was simply another acknowledgment of local maturation.

Civic smugness was short lived. Stories began to circulate a month after the convention's announcement that the contract might be canceled. Some 4,000 hotel rooms were needed, but this number might not be available. The convention hall was a problem, too. Though praised in 1900 at its construction for that year's Democratic convention, the building had not aged well. Crowds expected to number 20,000 would overwhelm its 11,000 seats. Convention delegates suggested that Kansas City had been selected not for its progressivism but only as a sop to disgruntled midwestern farmers who might otherwise bolt to the rival Democratic Party. They argued for relocation to Buffalo or Cleveland.[36]

Under the leadership of Conrad H. Mann, head of the local chamber of commerce, Kansas City managed to retain the convention and earn a passable grade from delegates, but the experience opened the eyes of civic leaders. They realized that the city had been figuratively sitting on its heels. Its last big project, the boulevard system, had been completed fifteen years earlier. Union Station had been largely a private undertaking, and so were Liberty Memorial, the planned art gallery, and the anticipated university. Public action was needed if the city hoped to remain competitive.[37]

The concern of 1928 led directly to the nation's most ambitious urban renewal program of the next decade. Modestly termed the Ten-Year Plan, its approach was at once broad based, fair minded, and pragmatic. Mayor Albert I. Beach set the tone in 1929 when he appointed a committee of 100 residents to draft a general strategy. His successor, Bryce B. Smith, enlarged the planning group to 1,000 on fifteen subcommittees and appointed the same Conrad Mann who had salvaged the Republican convention to head the overall effort. The group debated specific projects within a total budget of $50 million. Then, even as economic depression deepened across the nation, voters on May 26, 1931, approved the plan by a margin of four to one. Like Mann, they wanted "to make Kansas City the greatest inland city in America."[38]

The grand proposal included money for sewers, fire protection, public hospitals, roads, and more. But attention focused on a new, $4.5 million auditorium to replace the convention hall downtown and especially on an $8 million civic complex that would include a new city hall and courthouse. George Kessler and Jarvis Hunt's dream of 1910 could now become reality, but with two complexes instead of one. As the arts people settled on the Nelson property in a southern residential area, planners pondered their options for the governmental equivalent. Their decision, obviously, could greatly influence the future urban landscape.[39]

The matter of location for what came to be called Municipal Auditorium was resolved first. Although this building could have been incorporated into the civic complex, business demands were more pressing. Hotels already clustered near the old Convention Hall, and an adjacent full block of land was available at reasonable cost. This tract, south of Thirteenth Street between Wyandotte and Central, sloped to the south, and this, too, was advantageous. It allowed direct access from Fourteenth Street into a vast, 5-acre exhibition

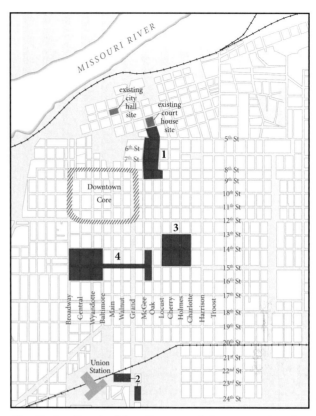

Map 33. *Sites Considered for a Governmental Center, 1930. Data from Chamber of Commerce of Kansas City,* Where These Rocky Bluffs Meet: Including the Story of the Kansas City Ten-Year Plan *(Kansas City, Mo.: Kansas City Chamber of Commerce, 1938), pp. 135–136.*

hall on the building's lower level. Thirteenth Street provided similar entry to the main floor.

The auditorium, with a functional limestone facade and a beautiful Art Deco interior, has served the city well for over seventy-five years. Its 13,000-seat arena remained viable for major sporting events through the 1970s, and its smaller Music Hall and Little Theater have never fallen from public favor. Architects intended the building to be viewed from a public plaza on its north, the site provided by a razing of the old Convention Hall. This goal was only partially accomplished. A park does exist (today's Barney Allis Plaza), but because of garage construction beneath, it is elevated several feet above street level and so obscures the sight lines.[40]

The planning subcommittee for the civic center was chaired by developer J. C. Nichols. His group initially considered twenty sites, but issues of public access trimmed the list to four for additional study (map 33). Predictably, all of these aligned closely with the traditional urban axis of Main Street and Grand Avenue. The choices extended from the southern edge of the original townsite to just beyond Union Station.[41]

The most conservative option, along Oak Street between Missouri Avenue and Ninth Street, abutted the existing courthouse. The old city hall sat only three blocks to the northwest. Buildings here would serve business well and interrupt familiar routines only slightly. They also would act as urban renewal, eliminating several blocks of lower-quality apartments and small houses, many of them occupied by Irish immigrants and African Americans.

A second option harkened directly back to Jarvis Hunt and the civic possibilities adjacent to Union Station. With Liberty Memorial now occupying the land south of the station, the Nichols committee looked closely at two nearly vacant tracts to the east, diagonal to one another across Grand Avenue. Businesspeople objected to the remoteness of this site, but planners saw Union Station as the city's new crossroads and predicted that the local population center soon would move this far south.

The final two sites were compromises, midway between business and residential sectors. One was six square blocks focused on Fourteenth Street east of Locust. This site would require removal of numerous homes plus two churches and a synagogue. The last site was the largest. Its core was another six-block tract, but this unit connected to a smaller, second piece of land along Fifteenth Street. Four blocks of this street then would be widened to create a linear plaza that would showcase the buildings at either end.

When it came time to make a recommendation, only two sites received votes. Sixteen committee members favored the Fifteenth Street location with its plaza; five preferred the one adjacent to downtown. The choice was obvious, but influential merchants objected. At a protest meeting, 170 such people urged reconsideration of the site at Sixth and Oak so as to "preserve the integrity of the downtown section."[42]

The protest produced a public hearing but no capitulation. Conrad Mann then suggested locations midway between the two sites. Such land would be more expensive, however, since it was nearer the business core, and so the budget would dictate either a smaller tract or less elaborate buildings. Seeing no alternative, officials approved the compromise. The new acreage was on Twelfth Street between Oak and Locust. Major commercial buildings stood only a block to the west, and streetcars provided easy access. On the negative side, the site was reduced to two square blocks, a severe handicap for any architect who hoped to create a symbolic landscape.[43]

Realizing that unified design offered the best possibility for visual impact from the cramped new complex, officials selected a single architectural firm for the entire project. The resulting courthouse and city hall face one another across Twelfth Street. They are large, formal buildings whose lower stories project outward. From these bases rise simple but elegant towers with Art Deco trim and small stepbacks on top. The tallest building, city hall, reaches thirty-two stories.[44]

In 1938, a year after the city hall was completed, funds became available to add a municipal courts building to the complex. Officials bought land just east of city hall, hired the same architect, and obtained a quality complementary structure. But there the momentum stopped. The city had three praiseworthy but space-starved buildings.

From the perspective of urban development, the Twelfth Street civic complex essentially preserved the status quo. This disappointed many planners who had seen greatness nearly within their grasp. Had the power of vested interests been only a little less, the center certainly would have been more monumental. Moreover, if construction had occurred near Union Station, it is possible (even likely) that the city's commercial district would have relocated there as well.

Ramifications of the Fifteenth Street plaza site favored by the Nichols committee are even more intriguing. That tract was close enough to both Union Station and the newer commercial buildings on Eleventh and Twelfth streets to allow a grand symbiosis. Fifteenth Street would have become the handsome urban centerpiece in this scenario, with warehousing and transportation to the south and Petticoat Lane shopping to the north. The area impacted most negatively would have been north of Ninth Street. The old city hall and courthouse were big employers in that aging section, and their potential loss was what sparked the merchant protest of 1930. The irony, of course, is that the area north of Ninth deteriorated just as fast with the constricted civic center on Twelfth Street as it would have with the more spacious site on Fifteenth.

Industrial Expansion

The increasing economic prominence of Kansas City in the 1900–1930 period that had prompted two presidential conventions and a new Union Station also encouraged manufacturers and wholesalers. Much of this latter activity remained in Argentine, Armourdale, and the West Bottoms where it previously had been concentrated, but four new industrial districts also opened to handle growth. Each of the four—in the valley near Union Station, in the Blue River valley, in the Clay County Bottoms, and in the North Bottoms of Wyandotte County—greatly influenced neighborhood image and residential character (map 2). The latter two were also trendsetters on the national scene.

The process began about 1884 when Santa Fe railroad officials laid tracks along OK Creek and created the Kansas City Belt Railway Company. At the time, these men were contemplating depot locations and direct routes to Chicago more than industrial development, and as a result, they did not actively recruit companies. Still, several entrepreneurs moved to the area, led by John W. Merrill, whose lumberyard near Twenty-fourth and Summit initiated a "Twentieth Street lumber district." Because the valley is narrow and was already laid out with residences in mind, its landscape by the 1920s was both linear and hodgepodge. Away from the carefully manicured grounds of Union Station and Liberty Memorial, one could find coal yards and blighted houses interspersed with bigger warehouses and the signature lumber companies.[45]

Because OK Creek adjoined the West Bottoms, expansion up that stream was easy. It also was necessary, since space in the West Bottoms was going at premium prices. The stockyard had grown huge, and railroads were enlarging their terminal facilities. By 1900, the tracks and freight depots of the Rock Island, the Missouri-Kansas-Texas, the Milwaukee Road, the Frisco, the Burlington, and the Santa Fe lines completely filled the lowland east of the stockyard and south of Fourteenth Street. This left no room for houses. The Annunciation Catholic church and school there, which had served 5,000 parishioners in the early 1880s, saw this number drop to 300 in 1897. Church officials sold out to the Rock Island the next year.[46]

Investors seeking industrial sites larger than OK Creek and less expensive than the West Bottoms found an appealing possibility in the lower valley of the Blue River, on the city's eastern edge. Growth was rapid in this direction, and excellent rail service was available via the Missouri Pacific's main line, which traversed the valley, and the new Belt Railway that entered its northern end. Financing was available, too, via the Lands Trust Company, an English syndicate that had invested in the area. Agents for this trust platted three subdivisions in 1887—Sheffield between Wilson Avenue and Seventh Street, Centropolis between Tenth and Fourteenth streets, and Manchester between Sixteenth and Nineteenth. Slightly later came Leeds between Thirty-fifth and Forty-second. Partly because of their newness, all the Blue Valley additions suffered greatly during the hard times of the 1890s. Yet they survived and eventually prospered.[47]

The injection of major British capital thrilled local residents, but its impact was somewhat muted because of a rival plan that was even grander and more speculative. Its author, predictably, was the city's leading dreamer, Willard E. Winner. Winner thought the best option for new industry lay just across the Missouri River from the original Kansas City townsite. Here were the Clay County Bottoms, some three times larger than the West Bottoms and already served by the Hannibal Bridge and two railroads (map 2). In typically bold fashion, he created the North Kansas City Improvement Company and purchased 10,000 acres. Simultaneously, he lobbied federal officials successfully for permission to construct a second railroad bridge over the Missouri, the same structure noted earlier in this chapter in connection with potential sites for Union Station.[48]

When Winner's companies failed in 1891 with the collapse of the real estate bubble, the land was not yet developed. Several years later, it was acquired by the Armour and Swift packing companies. This move, surprising on the surface, was part of a business maneuver. These packers wanted to increase efficiency by purchasing the Kansas City Stock Yards Company from Charles Adams and his Boston partners. When Adams proved reluctant, the packers threatened to start a rival yard across the river. In 1912, however, Adams capitulated. The Armour and Swift people then opted to use the Clay County acreage as Winner intended. Partnering with Burlington railroad executives to establish the North Kansas City Development Company, they systematically created one of the nation's first planned industrial communities.[49]

In order to better control the development process and keep taxes low, the company incorporated as a separate entity, North Kansas City, rather than joining politically with Kansas City, Missouri. Company officials built their own levee and drainage ditch and then platted two industrial districts and a residential/retail community (map 34). The internal geography was determined by railroad positions, particularly the existing Wabash yard and a new one planned by the Burlington people. Prime industrial space lay within the wedge formed by these two main lines. Part of it was platted in standard lots measuring 610 feet by 270 feet, each served by a road in front and a railroad switch track in back. Farther east in the wedge and throughout a second district southeast of the Wabash tracks, land was reserved for companies needing larger sites.[50]

Worker availability was the company's principal concern. No more than a few hundred people lived in the adjacent

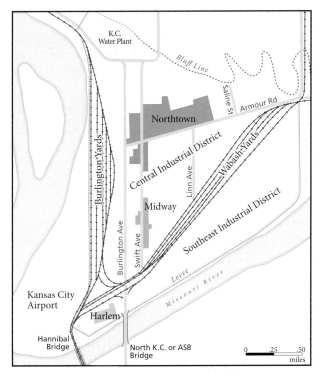

Map 34. North Kansas City, circa 1930. Modified from a map in John Q. Adams, "The North Kansas City Urban District," Economic Geography 8 (1932): 411.

communities of Harlem and Riverside, and commuting from Kansas City on the new, company-owned bridge was inhibited by tolls levied to recoup that huge infrastructure cost. To simultaneously avoid sacrificing needed toll income and attract a skilled class of laborers, officials decided to create their own residential center.

The new town purposely was sited away from Harlem's makeshift dwellings and near the intersection of (naturally enough) Swift Avenue and Armour Road. Shops lined these two main streets, with houses north of Armour. The officials christened the community Northtown, a name soon forgotten for the village itself but still popularly applied to North Kansas City as a whole and increasingly to areas beyond. The rules were many, designed to encourage order but seen by critics as limiting entrepreneurial initiative. Businesses, for instance, were forced to rent space within one of several large, two-story structures erected by the developers. Leases were signed, in fact, before construction began. These retail buildings, which still stand, created a unified and pleasing atmosphere not unlike that of a modern mall.[51]

To encourage worker stability, the company built houses only for sale, not for rent. The original ones, although not identical, all featured the bungalow styling popular at that

time. Most had five rooms and a basement. Residents praised the neatness of the neighborhood and the quality of parks and schools constructed nearby. Nobody mentioned another company policy also intended to attract "better" workers: African American, Mexican, and South European families all were excluded.[52]

North Kansas City was a moderate success in its first twenty years. Northtown grew to about 2,000 residents, both railroads erected big elevators, and several food and flour companies built mills. Nearer the townsite were a large Sears and Roebuck mail-order house and several equipment manufacturers. Still, some two-thirds of the company's land remained idle or in crops in 1929. Some people blamed this vacancy on the bridge toll, which had continued until 1927. Others cited centrality advantages of the older districts and the possibilities of a rival industrial area about to open in adjacent Wyandotte County.[53]

Upstream 2 miles from North Kansas City's ASB Bridge, the floodplain of the Missouri River switches to the Kansas side. This area is the North Bottoms, a smaller tract than the one in Clay County but still substantial at 1,300 acres (map 2). From an industrial perspective, this land had good access to two railroads. Missouri Pacific tracks ran along the entire upland border on the west, and the big Union Pacific yards lay only a mile to the south. Just as important (and in contrast with North Kansas City), a main residential section of Kansas City, Kansas, adjoined this land. Workers would be abundant without any necessity for new bridges or special housing.

Given Wyandotte County's strong historical connections with industry, one might expect government officials to have promoted the North Bottoms. Instead, success in Armourdale and other lowlands together with the newer competition in North Kansas City bred complacency. Overcoming this was the self-appointed task of a local attorney, Guy E. Stanley. Stanley had first glimpsed the potential of the bottoms in 1914 when he negotiated an ownership dispute there. Over the next eight years, he obtained options to purchase most of its acreage and created a drainage district to build needed levees and ditches. Next, he renamed the tract Fairfax and courted Union Pacific Railroad executives as his financiers and partners. Progress was slow but steady, and after a million dollar investment, the first tenant business opened in 1931.[54]

Fairfax was an immediate success despite its start during Depression times. Like North Kansas City, it coddled industry with flexible lot sizes and adjacent railroad spurs. But Stanley went even further. He banned retail operations and all residences. Kansas City officials promised to keep taxes low by not annexing the district for at least twenty-five years. They also pledged to widen Seventh Street as a major artery for workers and suppliers. That the district's welfare was paramount in the new trafficway was specifically acknowledged in 1933 when a viaduct across the Missouri River was named Fairfax Bridge.[55]

Fairfax breathed new life into Wyandotte County's industrial scene, its first big boost since the packers had arrived a generation before. Led by tenants such as the Loose-Wiles Biscuit Company, Sealright containers, and a Chrysler supply depot, the new businesses also belched less smoke and fewer smells than their older counterparts. Workers, as expected, applied in large numbers, and new housing soon filled in the last vacant tracts on the adjacent upland.

Elite Neighborhoods and Expansion to the South

Kansas City residents went from glimpsing the possibility of a metropolis in 1900 to the achievement of that lofty vision a generation later. Heavy investments in transportation and industrial infrastructure had produced Union Station, Fairfax, and North Kansas City, all of which were the envy of urban leaders across the country. The city's boulevards continued to draw lavish praise, and now a museum, a university, and a planned civic center were about to add a needed air of sophistication. Population figures for 1930 revealed exactly what boosters had expected. Adding 100,000 citizens per decade since 1900, the Missouri community ranked number nine-

Figure 21. Armour Road, 2010, Looking East from Swift Avenue. The corner of Armour and Swift is the business heart of Northtown, a worker community created by the North Kansas City Development Company. Six retail structures existed by 1931, each designed for particular lessees. Kelso's Restaurant occupies part of the Peoples Building, for example, constructed originally for a bank by that name and a Grand Union grocery. The development company controlled North Kansas City until 1985. Today, individual operators such as Kelso's are aided by new sidewalks, signage, and other improvements funded by fees from the city's casino (Harrah's). (Photograph by Barbara Shortridge)

teen in the country, and the Kansas one was number sixty-six. With a total of 521,603 residents, the two communities together placed fourteenth in the nation.[56]

Along with their growth, the two cities had enlarged their geographic footprints. In Kansas, Argentine (1909) and

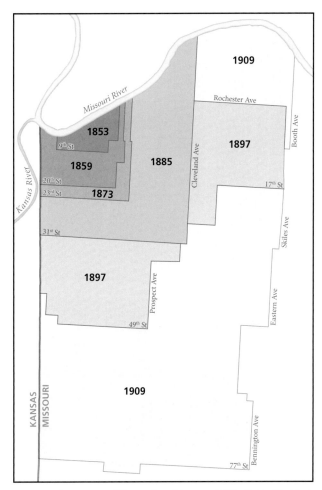

Map 35. City Limits of Kansas City, Missouri, 1853–1909. Modified from a map in Chamber of Commerce of Kansas City, Where These Rocky Bluffs Meet: Including the Story of the Kansas City Ten-Year Plan *(Kansas City, Mo.: Kansas City Chamber of Commerce, 1938), p. 86.*

Rosedale (1922) joined the Kansas City union, and officials had plans to expand the western corporate boundary from Eighteenth Street to Thirty-fourth. Missouri changes were even more dramatic. From being a compact square in 1885, this Kansas City nearly quadrupled its acreage with a major annexation in 1897 and another in 1909 (map 35). The shape changed as well. Whereas the 1897 additions had advanced east as much as south, the ones for 1909 stretched mainly to the south. The old town of Westport and the once-remote Swope Park now lay wholly within the city.

With so much space available, real estate investors had difficulty evaluating sites. A civic center on Twelfth Street, Union Station on Twenty-third, and the Nelson gallery on Forty-fifth each provided a competing growth pole. These potentials had been obvious from the intensities of debate over their own locations, and now the complexity multiplied as

house builders and other developers planned new strategies. Still more complication came from housing decisions that had been made before the new institutions were positioned. The story is best begun with a look at the choices of wealthy homeowners.

Of the three premier neighborhoods in the 1880s—Gladstone Boulevard, Quality Hill, and south Troost Avenue—Quality Hill was the first to change. Its location, though stately, elevated, and convenient to downtown, was small and nearly totally constricted by adjacent bluffs and businesses. Housing sites were unavailable for newly arrived nabobs or children of the original residents. Proximity to the West Bottoms was another problem. Every year brought more smoke and more smells plus further encroachment of jerry-built shacks up the bluffside.[57]

Moves from Quality Hill to the other two mansion districts were possible but rare. The small Troost neighborhood had been completely encircled by lesser homes during the boom of the 1880s, and cultural differences between "eastern" and "southern" money stymied relocations to Gladstone. The obvious alternative was a new Quality Hill. Creating such a place, however, would require both money and social tact. Charles F. Morse, Kansas City's supreme behind-the-scenes promoter, epitomized this combination. As a Quality Hill insider, he saw the need, and as agent for Charles Adams, he had the connections. Throughout 1885, he searched for a site large enough to allow expansion and guarantee exclusivity. Eastern Kansas City was developing too fast to provide such acreage, but the southland offered possibilities. Just beyond the city limits and adjacent to old Westport, he and several associates found 160 acres that extended from Thirty-fourth Street to Fortieth Street and from Broadway to Oak. The next year, they platted it as Hyde Park (map 36).

Morse was a meticulous planner. He partnered with the bankers at Jarvis, Conklin and Company and hired Frank J. Baird as developer, the same man who had subdivided Armourdale and other Adams properties. Next, Morse brought in two more specialists: architect Henry Van Brunt from Boston to design a series of tasteful mansions and an unknown George Kessler to landscape a ravine on the land's southern fringe (and thereby eliminate the possibility of squatter huts). Finally, Morse himself provided a critical demonstration, moving his family in 1887 to a 2.5-acre estate at the northeast corner of Thirty-sixth and Warwick.[58]

Hyde Park was an immediate success. Morse's biggest recruiting coup was packing magnate Kirkland Armour. Other prominent names included architect Van Brunt, railroad builder Arthur Stilwell, merchant Joseph T. Bird, and manufacturer Jacob L. Loose. Then, as the grand homes multiplied, their presence induced major changes elsewhere. Quality Hill, for example, went into rapid decline about 1906. In 1887, the neighborhood had been home to 75 percent of the city's social establishment, but this percentage fell to 42 in 1901 and just 2 in 1915. When old families left, new owners partitioned the villas into apartments and began to ignore needed repairs. By World War I, the once-proud neighborhood was approaching slum status.[59]

Just as Hyde Park's growth led to decline in one place, it boosted another. Developers platted 80 acres immediately east of Morse's land (between Oak and Holmes) as the Kenwood Addition, with homes only slightly smaller than those in the Hyde Park core. Part of Kenwood, in turn, became Janssen Place in 1897 (map 36). There, Arthur Stilwell laid out thirty-two large lots on a cul-de-sac with a formal median park. He named it after his Dutch financier and saw it fill quickly with wealthy lumber executives.[60]

Just south of Hyde Park lay the estate of William Rockhill Nelson. Like Morse, Nelson had considered buying land in eastern Kansas City, but he opted for 10 acres bounded by today's Forty-fourth and Forty-seventh streets, Oak, and Cherry. This was in 1886, the same year as the platting of Hyde Park. Nelson built his own mansion (Oak Hall) over the next four years while simultaneously purchasing adjoining acreage. Some of this property, across Oak Street to the west, he platted as Southmoreland—a development that was to be smaller than Hyde Park but even more exclusive. He

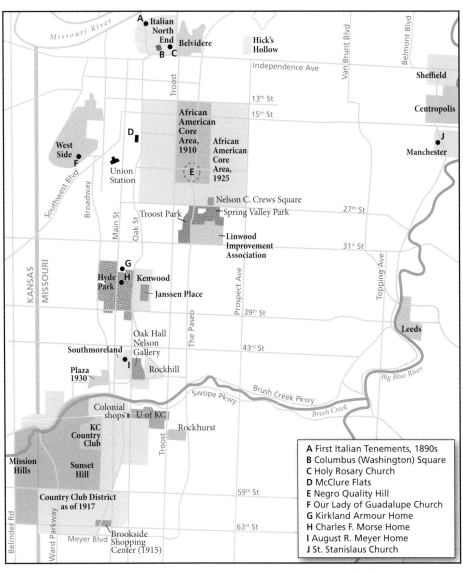

Map 36. Neighborhoods in Kansas City, Missouri, circa 1925. Compiled from multiple sources.

donated 4 acres for a park and lobbied successfully for a conversion of Warwick Avenue into a boulevard that terminated on his property. His coup de grâce, however, was convincing his influential friend August Meyer to relocate to this neighborhood from the Gladstone area in 1896. Shortly thereafter, the Armours, Cudahys, and similar elite families joined the trek south (map 36).[61]

The sequential creation of Hyde Park and Southmoreland swung the tide of development in Kansas City irrevocably to the south. The migrations there of Morse in 1887 and Meyer in 1896 symbolically ended two elite neighborhoods and started a third. More than a quarter of the city's business and social elite lived in the Hyde Park area in 1901, and nearly two-thirds resided there in 1915. The reason, in retrospect,

Figure 22. Apartments on Armour Boulevard, circa 1934, Looking West from Locust Street. This parkway was built in 1900–1901 to provide a crosstown link between Broadway and The Paseo at Thirty-fifth Street. Like its parallel boulevards Admiral and Linwood, it soon became a popular site for apartment hotels: six-to-eight-story structures with ornate entrances and elegant names. Visible here, left to right, are the Park Central (just beyond Gillham Road in the middle ground), the Georgian Court, and the Sombart. Note the wide right-of-way and the lines of graceful American elms. (Courtesy Missouri Valley Special Collections, Kansas City Public Library)

seems to have been razor-thin economics. Had the aggressive eastside promoter Willard Winner not tied up so much acreage there early in the boom years, Morse's and Nelson's estates might well have overlooked the Blue River instead of Brush Creek. From that circumstance, development could easily have moved farther east toward Independence.[62]

Hyde Park was the last real estate venture for Morse, who retired in 1898 and moved back to Massachusetts. Nelson,

though, remained active. Besides promoting the new system of boulevards, he continued to acquire and develop property south of Brush Creek. In the process, he befriended a younger developer named J. C. Nichols, who would soon entice the Kansas City elite several more miles to the south and west. With handoffs from Morse to Nelson and then from Nelson to Nichols, a geographic die was cast.[63]

Unlike Morse or Nelson, Nichols had few initial connections to Kansas City society. His first homes in 1903 were small, and he selected acreage south of Brush Creek primarily because of cost. This area was outside the city limits and so lacked water and sewer service. In fact, it had only two major assets. Just to the northeast lay Nelson's Rockhill properties, where Nichols observed how the older man's emphasis on quality construction and landscaping amenities such as rock walls paid off in sales. The site also happened to sit two blocks east of the Kansas City Country Club, a golf course created in 1896 that was increasingly popular with the city's elite. Nichols decided to trade on both images and thereby ratchet up his target audience. He blatantly employed the Rockhill name in three of his next developments, and by 1908, he was advertising properties south of Brush Creek as his "Country Club District."[64]

Nichols was bright, innovative, and hardworking. This combination soon attracted solid financial backing for his company from William T. Kemper, head of the large Commerce Trust Company, and Hugh Ward, whose family owned the land leased to the country club and most of the adjacent Missouri acreage north of Fifty-ninth Street, west of Wornall Road, and south of Brush Creek. The company's ascent was breathtakingly fast but solidly based. By 1908, Nichols controlled 1,000 acres and had lobbied successfully for annexation to get city water, sewers, and streets (map 36). He made houses available in many price ranges but always remembered his original idea of claiming value by association. To this end, he took care to develop two areas for the rich. The first, Sunset Hill in 1909, occupied the Ward property (map 37). The second, three years later, adjoined Sunset Hill across the state line in Kansas. He called these 229 acres Mission Hills.[65]

The two elite properties achieved immediate success. This feat is remarkable considering that both were remote from downtown's shops and jobs and came on the market while Hyde Park and Southmoreland were at their pinnacles. In addition, attempts to sell Mission Hills residences to Missouri buyers violated cultural codes dating to the Civil War and

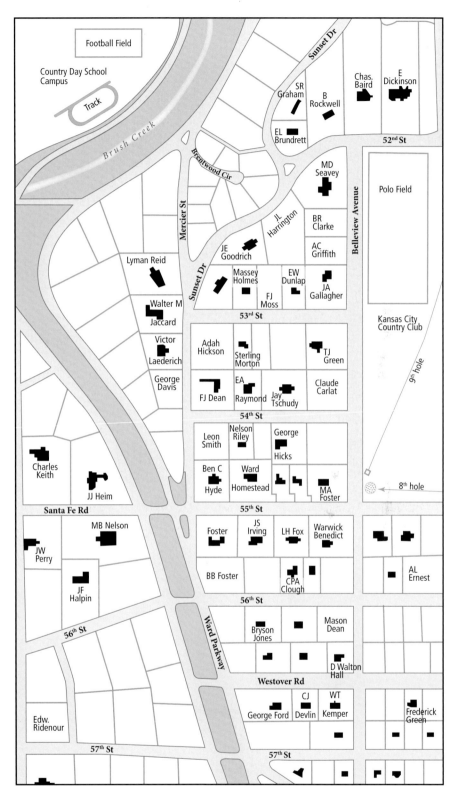

Map 37. Part of the Sunset Hill Neighborhood, circa 1917. Modified from the map "The Country Club District," published by the J. C. Nichols Company in 1917, a copy of which is in the Western Historical Manuscript Collection at the University of Missouri–Kansas City.

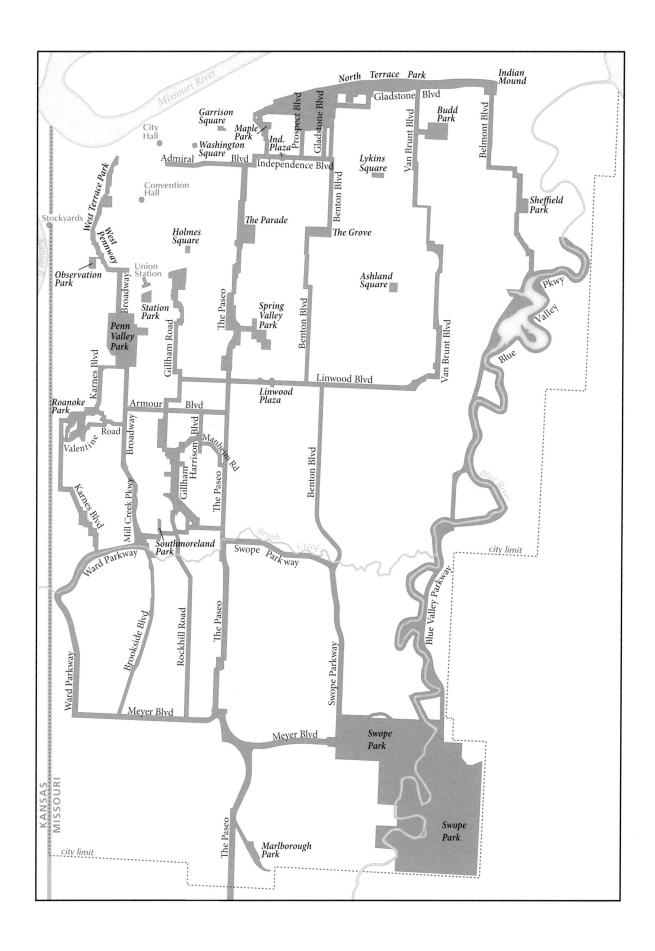

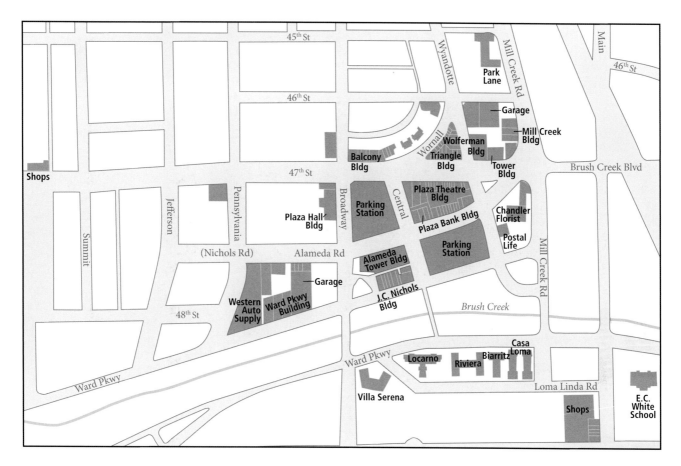

before. Nichols overcame these problems partly with innovative ideas and partly with good timing. The timing related to the advent of the automobile age. With this new invention, the alleys and horse stables of Hyde Park suddenly became anachronistic. Trolleys similarly went from being a universal urban necessity to déclassé transportation used only by those who could not afford motorized vehicles. Nichols saw the trend coming and shrewdly banned the old-fashioned alleys from his tracts, lobbied the city to extend a boulevard south from Penn Valley Park to Sunset Hill, and used company money to construct two additional parkways that would accentuate the Country Club District itself. One of these, Brookside Boulevard, marks the property's eastern limit; Ward Parkway bisects its heart (map 38).[66]

Nichols created a very appealing product. Liking the naturalistic features he saw on Nelson's developments, he hired George Kessler to consult on Sunset Hill. Together, they

Map 38 (facing page). The Park System in Kansas City, Missouri, 1915. Modified from a map in Board of Park Commissioners, Kansas City, Missouri, Report of the Board of Park Commissioners for the Fiscal Year Ending April 19, 1915 (Kansas City, Mo.: Board of Park Commissioners, 1915).

Map 39. Country Club Plaza, 1930. Modified from a map produced by the J. C. Nichols Company in 1930, a copy of which is in the Western Historical Manuscript Collection at the University of Missouri–Kansas City.

laid out curvilinear streets that respected the land's contours, planted thousands of trees, and encouraged the use of stone. They also elongated blocks east and west to allow sunnier rooms. On a larger scale, Nichols protected the integrity of his enclaves with a series of screens. The first of these, the Kansas City Country Club, was present by happenstance, but he was deliberate in Kansas where sales initially were more difficult. In 1913, he created the Mission Hills Country Club as a buffer on the north, the side nearest other housing. Five and thirteen years later, respectively, came similar golf courses on the western and southern flanks. The emphasis Nichols placed on such barriers also was demonstrated in 1922 when Hugh Ward's widow announced a termination of the Kansas City Country Club lease in favor of a housing development. Nichols promptly recruited another widow to purchase most of the land in memory of her husband. In this way, he retained his screen and Kansas City acquired the showplace Jacob L. Loose Memorial Park.[67]

83

Figure 23. Country Club Plaza, 1930, Looking West from Main Street. The 1923 opening of the Tower Building (inspired by a cathedral in Seville, Spain) and the larger Mill Creek Building to its right inaugurated the Country Club Plaza and brought national fame to developer J. C. Nichols. The area's slightly exotic, upscale design appealed to visitors and residents alike. Note the gasoline stations and a large, somewhat obscured garage, indications that Nichols foresaw the automobile age. The open space in the foreground has been filled since 1960 by a large memorial fountain. (Courtesy Missouri Valley Special Collections, Kansas City Public Library)

The fact that Sunset Hill and Mission Hills retain elite status today, a century after their establishment, is largely testimony to another Nichols innovation—self-perpetuating restrictions in the property deeds. He had observed that an absence of zoning laws contributed greatly to the rapid decline of earlier exclusive neighborhoods and so had lobbied locally and nationally for better urban planning. Deed covenants such as minimum house prices and special taxes for street maintenance were similar tools for stability. These restrictions had existed before Nichols, but they typically expired several years after construction. Nichols made them self-renewing unless a majority of homeowners disagreed. As a result, property values in his developments tended to remain high.[68]

Despite his innovations and initial sales success, Nichols worried that remoteness might limit the appeal of the Country Club District. Downtown, after all, was twenty-five minutes away by trolley or (by his calculation) thirty-two by automobile. To counter this concern, he placed shops near the houses. First was a combination grocery and drugstore at

Fifty-first and Brookside, where the trolley line ended. This business opened in 1907. When it prospered, he constructed three more elaborate centers, each with company ownership and leased shops. One, a neighborhood center unified by English Tudor design, arose at Sixty-third and Brookside in 1919. This, too, was well received.[69]

Nichols had even grander plans for his prized elite residents and so acquired 40 acres just north of Sunset Hill in the valley of Brush Creek. This site, at the nexus of Mill Creek Parkway, Brookside Boulevard, and Ward Parkway, was ideally positioned for growing automobile traffic. Allocating an amazing 46 percent of the space to wide streets and parking lots, Nichols created a festive, slightly exotic atmosphere with Spanish Colonial architecture (map 39). This Country

Club Plaza opened in 1923 with shops as upscale as their intended clientele. Soon acknowledged as the world's first regional shopping center, the Plaza firmly cemented Sunset Hill and Mission Hills as Kansas City's most desirable addresses. Research reveals that these neighborhoods housed 10 percent of the city's elite in 1915 and 59 percent in 1930. Hyde Park and Southmoreland, in contrast, together fell from 64 to 31 percent over the same period.[70]

Slums and Racial Enclaves

Neighborhood character, whether for slums or mansion districts, is often determined by long-forgotten events that initiate a complex series of decisions. The chance presence of the Kansas City Country Club pushed J. C. Nichols to

85

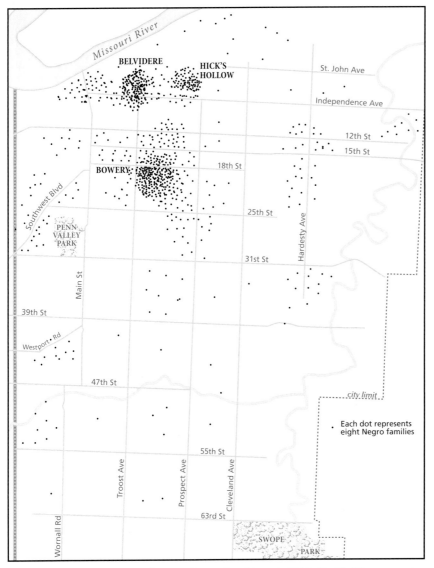

Map 40. *African American Population in Kansas City, Missouri, 1910. Modified from a map in Asa E. Martin,* Our Negro Population: A Sociological Study of the Negroes of Kansas City, Missouri *(Kansas City, Mo.: Franklin Hudson, 1913), p. 2.*

African American homes in 1900 were as widely distributed throughout the city as they had been two decades before. With exclusionary laws still in the future, location remained primarily a matter of affordability. Even so, several changes had occurred. Park construction had destroyed the slums along OK Creek and the escarpment below Quality Hill, and enlarged stockyard and railroad terminal facilities did the same to most of the residential blocks in the West Bottoms. The people residing in these areas had to find new homes. Some moved to the three remaining traditional black neighborhoods, but options there were limited. Belvidere and Hick's Hollow, north of Independence Avenue, were small and constricted. Church Hill, only six blocks east of Grand Avenue on Tenth Street, was losing its housing stock to commercial expansion.[71]

Because of job opportunities in the West Bottoms, many African Americans sought new homes in Kansas City's West Side, the upland neighborhood south of Quality Hill and west of Penn Valley Park. Some 880 black families lived there by 1910, with another 72 families nearby in the old Westport area (map 40). Competition was intense for these properties with Irish and other immigrant laborers, however, so most home seekers were forced to look elsewhere.[72]

Anybody who has experienced the current and longstanding poverty in the neighborhood between Troost and Woodland avenues and Twelfth and Twenty-third streets finds it hard to comprehend that area as it was between 1890 and about 1915. Its houses were new then, built mostly on speculation during the late 1880s for the middle-class market on either side of the upscale Paseo corridor, George Kessler's premier boulevard. The financial collapse of 1890 threw the contractors and underwriters of these homes into panic, for they held paper on some 7,000 properties with no buyers in sight. Their perhaps inevitable solution—dropping prices and

consider the construction of upscale houses nearby, for example, and his expansion across the state border to Mission Hills was because of the availability there of a defunct Hereford farm owned by descendents of packing magnate Kirkland Armour. Without Mission Hills, of course, the subsequent development of Johnson County likely would have been quite different. Regarding the other end of the economic spectrum, the pivotal event for the 1890–1930 period was the overdevelopment of Kansas City's east side with inexpensive and moderately priced houses during the boom of the 1880s. In so doing, Willard Winner and his colleagues unwittingly created an affordable setting for African American residents in an increasingly segregated community.

expanding the client base—was a boon to black Kansas City. This neighborhood was fully integrated by 1900, including 1,331 African American residents, about 29 percent of the total. It was middle class as intended, but it also included an emergent "Negro Quality Hill" near the intersection of The Paseo and Twenty-fourth Street.[73]

Why African Americans opted to buy in the area immediately east of Troost instead of in another section of the large East Side is unclear. Decisions of white realtors may have been a factor, but the site also enjoyed good public transportation with trolleys along Troost and Eighteenth streets and was relatively close to jobs at Union Station, downtown, and the West Bottoms. Once started, the movement grew rapidly. The area was 75 percent African American by 1920, but with barriers to ownership going up elsewhere, it was making a transition from residential area of choice to ghetto.[74]

Lincoln High School, the cornerstone of black education in the city, was particularly appealing to residents on the East Side. The school had been relocated in 1890 from Church Hill to the corner of Nineteenth and Tracy (map 41). Over the next three decades, many other businesses and institutions followed suit. Most clustered along The Paseo near its intersection with the trolley line on Eighteenth Street, creating a new center for the local black community. Attucks Grade School was one such landmark, moving to the corner of Nineteenth and Woodland in 1907.[75]

Many churches joined the schools at the new center, including the large Vine Street Baptist and Ebenezer AME groups, and the population soon became substantial enough to support a full range of entrepreneurs. Core operations along Eighteenth Street included the Street Hotel, the Lincoln Building (offices for doctors and attorneys), Matlaw's clothing store for men, and the *Kansas City Call* newspaper. Equally important were the Paseo YMCA and YWCA buildings, which provided much-needed community meeting rooms. For more complex reasons (including selective enforcement of the law), this area also came to house most of

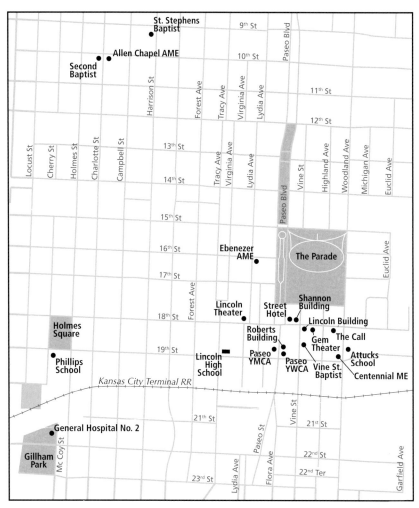

Map 41. *African American Landmarks on Kansas City's East Side, 1925. Modified from a map in Charles E. Coulter, "Take Up the Black Man's Burden": Kansas City's African American Communities, 1865–1939 (Columbia: University of Missouri Press, 2006), p. 54.*

the city's vice trade, with gambling, prostitution, and illegal drug operations barely concealed under cover of jazz clubs and other music venues.[76]

Kansas City people today are justly proud of their vibrant and innovative jazz heritage, an enterprise that flourished in the 1920s and 1930s. They conveniently forget its context. The story begins with political boss Tom Pendergast, who gained control of the city council and police force in 1925 and quickly saw how lucrative a carefully encouraged and regulated vice industry could be. Genteel society might object, but this risk could be minimized by a control on location. Protests arose from the black community, of course, but this voice was small and muted by gratitude for the new jobs created. Many residents worked as musicians and custodians, others as dealers and pimps.[77]

Pendergast's concentration of the vice trade in the black

Figure 24. Dick's Down Home Cook Shop, 1521 East Eighteenth Street, 1929. The 1500 block of Eighteenth Street, with The Paseo to the west and Vine Street to the east, formed the heart of the African American business district. The north side of the street featured the sophisticated Street Hotel with its 300-seat Rose Room for dining and secluded Blue Room for jazz. Dick's restaurant—a single-story building only 15 feet wide—was typical of the smaller-scale south side. A pawnshop is visible to the right, and a somewhat larger saloon abutted on the left. Note that the owner priced meals by size of portion. (Courtesy Missouri Valley Special Collections, Kansas City Public Library)

East Side created a physical association of African American people with unsavory behavior. This relationship was not causal, of course, but it could become seen as such by the surrounding white community in the absence of day-to-day contact. Black people, the reasoning evolved, somehow had to be responsible for the vice. And once started, such thinking easily escalated. One piece of evidence came in 1926—the decision to place the city's garbage-reduction plant adjacent to the black commercial district. Such a location implied that, for white public officials, poor sanitation had now joined vice as a trait easily associated with black residents.[78]

By the end of the 1920s, the illusory web of negativity held by white Kansas City toward the black East Side was augmented by a decline in infrastructure. The city's African American population had grown 119 percent since 1900, to a total of 38,574, and most of these residents were crowded into The Paseo corridor north of Twenty-seventh Street. What once had been spacious houses became crowded apartments, and one survey revealed an average of four and a half families per residence. Sewer and water lines rapidly became inadequate and poverty the rule.[79]

How did a neighborhood decline so quickly from promising in 1900 to completely overburdened two or three decades later? Why did some of its wealthier residents not simply move south or east to alleviate the crowding? Increases in black population and the loss of housing stock in the West Bottoms and elsewhere explain only a small part of the dilemma. So does out-and-out racial hatred. The salient issue, operating nationally at this time as well as locally, was the growth of restrictive covenants on many properties in combination with the subtle but powerful ideology mentioned earlier that suggested an African American presence somehow led to neighborhood deterioration and declining property values.[80]

Racially restrictive covenants first became common across the country in the 1910s. J. C. Nichols was a pioneer in this regard. White home buyers quickly accepted the logic that standards for building materials, lawn maintenance, and such would help to retain property values. They probably thought little about another item on the list, an item that banned African Americans and (often) other dark-skinned peoples. Restrictive covenants in new subdivisions did not cause the overcrowding on the East Side directly. Instead, they initiated a chain reaction. Thus, by 1933, race had been written into federal guidelines for creditworthiness on home loans. Somewhat earlier, the idea of retroactively adding covenants to existing neighborhoods became popular. The effect was as if walls had been erected around The Paseo corridor and similar ethnic communities throughout the country.[81]

The boundaries of the black East Side were fluid initially. Troost and Woodland, Twelfth and Twenty-third streets served as approximate delimiters in 1910 (maps 36 and 40), but population growth over the next fifteen years forced expansion in three directions. The north held firm as people moved east and west some seven or eight blocks along and south of the trolley line at Eighteenth Street. Prospect Avenue, Oak Street, and Twenty-seventh Street marked the new limits. No major conflicts occurred on the western frontier, since this advance abutted the business strip connecting downtown with Union Station. The southern and eastern edges were another matter.

The community spread fastest to the east, although in irregular fashion, as realtors (black and white alike) paid cash bonuses to white families willing to sell. Some violence took place, but most people saw the extension as inevitable (map 42). Resistance was much stronger in the south. There, white homeowners between Flora and Brooklyn and between Twenty-eighth and Thirty-first organized themselves in 1926 as the Linwood Improvement Association. Their power came partly because they organized ahead of blockbusting attempts in the neighborhood but even more because of a physical barrier.[82]

Troost Park happened to border the Linwood area on the

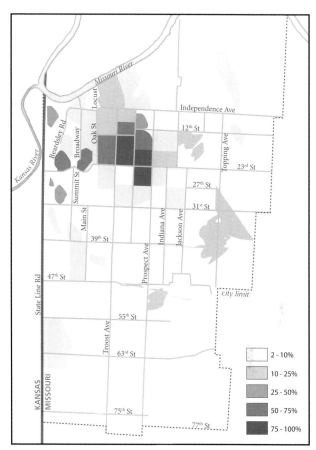

Map 42. African American Population in Kansas City, Missouri, 1940. Modified from a map in Charles E. Coulter, "Take Up the Black Man's Burden": Kansas City's African American Communities, 1865–1939 (Columbia: University of Missouri Press, 2006), p. 291.

west, whereas Spring Valley Park extended the greensward seven blocks east along Twenty-seventh Street to Brooklyn Avenue (map 38). Neither park had been created with segregation in mind, but they both played a part in maintaining the local color line for two decades. In 1927, the city bowed to white pressure and condemned land to join the two parks along Twenty-eighth Street. In 1941, officials acknowledged the other half of the racial divide by rechristening the northern part of Spring Valley as Nelson C. Crews Square. Crews was a longtime business and political leader of the local black community and publisher of the Kansas City Sun.[83]

Sometimes lost in discussions of the black East Side is its effect on Kansas City's boulevard system. Although houses along The Paseo north of Twenty-seventh Street retained their magnificence for a few years after 1920, they gradually declined along with the general neighborhood. This decline was followed by reduced maintenance of the street's fountains and gardens and then a functional repositioning of status. East

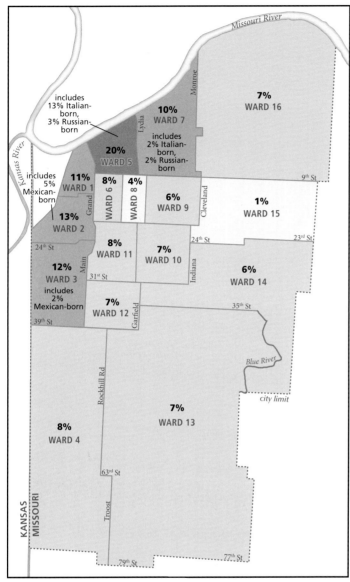

includes
13% Italian-
born,
3% Russian-
born

10%
WARD 7

7%
WARD 16

20%
WARD 5

includes
2% Italian-
born,
2% Russian-
born

includes
5%
Mexican-
born

11%
WARD 1

8%
WARD 6

4%
WARD 8

6%
WARD 9

1%
WARD 15

13%
WARD 2

8%
WARD 11

7%
WARD 10

6%
WARD 14

12%
WARD 3

includes
2%
Mexican-
born

7%
WARD 12

7%
WARD 13

8%
WARD 4

KANSAS
MISSOURI

Map 43. Foreign-Born Population in Kansas City, Missouri, 1920. Data from U.S. Census.

of the ghetto, the still-white Benton and Van Brunt boulevards saw property values rise, but most money went south. Nelson's Rockhill Road and Nichols's Brookside Boulevard were major beneficiaries, Ward Parkway even more. Ward essentially became the new Paseo (map 38).

Because of large numbers and segregationist tensions, African Americans dominated the city's ethnic discussions throughout the first decades of the twentieth century. Foreign-born people constituted only 6 percent of all residents by 1930, and Irish and German immigration had slowed greatly. These two groups also had largely assimilated themselves, living widely dispersed across the community. At the

same time, however, demand in the packinghouses, rail yards, and elsewhere attracted a new generation of manual laborers. Four nationalities predominated in this second wave, two on the Missouri side of the state line and two in Kansas. The 1920 census reported 3,848 Russians, 3,318 Italians, and 1,797 Mexicans in Kansas City, Missouri. Meanwhile, Kansas City, Kansas, was home to 2,039 Mexicans, 1,419 Croatians and other southern Slavs, and 1,076 Russians. None of their numbers were huge, but these groups gave distinctiveness to several neighborhoods.[84]

The Russian immigration is easiest to understand. It followed several brutal policy shifts in the homeland, especially after the assassination of Czar Alexander II in 1881. Jews, Catholics, Mennonites, and other non-Orthodox peoples felt increasingly unwelcome in their native country. Santa Fe railroad officials recruited settlers for central Kansas from these groups, but some of the migrants decided to try life instead at the entrepôt of Kansas City, Kansas. The Missouri contingent was largely Jewish. This group of about 1,800 was conservative in faith but unsophisticated and extremely poor. They nearly overwhelmed the existing Jewish community of 175 middle-class families. Trying to help but worried how the coarse newcomers might affect the faith's overall local image, the hosts searched for housing options.[85]

Two settlement areas emerged—the same Belvidere area near Independence Avenue and Lydia where African Americans occupied about a third of the houses and a full-block tenement between Grand Avenue and McGee, Nineteenth and Twentieth streets. The former area was unspectacular but enduring, largely because of the construction of the Tefares Israel Temple at the corner of Admiral Boulevard and Tracy. Three percent of the people in the city's Fifth Ward were Russian born in 1920 (map 43). The latter area, called McClure Flats, was notorious but shorter lived. Probably because of its location near the offices of the *Kansas City Star,* the newspaper identified it in 1893 as one of the city's worst slums. The block was a warren, containing ninety attached houses in three rows, with each unit having three tiny rooms. Some 500 people huddled within, "almost entirely Russian Jews" who made a precarious living as "rag pickers and junkmen's assistants."[86]

The Italians clustered together even more closely than the Russians. A few dozen families from the Genoa area moved

to Kansas City in the 1880s and found housing in the eastern part of the original townsite, an area of inexpensive houses popular with many immigrant groups. These northern Italians became reluctant hosts to several thousand Sicilians starting about 1890, part of a huge group of people who were fleeing extreme poverty in Italy's southern provinces. Track-repair jobs on the railroads were the original attraction, but the new migrants sought housing near their compatriots. By 1893, the phrase *Little Italy* was common in the city, referring originally to two tenements near the corner of Second Street and Locust. There, around 300 people crowded together, with up to a dozen said to share a single room.[87]

Employment shifted rapidly from railroads to fresh produce, led by women who saw opportunities in the nearby city market. By the 1910s, most men had turned to this work as well, becoming vendors and owners of bakeries and groceries. They made the North End their own, with a focus on Holy

Figure 25. City Market, 1906, Looking Northwest. The public square between Main and Walnut streets, Fourth and Fifth, was a gift from the William Gillis family in 1846. A farmers' market has operated here continuously since 1857. The facility photographed was built in 1898 and sits in the shadow of the community's second city hall (1892–1937). Italian immigrants, whose homes were nearby, became closely identified with market operations starting about 1900. (Courtesy Library of Congress, Prints and Photographs Division)

Rosary Church at the corner of Missouri Avenue and Campbell Street. This church was constructed in 1895, followed soon by a school next door. Italian natives constituted 13 percent of the people in Ward Five by 1920, or 25 percent if one adds second-generation immigrants (map 43). City officials formally recognized their presence in 1926 by rechristening the local Washington Square park as Columbus Square and eventually equipping it with lawn bowling (boccie) greens.[88]

Mexicans, comprising the third-largest immigrant group on the Missouri side in 1920, were the most recent arrivals.

Figure 26. The 300 Block of Askew Avenue, circa 1905, Looking Northeast. This Chautauqua Place section of the city's Northeast neighborhood was less than a decade old at the time of the photograph. Its streets are paved and guttered and the houses trim. The smaller, gable-front dwellings contain five rooms; the larger, pyramid-roofed ones have eight. Askew was (and is) home to clerks, factory workers, and lots of children. Scarritt School is less than a block away. (Courtesy Johnson County Museum)

The census lists only 27 Mexican residents in the entire metropolitan area for 1900 and 335 in 1910. Some 3,000 more immigrated in the next decade, most of them recruited by Santa Fe railroad officials, but some were political refugees from the Mexican Revolution of 1910. Kansas City jobs were of two types, and each produced a residential cluster. In Missouri, the construction of Union Station between 1910 and 1914 demanded many laborers. Mexicans there found housing available on the West Side, between State Line Road and Summit, Fourteenth Street and Southwest Boulevard. This area of hilly terrain and small homes was in the process of transition as upwardly mobile Irish families moved elsewhere. Mexicans had become numerous enough by 1914 to create a new parish, Our Lady of Guadalupe. Its church building, purchased five years later from a Swedish Lutheran group, became the community's focal point at the corner of Twenty-third and Madison. It remains so today. An annual fiesta fund-raiser has cemented identity since 1926.[89]

One other significant ethnic grouping existed in Kansas City, Missouri, at that time, although its isolation and heterogeneity made it relatively unknown. This area was on the far east side, atop bluffs that overlook the Blue River valley and down the hillside toward the factories of Sheffield, Centropolis, Manchester, and Leeds. The Sheffield Car Company and the Kansas City Switch and Frog Company brought German and Irish workers with them to this neighborhood from their previous locations in Pennsylvania. The American Radiator Company did the same with Polish iron molders from Buffalo, New York. Over 900 Poles lived in Kansas City, Missouri, in 1920, enough to merit their own church, St. Stanislaus, in Manchester.[90]

The Blue River ethnic mosaic expanded in 1904. The Standard Oil Company built a large refinery 3 miles northeast of Sheffield and created a company town around it called Sugar Creek. Croatian and Ruthenian workers brought in from company headquarters in Indiana gave added identity to the area. Each group built a church there on Chicago Street—St. Cyril by the Croatians and St. Luke (Byzantine Rite) by the Ruthenians.[91]

Kansas City, Kansas

In the 1930s, as in earlier decades, the Missouri portion of Kansas City appeared to observers to be a complete community. It had a thriving downtown, several industrial districts, and a full range of residential neighborhoods. Between the extremes of Sunset Hill and poor ethnic areas such as the Italian North End and the African American Paseo corridor, a vast swatch of middle-class housing extended for 7 miles between the North Terrace bluffs and Swope Park and then west to encircle the grander homes near the Country Club Plaza. Missouri-side residents, whether rich or poor, had little reason to go to Wyandotte County or even to have it enter their minds.

The perspective and reality were quite different in Kansas. Though people in that Kansas City had reasons for pride—including a ranking as the number two meatpacking and stockyards center in the country, number three in soap manufacture, and number five in grain storage—they also knew that theirs was only a partial city. Minnesota Avenue might offer all the basic retail services, but any quest for specialty or luxury items meant a trip across the state line. Similarly, a lack of stately homes was increasingly obvious. Managers and owners of the factories in Armourdale and Fairfax had decided to live in J. C. Nichols developments outside the county.[92]

Political leaders who wanted to tout Kansas City, Kansas, found they had much to overcome. Name confusion with the larger city was always a problem. More often, the key fact was that most visitors entered town via the West Bottoms. Any trip across the Intercity Viaduct there revealed the packing district in "all its ugliness." A stench was omnipresent, one that was said to be "the quintessential extract of all the malodors that ever assailed the nostrils of frail humanity." This smell, the city's "deep dark secret," was never to be mentioned "in the business tour of the Chamber of Commerce or the good fellowship propaganda of the Rotarians and Kiwanians." With image problems galore and potential leaders opting to live in Missouri, it was not surprising that graft and cronyism took root in county politics. By 1925 or so, middle-class residents had learned to distrust any government initiative and to accept the view that they were indeed the unloved (but dependent) stepchildren of their neighbor to the east.[93]

Although the inferiority complex perceived by Wyandotte County's bourgeois community was real and enduring, it is essential to realize that most local residents felt otherwise. For the 80 percent or so who depended directly on the packinghouses, soap factories, railroads, and Fairfax plants for their livelihood, the city was opportunity personified. If rich folks wanted to move elsewhere, this meant more housing was available at affordable prices. If politics were somewhat

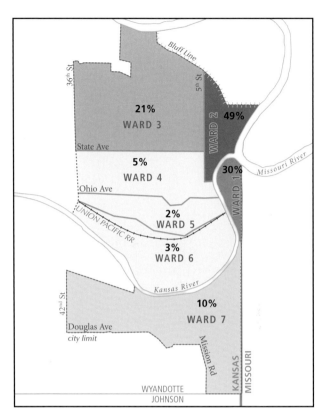

Map 44. African American Population in Kansas City, Kansas, 1920. Data from U.S. Census.

corrupt, that was how politicians usually acted and was no reason for particular alarm. For all these blue-collar people, Kansas City, Kansas, was a comfortable place to be.[94]

The unity of Wyandotte County provided by factory jobs and a firm work ethic was countered by sharp ethnic divisions. The city had grown rapidly between 1900 and 1930, roughly doubling its size to 121,857 residents. African Americans constituted some 15 percent of this total, first- and second-generation South European immigrants about 10 percent, and first-generation Mexicans another 5. People from each of these groups regularly worked together in the various rail yards and factories, but they lived in distinct sections of the city. African Americans predominated in the northeast, South Europeans just south of the business district, and Mexicans in parts of Argentine and Armourdale. Less ethnically identified residents, many of German and Irish descent, occupied the interstitial spaces and predominated in the city's western half.[95]

African American numbers in Kansas City, Kansas, tripled between 1890 and 1930, an increase of over 14,000 people. Job availability accounted for part of this growth, but social issues were important as well. Kansas was seen as a racially

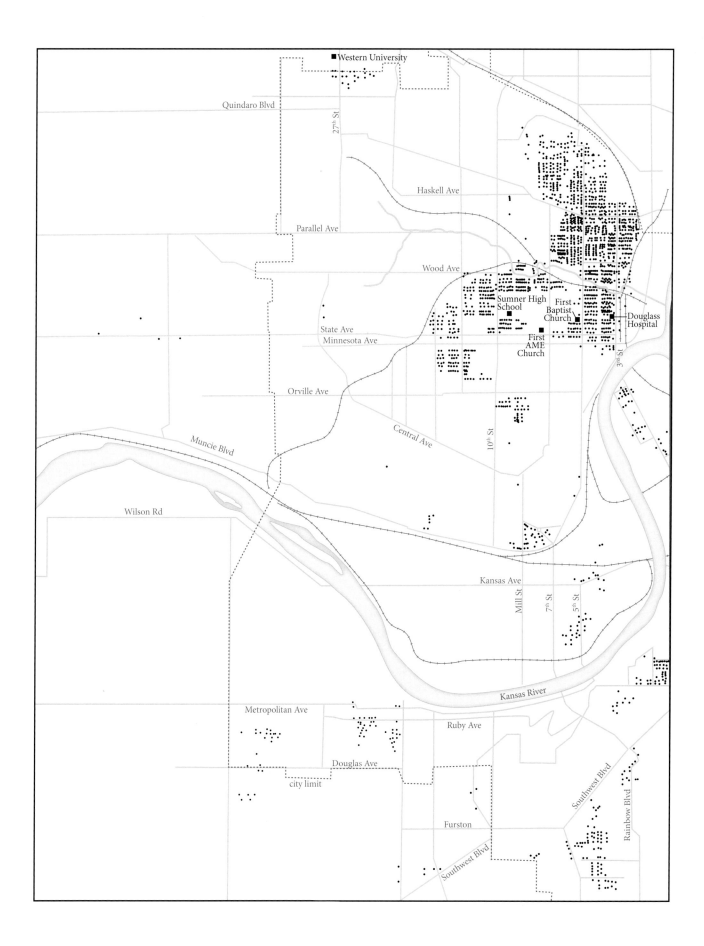

■ Western University

Quindaro Blvd

27th St

Haskell Ave

Parallel Ave

Wood Ave

Sumner High
School

First
Baptist
Church

Douglass
Hospital

State Ave

Minnesota Ave

First
AME
Church

3rd St

Orville Ave

Central Ave

10th St

Muncie Blvd

Wilson Rd

Kansas Ave

Mill St

7th St

5th St

Kansas River

Metropolitan Ave

Ruby Ave

Douglas Ave

city limit

Southwest Blvd

Rainbow Blvd

Furston

Southwest Blvd

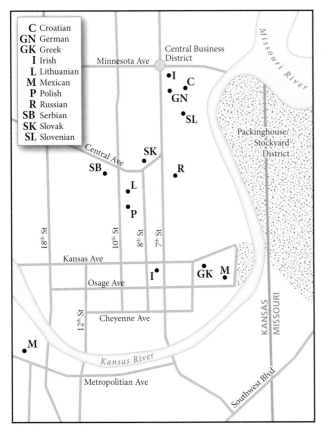

Map 46. *Immigrant Catholic and Orthodox Churches in Eastern Kansas City, Kansas, circa 1937. Modified from a map in Susan D. Greenbaum, "The Historical, Institutional, and Ecological Parameters of Social Cohesiveness in Four Urban Neighborhoods" (Ph.D. diss., Department of Anthropology, University of Kansas, 1981), p. 144.*

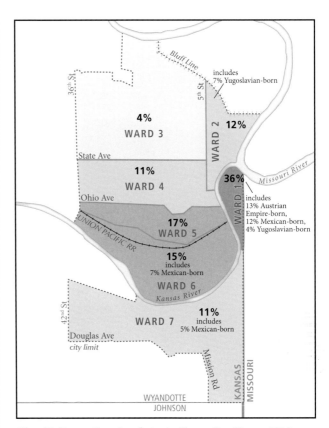

Map 47. *Foreign-Born Population in Kansas City, Kansas, 1920. Data from U.S. Census.*

progressive state, and this image had attracted a core group of black civic leaders to the city in the 1880s. These people established businesses and then banded together to create two nationally famous institutions. The first, in 1895, was Western University. This effort involved convincing leaders of the AME Church to revive an older, nearly moribund school located 4 miles northwest of downtown. Then, three years later, came Douglass Hospital at 312 Washington Boulevard, the first black institution of its type west of the Mississippi.[96]

Western University was too remote at the time to serve as a focus of settlement, but Douglass Hospital was near Juniper Bottoms, the larger of the two Exoduster centers from the early 1880s (map 26). The most prestigious of the

Map 45 (facing page). African American Population in Kansas City, Kansas, 1936. Modified from the map "Distribution of Negro Population," published by the Wyandotte County government in 1937, a copy of which is in the Kansas Collection of the University of Kansas Library.

black churches (First AME and First Baptist), Sumner High School, and middle-class black residences clustered just west of the hospital along Washington Boulevard and Nebraska Avenue to Fourteenth Street. Most African Americans lived northeast of this relatively elite core, however. They filled in the half mile that originally separated Juniper Bottoms from the second Exoduster center to the north, and by 1920, they constituted 49 percent of the residents there (map 44). This trend continued over the next decade. The group's share of the Ward Two population rose to 73 percent, and people moved west to Eighth Street (map 45).[97]

The South European presence in Kansas City, Kansas, grew out of a major strike at the packinghouses in 1893. Owners crushed this movement and then recruited new workers from abroad. They concentrated on peoples chafing under the rule of the Austro-Hungarian monarchy, first Croats and Poles and then Slovenes, Slovaks, Serbs, and Russians. Some 4,000 émigrés had arrived by 1920. Most of these people lived initially in the West Bottoms near the Armour plant, where housing costs were cheapest. But the big flood of 1903 forced abandonment there and prompted movement to the adjacent upland across the Kansas River. This area, Strawberry Hill,

Figure 27. The Santa Fe Yard at Argentine, 1943. Argentine has hosted a major railroad switching and repair facility since 1906. Its scope has expanded greatly over the years, becoming more efficient but continuing to employ about 1,300 local people. This view shows two steam locomotives known as Mikados, conservative but reliable engines used to pull freight. Beyond them is the yard's towering coal and sand chute. Jack Delano's photograph is from the files of the Farm Security Administration's Office of War Information. (Courtesy Library of Congress, Prints and Photographs Division)

consisted of small houses built in the 1880s for earlier immigrants. It was also the site of St. Mary's, St. Anthony's, and St. John the Baptist Catholic churches.[98]

New parishes followed quickly for the various groups, joining St. John the Baptist at Fourth and Barnett that had served Croats since 1898. Sts. Cyril and Methodius for Slovaks, Holy Family for Slovenes, St. George for Serbs, and Holy Trinity for Russians all opened before 1920 (map 46). Their locations, in turn, influenced the housing decisions

of later migrants. By 1920, Slavs were the most prominent group south of Minnesota Avenue and east of Seventh Street, an area split by ward boundaries (map 47). They also had expanded west to Twelfth Street in the neighborhood south of Central Avenue and had opened several businesses along Fifth Street.

While the packing companies recruited in Europe, Santa Fe and other railroad officials sought labor in Mexico. This movement began about 1910, and census people counted 2,039 migrants in 1920. Racial discrimination was common at first, including restrictions on housing and jobs. The Santa Fe town of Argentine proved most hospitable, but as jobs opened in the packinghouses during the 1920s, Mexican people also moved to the eastern portion of Armourdale. The group's first church—Our Lady of Mt. Carmel—was built in Armourdale in 1925. St. John the Divine, in Argentine, opened in 1937.[99]

5 The City in the Gray Flannel Suit, 1940–1967

May 29, 1939, marked the end of an era in Kansas City. As Thomas J. Pendergast, one of America's most powerful political bosses, entered federal prison for income tax evasion, his entire governmental machine collapsed. Citizens were visibly shaken and unsure how to react, for Pendergast had generated both fame and infamy for the community. Nobody lamented the passing of extortion payments routinely needed to acquire city contracts, but feelings were mixed about the selective police action that had allowed gambling businesses to proliferate and, with them, jazz clubs and other hallmarks of a "wide-open" town. Had this atmosphere helped local prosperity or hindered it? Pendergast also had been the prime mover in the massive Ten-Year Plan that had generated the much-praised Municipal Auditorium, new roads, and other public works. This effort, too, had been graft infested, but its jobs were valuable to local people trying to survive the bleak years of the Depression.[1]

With their past corruption fully exposed, citizens opted for political cleansing and found able leaders in Mayor John B. Gage and City Manager L. Perry Cookingham. Together, these men cut the bloated city payroll in half, instituted careful auditing procedures, and reduced cronyism. Then, they began to think about the future, especially challenges posed by rapid increases in airplane and automobile travel. Cookingham, a cool and efficient planner, soon secured an auxiliary airport site with room to accommodate the newer, larger planes expected in the future. Similarly, he anticipated federal programs for highway construction and slum clearance and therefore had plans in place as soon as the dollars appeared.

The city received kudos for this progressivism and even more for a program of aggressive annexation. Acreage within the city limits quintupled between 1950 and 1963.[2]

Planning successes were only part of the city's surge during the 1940s and 1950s. New industries acquired during World War II provided a solid manufacturing component to the economy, and the J. C. Nichols Company continued to lead the nation in stylish, suburban development. The capstone came in 1955 when a relocation of the struggling Philadelphia Athletics baseball franchise officially made Kansas City a major-league community. Cookingham was asked to write an article entitled "The Kansas City Story" for a leading planning magazine, and the popular press itemized "Ten Lessons Kansas City Can Teach the Nation."[3]

Despite the obvious accomplishments of the period, Kansas City was not a totally healthy city by the end of the 1950s. Seven years later, in fact, serious troubles were obvious, with a previously vibrant downtown now "dull and gray" and originally praised public housing projects so dirty and crime ridden as to be almost uninhabitable. The new reality caught leaders off guard and took years to fully understand. In retrospect, the largest error appears to have been a planning philosophy that was too steeped in skyscraper construction and traffic efficiency and too little concerned with cultural values and the appreciation of difference. Sloan Wilson's 1955 novel, *The Man in the Gray Flannel Suit,* provides an apt metaphor. It was (and is) all too easy to sacrifice human dignity in an environment dominated by the bottom lines of account books.[4]

War Plants and Their Aftermath

Historians agree that it was wartime production during the 1940s that finally ended the Great Depression. Certainly this was true in Kansas City, although the community's full participation required skilled salesmanship. Once it had become obvious that massive industrial expansion would occur in the United States as part of the war effort, various regional interests began to lobby federal officials. Standard wisdom held that contracts would go mostly to existing manufacturers on the east and west coasts. To counter this attitude, the Kansas governor created a special commission to argue for local inclusion. In Washington, D.C., this delegation joined with two Kansas City representatives, the ubiquitous developer J. C. Nichols and Richard Robbins, former president of Trans World Airlines. Nichols and Robbins were nationally respected men with influential contacts. Their case also appealed to logic—that a dispersal of industry nationwide would make it less vulnerable to enemy attack and that interior, midwestern locations were especially safe. Less honorably, albeit effectively at the time, they added a dose of fearmongering, noting the all-American character of Kansas City people and the unlikelihood that they would absorb any "foreign 'isms' or strange doctrines."[5]

The metropolitan area ended up with about 1 percent of the total war production dollars, an outsized share compared to its population. Contracts went to many existing companies, including Kansas City Structural Steel in Argentine for landing craft, Cook Paint in North Kansas City for camouflage paint, and the Ford automobile assembly plant in the Blue River valley for cylinder assemblies for aircraft. Dwarfing these, however, were four mammoth new operations. First came an ordnance plant called Lake City on 3,200 rural acres 10 miles east of Independence. Costing $18 million, construction of the plant required 6,000 workers, the largest single labor crew in city history. But these impressive numbers soon looked small. A second, even larger ordnance plant called Sunflower rose 20 miles west of the city near De Soto. There, 12,000 employees made explosive powders and rocket propellants. Larger yet were two factories in Kansas City proper. One was built in Fairfax in 1941, an $87 million facility for North American Aviation. Over 26,000 workers there assembled giant B-25 bombers, making 13 per day and over 6,000 for the war. Not far away, on 400 acres in the Blue River valley near the intersection of Bannister and Troost, the government built a similar-sized plant for the Pratt and

Whitney Corporation. There, with 80 acres under roof, another 24,000 people made aircraft engines for the U.S. Navy. Testing created a round-the-clock drone that could be heard for miles.[6]

At their peak, the four big plants together required nearly 70,000 men and women to operate, an almost impossible number to find in a metropolitan area of 634,093 residents that had already contributed thousands of people directly to military service. The jobs acted as a magnet, of course, hastening rural-to-urban migration. They also converted many farmhands and waitresses into highly skilled workers. In these ways, Kansas City was positioned well for the postwar boom economy.[7]

Observers felt that wartime industrialization had renewed the community's spirit. They compared the aggressive pursuit of such companies to a previous generation's quest for railroads, and they contrasted local fervor with a complacent, "mildewed" air in neighboring St. Louis. Kansas City people, according to the influential *Fortune* magazine, now regarded their position "not as the second city of Missouri, but as the natural metropolis of the whole Southwest."[8]

The vision of 1945 featured a complete city in economic terms, one that was adding a sizable manufacturing sector to its traditional roles in agribusiness, transportation, and wholesaling. This hope was borne out almost immediately. The General Motors Corporation agreed to take over the mammoth North American Aviation plant in Fairfax, converting it to an assembly line for Buick, Oldsmobile, and Pontiac automobiles. Pratt and Whitney's space was subdivided, but the effect was the same. Westinghouse, starting in 1948, manufactured aircraft engines there. The Bendix Aviation Corporation joined the complex the next year to fabricate electronic parts for the Atomic Energy Commission.[9]

The conversion of war plants merely initiated the process. Sunshine Biscuits, Inc., built a large, $1.75 million plant in Fairfax just west of the General Motors site, and that entire industrial district was said to be nearly full by 1947. Seeing this situation, a group of New York investors purchased the adjacent lowland. This site, the entirety of North Kansas City, included 1,500 acres of land plus thirty-three industrial buildings, eleven retail buildings, and a housing development. Aggressive marketing led to new commitments there from major manufacturers such as General Electric, Frigidaire, and Goodyear. An even bigger employer, the Ford Motor Company, selected a site several miles to the northeast, between North Kansas City and Liberty. In 1950, Ford

announced plans for a $30 million assembly plant to replace a much smaller factory that had operated at Centropolis near the Blue River since 1912. Together with two General Motors plants (one in Fairfax and an older Chevrolet one in Leeds), Ford helped Kansas City become the country's most important automobile assembly point outside Michigan.[10]

When J. C. Nichols and others were lobbying to secure war contracts for the city, they encountered doubts that the area could provide the technical support needed for such work. The men succeeded in allaying these concerns sufficiently to get the plant contracts, but they worried that the partial truth behind the doubts might curtail future growth. To prevent that from happening, they rallied support for an independent scientific laboratory that could assist and promote regional industrial and agricultural interests. The result, modeled on similar organizations in Ohio and Illinois, was the Midwest Research Institute. Started in 1943, it grew rapidly and came

Figure 28. Pratt and Whitney Complex, 1945, Looking Southeast. This gigantic war plant, built in 1942–1943 by the federal government to manufacture airplane engines, transformed the city's south side. The main building, seen here, stretched for half a mile, enclosed 57 acres, and employed 24,000 workers. People traveled from the north via Troost (in the foreground) and from the east and west via Bannister Road. After the war, when the Bendix and Westinghouse corporations took over the facility, continued employment led to a housing boom. (Courtesy Missouri Valley Special Collections, Kansas City Public Library)

to symbolize Kansas City progress. Ten years later, the institute's officials broke ground for their current building, impressively located across from a fountain on Volker Boulevard and adjacent to both the Nelson-Atkins Museum of Art and the University of Kansas City.[11]

As the city celebrated its centennial in 1950, the local mood was as bright as it had ever been. Manufacturing had indeed expanded to fully complement the older economic

Figure 29. Petticoat Lane, 1956, Looking East from Main Street. For nearly eighty years, the city's retail focus was a two-block section of Eleventh Street. Large department stores anchored the ends: Macy's (née John Taylor) and Peck's on Main and Emery, Bird, Thayer on Grand. In between, shoppers could inspect fine clothing at Harzfeld's (right foreground) and Woolf Brothers, jewelry at Helzberg's, and shoes at Showalter's. The focus, perhaps, was a sophisticated tea room at Emery Bird's. Everything functioned normally in 1960 but disappeared a decade later as downtown become exclusively an office center. (Courtesy Missouri Valley Special Collections, Kansas City Public Library)

sectors, and population was on the rise. Retailing, too, was healthy. The key marketing event was a change at John Taylor's, the city's principal department store, located at the intersection of Main Street and Petticoat Lane (Eleventh Street). When New York's R. H. Macy and Company purchased this business in 1947 and rechristened it with the corporate name after a $7 million modernization, local reaction was positive. Instead of complaining about unfair competition, people felt pride that savvy outsiders had invested in their city, which

validated their own faith in the future. Almost immediately, Macy's "completely coordinated escalator and elevator system" inspired capital expenditures in other stores.[12]

July 13, 1951, brought a challenge to the optimistic attitude. Heavy rains in northern Kansas poured more water into the Kansas River than anybody could remember. Topeka and Lawrence flooded in quick order, and then water surged through the Kansas City bottomlands. People in Armourdale saw levels rise past second-story windows, stockyard animals perished, and all east-west rail traffic was suspended. Twenty thousand residents became homeless.[13]

The Corps of Engineers judged the 1951 flood as the worst in the nation's history. The total bill for Kansas City came to $426 million, with a third of the damage in the West Bottoms and most of the rest in Armourdale, Fairfax, and Argentine. Cudahy, one of the city's major meatpackers, elected not to reopen, and scores of smaller companies did the same. Still, the disaster did little to derail the overall sense of growth

Figure 30. Municipal Stadium, 1955, Looking Southwest. Local pride reached a peak when major-league baseball debuted on April 12 and the hometown Athletics beat the Detroit Tigers. The stadium, at Twenty-second Street and Brooklyn Avenue (Brooklyn runs near the scoreboard), was an old minor-league park hastily refitted with a second deck. Grass and parking conditions were less than ideal, but the games brought needed money to the city's East Side. Play continued through the 1972 season, and the park was demolished in 1976. (Courtesy Missouri Valley Special Collections, Kansas City Public Library)

and accomplishment throughout the city. Civic leaders handled the disaster relief effort with generosity and efficiency, and many observers drew an analogy to the can-do effort two generations before that rebuilt a burned Convention Hall in time for the 1900 Democratic National Convention. Joyce Hall, head of a growing local company called Hallmark, gave form to the mood by commissioning a painting called *The Kansas City Spirit*.[14]

Postwar pride peaked locally in 1955. Although the acquisition of new factories and the successful relief efforts after the flood had brought smiles of satisfaction, neither compared with news that the Philadelphia Athletics baseball franchise would relocate to Mid-America. Baseball was just a game, of course, but residents saw the move as highly symbolic. With the team's presence, Kansas City would join the nation's urban elite and become "major league" in a larger sense of that phrase.

The baseball movement had started in 1953 when declining profits led the Boston Braves to shift operations to Milwaukee. That summer, a rumor circulated that the similarly struggling St. Louis Browns would go to Kansas City. This shift did not occur, but it raised local expectations. In 1954, city officials authorized funds to purchase and enlarge a stadium at Twenty-second Street and Brooklyn, where the New York Yankees housed their Kansas City Blues farm team. Residents pledged to buy thousands of tickets should a

101

major-league team materialize. No sooner had these acts been completed than they yielded success. Local people rejoiced and naturally interpreted the decision from their own perspective. Nobody talked about the debts and poor quality of the Athletics organization. Instead, they stressed how Kansas City's potential had been recognized by astute Philadelphians and by Arnold Johnson, a Chicago businessman who was to become the new owner. No wonder 200,000 residents attended a welcoming parade for the new team in April 1955. And no wonder a *Kansas City Star* reporter called opening day "one of the most momentous events of the city's existence."[15]

Annexation

Following the trend of most cities, the postwar boom brought not only people and industry to Kansas City but also an acceptance of ideas regarding the superiority of suburban living. The wholesale quest for grassy, quarter-acre lots implied a more dispersed population, and nobody worried about transportation issues because of a concurrent increase in automobile ownership. Such developments brought joy to building contractors and car dealers, but they posed serious problems for officials of the core city. If large numbers of people were to move to surrounding suburban communities or to the open countryside, city tax revenues would plummet. In turn, schools, roads, and basic police and fire protection all would deteriorate.

Some city managers did not grasp the full negative implications of suburbanization until it was too late for action. In cities such as San Francisco, with its peninsular setting, or St. Louis, where officials had separated their city politically from St. Louis County in 1876, annexation was nearly impossible. Kansas City, in contrast, had options, and city manager Perry Cookingham was prescient in his thinking.[16]

Cookingham knew that annexation would be unpopular with some people, but he vowed to push ahead and to do so aggressively before opposition could become well organized. His decision was based largely on the tax considerations noted earlier, but it was influenced also by specifics of Kansas City's geography. The city, by law, could not annex land across a state line. Consequently, no possibility existed for capturing the exclusive Mission Hills development in adjacent Kansas or J. C. Nichols's newer Prairie Village community there for middle-class families. Instead of a full circle of land available for possible expansion, Kansas City's political options were reduced by half.[17]

In reality, restrictions on annexation involved more than

the state line. An earlier extension of the city limits, in 1909, had incorporated land just east of the Blue River (map 35). Beyond that valley lay Independence and therefore an end to expansion. South was a possibility, but growth in that direction had been strong for decades. To push much beyond the existing limit at Seventy-seventh Street would isolate downtown Kansas City (in the municipality's extreme northwestern corner) even further. By a process of elimination, north emerged as the most logical choice for growth. Expansion there obviously would improve the centrality of downtown businesses within the city, but few people gave the idea serious consideration. It would entail a jump across the Missouri River. It would require inclusion of a new county (Clay) into the urban mix. It also would necessitate a leapfrogging of the politically independent North Kansas City.

Cookingham began his annexation strategy with a small test case. In 1944, with development about to push south of the city limit, he asked voters to approve incorporation of acreage between Seventy-seventh and Eighty-ninth streets as far east as Indiana Avenue. Opposition arose immediately in the affected area, especially over tax increases and a Missouri state law that denied ballots to residents of the unincorporated place being annexed. City officials countered by citing the need for comprehensive planning, but they finally agreed to scale back the expansion from Eighty-ninth to Eighty-fifth Street. The measure passed and took effect on January 1, 1947 (map 48).[18]

The big move to the north began in August 1946. News reached Cookingham that the city of North Kansas City was about to annex 14 square miles of land on its northern border, an area extending from Thirty-second Avenue to Englewood Road (Fifty-sixth Street). If successful, this move would end any hopes of Kansas City expanding into Clay County. Cookingham studied state law on the issue and found that, if a given parcel of land was desired by two cities, priority would go to the one that first proposed an ordinance for annexation. He therefore pushed his agenda swiftly but quietly, and the city council in Kansas City passed its ordinance days before North Kansas City officials did theirs. The two proposals differed only in that the Kansas City version included the tract occupied by Municipal Airport. Then, even though the actual election on this issue was held in North Kansas City two months before the one in Kansas City (it passed 801 to 33 and 39,978 to 37,920 in the two cities, respectively), state officials ruled for Cookingham.[19]

Clay County people were livid at what they viewed as a

show of raw power. The mayor of North Kansas City initiated a lawsuit that took three years to resolve. Several writers called Cookingham a dictator comparable to Adolph Hitler, and the Clay County Self-Defense League offered to finance a referendum. Bitterness was widespread. Kansas City's mayor, William E. Kemp, self-righteously asserted that his people deserved a choice on "whether their city should grow to the north or be cut off forever," but the pragmatic Cookingham set out to make things better. Immediately after the annexation was official in 1950, his crews built police and fire stations and laid out public parks. He also pushed successfully for three new bridges to better unify the redefined city. First, in 1953, he authorized conversion of the Chouteau Bridge on the city's eastern edge from railroad to automobile use. A year later came the opening of the $18 million Paseo Bridge and in 1956 the $13 million Broadway Bridge to the airport and beyond.[20]

The three-year wait to decide the legality of Clay County annexation provided time for Cookingham to plan his next moves and for opponents to consider defensive strategies. The results largely favored the city manager, but people created sizable new suburbs in two areas and expanded community limits in several others. The new entities, Raytown southeast of the city and Gladstone to the north, actually were preexisting but unincorporated places. Raytown had been a stop on the Santa Fe Trail, whereas Gladstone sprang from an 1880s community called Linden. Raytown people first petitioned for incorporation in 1950, ahead of any Kansas City threat. Their success prompted nearby homeowners to join the union, and by 1961, the original town near Sixty-third Street and Raytown Road had expanded to 8.5 square miles. The Gladstone incorporation began in 1952 on a rumor that Cookingham was about to annex more land in Clay County. From Linden's original core at what is now Seventieth Street North and Holmes, petitioners claimed about 10 square miles of territory abutting Kansas City on the north and west. The name Gladstone was that of the local telephone exchange.[21]

Cookingham's annexations after 1954 took place swiftly and largely without incident. He operated ahead of suburbanization for the most part and gained credibility by the

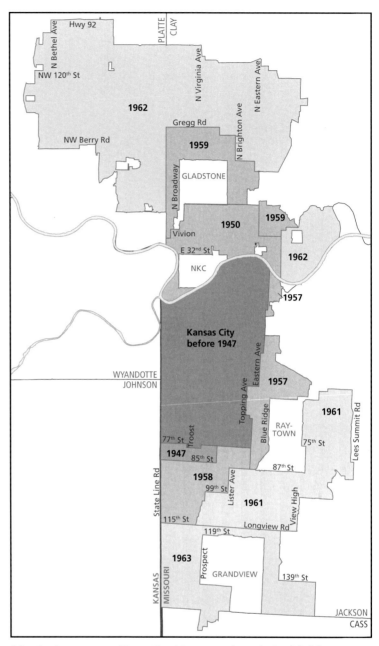

Map 48. Annexations to Kansas City, Missouri, 1947–1963. Modified from maps in William L. McCorkle, "Annexation: The Way Kansas City Has Continued to Grow," Kansas City Times, August 13, 1970, p. A5.

quality of ongoing improvements to his new Clay County acreage. The first expansion, taking effect in 1957, extended the city to the southeast considerably beyond the Blue River. This move fixed common boundaries with both Independence and Raytown (map 48). An addition on the southern border in 1958 was routine, but Cookingham showed his boldness again in two last annexations planned before his resignation in 1959. Gladstone formed a nearly complete blockade to further expansion northward, and Raytown did the same

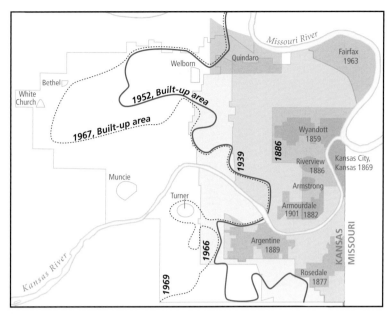

Map 49. Annexations to Kansas City, Kansas, 1886–1968. Modified from pl. 0–1 in Historical Profile, *Part 1-A of the Community Renewal Program: An Analysis of Community Need and Renewal Potential (Kansas City, Kans.: Kansas City, Kansas, Planning Department, 1969).*

toward the southeast. Still, small openings existed. In his penultimate move, the city manager seized this opportunity and deftly encircled both communities. He added 18 square miles in the north and 38 in the southeast.[22]

The final phase of Cookingham-era expansion concentrated on northern territory and was carried out by his successor managers. They added some acreage on the south, but simultaneous annexations there by the cities of Grandview and Lee's Summit limited the possibilities. In contrast, lands in Clay County and in Platte County to its west were largely open. Consequently, Kansas City officials claimed 42 square miles east and north of the existing boundary in Clay County and an unprecedented 68 in Platte.[23]

Cookingham's aggressive annexation work is a critical but underappreciated aspect of local history. His vision, unequaled in other large American cities of the time, earned high praise from fellow city managers. Kansas City people, in contrast, accepted as standard issue their well-planned land base for future expansion and their continuous inflow of dollars to maintain city services. Comparisons with most other major cities show the problem of a laissez-faire planning attitude in the automobile age. In fact, a prime example existed just across the state line in Kansas.[24]

Despite the construction of major new plants for General Motors and Sunshine Biscuits just after the war, the population of Kansas City, Kansas, actually declined during the

1950s. This paradox contrasts with a substantial gain for Wyandotte County as a whole (from about 165,000 residents to 185,000) and is directly attributable to annexation decisions. Inaction was the word in this Kansas City. The western city limit established at consolidation in 1886 remained in place for over fifty years (map 49). By the time officials moved the line from Eighteenth Street to Thirty-fourth and Thirty-sixth in 1939, developers already had subdivided this acreage in haphazard fashion. New homes without city regulation meant lower taxes for buyers—but also septic tanks and a nonintegrated road network. Then, learning nothing from the high cost of retrofitting modern services into this area, officials repeated the process. Not for another twenty-seven years did the city limits move again, and then it was only by fifteen blocks. Finally, in 1968, the policy changed. Pushing the boundary another 4 miles west, the city at last began to annex land ahead of mass development.[25]

Why was annexation so different in the two Kansas Cities? Part of the reason was Cookingham's unique foresight and will; part was the strong city manager system in which he worked. A contrast in land competition for the two governments was pivotal, too. Whereas Cookingham faced multiple barriers to expansion that forced him to act early and decisively, his counterparts in Wyandotte County had no rival cities to their west for at least 15 miles. The decision to expand or not was entirely in their hands, and their slowness was a product of patronage government. Voters had been given an opportunity to hire a city manager in 1947 but opted instead to stay with a three-person commission whose interests were tied closely to ethnic power bases. Corruption was the rule and inefficiency the result.[26]

Airports

Although suburbanization was a prime mover behind annexation, it was not the exclusive rationale. Airports were another big user of land, and demands for their expansion increased as planes became larger and traffic heavier. From a city planner's perspective, thinking about airports in the 1940s and 1950s actually involved much more than assessing space availability for landings. Airways were rapidly replacing railroad tracks as the country's primary means of long-distance travel, which implied that airports likely would become analogous to Union Station and other depots of the recent past. Their position would influence future locations of highways, industry, and suburban housing.

The first sign that Kansas City people were aware of air transportation came in 1925, via a $500,000 proposal to construct an "aviation field." This bid failed to gain approval, but change in attitude came rapidly. Three years later, voters not only approved the funding but also doubled the original amount. Out of this came Municipal Airport, built on 687 acres of Missouri River floodplain across from the downtown business district. The site, larger than most of its peers and unmatched in accessibility to local manufacturers and retailers, was praised highly. It was also highly successful. Within months after opening in 1929, the first airline to contemplate coast-to-coast routes selected Municipal as its headquarters. This company, Transcontinental Air Transport (soon to be renamed Transcontinental and Western Air and then Trans World Airlines [TWA]), became one of the nation's leading carriers.[27]

Given the pace of change in the air industry, even an airport that looked big in 1929 seemed small by the war years. Nobody was yet ready to abandon convenient Municipal, but realistic planning demanded a second, auxiliary facility on a flood-free site of several thousand acres. In theory, the suburban possibilities were many. Although sites to the east and west were blocked by Independence and the Kansas border, one could look to the southeast. Richards Flying Field, the main predecessor to Municipal Airport, had been located there on property later incorporated into Raytown. The area north into Clay County was open, too, although few Kansas City people thought about this direction seriously before Cookingham's annexation of 1946. These scenarios, however, overlooked the potential influence of politics. Kansas City actually received its new airport quietly via the 1941 purchase of acreage in the southwestern corner of Jackson County. Known officially as Grandview Airport when it opened in 1943, its origins are better revealed by a nickname: this was "Harry's Airport," as in Harry Truman, a U.S. senator at the time whose family farm was in the neighborhood.[28]

Grandview was not a bad location. U.S. Highway 71 ran nearby, as did several railroads. Property was available for industry and housing, and developers assuaged the doubts of downtown merchants by labeling this site as "auxiliary" and talking about helicopter taxi service to the hotel district. The airport's planners received special applause in July 1951. As floodwaters threatened Municipal Airport, officials transferred all operations to Grandview. Everything worked smoothly.[29]

One could speculate at length on how the new airport at 135th Street might soon affect the neighboring Grandview and Belton communities plus the entirety of south Kansas City. Certainly, it would act as a growth pole, drawing urban development even farther in that direction and consequently slowing expansion north of the river. But the question quickly became moot. Just three months after the big flood and again without forewarning or fanfare, city officials sold the facility to the federal government. On the face of it, the move made little sense because the city clearly would require an airport of this size in the near future. Pilots of larger planes already complained about difficulties clearing the downtown office buildings near Municipal and then descending sharply to runways that were barely long enough under ideal conditions. TWA also had threatened to leave if improvements did not come soon.[30]

The answer to the mystery behind the sale again involved Harry Truman, who now occupied an even loftier political position. President Truman learned that the Aerospace Defense Command required a site in this general area for an interceptor base. Although suitable, federally owned fields for this purpose already existed in Ottumwa, Iowa, and St. Joseph, Missouri, Truman pushed for the more expensive Grandview site. Critics said the reason was to ensure profits for local land developers (including many friends of the president), but this charge rings false, for real estate gains would have been as great for a metropolitan airport as for a federal base. A more charitable view is that Truman saw a way to provide two plums for his city—a military post on its southern fringe and a chance to create additional growth (and speculator profits) with a new public facility somewhere else.[31]

Truman's vision came to pass but not without additional drama. Things went smoothly at Grandview as the Aerospace Defense Command gave way to the U.S. Air Force in 1953. The site was made a permanent base in 1955, and two years later, its name changed from Grandview Air Force Base to Richards-Gebaur to honor two local men. As for a new Kansas City airport, City Manager Cookingham considered fifteen possible sites in Jackson and Clay counties before recommending a 2,850-acre tract in Clay. Land was cheaper north of the river, and Cookingham thought a facility there would ease the bad feelings that lingered after his recent annexation. The actual site lay just northeast of the annexed area, near Liberty and U.S. Highway 69.[32]

Cookingham's plan was solid, but he underestimated the distrust of Clay County residents. Seeing an avaricious city at work, people refused to sell their land and threatened lawsuits if the issue were forced. As the city manager pondered his options, he got a call from Jay B. Dillingham, president of the Kansas City Stock Yards. Dillingham, one of the city's most trusted leaders, suggested his native Platte County as a new site and offered his influence to help calm local fears. Since Platte County would be the equal of Clay for integrating the north country into the city, Cookingham agreed. In May 1953, he announced the purchase of 4,590 acres southeast of Platte City. The property lay adjacent to U.S. Highway 71, about 15 miles from downtown Kansas City.[33]

Work on the airport began in 1954, and the facility opened in 1956. As with Grandview before it, officials were careful to avoid the appearance of competition with the convenient Municipal terminal. During construction, the new facility was labeled the city's "industrial" airport and said to be home primarily to an $18 million overhaul base built for TWA. The official name for the field—Mid-Continent International—also was carefully chosen. It suggested the location and honored the airport's other major client, Mid-Continent Airlines, while simultaneously avoiding use of the potentially antagonistic words *Kansas City*.[34]

Subterfuge continued at Mid-Continent until the middle 1960s. Then, after federal officials finally deemed Municipal unsafe for large jet aircraft, voters approved a bond issue to expand Mid-Continent into the city's primary facility. Retaining its airport code of MCI but now becoming known officially as Kansas City International, the enlarged airport opened in October 1972. The city eventually annexed the area, but because of the distance from other built-up acreage, local development did not follow immediately.[35]

Expressways and Urban Renewal

L. P. Cookingham and his planning associates saw three primary needs for Kansas City. Industrial jobs and room for growth via annexation were critical, but so were new highways to serve an increasingly mobile public. Road improvements were especially vital for the downtown area, where congestion reached its peak and where the existing infrastructure was oldest.

Roads are a perennial concern for any community. As Kansas City entered the automobile age in the 1920s and began to spread east and south, leaders saw the first need as being better access to the downtown area. Consequently, they proposed two major arteries in the Ten-Year Plan of 1931. One, called the Southeast Trafficway, would run from Linwood Boulevard (U.S. 40) at Jackson Avenue to Blue Parkway (U.S. 50) at its Blue River crossing. The other, Southwest Trafficway, would connect downtown with Ward Parkway along the general route of Summit Street.[36]

When Cookingham arrived in Kansas City in 1940, he oversaw completion of the Southwest Trafficway but folded the other route into a more comprehensive plan. Downtown remained central in the thinking but was now linked with twin goals—accessibility plus renewal. In contrast to the gleaming and automobile-friendly Country Club Plaza, downtown streets had come to seem "cramped and narrow." The solution, he said, was a system of express highways that would loop around some 120 blocks of the business district. When paired with a series of new parking garages at this loop's edge, the roads would simultaneously allow easy access for shoppers and uninterrupted passage for through drivers.[37]

The conception of an expressway loop was not unique among planners. Its Kansas City expression, however, was part of a much larger strategy that was indeed groundbreaking. In 1947, Cookingham instructed his planning engineer, Philip E. Geissal, to create a comprehensive highway system in cooperation with neighboring Kansas City, Kansas, and North Kansas City. The resultant plan was a prescient document, anticipating not only future traffic but also federal assistance programs for land condemnation and interstate highway construction. When the needed legislation materialized in 1949 and 1956, respectively, Kansas City was ready. Contracts were let early, and the designs matched those of the original proposal almost exactly.[38]

Consider first the expressways (map 50). Geissal's patterns look familiar to modern eyes everywhere except in Kansas City, Kansas. There, the Kansas Turnpike, authorized in 1953, was an unforeseen factor. The lowland path selected by turnpike engineers near the Kansas River served Cookingham's Missouri interests nearly as well as had the original design. Kansans were less sure about the change. The original plan, with expressways almost encircling the Minnesota Avenue business district, would have aided retailers. But such a gain would have come at the cost of several thousand homes, far more than had been lost to the turnpike.

Expressways were easiest to plan north of the Missouri River, where population density was low. Geissal's chart was perfectly executed there, with what became Interstates 29 and 35 jointly crossing the river on the new Paseo Bridge and

then diverging along the preexisting paths of, respectively, U.S. 71 and U.S. 69. The new airport and North Kansas City industry both were served well.

In Jackson County, Cookingham concentrated first on the downtown area and the route that would become I-70. Work on the Intercity Freeway over the West Bottoms and along Sixth Street to the Paseo Bridge was complete by 1958, and construction was under way for the east side of the downtown loop and its extension east and south to Linwood Boulevard. Near the state line, the Kansas Freeway (today's I-35) was completed in the late 1960s along a path separate from the Southwest Trafficway south of Twenty-seventh Street, but most of Geissal's other ideas were implemented as written. These projects include the expensive Crosstown Freeway and the South Midland Freeway, both of which passed through established neighborhoods. Officials deleted only three road segments: the Crosstown spur eastward into the partially in-

Figure 31. Downtown Kansas City, Missouri, 1950, Looking North from Liberty Memorial. A series of office towers built between 1919 and 1937 gave the city its first definitive skyline, one that would endure for decades. Standing alone west of Main Street is the graceful Power and Light Building with its lighted finial (1931). The center cluster includes the slender, twin-turreted Fidelity Bank and Trust Building (1931) and the bulkier Bryant (1931) and Federal Reserve Bank (1919) structures. Finally, to the east are the Southwestern Bell Telephone Building (1929), city hall (1937), and the county court-house (1934). (Courtesy Missouri Valley Special Collections, Kansas City Public Library)

dustrialized valley of OK Creek, the Twenty-seventh Street connector between the South Midtown Freeway and I-70, and the Southeast Trafficway south from I-70 to U.S. 50 via the Leeds industrial area.

As impressive as the expressways were, writers and planners of the time always couched discussions of them within the context of what they considered "America's Number 1

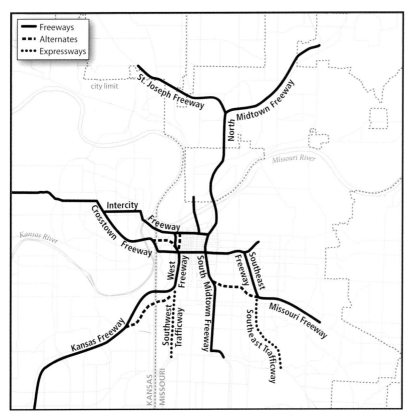

Map 50. Proposed Expressway System for Greater Kansas City, 1950. Modified from a map in Philip E. Geissal, "Kansas City Sees Expressways Preventing 1970 Traffic Jams," American City 67 (March 1952): 141.

urban problem—downtown congestion and blight." Consequently, parking garages were promoted to accompany these pavements, and so were new or renovated stores and residential structures. Less discussed but always implied was the concurrent removal of slums.[39]

New construction downtown began in 1950, just after Congress passed the Housing Act of 1949. This landmark legislation granted local governments the power of eminent domain over blighted areas and provided subsidies for property acquisition and demolition. Quality Hill, the mansion area of the 1870s that had fallen into decay, was an obvious first target. Realtor Lewis Kitchen assembled tracts there on Pennsylvania and Jefferson streets between Ninth and Eleventh and constructed five apartment buildings of ten stories each. A few years later, he expanded the project, adding a hotel, several office buildings, and more apartments south to Fourteenth Street (map 51).[40]

While Kitchen worked on downtown's western fringe, Cookingham tackled the rest. First came a much-needed, 1,200-car parking garage to serve Municipal Auditorium and adjacent hotels. The structure occupied the entire block just

north of the auditorium, and all three levels of its parking were underground. This design, inspired by Union Square in San Francisco, allowed the surface to be landscaped as a park. Eventually named Barney Allis Plaza, the facility opened to high praise in December 1955. Parking also was central to the next project, 8 acres at the Main Street exit of I-70. This work eliminated one of the city's most photographed intersections, where Main and Delaware streets had merged at Ninth, but it yielded another large garage in the lower six floors of a new office tower (the Eight Eleven Main Building) occupied by the American Telephone and Telegraph Company.[41]

The eastern edge of downtown, between Locust Street and the freeway loop, had always been more residential than commercial. The old Kerry Patch around St. Patrick's Catholic Church and the African American Church Hill district formed its traditional core (map 22). But by the 1950s, this entire neighborhood was seriously blighted and therefore a target for renewal by Cookingham. He completely cleared the area south of Twelfth, dubbed South Humboldt, to allow space for a series of public buildings that would complement the existing city hall and county courthouse (map 51). The area's anchor was a large Federal Office Building completed in 1966. North of Twelfth, in a 58-acre project called Eastside, about two-thirds of the buildings were razed, leaving St. Patrick's and other symbolic and solid structures as a nucleus for renovation. The primary aim here was the creation of new, middle-income housing, mostly apartments.[42]

The remaining renewal projects of the time lay just outside the downtown loop and therefore received less media attention. The first of these, a 53-acre tract named after Attucks School, began in 1955. Bounded by Fifteenth and Nineteenth streets, Paseo and Brooklyn, this area was the heart of black Kansas City (maps 41 and 42). The mainstream press glossed over this cultural significance, however, implying that Attucks was a peripheral project where "Negro occupied slums have been razed to make way for 500 units of middle-income rental housing."[43]

Viewed dispassionately from an office in the city hall tower, Attucks made sense. The area was seriously blighted, and a

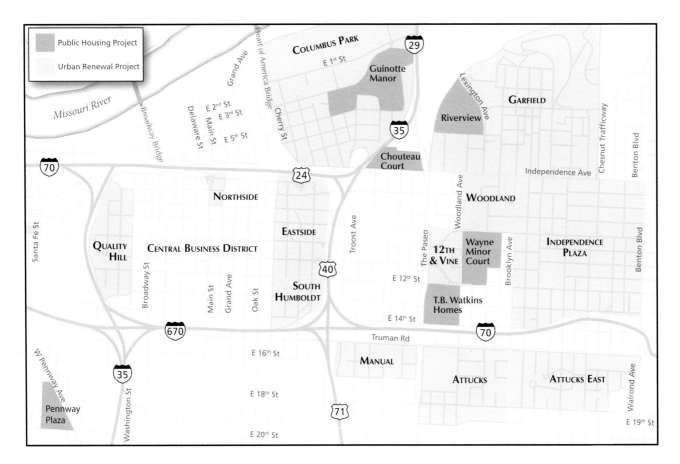

Map 51. Urban Renewal and Public Housing Projects in Downtown Kansas City, Missouri, 1953–1969. Modified from a map in Kevin F. Gotham, Race, Real Estate, and Uneven Development: The Kansas City Experience, 1900–2000 *(Albany: State University of New York Press, 2002), p. 81.*

plan that saved historical buildings at the Eighteenth and Vine commercial core while erecting hundreds of new housing units could lead to a brighter future. Such logic actually allowed the Attucks model to be extended to seven adjacent neighborhoods in the 1960s (map 51). Yet a renovated Attucks could accommodate far fewer people than had lived there before, and the same was true for Eastside, Quality Hill, South Humboldt, and subsequent targeted districts. What would happen to this "surplus," typically poor population?[44]

Writers of the federal Housing Act of 1949 knew that dislocation would be a problem and so required any city that accepted the government's renewal funds to construct replacement dwellings. The simplest way to fulfill this obligation was with apartment complexes, and again, Kansas City was a leader in this regard. By 1954, three such entities existed: Guinotte Manor near Fourth and Troost (454 units), Riverview near Fifth and The Paseo (232 units), and T. B. Watkins Homes (462 units) near Thirteenth and Vine (map 51). Four other complexes were under construction, including the large Wayne Minor Court near Ninth and Woodland (738 units). Started as they were in the years of segregation, each complex was race specific. T. B. Watkins and high-rise

Wayne Minor, located within traditionally black neighborhoods, were designated "for Negro families," the others for white occupancy.[45]

Flaws in the Renewal

City planning in a time of rapid technological and social change is necessarily an imperfect art. Mistakes, sometimes serious and long lasting, will occur even with the best of leaders and the best of intentions. Such was the case with Kansas City during the 1950s. L. P. Cookingham was a visionary in many ways. His bold plan for annexation ahead of suburbanization saved the city's tax base, for instance, and provided an enduring point of pride in comparisons made with "landlocked" St. Louis. Similarly, his expressway system and suburban airport have allowed the city to remain competitive nationally in these critical arenas.

Downtown Kansas City was Cookingham's focus. Believing

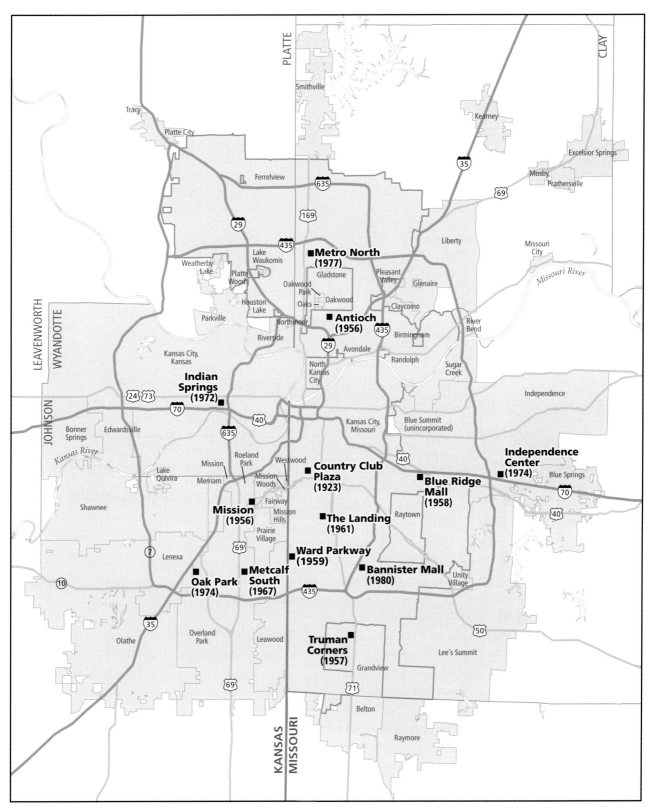

Map 52. Major Suburban Shopping Centers, 1923–1980. Compiled from multiple sources.

Figure 32. Prairie Village Shopping Center, 1960, Looking West. The J. C. Nichols Company constructed this small retail center alongside the Indian Hills Country Club in 1955 to extend the buffer between the mansions of Mission Hills and the modest Cape Cod homes of Prairie Village. The forty or so shops at the corner of Mission Road (running left to right) and Seventy-first Street continue to serve the area well. Note the curvilinear streets of 1960s suburbia and how tree size reveals the age of home construction. (Courtesy Missouri Valley Special Collections, Kansas City Public Library)

that it "should be as attractive and beautiful as the best planned and developed outlying shopping centers," he wanted to augment the freeway loop and garages by converting several streets into plazas. These would feature fountains and outdoor cafés and be linked to the parking structures by "a series of moving sidewalks." This vision did not materialize. In fact, only eight years after he revealed his intentions, officials deliberately passed over downtown as a site for a massive new sports and entertainment complex. The year after that, the decline in foot traffic was obvious enough to receive comment in national magazines. Big conventions arrived in town less frequently because Municipal Auditorium was now too small to meet their needs. Shoppers stayed away, too, even though parking was abundant. And "one after another, retail stores have folded . . . and gathering dust has turned the windows of empty shop fronts to an opaque gray."[46]

What happened to downtown Kansas City? Partly, of course, the story is that of suburbanization. Cookingham alluded to the competition of new shopping centers in the

quotation just cited, and such malls were inevitable as the automobile culture dispersed residents over a widening area. What J. C. Nichols had started with his Country Club Plaza in 1923 mushroomed in the late 1950s. In fact, the same expressways that were intended to save downtown became prime sites for suburban shopping developments (map 52). Between 1956 and 1958, a new mall claimed each of the cardinal directions. Antioch Center along U.S. 69 in the north and Mission Center along U.S. 50 in the west were each anchored by a Macy's department store. Truman Corners along U.S. 71 in the south championed a J. C. Penney outlet, while

111

the Blue Ridge Mall along U.S. 40 and I-70 in the east set the local standard with eighty-five tenants, including J. C. Penney, Montgomery Ward, and the Jones Store.

Downtown Kansas City as a shopping district obviously would have to change in the face of suburban competition. But adaptation is not the same thing as collapse, and downtown merchants already had successfully accommodated the presence of the Country Club Plaza over the previous forty years. It would have been reasonable to predict another round of thoughtful adjustment circa 1960, especially given the encouragement provided by new highways, garages, and slum clearance. Again, what happened to downtown Kansas City?

One overly simplistic answer blames the new city administration that took office in 1959. The nonpartisan Citizens Association that had hired Cookingham and established a progressive agenda for the previous twenty years was defeated when it pushed for a new earnings tax to continue improvements. Cookingham resigned under pressure two weeks after the election, and cost-saving philosophies meant a quick death to plans for downtown plazas and moving sidewalks. With nine different city managers trying to steer the local ship of state between 1959 and 1963, it is little wonder that stagnation became the rule.[47]

The 1950s and 1960s were pivotal decades for downtowns in all American cities. With good leadership, these districts could remain vibrant even amid the lifestyle changes. Without it, however, the business community could easily follow the new housing developments to the urban fringe. For Kansas City, the change from progressive to conservative government came at a terrible time in this regard. Cookingham's initiatives, had they been fulfilled, would have prevented at least some of the steep retail decline that occurred in the 1960s. More speculative but equally significant is how successfully that former administration might have pushed downtown as the site for a massive $109 million sports and entertainment facility being discussed in 1966.[48]

When Kansas City acquired a major-league baseball team rather suddenly in 1954, not much thought was given to stadium location. The field where the previous minor-league team had played was available at Twenty-second Street and Brooklyn Avenue, and so, officials simply purchased it and added extra seats. This field, Municipal Stadium, worked well for the new franchise, and the adjacent residential neighborhood benefited from parking fees on lots and lawns.

Municipal Stadium was built for baseball, but starting in 1964, it was modified to accommodate football as well. Lamar

Hunt, a millionaire cofounder of the new American Football League, decided to relocate his team from Dallas. This move, unlike that of the Athletics in 1955, was accompanied by little fanfare, but the new Chiefs team quickly became popular. Soon, Jackson County officials began to ponder a new stadium. A design better suited to football was one consideration; greater size was another. Less discussed publicly but important nonetheless was the perceived discomfort of the predominately white, middle-class fan base with a stadium located in a poor, black neighborhood.[49]

Architects were told to design a 60,000-seat, domed athletic center suitable for baseball and football. They also were to assess the relative worth of two possible sites: the first downtown just south of Municipal Auditorium and the second near Leeds where I-70 crossed the Blue River. As expected, land proved to be more expensive downtown ($21.7 million versus $13.9 million), and a multilevel garage would be a necessity there as well. Total costs were $109.5 million in the city and $85 million on the fringe. Yet when benefits were weighed against these numbers, the urban site came out ahead. Planners thought that by attracting people to the downtown area, such a stadium would boost existing businesses, prompt the development of new ones, and enhance the city's overall public image. As for the Blue Valley location, the main benefit it provided apart from lower cost was ease of access.[50]

Debate over the two sites was intense in 1966, but the cards were stacked against the downtown location. Without Cookingham, that site lacked a strong advocate, and people seriously underestimated the need to stimulate this core region. Several business owners there who would be displaced by construction also threatened to move to Kansas. The suburban site, in contrast, offended nobody and came at a cheaper price. The case was sealed when estimates to heat and cool the dome proved high enough to shift plans from a single stadium to a paired arrangement. Now, acquiring suburban space would be essential.[51]

In retrospect, the sports complex can be seen as a last chance to save a downtown that already was dying. It might

Figure 33 (facing page). Truman Sports Complex, 1973, Looking Southwest. By designing separate facilities for baseball and football at a single site, the architectural firm Kivett and Myers was able to optimize the seating at each and yet share access roads and parking lots. Both stadiums were highly praised at their opening in 1972–1973 and remain so today. Note their axial alignment, the result of an unfulfilled plan to install a common, movable roof. (Courtesy Missouri Valley Special Collections, Kansas City Public Library)

have provided a miracle cure, but its story offers little insight into the core illness (beyond suburbanization) that afflicted this recently vibrant place. The basic problems, poorly understood at the time, revolved around flawed social policies and centered on race. They were most apparent in urban renewal, real estate loans, and the creation of school districts.

The efficiency of L. P. Cookingham that made Kansas City a pioneer in annexation and urban renovation came with a downside. Pioneers make mistakes that slower-acting communities can partly avoid. The policy of segregation in public housing that existed before 1964 was the city's most obvious blunder. Rigidity was codified in this way just at the time that racial barriers were beginning to fall in schools, restaurants, and similar public places. Compounding the issue was a decision to concentrate public housing, especially units designated for African Americans, in a single inner-city area. Such concentration inhibited social interaction between races and thus contributed to stereotyping. This particular positioning also hurt the viability of downtown as a shopping district. The fashionable stores on Petticoat Lane were now nearly encircled by a ring of poor neighborhoods (map 51). By definition, public housing residents had little money to spend, and their presence inhibited others from wanting to pass through their areas. Moneyed shoppers, of course, now had alternatives, and they opted instead for the Country Club Plaza and the newer malls.[52]

Kansas City's problems of residential segregation were not limited to public housing. They were just as severe with private real estate, although controls in this realm were more subtle than a blunt policy of "no blacks allowed." From the perspective of white America, this movement began with a certain innocence. One source was the deed restrictions popularized by J. C. Nichols as a way to maintain suburban property values. Because this concept worked, it spread rapidly across the country during the interwar years and was nearly universal by 1945. Such covenants routinely included race, but since few African Americans could afford new homes in, say, Prairie Village, Kansas, little outcry was heard.

Racial deed restrictions arose from prejudice, of course, and a confusion of skin color with issues of poverty, crime, and disease. Then, lobbying efforts by the national real estate industry turned these same negative associations into government policy. Landmark legislation came in 1934 with the establishment of the Federal Housing Administration (FHA). This agency created the country's modern mortgage system by guaranteeing loans for millions of families. But such loans

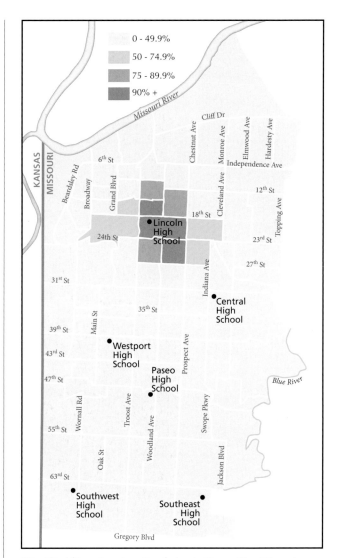

Map 53. *African American Population in Kansas City, Missouri, 1950. Data from U.S. Census.*

were to be made only in "stable" neighborhoods, meaning only those with restrictive covenants, racially homogeneous populations, and no blight. These preconditions were made to order for new suburbs and fueled their expansion, but they did not match reality in older sections of any city. Although not absolutely precluding loans to African Americans, they did so in practice. Covenants forbade black residence in the suburbs, and homes in either a mixed-race neighborhood or an older, African American (and inevitably blighted) one did not qualify for mortgage insurance.[53]

Restrictions on property deeds and loans produced radical and largely predictable changes on the Kansas City landscape starting about 1945. First, new and spacious developments in Gladstone, Grandview, Prairie Village, Raytown, and similar areas began to attract thousands of middle-class whites.

114

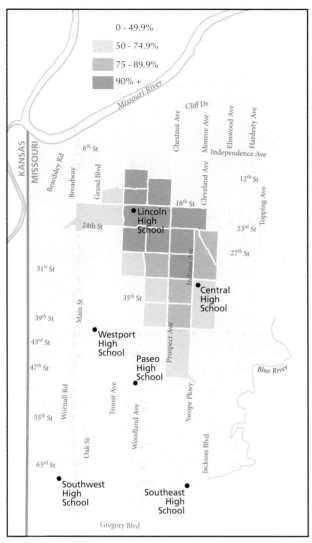

Map 54. *African American Population in Kansas City, Missouri, 1960. Data from U.S. Census.*

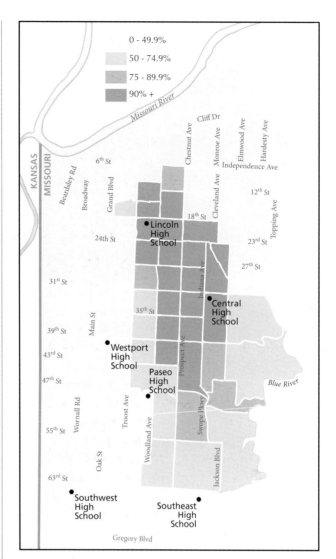

Map 55. *African American Population in Kansas City, Missouri, 1970. Data from U.S. Census.*

With this trend came increased segregation, of course, but in the absence of the FHA guidelines, one might have expected a simultaneous expansion of mixed-race neighborhoods throughout the older city. Middle-class African Americans presumably would have filtered into homes recently vacated in the suburbanization process, where they would live alongside white families who had decided to stay put. Such a change would at once remove the racial division line at Twenty-seventh Street and promote racial harmony.

But mixed-race neighborhoods never happened. Unscrupulous real estate agents used the same racial stereotyping that had produced the FHA guidelines to frighten white homeowners. Houses should be sold quickly, the litany went, because crime would increase along with the African American population, and then property values would tumble. This

practice of blockbusting played to people's worst fears, but homes so purchased at reduced prices could be resold at a premium to incoming black families. With brokers accumulating big profits, the process continued for decades, with neighborhood after neighborhood metamorphosing from nearly all white to nearly all black (maps 53, 54, and 55).[54]

The timing and scale of racial change are perhaps best seen through school enrollments. Central High School at 3221 Indiana Avenue was 17 percent African American in 1956–1957 but 90 percent black in 1960–1961. Fifteen blocks farther south, a similar transition occurred at Paseo High (4747 Flora) between 1961–1962 (16 percent black) and 1969–1970 (88 percent). Another sixteen blocks south at Meyer Boulevard and Bales, the numbers at Southeast High were 3 percent in 1965–1966 and 92 percent in 1971–1972.[55]

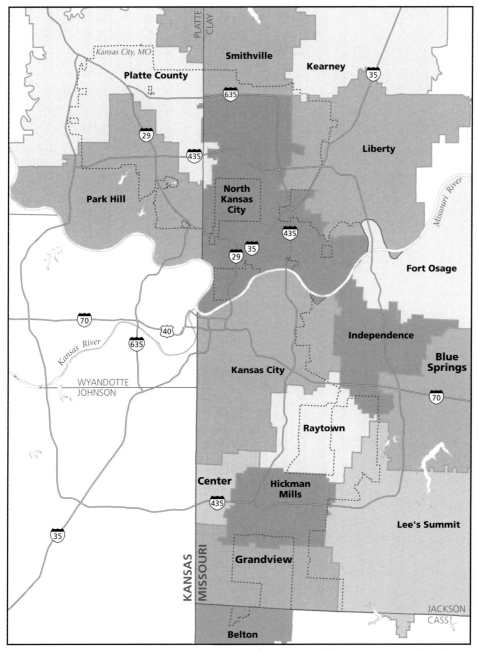

Map 56. School Districts Serving Kansas City, Missouri, 2007–2008. Modified from a map on the website of the city's Office of Planning and Development, available at http://kcmo.org/planning.nsf/web/schoolmap (accessed January 20, 2009).

cant cultural divide in the late 1950s and remains so today.

Troost Avenue, a traffic artery that dates back to Kansas City's beginnings, developed its racial overtones through actions of the local school board. This board, all white until 1968 and mostly so through the 1970s, did not resist mandatory school integration when it became federal law starting in 1955. But it did manipulate attendance boundaries to effectively separate white schools from black schools. Troost, the board members decided, was to divide the attendance zones for Westport High and Southwest High on the west from Central High, Lincoln High, Paseo High, and Southeast High on the east. Their work was highly effective. In contrast to the transformative figures cited earlier for the eastern schools, Southwest High at 6512 Wornall Road remained more than 97 percent white through the 1972–1973 year. The use of Troost as a boundary also kept most of the city's cultural institutions and elite residences safely within white neighborhoods. Places just west of the line included the Hyde Park and Rockhill districts, the Nelson-Atkins Museum of Art,

Given that Twenty-seventh Street had long served as a pressure point within the black community, it is logical that neighborhood expansion pushed toward the south more than the north (maps 53, 54, and 55). Interstate 70 also formed a barrier of sorts in the latter direction. As outward growth continued, however, an unexpected, abrupt, and persistent border arose on the west. Known locally as the Troost Wall, this line has insidious origins. It became the city's most signifi-

and the University of Kansas City.[56]

As the geographic implications of regressive attitudes toward public housing, home loans, and school boundaries evolved on the landscape in the late 1950s, their patterns were reinforced by still another set of public policies. This plan concerned schools as well but involved a competition between school systems rather than one within the Kansas City district itself.

The relationship between areas controlled by an American city government and its public school system is typically conformal. Though officially independent of one another, the two systems develop in tandem, with educators often setting the pace via consolidations with rural school districts. Kansas City followed this model for its first century. When city officials made their first big political annexation in 1885, for example, the school district already extended several blocks farther to the east (map 35). The same thing was true for the annexations of 1897 and 1909. Kansas City schools were seen as progressive, and people wanted to join the success.[57]

But a new pattern rapidly emerged after 1954, corresponding with the federal mandate for integrated education and L. P. Cookingham's program of annexation. Cookingham did not have to think much about local feelings in the areas he annexed because political additions depended solely on the votes of people already in the city. In contrast, any school merger had to be initiated and approved by voters in the outlying locale. And after 1954, these people judged the appeal of Kansas City differently.

The Center School District in south Kansas City came to be the new model. A small rural high school by that name had existed at 8434 Paseo since 1925. Then, as the city neared in the 1950s, residents of the nearby Boone and Dallas districts petitioned to consolidate with this school instead of with the larger city. New housing brought more students, and by the middle 1960s, the Center District taught some 6,000 children, all of them residents of Kansas City.[58]

The sequence of events at Center was repeated throughout the urbanized area, and soon, more Kansas City residents attended school in suburban districts than in that of the city itself (map 56). This transition was remarkable and important, but it was rarely discussed. Begun ostensibly just to assure quality, locally controlled education, the move clearly was fueled by racial fears. The trend was strong in the south, with Grandview, Hickman Mills, and Raytown joining Center on Kansas City soil. It reached even greater heights north of the Missouri River. Nobody in that area forcibly annexed by Cookingham wanted anything to do with Kansas City schools. Instead, the North Kansas City system expanded far beyond that city's political limits, and the small town of Parkville transformed its district into the sprawling Park Hill system.

The expansion of suburban school districts deep into Kansas City's political territory had little immediate impact in the 1950s but a tremendous one in succeeding decades. The

principle was the same as that Cookingham had espoused for annexation—grow with the population or see the tax base decline and services suffer. By 1970 or so, although the enlarged city had plenty of money for road repair and police protection, the shrunken school district was beginning to fall behind in facilities, teacher salaries, and standardized test scores. New suburban schools in Johnson County, Kansas, added to the challenge, and the Kansas City system deteriorated from troubled to truly desperate. People moving into the metropolitan area tried to avoid the district entirely if at all possible.

Missouri Neighborhoods

Suburbanization, urban renewal, and housing segregation combined to modify Kansas City's neighborhood structure substantially during the 1950s and 1960s. Most obvious, of course, was the greatly expanded African American East Side. Movement south from the old racial divide at Twenty-seventh Street relieved population pressure in the core district, but it also created an economic schism. Only upper- and middle-class people could afford the larger homes being offered by blockbusting realtors, especially those near the fashionable boulevards of Benton, Linwood, and The Paseo. The poorest families were similarly concentrated but north of Truman Road (Fifteenth Street). This was the site of the Wayne Minor and T. B. Watkins public housing projects.

The expansion of black housing prompted other economic and social changes. The segregated business and entertainment district at Eighteenth and Vine began to suffer, for instance, a victim of population dispersion and the desegregation of formerly white-only stores downtown. Businesses along Prospect Avenue and Thirty-ninth Street, in contrast, adapted quickly to the new customer base, as did most area churches. New ownership produced new signage, but the same general products and services were offered. Still, inevitably, a few white-controlled neighborhood institutions closed without replacement, among them baseball's Municipal Stadium and the imposing, X-shaped St. Joseph's Hospital at the northwest corner of Linwood and Prospect. In terms of upkeep, observers noticed little change. New black homeowners south of Linwood lavished care on their purchases, whereas blight continued to be the rule between Fifteenth and Twenty-seventh streets. Decades of poverty had pushed most buildings there past the point of possible restoration, even those that lined the once-genteel Paseo.

Besides African Americans, two other ethnic groups held

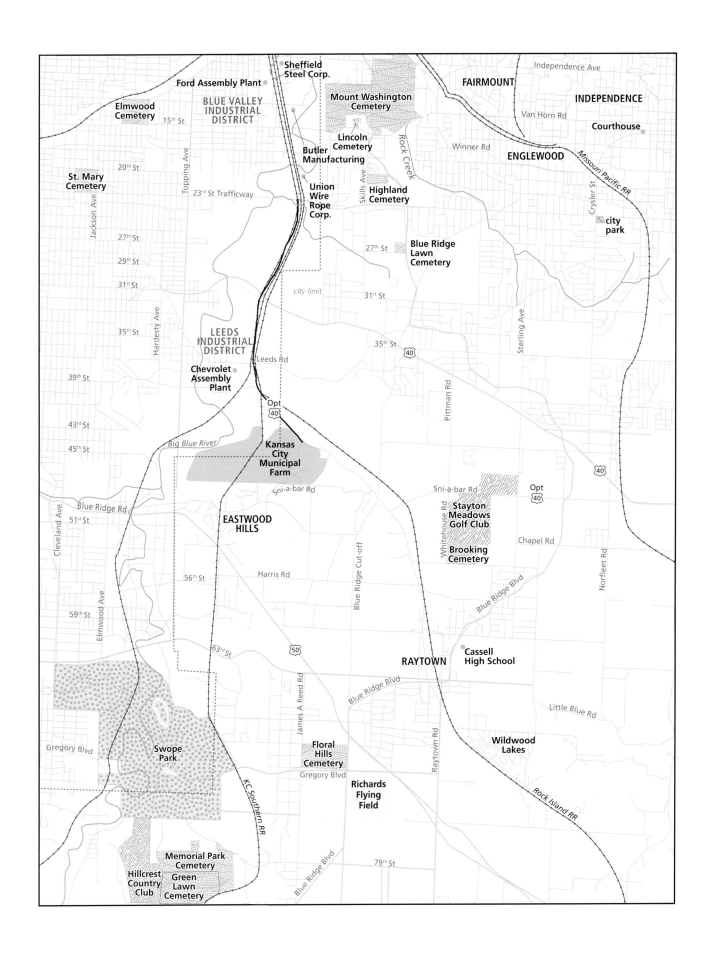

strong place identities at this time. Some 1,100 Mexican immigrants resided in the city in 1950. Just over half of them, plus a much larger number of second- and third-generation people, lived in the same West Side neighborhood they had occupied since 1910. This hilly area, west of Broadway and north of Southwest Boulevard, focused on Our Lady of Guadalupe Catholic Church at Twenty-third and Madison (maps 36 and 43).[59]

The Italian community, twice as large as the Mexican one in 1950 and still attached to its North End origins, was severely disrupted by urban renewal. The Guinotte Manor and Riverview housing projects in the area welcomed Italian residents, but many small homes were destroyed north of Independence Avenue and west of Benton Boulevard (map 51). The group's mother church, Holy Rosary, survived, but many families moved eastward. There, north of Truman Road and east of Benton, they became part of the city's diverse Northeast neighborhood.[60]

The Northeast, centered around the high school by that name at 415 South Van Brunt Boulevard, epitomized blue-collar Kansas City. Some residents, among them my cousin Robert Thomson of 1020 Askew, owned small retail shops along Independence Avenue and similar streets. Others commuted downtown, but the biggest employers were nearby industries in the Blue River valley and the East Bottoms, especially Sheffield Steel and Montgomery Ward (map 57). Residents took pride in the neighborhood's self-sufficiency and developed a strong sense of place.[61]

In many ways, the Northeast neighborhood could be seen as a western extension of Independence. My Thomson cousin had roots in that older city, for example, and residents of both places had working-class mentalities. The reorientation of Independence from an autonomous community to a part of Greater Kansas City had begun with the industrialization of the Blue Valley in the 1880s. The Ford Motor Company, Sheffield Steel, and (starting in the 1930s) General Motors at Leeds provided wages that were too good to resist, plus only short commutes. A big refinery built just north of town at Sugar Creek by Standard Oil of Indiana expanded the job possibilities in 1904 (map 57). Then, in 1940, the encirclement became nearly complete when the federal government constructed a huge ordnance plant at Lake City, a few miles to the east.

Map 57 (facing page). The Eastern Urban Fringe, 1944. Modified from the "Map of Greater Kansas City," included in Official Guide and Map of Greater Kansas City *(Kansas City, Mo.: Gallup Map and Stationery, 1944).*

A series of articles written as native son Harry Truman assumed the U.S. presidency in 1945 characterized Independence as a folksy, middle-class community. Its southern heritage was still obvious, people all seemed to be kin to one another, and the pace of life was slow. The inward focus was reflected in school district boundaries. In contrast to the aggressiveness of people from Raytown and Hickman Mills in terms of retaining their own schools, Independence residents did not object when, between 1910 and 1958, Englewood, Fairmount, and other of their western neighborhoods joined the Kansas City school district rather than their own (map 56). This phenomenon occurred nowhere else in the metropolitan area.[62]

Changes in Independence are obvious from population figures (table 1). Starting with 16,000 or so residents in 1945, the number doubled by 1950 and did so again in each of the following two censuses. Less than 1 percent of the 1970 total was African American. Much of this growth was a by-product of industrial jobs near at hand, but some came via the annexation of existing subdivisions south and west of the city and some via new suburban development. Interstate 70 passed through southern Independence, easing commutes. The large Blue Ridge Mall and the appropriately named Truman Sports Complex for the Royals and the Chiefs were both nearly on Independence soil (map 52).

West of Troost, Kansas City's older neighborhoods changed relatively little during this time. Downtown merchants, though definitely feeling the impact of new suburban malls, maintained faith in the restorative powers of urban renewal. Even in the late 1960s, as retail stores began to close, the merchants' Redevelopment Corporation unveiled a $100 million project called Towne Center. Focusing on eleven blocks between Twelfth and Fifteenth streets and Wyandotte to Oak, the design called for inserting new buildings among the old and adding 8,000 parking spaces. This plan, supplying useful office space but not restoring overall vitality, turned out to be the area's last hurrah for several decades, but it boosted confidence for a time.[63]

The old North End, the city's birthplace, had always been divided at Locust Street between a commercial district in the west and houses in the east. Urban renewal transformed this eastern half, replacing hundreds of small homes with the Guinotte Manor project. Rickety porches gave way to garden-style apartments, and by forcing African Americans south into other public housing units, the neighborhood lost diversity. Amid this change, the rest of the North End stayed

Figure 34. *Sheffield Division, ARMCO Steel Corporation, 1955, Looking Northwest across Independence Avenue. With its sprawling mill in the Blue Valley, Sheffield epitomized heavy industrialization in the city. The company started in 1888 as Kansas City Bolt and Nut and employed 4,500 people at its peak about 1970. Most of the buildings seen here are now demolished. Beyond Sheffield sits a large Montgomery Ward warehouse at the edge of the lowland. It employed an additional 550 local workers before closing in 1977. (Courtesy Missouri Valley Special Collections, Kansas City Public Library)*

as it was. The city market operated at a leisurely pace on the public square at Fourth and Main; a few warehouses did well; and most famously, so did "a hushed and underground red-light district."[64]

The most stable portion of the city, without question, was J. C. Nichols's Country Club District. Proving the value of restrictive covenants, the twin Sunset Hill and Mission Hills developments retained their appeal as everybody's residential addresses of choice. People with slightly less money saw similar stability in Armour Fields and other Nichols subdivisions farther south, as well as in the slightly older Rockhill neighborhood around the Nelson Gallery and the University of Kansas City. Anchoring all this was Nichols's Country Club Plaza, a shopping center praised from its outset for innovation and sophistication. In the words of one outside observer, "Kansas City is immensely proud of the whole thing."[65]

If the Country Club District represented an idealized but largely unattainable vision of Kansas City for an average white resident and if the East Side was an area to ignore, suburban developments to the south, southeast, and north were practicable realities. Here were new and affordable homes, green grass, good schools, and convenient shopping centers. With postwar prosperity, growth came rapidly (table 1).

Southeast of the city proper, the Blue River curtailed expansion until the middle 1950s (map 57). This river's broad valley had become a smoky industrial zone north from Thirty-ninth Street and home to the city's Municipal Farm for paupers between Forty-third and Forty-seventh streets. Then came Swope Park south of Sixty-third Street and the Bendix and Westinghouse plants at the old war-plant site on Bannister Road (Ninety-fifth Street) before the stream angled close to the Kansas state line. As population pressure and road improvements combined to overcome this barrier, Raytown and Grandview boomed. These tiny communities, like Independence, occupied a ridge of high ground that separated the valleys of the Blue and Little Blue rivers (map 3). The prairies there that once had sustained oxen on the Santa Fe Trail were now converted to bluegrass lawns, and the old trail route was rechristened as Blue Ridge Boulevard.

Raytown, closer than Grandview to downtown Kansas City and to most Blue River jobs, was the first to grow (table 1). Its incorporation in July 1950 came a few weeks too late for an official census count but soon enough to thwart Cookingham's plans for annexation in the area. The community was small at the outset, encompassing 2 square miles and perhaps 300 people, but it was well connected to the larger city via U.S. Highway 50. Most of the growth extended northeast and southwest along the ridgetop as developers built $10,000 ranch houses for working-class families. It was Middle America personified, an appropriate setting for the 1980s television series *Mama's Place*, staring Vicki Lawrence and Ken Berry.[66]

Grandview was incorporated in 1889 as a station on what became the St. Louis and San Francisco Railroad. Fourteen miles from downtown Kansas City, it remained a farm town of several hundred residents until 1941. Then, in quick succession, Senator Truman helped to create the big Grandview

Table 1. Population of Selected Cities in the Kansas City Metropolitan Area, 1950–1970

Missouri Communities	1950	1960	1970
Kansas City	456,622	475,539	507,330
Clay and Platte Co. part of K.C.	21,802	42,868	66,561
Claycomo	808	1,423	1,841
Gladstone	—	14,502	23,422
Grandview	1,556	6,027	17,456
Independence	36,963	62,328	111,630
North Kansas City	3,886	5,657	5,183
Parkville	1,186	1,229	1,253
Raytown	—	17,083	33,306
Riverside	—	1,315	2,123
Sugar Creek	1,858	2,663	4,755
Kansas Communities			
Kansas City	129,553	121,901	168,213
Fairway	1,816	5,398	5,227
Leawood	1,167	7,466	10,645
Lenexa	803	2,487	5,549
Merriam	—	5,084	10,955
Mission	—	4,626	8,125
Mission Hills	1,275	3,621	4,198
Overland Park	—	28,085	77,934
Prairie Village	—	25,356	28,378
Roeland Park	—	8,949	9,760
Shawnee	845	9,072	20,946

Source: U.S. Census records.

Airport just to the south and the wartime Pratt and Whitney engine plant 4 miles to the north. As the airport evolved into Richards-Gebaur Air Force Base and the war plant into Bendix and Westinghouse operations, Grandview joined the metropolitan area (table 1). U.S. Highway 71 provided direct access to the larger city, and the 1957 creation of Truman Corners Shopping Center made Grandview itself a destination. Local growth would have been even faster had not considerable undeveloped acreage remained just to the north and west in Kansas City proper.[67]

121

Although Grandview and Raytown offered the traditional appeals of suburban life, some potential white buyers there worried about future racial tensions. Kansas City's African American neighborhoods were expanding rapidly, especially toward the south and southeast. Race clauses in suburban property deeds allayed such fears for the moment, as did the possibility that the line of Blue River industries might serve as a permanent population barrier. But then, talk about fair housing legislation raised concern again.

Many middle-class residents in search of white-only suburbs reasoned that their safest option lay north of the Missouri River. Clay and Platte counties, an area becoming known as the Northland, offered a double layer of protection—the river and then 2 miles of industrial North Kansas City. Although some jobs were available locally and the ASB and Paseo bridges provided decent access to the south, neither employment nor transportation was as promising as in other suburban locations. Racial fears are by far the most plausible explanation for the northward migration of 67,000 people by 1960 and 100,000 by 1970 (table 1). An observer in 1968 flatly asserted that "there are no Negroes north of the river" and found universal agreement there with the sentiment that "it's my right as to whether or not I want to live next door to a colored person."[68]

Kansas Neighborhoods

A major cultural divide has existed at the state line in Kansas City since the 1830s. This distinction always has been based on social class, with Missourians looking down first at Indians and then at more complex ethnic patchworks as the big packing plants and rail yards began to import laborers. Differences might have been expected to fade over the years via assimilation and a greater choice of jobs, but this was not the case. One reporter in 1945 still saw a lack of "éclat" in Wyandotte County, while another described people there as the "less worldly country cousins" of the sophisticated Missourians. Kansas City, Kansas, a third observer concluded, felt like a small town with "comparatively little traffic [and] a noticeable lack of bustle."[69]

The reporters' comments were not exaggerated. If anything, they were kind in that they ignored the self-destructive nature of Wyandotte County politics during this period. As noted in the earlier discussion of annexation, the city and county governments were blatantly corrupt. Whereas a planning document from 1957 hopefully had forecast 300,000 residents for the county by 1980, the city actually lost over 7,000 people in

the 1950s (table 1). The county population peaked at about 186,000 in the 1960s and then began a forty-year fall.[70]

Some of the Wyandotte County problems were beyond local control. Most of the damage from the big flood of 1951 occurred on the Kansas side of the metropolitan area, for instance, especially in Armourdale, Argentine, and the West Bottoms. Armourdale was hit the hardest, with a forced evacuation of 9,100 people and damage of $121 million. From a total population of about 10,000 before the deluge, only 3,000 ever returned. And since these returnees faulted Wyandotte County officials for not doing enough to help, they no longer patronized stores in that jurisdiction.[71]

The decision of Kansas Turnpike engineers to bypass the Minnesota Avenue business district instead of focusing on it was a second blow that local efforts could not overcome (map 50). So, too, was the white flight associated with forced integration after 1954. Still, the completely reactionary approach of local officials to suburban development overrode all other problems in the county. Officials refused to annex any land between 1939 and 1966 on the premise that it would cost money to extend sewer and water lines. Developers were appalled, and most went elsewhere. The few subdivisions that did materialize were largely unregulated and therefore of suspect quality. The city's built-up area in 1952, seven years into the postwar boom, was nearly the same as it had been in 1939. Even by 1967, it had advanced only modestly, 2 miles west along Leavenworth and Parallel roads and 1 mile southwest toward Shawnee in adjacent Johnson County (map 49).

Two examples of mismanagement stand out to longtime observers. The reputable Winn-Rau Corporation, headed by the future congressman Larry Winn, proposed large housing projects along State Avenue at Ninety-eighth Street in 1951 and at 110th in 1954. At neither time would public officials agree to extend water lines that far out, so the projects died. In contrast, protestors in 1951 tried in vain to stop the 200–unit Wyandotte Village development at Forty-seventh and Garfield. Responding to the argument that construction would be shoddy, county commissioners replied that they were powerless to prevent that because no building codes existed for homes outside the city limits.[72]

Given such attitudes, it is no wonder that Wyandotte County lagged fifteen years behind the rest of the metropolitan area in the development of a major shopping mall and that much of its middle- and upper-middle-class white population moved out almost en masse. Locations just across the Johnson County line to the south offered quality homes and sup-

Figure 35. Downtown Kansas City, Kansas, 1950, Looking East from Ninth Street. The five blocks of Minnesota Avenue between Fifth and Tenth streets thrived as a retail center through the 1950s. Three department stores operated here, two large drugstores, and three movie theaters, including the Avenue midway along the corridor. Major automobile dealerships, such as Feld Chevrolet, also were able to afford the rent. The 1971 opening of Indian Springs Shopping Center 3 miles to the west ended the halcyon years. (Courtesy Missouri Valley Special Collections, Kansas City Public Library)

porting infrastructure with only a slightly longer commute to work (map 58). The city's median family income, $5,583 for 1960, was the metropolitan nadir. In contrast, Independence, the Kansas City Northland, and Prairie Village recorded figures of $6,535, $7,050, and $10,225, respectively.[73]

The loss of a major segment of its population made Kansas City, Kansas, ever more an ethnic and working-class city. Most obviously, the African American population grew from 29,367 to 35,707 in the 1950–1970 period (about 19 percent of the county population) and expanded spatially as well (maps 45 and 59). From the traditional core area in the northeast, people moved west to Eighteenth Street and northwest to the old Quindaro neighborhood near Twenty-seventh and Sewell. Numbers also increased in Rosedale near the University of Kansas Medical Center and just north of downtown between Third and Fifth streets, where officials replaced shacks with the Juniper Gardens public housing project in 1958.[74]

The city's two other sizable ethnic groups, East European Slavs and Mexicans, also increased their presence. The Slavs, perhaps 4,000 strong now and nearly all second- and third-generation residents, maintained their domination over the Strawberry Hill neighborhood just south of downtown. Some of them also moved to newer homes near Christ the King Catholic Church, established in 1949 at 3024 North Fifty-third Street. Twenty-three hundred Mexican immigrants and at least three times that number of American-born Hispanics also stayed close to their traditional churches and railroad

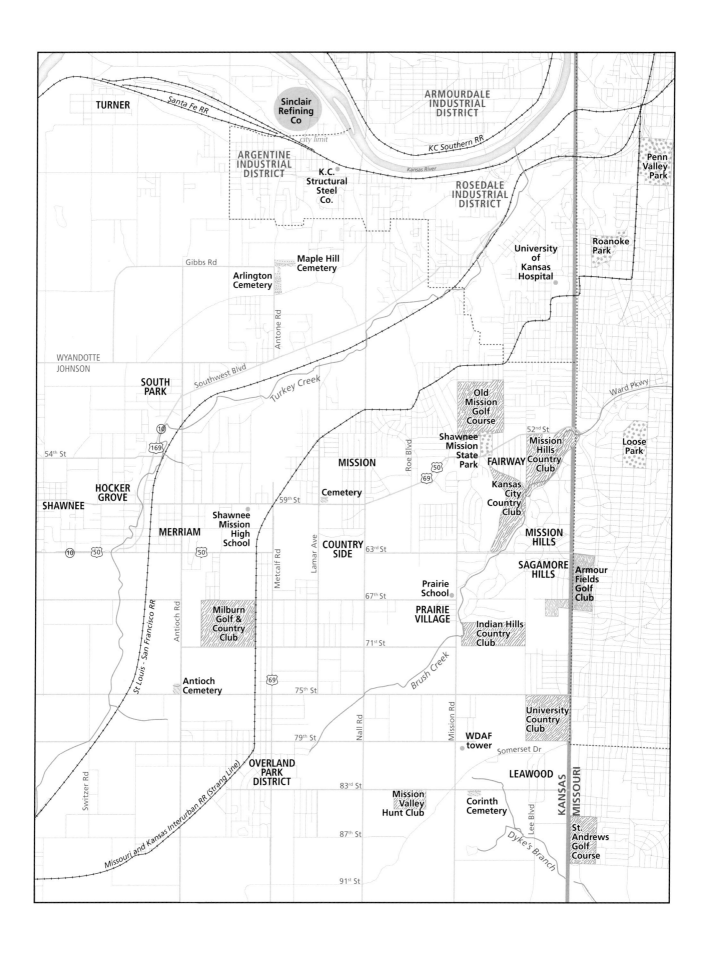

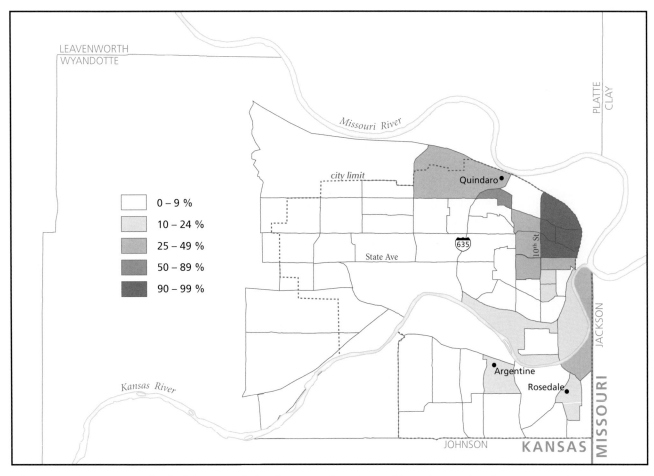

jobs (map 60). In 1960, a third of these people lived in Argentine, a third in eastern Armourdale and Armstrong, and a third in Strawberry Hill and the West Bottoms.

A person who travels south from Wyandotte County into Johnson County notices an abrupt change in the orientation of numbered streets. Instead of these routeways running north-south in the pattern begun at the city of Wyandott in 1857, they extend east-west. The change makes them fit seamlessly into the road grid of Jackson County to the east and suggests a closer economic and social connection to Kansas City, Missouri, than to Kansas City, Kansas. In fact, ever since the founding of Mission Hills in 1912, northeastern Johnson County has been the entire area's suburb of choice.

Having a city's elite housing district across a state line from its commercial and cultural core is rare, perhaps unique on the American scene. It certainly was not a scheme hatched by any Missouri politician because laws prohibited the annexa-

Map 58 (facing page). The Western Urban Fringe, 1944. Modified from the "Map of Greater Kansas City," included in Official Guide and Map of Greater Kansas City *(Kansas City, Mo.: Gallup Map and Stationery, 1944).*

Map 59. African American Population in Kansas City, Kansas, 1960. Data from U.S. Census.

tion of such property into the city—and therefore its taxation. The Kansas City school district was similarly prohibited from expansion of this type. Political isolation acquired a positive spin in the late 1950s, however, at least among many of the region's white residents. Separate school districts and separate governments promoted peace of mind in that time of racial tension.

It would be foolish to argue that racial issues were irrelevant to Johnson County's growth, given that the area's population was still 99.2 percent white in 1968. Certainly, these matters played a role. Yet the area's suburbanization goes back to before 1910, and its pattern of development through the 1960s likely would have been little different had the region's racial issues somehow disappeared. The original allures of the site, promoted separately by two different men, were statuary-laden estates geared to the wealthy and 1-acre tracts for people wanting more modest homes with space enough for swing sets and vegetable gardens.[75]

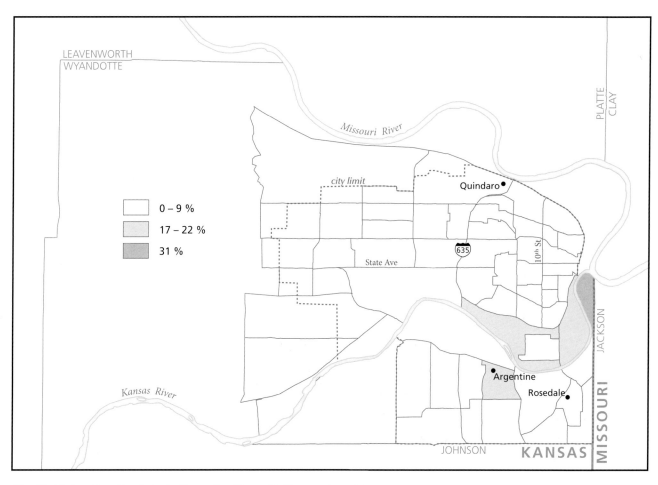

Map 60. Mexican-Born Population in Kansas City, Kansas, 1960. Data from U.S. Census.

I have already related the early story of J. C. Nichols and how he came to develop Mission Hills. This property lay adjacent to his Missouri holdings and was available at a reduced price because Kansas land was less prestigious. Turning undervalued fields into premium suburban holdings via a mansion district was risky but inspired real estate development. Not only did the maneuver yield profits from Mission Hills itself, but it also raised the value of adjacent acreage. Nichols, of course, had previously purchased nearly all of this land. It became the basis for Mission Woods, Westwood Hills, and Fairway to the north starting in 1937–1938; for the Sagamore Hills addition to Mission Hills to the south (1937); and for Prairie Village to the southwest (1941). The two largest of these developments—Fairway and Prairie Village—were designed specifically for the middle class as places where young families could enjoy tasteful bungalows and Cape Cod homes while basking in the reflected glory of country club life. In 1944, all these communities were still works in progress (map 58). Prairie Village, for example, consisted of only four blocks

of homes at the southwest corner of Sixty-seventh Street and Mission Road. Its name had been appropriated from the adjacent Prairie School.[76]

Although the Nichols developments were well positioned and early on the scene, several competitor communities existed. One of them—Shawnee, along the old ridge road between the Kansas River and Turkey Creek—dated to 1857 (maps 7 and 58). Two others started as nineteenth-century stations on the Missouri River, Fort Scott and Gulf Railroad as it ascended the valley of Turkey Creek. Merriam (named after a railroad official) served as the depot for Shawnee; Lenexa lay 4 miles farther to the southwest. All of these towns were relatively remote from urban jobs, however, and so they remained small villages for nearly a century.[77]

J. C. Nichols's chief rival in early Johnson County development was William B. Strang. Strang, the story goes, witnessed the devastation of Kansas City's working-class neighborhoods by the major flood of 1903. He saw the superiority of upland homesites and reasoned that construction of one of the newly popular interurban rail lines would allow him to create the suburb of his dreams. Quickly finding the needed financial backers, he purchased some 600 acres near the corner of what is now Seventy-ninth Street and Metcalf Avenue. His electric railroad, officially the Missouri and Kansas Interurban but known to all as the Strang Line, opened in 1906 (map 58). It started in Lenexa and paralleled the Gulf railroad (by then part of the St. Louis and San Francisco system) for a distance before turning east through Strang's properties. Next, the line went north, parallel to Metcalf, and then northeast along the upland between Brush and Turkey creeks. It entered Missouri just south of the University of Kansas Medical Center.[78]

Strang's commuter line proved popular. It encouraged the establishment of scattered housing developments along its route in what was to become Roeland Park and Mission, but through skillful promotion, Strang's own acreage drew the most interest. He liked the word *overland* because of its flood-free connotation and used it for six separate subdivision names. He constructed a large hall for dances and auctioned off as much as $30,000 worth of land during weekend promotional festivals. With many lots as big as an acre, Strang told buyers that they could have the good life—a new home, a family cow, and an easy trip to work. His Overland Park District had several thousand residents by the time of his death in 1921.[79]

Figure 36. Strawberry Hill Residences, 2010, the 400 Block of Ann Avenue. Although this neighborhood is strongly associated with Croatian culture, it was built in the 1880s for North European laborers. A German Methodist church used to occupy the west end of the block. Once Croats arrived after 1893, however, they stayed. Strawberry Hill homes are small but well maintained. Most, like the two frame ones here, sit on 25-foot lots and provide about 800 square feet of living space. (Photograph by Barbara Shortridge)

Nichols and Strang both believed in quality, and their reputations attracted other developers to the area. A few were active in the 1915–1929 period, including banker Richard W. Hocker, who laid out Hocker Grove just northwest of Merriam, and Louis D. Breyfogle, whose Mission Hills Acres

became the core of the future city of Mission (map 58). More promoters arrived in the late 1930s when Depression days were ending and federal home loan guarantees were beginning. Shawnee received a boost at this time via a subdivision built by realtor Richard O. Larsen. Roeland Park and Leawood also emerged. The development of Roeland Park,

Figure 37. Seventy-fifth Street and State Line Road, 1945, Looking Southwest. The pace of change has been fast in Johnson County. This view focuses on a vacant, 160-acre square that until recently had been the Meadow Lake Country Club. Piecemeal development exists in the foreground and along the new Lee Boulevard in the left distance. Somerset Drive angles south and west on the right horizon toward another golf course, Bel-Air. Plans existed briefly in the 1920s to convert the Meadow Lake tract into a university campus. (Courtesy Missouri Valley Special Collections, Kansas City Public Library)

across U.S. 50 north from Fairway, was an imitation of J. C. Nichols's approach, spearheaded by investor Charles E. Vawter. He borrowed the Roe name from a pioneer family in the area and sold homes in the price range of $4,000 to $6,000. Farther south, the brothers John and Gene Kroh purchased a 1,000-acre farm from retired oilman Oscar G. Lee. This land abutted J. C. Nichols property on the north at Seventy-ninth and State Line Road and ran .5 miles west and 3 miles

south. The brothers' plan, taking advantage of proximity to Mission Hills, was to pursue the upper-middle-class market. Naming their development Leawood, they platted lots with a minimum frontage of 100 feet and built individualistic homes selling for several thousand dollars more than those in Fairway or Roeland Park.[80]

Johnson County home buyers before about 1950 thought in terms of neighborhoods, not cities. Volunteers handled what few civic duties existed, schools were left to independent boards, and public utilities were purchased from adjacent Kansas City. Then, when the service burden on the rural township structure grew too heavy, the state legislature approved the creation of urban townships in 1951. This move would allow Mission and Shawnee townships (Antioch Road was the boundary) to function essentially as cities, but jealousies soon prevailed and separate incorporations began.[81]

Postwar growth was unprecedented in northeastern Johnson County. Officials issued over a thousand building permits annually between 1946 and 1949. Six communities had incorporated by 1950 with a population total of 6,472, and another 26,492 people lived elsewhere in the two townships. Builders under contract to the J. C. Nichols Company were completing a new home every day in Prairie Village, and local wags had nicknamed the town Pregnant Village. By 1960, the inner ring of suburbs—including Fairway, Mission Hills, Prairie Village, and Roeland Park—was essentially full, and people were rethinking how best to manage the expansion (table 1). One influential group, the Johnson County Junior Chamber of Commerce, reasoned that bigger cities could provide more efficient services. Leaders therefore petitioned to ensure that the next new incorporation, Overland Park, would include enough subdivisions to encompass at least 25,000 people. They were successful in a vote held on May 20, 1960.[82]

Once begun, Johnson County growth never faltered. Five thousand people arrived each year throughout the 1950s and 1960s, and the outer suburbs led by Overland Park annexed new land to accommodate the influx. Beyond the elite image of Mission Hills and the continuing good reputations of the Nichols and Kroh Brothers companies, at least three

other forces aided the trend. One was Interstate Highway 35, which opened in 1959 following the St. Louis and San Francisco rail route up Turkey Creek. Essentially an automobile version of the Strang Line (which had ceased service in 1940), it created easy commutes into the central city from Overland Park, Lenexa, and even the county seat of Olathe.[83]

Two other factors were interconnected. During the time when cooperative neighborhood agreements still predominated over formal city governments, a consolidated school system emerged in northeastern Johnson County. The process began in 1922 with the opening of Shawnee Mission Rural High School on Johnson Drive just east of Merriam (the name came from the two townships being served by the alliance). Voters kept the unified spirit intact when enrollments necessitated a second high school in 1958 (Shawnee Mission East in Prairie Village) and a third in 1968 (Shawnee Mission West in Overland Park). This system, strongly supported by the young families who had just moved to the area, stood in stark contrast to the public schools of both Kansas City, Missouri, and Kansas City, Kansas. Johnson County had money and, with a nearly homogeneous population, no racial tensions. White newcomers to the Kansas City area, whether racially prejudiced or not, found the advantages of life in Leawood, Overland Park, and Shawnee hard to resist.[84]

6 Geography in Black and White, 1968–1991

As postwar suburbs and new interstate highways ushered in a full-blown automobile culture in the 1960s, 1970s, and 1980s, the landscape that was created came to dominate American urban discussions. Edge city, as people called this new growth on the periphery, generally was assessed in positive terms. Business parks were bringing jobs to the suburban beltways, where they joined with preexisting shopping centers to produce a nearly self-contained life for middle- and upper-class residents. Everything seemed fresh and hopeful.[1]

Still, the very phrase *edge city* suggests a limitation to overly optimistic thinking. If the edge of a community is prospering, what has happened to its core? The answer for metropolitan Kansas City and many other communities was decay, partial abandonment, and an increasingly segregated African American population. This emerging pattern, clear in retrospect, nevertheless caught many white residents by surprise. Enjoying the new amenities of the urban periphery, they naively assumed that life in the central business district, the West Bottoms, and the residential neighborhoods immediately east and west of this core remained much as it had been in the early 1950s. Other suburban people undoubtedly knew of the inner-city regressions but chose not to acknowledge them fully. Either way—conceded or not—a new and profound bifurcation of the city had occurred.[2]

Kansas City's traditional division into Missouri and Kansas segments did not disappear in the new reality. It remained a deterrent to efficient planning and political action, but in other ways, it retreated to being little more than a rationale for university sports discussions. Much higher priority now

was accorded to a racial and income chasm that followed along Troost Avenue (map 61). A person could extend this line of demarcation north to the railroad tracks along OK Creek where it turned west and southwest to follow near Interstate 35 and Southwest Boulevard to about Steele Avenue in Kansas. Steele separates the industrial sections of Rosedale, Argentine, and Turner from newer subdivisions. To the north, in central Kansas City, Kansas, the line between haves and have-nots blurred, but it was approximated by Fifty-ninth Street. It sharpened again at the Missouri River, and this stream served as the divide all the way east to the Blue River valley and Interstate 435. Finally, on the metropolis's south and southeastern sides, indistinctness returned. This was (and is) an area of inner-city expansion, with Raytown and Grandview changing character over the 1960–1990 period. Looking inside this meandering and unmarked but ever-clearer socioeconomic boundary, the obvious core was and is the central business district of both Kansas City, Kansas, and Kansas City, Missouri. These former rivals were now united in common struggle. Allied with them were most of the older industrial districts in the river bottoms, their flanking blue-collar residential areas, and two much-enlarged African American ghettos.

Before exploring the nature of the shiny and the shabby sides of Kansas City, it is important to consider how such a major divide could have developed with relatively little public comment or apparent concern. Part of the reason, of course, is that the impoverished people of the inner city lacked a voice in major media outlets. Another part is that sufficient

130

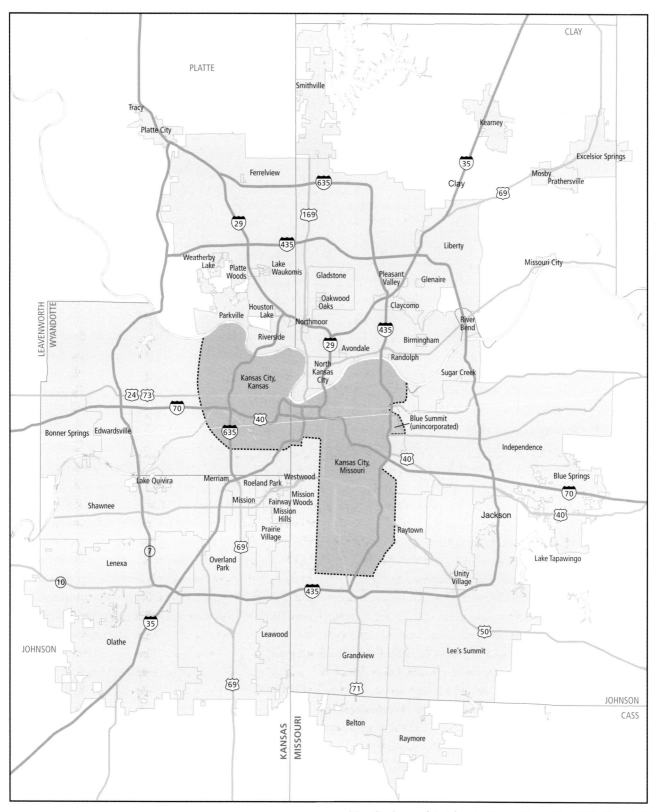

CLAY

PLATTE

Smithville

Tracy

Platte City

Kearney

Excelsior Springs

Ferrelview

35

Mosby
Prathersville

Clay

69

169

29

435

Liberty

Missouri City

Weatherby
Lake

Platte
Woods

Lake
Waukomis

Gladstone

Pleasant
Valley

Glenaire

Oakwood
Oaks

Parkville

Houston
Lake

Northmoor

Claycomo

River
Bend

435

Riverside

29

Avondale

Birmingham

LEAVENWORTH

WYANDOTTE

Kansas City,
Kansas

North
Kansas
City

Randolph

Sugar Creek

24 73

70

40

Blue Summit
(unincorporated)

635

Independence

Bonner Springs

Edwardsville

Lake Quivira

Merriam

Westwood

Kansas City,
Missouri

Blue Springs

Roeland Park

70

Mission

Shawnee

Mission

Fairway Woods

40

40

Mission
Hills

Jackson

Prairie
Village

Raytown

Lake Tapawingo

7

69

Lenexa

Overland
Park

10

Unity
Village

35

50

Olathe

Leawood

Lee's Summit

JOHNSON

Grandview

69

71

JOHNSON

KANSAS

MISSOURI

CASS

Belton

Raymore

*Map 61. Core and Periphery in Greater Kansas City, 1990. Compiled
from multiple sources.*

economic and political progress was being made within the city's black community to forestall protests on the vaguer issue of regional isolation. Still another set of explanations emanates from the city's white establishment. Suburbanites obviously could live isolated in their edge-city cocoons. Understanding the motives of business leaders is a more complex undertaking. Speaking out about problem areas might not have been good for commerce, yet the downtown area where banks, advertising agencies, and other offices were concentrated was definitely part of the inner-city dilemma. Could these nabobs somehow alleviate the decay without having to broadcast that it actually existed?

The quandary of Kansas City business leaders was in many ways that of the community as a whole. Residents had become immensely proud of their collective hometown during the immediate postwar years and throughout the 1950s. As the military industries transformed themselves into successful civilian manufacturers, they and the innovative Midwest Research Institute promised a diversified and growing economy. A united effort to recover from the great flood of 1951 boosted self-esteem further, and people felt rewarded in 1955 and 1964 when baseball and then football authorities declared Kansas City to be officially major league. Innovative and ambitious designs for a new international airport and a sports complex continued the good feelings into the next decade. The city, residents reasoned, was about to escape its long-standing and limiting image of an agricultural processing center.[3]

Local publicists supported claims to sophistication first by pointing to steady growth. From 468,622 residents in 1950, annexation had enabled Kansas City, Missouri, to increase to 507,087 by 1970 even without counting the suburbs. Kansas City, Kansas, saw similar progress, from 129,553 residents to 168,213. With the two numbers combined, the metropolis ranked as the fifteenth largest in the nation, ahead of old rival St. Louis and also such established communities as Boston, Cincinnati, New Orleans, and Pittsburgh. Boosters next touted new industries, citing the city's number two position in automobile assembly behind Detroit, and then the wonders of the Country Club District and the Nelson gallery. Their best efforts notwithstanding, however, the boosters knew that article after article by outside observers still began with an old stereotype. As one writer worded it, the city was "a cowtown isolated mid dry dusty plains and prairies, [and] impervious to cultural currents from the coast."[4]

The stubborn persistence of country hick symbolism despite a host of achievements frustrated many residents. Some worked directly to allay this image. In 1972, they initiated a campaign called Prime Time, which stressed the high quality of life in the Midwest. Its slogans, that Kansas City was "one of the few livable cities left" and "the nation's inland capital," were popular locally. But to outsiders, these phrases inadvertently reinforced an out-of-the-mainstream image. Sensing that the target had been missed, chamber of commerce officials quickly retooled their ads to stress glamour and sophistication. Now the slogans touted Kansas City as having "more fountains than Rome, more boulevards than Paris." Many national publications repeated this phrase, but again, the effect was minimal. Outsider opinion remained fixed, and a few inside observers began to accuse the promoters of pretention.[5]

The most damaging repercussion of the gap between local achievement and outsider response involved its effect on the self-confidence of residents. These people "yearn for compliments," wrote a New York reporter in 1973. "One of the first things an outsider notices about this city is its deep-seated inferiority complex, its Babbitt-like desire to be accepted, its paranoia about its wallflower reputation." Such an attitude, reported widely by observers, produced an overanxious questioning of visitors—"How do you like it here?"—and, according to one account, an odd obsession with imperial names: the Monarchs and Royals baseball teams, the Kings in basketball, the American Royal Livestock and Horse Show, and the crown symbol for Hallmark Cards. Much more significant, this mind-set led to a cult of conservatism. An expatriate writer, Richard Rhodes, went so far as to call suburban Kansas City the core of "cupcake land," a place of well-scrubbed blandness where critical-thinking skills atrophy and people judge serious social problems too unpleasant for conversation.[6]

Downtown

Because leaders of American cities in the 1950s were obsessed with annexation, suburban shopping centers, and interstate highways, downtown business districts were inevitably neglected. The Kansas City situation was better than most, for a new freeway loop provided good access and an accompanying garage beneath Barney Allis Plaza offered convenient parking. Still, decay was evident by the middle 1960s, especially a loss of retail stores to suburban malls. This situation could be ignored for a while so long as anchor stores remained; I remember my mother persistently making pilgrimages to Harzfeld's, Woolf Brothers, Emery Bird's, and the Forum cafeteria in those years just as she had in the 1940s. It ended quickly, however. The symbolic year was 1968 when Emery Bird's, the city's premier department store, closed its six-story, full-block operation on Petticoat Lane.[7]

This is not to say that downtown died in the 1960s, but its character did change drastically. A guide for visitors to the Republican National Convention that the city hosted in 1976, for example, recommended a trip to the Country Club Plaza for shopping, since "downtown Kansas City, like most downtowns, offers little these days." Some smaller stores persisted, but these repositioned themselves away from a general middle-class clientele and toward one of two specialty audiences—office workers or low-income minorities from the adjacent public housing projects. By 1978, downtown had become the city's principal black shopping district. Still another set of enterprises served the down-and-out. Transient hotels were common at the time, including the Cordova at Twelfth and Pennsylvania and the New Frederic at 312 East Ninth. The north side of Twelfth Street between Wyandotte and Central was a continuous row of seedy bars and peep shows, and Sanderson's Lunch at 104 East Eighth Street served as a gathering place for the area's homeless, desperate, or eccentric citizens. It was an interesting neighborhood but not one that city officials wanted to advertise.[8]

Sheer distance from the suburbs and the low incomes of more proximate residents would have forced changes on downtown Kansas City regardless of the wishes of political and economic leaders. Nevertheless, the transition from general center to a more specialized role could have been planned and executed better were it not for jealousies among the local elite. The key players once city manager L. P. Cookingham had departed the scene in 1959 were banker James M. Kemper (head of the Commerce Trust Company) and his brothers R. Crosby Kemper and William T. Kemper, Jr. Together with sons R. Crosby, Jr., and James M., Jr., these men controlled two of the city's largest banks and some seven blocks of core real estate downtown. In 1965, they built the tallest structure in the state, the thirty-two-story Commerce Tower at the corner of Ninth and Main (map 62). So far so good, for this building anchored the northern end of downtown as Cookingham had envisioned, and a freeway ramp funneled traffic to its doorstep. In the same way, Congressman Richard Bolling

secured the eastern portal. In 1963, he obtained funding for a massive new federal office building at 601 East Twelfth Street. This structure fit in well with the city hall–courthouse civic complex that dominated that area and greatly increased the number of government workers in the urban core.[9]

The coordinated planning fell apart at the next stage. James Kemper hoped to develop a city garage across Main Street from his new tower to complete another part of Cookingham's blueprint. But he was thwarted in this when an independent local developer, Robert Ingram, proposed a more elaborate solution for the site—a garage topped by another office tower. Ingram obtained the contract along with a promise from the Kansas City Board of Trade to relocate offices there from an outdated building at Tenth and Wyandotte. An angry Kemper used his influence to delay this project for several years. The obstruction nearly forced Ingram into bankruptcy and caused Board of Trade officials to build instead near the Country Club Plaza. Ingram's skyscraper, TenMain Center, finally opened in 1968, but downtown redevelopment lost critical momentum.[10]

Encouraging new construction to keep corporate offices and major law firms downtown was a sound strategy for planners. So was the complementary pursuit of modern hotels and meeting sites to attract conventioneers. Municipal Auditorium and the nearby Muehlebach Hotel had functioned admirably in this role since the 1930s, but both were undersized in the current market. A timely solution emerged in 1963 when Lewis Kitchen, a local realtor with financing from the New York firm of Kidder, Peabody and Company, proposed a $16 million hotel and convention center. This complex, with management from Hilton Hotels, was to be just west of Municipal Auditorium (which would be retained for smaller events) and adjacent to Kitchen's earlier renewal projects on Quality Hill. Again, though, jealousies prevailed. Owners of existing hotels claimed that a state law to extend the powers of eminent domain to renewal projects did not apply in this case. The suit proved baseless, but it took two years to clear the Missouri Supreme Court and then two more at the federal level.[11]

The delays caused Kitchen to pull his plan, and almost immediately, most of the city's major convention clients departed en masse. Although the owners of the venerable Muehlebach at Twelfth and Baltimore refurbished their rooms and added on a $4 million convention hall, these efforts were inadequate. Bartle Hall, a city-sponsored arena

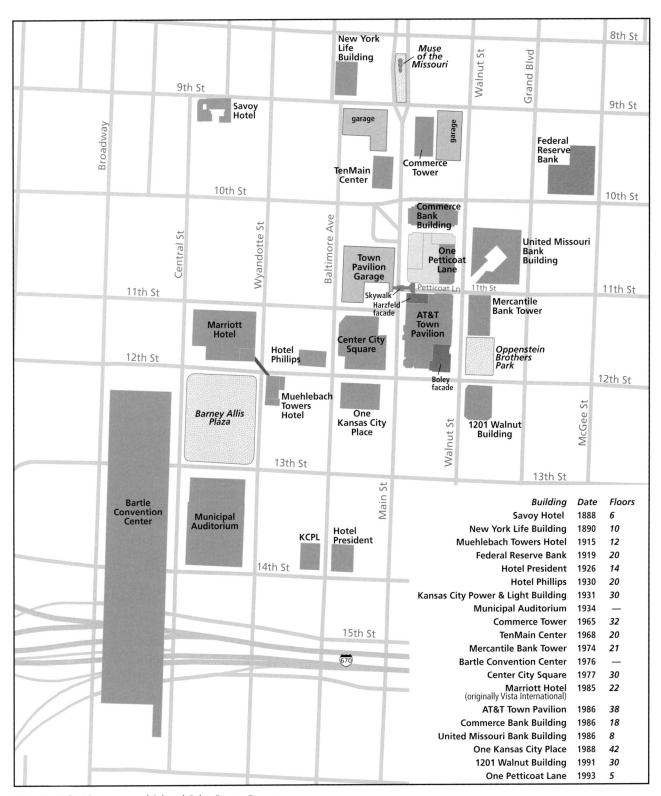

Building	Date	Floors
Savoy Hotel	1888	6
New York Life Building	1890	10
Muehlebach Towers Hotel	1915	12
Federal Reserve Bank	1919	20
Hotel President	1926	14
Hotel Phillips	1930	20
Kansas City Power & Light Building	1931	30
Municipal Auditorium	1934	—
Commerce Tower	1965	32
TenMain Center	1968	20
Mercantile Bank Tower	1974	21
Bartle Convention Center	1976	—
Center City Square	1977	30
Marriott Hotel (originally Vista International)	1985	22
AT&T Town Pavilion	1986	38
Commerce Bank Building	1986	18
United Missouri Bank Building	1986	8
One Kansas City Place	1988	42
1201 Walnut Building	1991	30
One Petticoat Lane	1993	5

Map 62. Office Skyscrapers and Selected Other Sites in Downtown Kansas City, Missouri, 1993. Compiled from multiple sources.

large enough to be competitive, did not open until 1976, and a similarly large convention hotel was delayed nine years more. Complete civic embarrassment on this front was avoided only when a consortium led by Irvine Hockaday of Kansas City Southern Industries and R. Crosby Kemper, Jr., finally assembled $54 million to construct the Vista International Hotel. When this facility opened in 1985 on Twelfth Street north of the Allis Plaza, leaders took the expected bows. The project did indeed restore a measure of competitiveness for national meetings and, as a bonus, removed the worst of the Twelfth Street bars. Still, damage had been done, and Kansas City lost its reputation as a top convention destination.[12]

The eminent domain lawsuit over Kitchen's hotel affected renewal efforts of all types, but the delay allowed time for ambitious planning. Builders saw a need for additional office space downtown and, increasingly, for projects that might revive retail sales and promote entertainment. In fact, as soon as the U.S. Supreme Court reaffirmed the state's development laws in 1967, a Kemper-backed group announced an extremely ambitious venture called Towne Center. This project would involve a selective clearing of about eleven square blocks between Twelfth Street and Truman Road, Wyandotte to Oak. Promoters planned a new department store along with an entertainment district, a covered shopping mall, offices, apartments, and garages. The total cost would be $100 million, with a completion date of 1976. This was development on a scale never seen before in the urban core. It had solid financial backing and a chance to truly revive the entire district. Following a familiar pattern, however, Towne Center never materialized. The problem this time was not jealousy but instead the unexpected and nearly simultaneous announcement of a comparable project ten blocks farther south.[13]

The rival project, also $100 million in scope, was what became Crown Center. This development was a private undertaking by the Hall family, owners of Hallmark Cards, Inc. Seeing decay invade the neighborhood of their corporate offices just southeast of Union Station on Grand Avenue and

Figure 38. Crown Center Square, 2008. Looking Southeast. A large plaza at the center of the Hall family's $400 million complex of offices, shops, residences, and hotels has become popular as a community gathering spot. It features seasonally an ice-skating rink (under the white tent) and a "dancing waters" fountain complete with forty-nine synchronized jets and colored lights. An office building (left) and the Hallmark offices frame the open area. (Courtesy Wikimedia Commons)

yet strongly believing in the future of the city, the Halls decided to redevelop rather than relocate. Their scale was nearly unprecedented—fifty buildings on 85 acres—and their planning meticulous. Using medium-height structures to symbolize a position between downtown and the suburbs, this city within the city included an office complex, a substantial hotel, apartments, and a shopping center. The Halls hid most of the parking underground and created sight lines to highlight a terraced, 10-acre "village square."[14]

Although cost estimates escalated to $200 million and then to $400 million, the Halls persisted with their dream and even added a second major hotel. Their work garnered praise across the country, and local people admired and patronized the center's international-themed shopping and upscale entertainment. Essentially a second Country Club Plaza, Crown Center bolstered everybody's self-esteem. Yet when questions are asked about the project's effect on its broader neighborhood, the answers are mixed. Certainly, its luster helped to preserve the appeal of Liberty Memorial on its western flank and the city's complex of health care buildings on the east. But the development hurt downtown proper. Several corporate headquarters moved the ten blocks south, and so did numerous conventions. More important, Crown Center's shopping center, including Hall's namesake

Figure 39. R. Crosby Kemper Memorial Arena, 2012, Looking Southwest. Although only a mile from the city center, the arena's location in the West Bottoms is actually quite isolated. A futuristic design with bold outside trusses won architectural awards, but a dramatic roof collapse in 1979 hurt the arena's credibility as a sports venue. The building was expanded in 1997, but when the new Sprint Center opened downtown in 2007, Kemper's role was reduced even further. (Photograph by Barbara Shortridge)

Intercollegiate Athletics (NAIA). A new facility was needed by about 1970, however, and sites were available downtown in the district's northwest or northeast corners. This option, in fact, had recently been considered for a baseball field before the suburban site east on Interstate 70 was selected. Now, with downtown clearly in need of attention, the decision should have been easy.

Kansas City received its sports arena in timely fashion when the Kemper family generously adopted this cause as its own. But with money comes power, and R. Crosby Kemper, Jr., chose to build elsewhere. Prices in the urban core were high, of course, but this apparently was not the deciding factor. Saying that "symbolically, the guts of the town are down there," he decreed that the R. Crosby Kemper Memorial Arena would be on former stockyard land in the West Bottoms. The site, just north of the Twenty-third Street Trafficway, permitted easy access and parking but had little else to recommend it. People complained about the isolation and bleak surroundings at the grand opening in 1974, and the grumbling continued even as the building's sleek, futuristic design won architectural awards. At the Republican National Convention held there in 1976, a reporter slyly observed that "delegates heading for the hall will encounter such scenery as the Columbia Burlap Co. and the Sweet Lassy Feed Co."[16]

When Kemper Arena opened, the West Bottoms was nearly vacant. The giant packers were in the process of relocating to smaller cities on the Great Plains, and warehouse owners were moving to new industrial parks along the interstate highways. Perhaps the philanthropist hoped that his gift

department store, inhibited the revival of a similar retail forum on Petticoat Lane.[15]

Just as the rebirth of upscale retail stores downtown was sidetracked by Crown Center, another unilateral decision at the time did the same to sports entertainment. Municipal Auditorium contained an arena nicely suited to basketball, and the city used it annually to host both a profitable, preseason tournament for the surrounding Big 8 Conference and the small-college championship of the National Association of

might inspire other investment there, but like Crown Center, the effort was flawed: it dispersed the limited resources of the city over too wide a geographic area. Had the largesse of Kemper and that of the Halls both been applied to downtown proper, that district likely would have flourished. As it was, downtown continued to struggle, Kemper Arena's isolation became a source of jokes, and Crown Center survived only with massive infusions of the owners' money.

With a sports arena and a major shopping and entertainment facility no longer possibilities for downtown, a corporate office center became the primary objective. This was a narrow economic platform, and it made local planners of the time susceptible to a dubious proposal from a Philadelphia developer. Thomas McCloskey had gained control of the entire block bounded by Eleventh and Twelfth streets, Baltimore and Main (map 62). On this, he erected City Center Square, a thirty-story office tower atop a four-story base building dedicated to retail shops. Kansas City officials liked this combined usage, thinking that stores tied directly to corporate offices would now be the best way to broaden the range of downtown offerings. The building opened in 1977

Figure 40. Downtown Kansas City, Missouri, 1999, Looking Northwest from Thirteenth and McGee. With shopping and sports activity removed to other sites by the 1970s, the central city was left as a land of business suits. New glass-skinned skyscrapers signified the change. From the left, these include One Kansas City Place (1988), City Center Square (1977), the 1201 Walnut Building (1991), AT&T Town Pavilion (1986, partly hidden), and the Mercantile Bank Tower (1974). Much of the rest is parking garages and vacant lots. (Courtesy Missouri Valley Special Collections, Kansas City Public Library)

to plaudits about "bringing new life to the area," but struggles began almost immediately. Because the design had skimped on parking, shoppers were fewer than anticipated and corporations reconsidered their leases. When the occupancy rate dropped below 50 percent in 1991, the owners defaulted on their loan. Conditions improved after that point but only marginally.[17]

Two more skyscrapers, each in turn being the city's tallest building, completed the conversion of the downtown district into a sleek and shiny office world. Both structures were constructed by local firms during the national business boom of the 1980s. Each had major tenants lined up from the start and incorporated space for adequate parking. The first, the

137

AT&T Town Pavilion, opened in 1986 on the block adjacent to City Center Square on the east. It was a joint venture of the namesake company with entrepreneur Frank Morgan and the developers Copaken, White and Blitt. The second, One Kansas City Place, was financed primarily by Morgan and adjoined City Center Square south across Twelfth Street. Both buildings are encased within blue stained glass, and they soar into the air for thirty-eight and forty-two stories, respectively.

Although the pair of massive buildings are of similar size and appearance, their construction evoked different symbolic messages. Work on the earlier Town Pavilion carried with it a last round of hope for a downtown renaissance; One Kansas City Place, although only two years younger, was seen as a capitulation of that hope to the narrower world of suits and briefcases. With the Town Pavilion project, Kansas City leaders saw themselves finally united after earlier miscalculations and petty jealousies. This was to be City Center Square done right. They reasoned that AT&T's commitment to downtown would inspire other major companies to sign on as well, and quality shops would bring in outsiders. Part of the retail optimism stemmed from the fact that the Dillard's company had agreed to establish a department store in the complex. Another factor was that Town Pavilion was physically part of the iconic Petticoat Lane, with a design that preserved the facade of the old Harzfeld's building. Officials predicted a shopping volume that would rival that of the Country Club Plaza and the new Crown Center.[18]

The elaborate hopes for Town Pavilion proved unsustainable. The project was a success in that AT&T's decision to remain downtown created the desired corporate domino effect. Both Kemper-owned banks—Commerce and United Missouri—constructed new facilities between Tenth and Eleventh streets, for example, and firms bid against one another to secure spots in the new One Kansas City Place. But the shopping venture was largely a failure. Suburbanites would not drive so far for goods they could purchase closer at hand, office workers ordered little more than lunch, and the urban poor looked in vain for less expensive selections. Dillard's soon withdrew its commitment.[19]

One Kansas City Place was more a product of speculation than civic pride. This building was conceived during the flush 1980s, and secretive developer Frank Morgan hoped to transform the entire south side of downtown into a business paradise called Kansas City Place. His proposal for four office towers interspersed with apartment and retail buildings struck many observers as overly ambitious. Suspect funding together with the collapse of an economic bubble in 1987 forced a scaling back to the single skyscraper.[20]

Questions about the changing role of downtown Kansas City can be given useful context by contrasting that area's recent history with that of three nearby neighborhoods: the original business district between Sixth Street and the river; downtown Kansas City, Kansas; and the old Westport business district near Forty-second and Broadway. As on Petticoat Lane, local leaders in these places saw the need to reimagine their traditional roles. In two cases, the efforts were low-budget, grassroot affairs, whereas the third—Kansas City, Kansas—involved big federal money. Ultimately, the degree of success correlated more with the type of plan envisioned than with the number of dollars spent.

In 1970, all three neighborhoods faced declines at least as severe as those at Twelfth and Main. Sales at the traditional retailers along Minnesota Avenue in Kansas were stagnant, Westport's population was aging rapidly, and the stores in the North End were small and largely decrepit. Residents saw a need for action, but only those in Kansas City, Kansas, had an independent government and therefore a means of raising substantial money on their own.

An outside threat aroused the people of Westport. When a business group in 1971 proposed replacement of an older housing area with condominiums and shops, residents lobbied for preservation instead. The neighborhood won and then wisely used its organization to promote a broad-based renovation of sidewalks, parks, homes, and small businesses. As improvements began to appear, county and city officials contributed modest amounts of money to the cause. By the late 1970s, Westport had been transformed from a near slum into a healthy, diversified neighborhood with a business emphasis on art and entertainment.[21]

Development in the North End, like that in Westport, came largely through private investment. This time, however, the initiative was individual rather than group. Marion A. Trozzolo, an entrepreneur who relocated from Chicago to run a plastics factory, saw economic potential in the low commercial buildings near Market Square. His model was Old Town Chicago (and, by extension, the French Quarter in New Orleans and Ghirardelli Square in San Francisco), where a rich intermixture of townhouses with restaurants, art studios, craft stores, upscale bars, and the like had created an entertainment district close enough to downtown to attract convention attendees.[22]

Trozzolo acquired twenty-one pieces of property by 1972 and began to market his dream. The River Quay, as he called it, was an immediate success—"a quaint jumble of boutiques, renovated cabooses, restaurants . . . and scenes of rollicking nightlife." Activity peaked in 1974. Trozzolo realized that he lacked the time and resources to manage the somewhat unconventional enterprise, but he could not find a local partner. Without firm leadership, promoters clashed over how many saloons to license and whether to allow striptease operations. Possibly because of links to organized crime, their conflict then escalated to violence, with at least four local murders, two dynamite blasts, and two cases of arson. The River Quay's fall was as rapid as its rise, and only one of the new businesses still operated in 1977.[23]

Merchants in Westport were the primary beneficiaries of River Quay's decline. As for the North End itself, storefronts remained largely empty for some nine years. Then, the same wave of economic prosperity that produced skyscraper construction downtown generated dollars for the renewal of old Delaware Street and the city market. This time, the goal was less entertainment and more a mixture of townhouses and small shops that might appeal to a new generation of urban sophisticates. Greenwich Village was now the model rather than the French Quarter. This movement stalled somewhat when money became tighter in the late 1980s, but otherwise, it has continued to the present.[24]

Merchants on Minnesota Avenue always knew that Wyandotte County residents spent part of their money in downtown Kansas City, Missouri. These retailers could accept such behavior for luxury goods, but they worked hard to retain basic middle-class services. Montgomery Ward and J. C. Penney were their signature stores. This strategy worked well through the 1950s, but after accounting for inflation, sales became nearly flat over the next decade. The solution, leaders decided, was an urban renewal grant from the federal government.[25]

The ease of obtaining federal money at the time made a renewal experiment almost inevitable. So did the acknowledged success of the city's initial foray of this type—Gateway Center—which by 1968 had replaced the slum-filled area north of Minnesota Avenue between Third and Fifth streets with a gleaming new bank, a ten-story office building, a Holiday Inn, and low-income housing. Local architects therefore conceived a $20 million project called Center City. This development would convert the 600 and 700 blocks of Minnesota Avenue into a mall. Cars would be shunted to off-street garages, and in their place, the street would become a stylized homage to the Kansas landscape. For instance, stainless steel pylons were designed for the Seventh Street intersection to symbolize either grain elevators or city skyscrapers. A split hemisphere farther west could represent an Indian mound or a hill penetrated by a highway cut.[26]

Construction began in 1969 amid hopes that the result would be "so attractive that people for miles around will come to look and shop, and merchants will be attracted to bid for space." Nothing close to this vision materialized. In fact, shoppers and merchants alike judged the project a failure even before it was completed. Montgomery Ward relocated its store to the suburbs in the early 1970s, followed quickly by Adler's, Helzberg's jewelry, and J. C. Penney. Although some people at the time blamed such moves on the chaos of construction, it is more accurate to see the Center City project as a last, desperate attempt to reverse long-term trends. The situation on Minnesota Avenue was similar to that across the Intercity Viaduct: suburbanization and shopping malls attracted former patrons, and nearby low-income housing projects yielded customers who required different types of stores.[27]

By the mid-1980s, a new economic strategy was obvious downtown. First, the split hemisphere and pylons were removed in order to once again allow streetside parking. A different set of businesses then emerged. Many of these—cafés, savings-and-loan offices, dollar stores—catered to the immediate neighborhood rather than to the larger municipality as before. Other entrepreneurs followed the lead of their sister city and worked to entice corporate and governmental clients. The mix of offices came to include headquarters for two large banks that remained from previous decades plus the Board of Public Utilities and the municipal library. The biggest coup, however, came in 1985 when Senator Bob Dole relocated the regional office of the Environmental Protection Agency from Missouri. The federal bureaucrats initially occupied one of the vacant department stores, but in 1998, they moved into a new $30 million building at the corner of Fifth and Minnesota.[28]

School Desegregation and Inner-city Neighborhoods

Common sense in the automobile age would suggest that the oldest parts of a city would be the poorest. New developments occur on the urban periphery, of course, and restrictive covenants designed to maintain housing status date back only

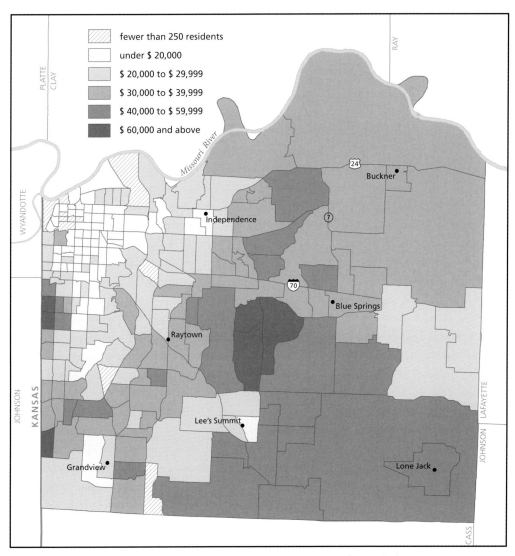

Map 63. Median Household Income in Jackson County, Missouri, 1990. Data from U.S. Census.

as far as the 1910s. Earlier construction, most of it found in a loose ring around the downtown core, would gradually deteriorate and be occupied by residents with incomes too low to allow them alternatives. This generality fit much of Kansas City in 1990. A zone of poverty encompassed eastern Wyandotte County, while the urbanized portions of Clay, Johnson, and Platte counties escaped such a fate because of their relatively recent development (maps 61 and 63). In contrast, the model partially fails in Jackson County. The area just east of downtown was poor as expected, but the situation to the south was more complicated. Near the state line, high-income people lived close to downtown. East of Troost Avenue, this wealth disappeared, and a low-income zone extended all the way to Ninety-fifth Street.

The Troost Avenue boundary provides a key to this anom-

aly. In the 1950s (as I described in chapter 5), this street had become the dividing line between black and white school districts, and its persistence more than a generation later as a major cultural divide is evidence that Kansas City people never dealt successfully with segregated schools. Indeed, educational policy explains much of the community's current cultural geography.

Integration began in 1955 with hope and goodwill on all sides. A sixth of the district's 61,000 pupils were African American, and as elementary school boundaries were reconfigured to ensure mixed populations at most sites, requests from parents to change districts were no more numerous than in previous years. Two years later, the report was much the same, although the percentage of black students citywide had risen to 22. The faculty was now integrated, and leaders were proud that racial mixing in the schools exceeded that of the community at large.[29]

Optimism about the school system persisted into the early 1960s. Although the "Troost Wall" was now a fact of life and although enrollment at Central High School (the city's long-time premier institution) had jumped from 42 percent black in 1958–1959 to 90 percent black in 1960–1961, the quality of instruction remained high. Central sent as many students on to college as it had during the all-white years. People also praised increases in the percentage of African American teachers and administrators.[30]

True villains are hard to find in the story of Kansas City's schools, but the program of racial integration that had started so smoothly stumbled badly over the next five decades. First, in the name of providing neighborhood schools, the board decided not to force racial balance through extensive busing. This action was rational, but it led many white families to move. Some did so out of prejudice, others because of fears of conflict or falling educational standards. These people often remained within the overall Kansas City school district initially, but the majority eventually affiliated with adjacent suburbs (map 56).

In retrospect, 1969 was a pivotal year. Voters that spring approved a routine tax increase for a school system in which white students had just lost their long-standing majority status. Nineteen additional proposals for school-support money would appear on the ballot over the next two decades, but none of them passed. A downward spiral thus began that soon collapsed the entire system: Good teachers took jobs elsewhere, paint peeled, parents with even moderate incomes moved out, and test scores fell. One federal judge who became involved with the issue said later that he had never seen a prison in such bad shape as the Kansas City schools of the early 1980s.[31]

To understand the crumbling schools, it is important to note that no parallel crises occurred with other city services such as road repair or police protection. The difference was not overt racism but rather a basic (and often overlooked) geographic difference between the territory politically part of Kansas City and that included within the Kansas City school district (map 56). Because of annexations and the rise of suburban schools, the city's school district by the 1970s encompassed less than half the acreage of the total city. Moreover, this district's population was and is disproportionately poor and black. The negative votes on school levies in the 1970s and 1980s largely reflected local incomes.

How could the crisis be resolved? Kansas City's schools had become some of the most segregated in the nation by 1976, so much so that government officials that year cut off the district's federal funds in order to force a solution. The local board responded by hiring its first African American superintendent, Robert R. Wheeler, and expanding its busing program to include some 29,300 children. This tactic was expensive for a poor district and had limited potential anyway, since the total pool of white students was shrinking fast. Realizing these facts and seeing no solution within their own means, members of the school board decided to file a suit in federal court.[32]

The board argued that the governments of Missouri and Kansas, through their segregation laws of the past, had contributed to the high concentration of poor minorities within the school district. Both states, it contended, should be held accountable. So should the federal government (for its locationally concentrated public housing projects) and eighteen suburban school districts in Missouri and Kansas. The hope, of course, was to secure court endorsement for a metropolitan-wide plan of consolidation. This had been the ruling in a similar case for Louisville, Kentucky, although another case had been denied in Detroit.[33]

Had the lawsuit been decided in the way the plaintiff intended, metropolitan Kansas City today surely would look and feel quite different than it does. School levies likely would pass regularly, and the quality of instruction would be high across the region. Such equity would have come at a cost to suburban districts, obviously, but the burden would be spread widely. The biggest gains would have come in the poorest areas of eastern and southeastern Kansas City, where hope would replace despair. The presence of good schools there would have gradually reduced the population exodus and encouraged new economic development. Reality proved not to be so rosy.

The dream of a single school district for the entire metropolis endured for eight years. The courtroom trial did not begin until December 1983, and it was January 1985 before Judge Russell G. Clark ruled that the suburban districts were not responsible for Kansas City's problem and therefore could not be forced into a consolidation. Although the judge did appear sympathetic to the utopian possibilities of a single-district plan by calling it "thorough and thoughtful," he nevertheless ruled that responsibility for an acceptable desegregation plan lay entirely with the Kansas City district and the state of Missouri.[34]

Any strategy designed to create integrated schools in a district where minority students constituted 73 percent of the total enrollment would have to involve a lot of money. To its credit, the court realized this and so ordered a near tripling of the budget. First, the judge raised local property taxes from $2.05 per $100 of assessed valuation to $4.96, but this covered only a quarter of the new cost. He directed the state to fund the remainder. Soon, an extra $200 million were flowing into the district every year, and hopes for social equality began to rise.[35]

With the superabundance of new money, leaders planned to make Kansas City schools the best in the nation. They erected fifteen new buildings and renovated fifty-four old ones. People argued that if the quality of instruction was high, the buildings modern, and the programs innovative, students from all over the region would want to attend. A racial balance of perhaps 40 percent white and 60 percent minority would result, and all would be well. Much attention focused on the idea of "magnet" schools, ones with curricula specialized in fields such as foreign languages, performance art, and science. Nearly every school was given such a focus, but the showpiece was to be Central High School. Officials designated Central as the Computers Unlimited/Classical Greek Magnet and invested $32 million in its creation. To start, they purchased a computer for every student. Then, to promote the Greek ideal of a sound body to complement the mind, they built athletic facilities so elaborate that they rivaled those of a true Olympic village. The complex included an indoor pool and specialized rooms for gymnastics and wrestling.[36]

Although the district's facilities were indeed superb and the budget included $900,000 for advertising, $6.4 million for busing, and even money for a taxi service, the program failed miserably. No more than 1,500 white suburban students ever enrolled in the schools in any one year, and it was rare for any of these pupils to stay longer than a semester. Beyond that, the quality of instruction for the district's own students failed to improve throughout the 1980s and 1990s. Scores on standard performance tests were so bad, in fact, that the district lost state accreditation in 2000.[37]

What had happened? Many critics have argued that attempting to integrate through magnet schools was foolhardy from the beginning. Given the high quality of most suburban schools, why would parents there bus children to the inner city? But a failure to raise student performance within the district was the real problem, and here, racial politics was pri-

marily responsible. It was far easier to put dollars into buildings than to make appropriate decisions about personnel. The pool of jobs in the school district was and is important for the black community, and board members and church leaders alike resisted attempts to fire incompetent people. Facing this situation, superintendents became frustrated and regularly quit shortly after assuming their positions. It is a sad story, but Kansas City people sacrificed quality of education to the shorter-term goals of integration and job retention. Despite the influx of some $2 billion in extra funding for education, the city in the 1990s remained as deeply divided racially, economically, and geographically as it had been before.[38]

Spatial correlations between maps of household income and African American population in Jackson County were strong for 1990, and both patterns can be related to boundaries of the school system (maps 56, 63, and 64). The correspondence is not exact, however, yielding a complex cultural geography. Low incomes defined the most extensive area. Using a measure of $20,000 per household, this zone sometimes reached south to Ninety-fifth Street and east as far as downtown Independence.

The outline of the school district matches the income distribution almost perfectly on the south and east, as the district at that time incorporated the western neighborhoods of Independence. The principal discrepancy lay in the southwest, where J. C. Nichols's Country Club District continued to house moneyed people. These residents generally paid twice for their privileged location—the cost of the housing itself plus tuition at a private school. It is no coincidence that the city's five most prestigious academies all are in this neighborhood—Barstow (11511 State Line Road), Notre Dame de Sion (10631 Wornall Road), Pembroke Hill (5121 State Line Road), Rockhurst (9301 State Line Road), and St. Teresa's (5600 Main Street).[39]

Kansas City people routinely speak of the city's African American East Side. Everybody knows that Troost Avenue marks this area's western limit, but the other boundaries are poorly understood. On the south, this vagueness is caused by neighborhood expansion. Whereas in 1970, African American majorities were the rule only north of Sixty-third Street (map 55), this zone extended south another sixteen blocks by 1990 (map 64). Misunderstanding of the neighborhood's eastern and northern limits has nothing to do with dynamics, however, for this border has been stable for decades. The problem is that at least some outsiders assume any low-income neighborhood is necessarily a black one.

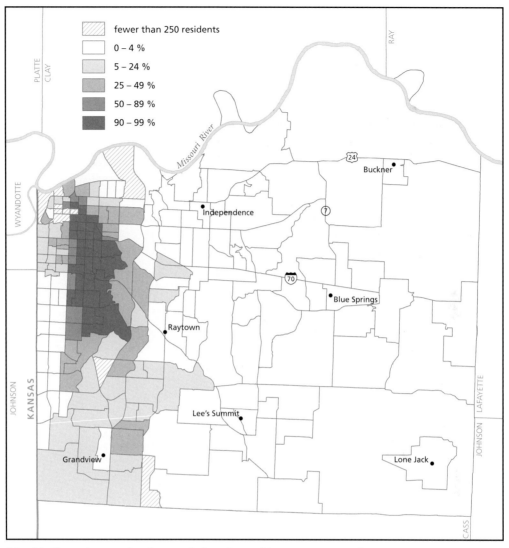

Map 64. African American Population in Jackson County, Missouri, 1990. Data from U.S. Census.

When Kansas City leaders of a century ago constructed their elaborate grid of boulevards, they hoped that these roads would serve as a de facto zoning system to reduce social friction and maintain housing values. This hope was only partly realized. Ironically, when engineers designed Interstate Highway 70 five decades later, they had no such social agenda but inadvertently created an effective racial divide. Data for 1990 show a strong African American presence northeast of this expressway only in the neighborhood adjacent to downtown. But from the road's intersection with Benton Boulevard eastward to its crossing of the Blue River, Interstate 70 separated census tracts that were 90 percent or more black from ones a quarter to a third African American. Southward from about Thirty-first Street, the Blue River served as an equally effective racial barrier as far south as Seventy-ninth Street at Swope Park.

The presence of two well-defined physical limits to the east and the absence of anything similar to the south help to explain the direction of African American expansion. South was the path of least resistance. Many white families that traditionally had found employment in the industrial Blue Valley became too poor to move once General Motors, Montgomery Ward, Sheffield Steel, and similar companies shuttered their operations in the 1970s and 1980s. Like most African Americans, they wanted to escape the problems of the Kansas City school district but could not afford to do so.[40]

Neither the black nor the white section of the East Side was uniform. Economics divided the African American community. Even though most of the truly prosperous black families had long since left the school district by 1990, a more modest north-south difference remained. Median household

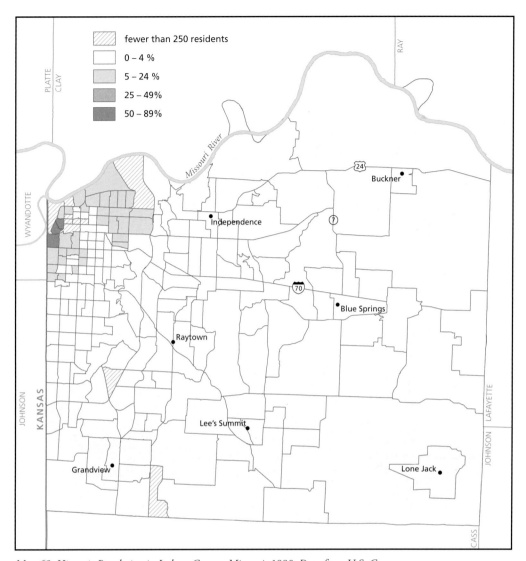

Map 65. Hispanic Population in Jackson County, Missouri, 1990. Data from U.S. Census.

income in the decrepit area north of Truman Road and west of Woodland was under $7,000. South of Forty-seventh Street, in areas just east and south of the University of Missouri–Kansas City, this figure was three times higher and the homes considerably newer and better maintained.

Racial politics kept the two economic groups united in many ways. The biggest issue concerned the route for the proposed South Midtown Freeway, a north-south link for U.S. Highway 71 through the heart of the city (map 50). One possibility would have followed the old Country Club streetcar tracks along Brookside Boulevard and the early J. C. Nichols developments, but city officials opted instead for a corridor near Prospect and Euclid avenues. This latter route, although cheaper and more direct, displaced some 10,000 people, nearly all of them poor and African American. Construc-

tion began in 1968, but disputes delayed completion for over thirty years. Naming the project after black leader Bruce R. Watkins did little to restore community harmony.[41]

The area north and east of Interstate 70, Kansas City's venerable Northeast district, increased its diversity over these years. The Italian presence remained strong, but as the local blue-collar economy deteriorated along with the school district, housing vacancies occurred. Some of these affordable units were acquired by black families, some by Kansas City's newest immigrant peoples. The 1990 census caught this change in progress. One set of newcomers—Vietnamese and other East Asians—clustered tightly in the public housing projects near Columbus Square in the North End. That census tract was the most complex in the city, with nearly equal populations of Asians, African Americans,

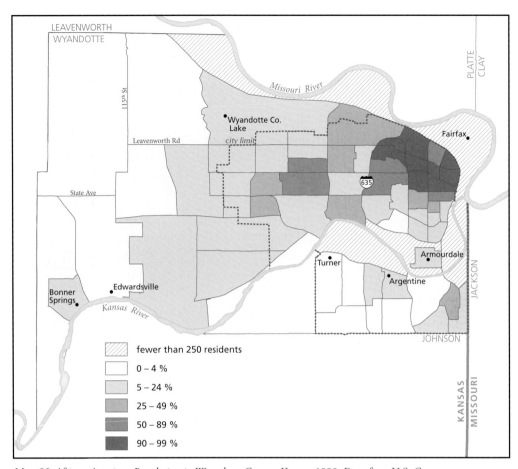

Map 66. African American Population in Wyandotte County, Kansas, 1990. Data from U.S. Census.

and whites, plus 8 percent of respondents who termed themselves Hispanic.

Mexicans and other Hispanic immigrants comprised the most numerous new group (16,819 citywide versus 4,903 Asians). This volume, together with support and advice from church officials and Latin families already in the area, produced fairly dispersed settlement (map 65). The traditional Mexican neighborhoods on the West Side were nearly full by this time and lacked easy avenues for expansion. The Northeast, physically separate but near enough to be known and understood, became the destination of choice. By 1990, Hispanic markets and other small businesses were common along Independence Avenue and Truman Road. Latinos constituted between 6 and 12 percent of every census tract in the extended neighborhood, and these figures increased yearly.

The Inner City in Kansas

Inner-city neighborhoods in Kansas had much in common with those in Missouri. Suburbs lured affluent, mostly white residents, and the two core cities lost population. As the

Missouri numbers fell from 507,087 in 1970 to 435,146 in 1990 and the Kansas ones dipped from 168,213 to 151,488, Kansas City boosters no longer spoke about national rankings. At the same time, both communities experienced sizable and parallel increases in minority populations. In 1990, African Americans constituted 29 percent of the population in each city; Hispanics totaled 7 percent on the Kansas side and 4 percent in Missouri.[42]

Despite the surficial similarities, Wyandotte County people adjusted better to changing social circumstances than their neighbors to the east. Their flight to the suburbs was not nearly as fast, for example, and their school troubles did not have to be argued before the Supreme Court. This relative tranquility, I think, derived from greater economic homogeneity in the population and a policy of keeping school district boundaries in general accord with those of the political unit. Throughout the late twentieth century, Kansas City, Kansas, remained a "hard-working" town that was "hemmed in by looming grain elevators and industrial smokestacks and underlaid with after-hours joints." Missouri might be a "far

145

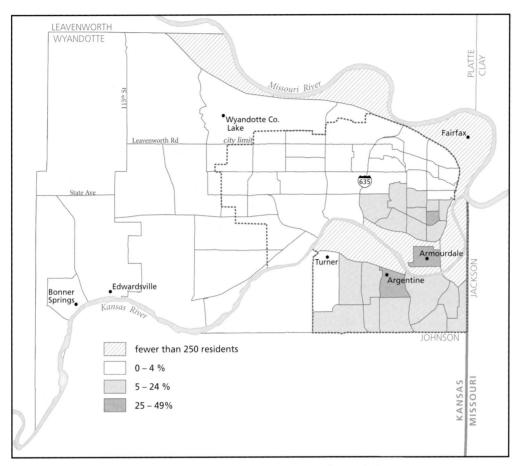

Map 67. Hispanic Population in Wyandotte County, Kansas, 1990. Data from U.S. Census.

livelier" place, but Kansans better understood their various neighborhoods. The median household income for 1990 was $3,000 lower on the Wyandotte County side of Kansas City, and salaries clustered heavily in the working-class ranges.[43]

At the close of the twentieth century, the traditional ethnic neighborhoods of Wyandotte County remained in place. African Americans still dominated the northeast part of town, and Eastern Europeans prevailed in the east-central section; the two groups were separated from one another by the Minnesota Avenue commercial district. Mexican Americans were numerous in Argentine, Armourdale, and Rosedale, while wealthier, mostly Anglo residents clustered near the city's western limits. Still, each of these units had changed from a generation before.

African American neighborhoods expanded greatly. Whereas Eighteenth Street had been the limit of black-majority populations in 1960, thirty years later this boundary stretched another twenty blocks westward to Interstate 635 (map 66). This movement incorporated the formerly isolated settlement at Quindaro into the larger whole and made

Quindaro Boulevard the local business strip. Black families also moved into majority white neighborhoods even farther west without significant incident. Washington High School at 7340 Leavenworth Road now began the integration process, just as Wyandotte High at 2501 Minnesota Avenue had done several decades earlier.

Although few African Americans moved south of Minnesota Avenue during the expansion process, life on Strawberry Hill was nonetheless in metamorphosis. Steeples of East European churches still dominated the skyline, but the congregations had largely relocated to the suburbs. Poorer, older people remained, together with a surplus stock of small, well-maintained homes. These houses quickly went to newer Hispanic immigrants. The 1990 census recorded the early stages of a diffusion northward from established Mexican neighborhoods (map 67). Central Avenue, running west from the old stockyard district, was the public face of the new settlers. Nearly everybody welcomed their bodegas and other businesses, since the storefronts previously had been mostly vacant.

South of the Union Pacific tracks, Argentine remained the

core of the Wyandotte County Hispanic community. Two other sites served as complements. Rosedale, just to the east in the valley of Turkey Creek, presented a situation similar to Strawberry Hill—small houses available via the process of suburbanization. A special allure there was the University of Kansas Medical Center, whose payroll of 5,000 included many positions for unskilled labor. Armourdale, in the Kansas River bottomland, was 27 percent Hispanic in 1990, one of the highest concentrations in the city. All of these people lived west of the Seventh Street Expressway. This was ironic in that laws once permitted Mexicans, African Americans, and East Europeans to reside only east of this street. Extensive flood damage in 1951, urban renewal in 1960, and new attitudes changed all this. City officials razed the housing district east of Seventh Street (Lower Armourdale, or LA, in local parlance), and many former residents moved a few blocks west.[44]

Not surprisingly, lower income levels in Wyandotte County corresponded almost perfectly with minority populations in 1990 (map 68). The "island" of moderate wealth south of the Kansas River and west of Interstate 635 is the Turner neighborhood. Like Argentine, Turner was and is a Santa Fe railroad town. As the silver smelter that gave Argentine its name di-

Figure 41. Central Avenue, 2010, Looking East in the 1400 Block. Central Avenue is the retail face of a growing Mexican population in Kansas City, Kansas. Businesses here offer a wide range of goods and services, including special fruit-flavored ice pops (paletas) at the Paleteria La Michoacana. El Torito #2 is one of the larger stores, a combination meat market (carniceria) and taco restaurant. The street is economically healthy by day, but suffers at night from a prostitution problem. (Photograph by Barbara Shortridge)

minished air quality, Turner became a refuge for families who could afford a longer commute to work. This refuge quality remains, now expressed largely in racial terms (the community was over 90 percent white in 1990). The highest income areas in the county reflect newer havens. The two most northwestern census tracts, largely west of the new Interstate

435, were sparsely settled in 1990, the houses middle class but mostly new. The southwestern tract is the suburban portion of Bonner Springs, a town conceived in the nineteenth century as a resort centered around its mineral waters. More recently, this community developed largely as a haven from the traditionally corrupt politics of Kansas City, Kansas.

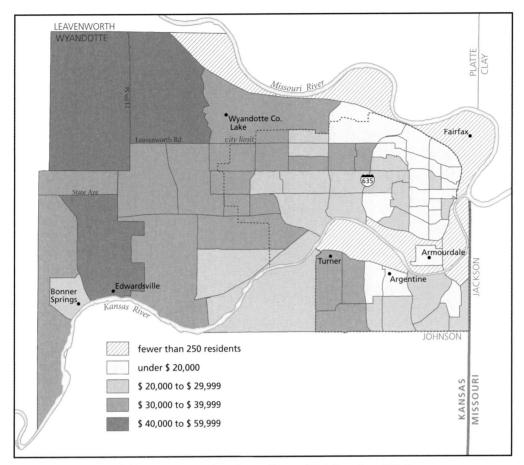

Map 68. Median Household Income in Wyandotte County, Kansas, 1990. Data from U.S. Census.

The Burbs

Kansas City development in the 1970s and 1980s can be summarized easily at the county scale (table 2). Wyandotte formed one extreme, losing more people than it attracted. Income levels there declined in relative terms, as did the white racial majority. Jackson County was much the same. Population declines in its inner city were greater than on the Kansas side, but gains in Blue Springs, Lee's Summit, and other emergent suburbs provided a counterbalance. That county's median income figures hid an unusually large gap between rich and poor. The contrast between the city's two core counties and their suburban neighbors was obvious. Johnson County, expanding from its Mission Hills development early in the century, passed Wyandotte in total population during the 1960s and never looked back. The booms in Clay and Platte counties (Kansas City's Northland) started later but advanced at a similar pace.

When examined more closely, the inner city–suburb comparison hides as much as it reveals (tables 1 and 3). Some

suburbs, mostly those adjacent to the core city, grew rapidly during the 1950s and early 1960s but then leveled out. Gladstone, Independence, and Raytown fit this pattern in Missouri; so do Fairway, Merriam, Mission, and Prairie Village in Kansas. In 1990, many families in such communities still lived in the homes they had built thirty years before. Local income levels remained relatively the same as well, but school enrollments dropped.

Newer housing developments ringed the older communities and accounted for virtually all the metropolitan growth during this period. Because Kansas City's freeway system was well developed in all directions (officials claimed more interstate highway miles per capita than in any other metropolitan area), this expansion was fairly even geographically.[45]

The beltway formed by Interstates 435 and 470 some 15 miles from the urban core can be used as a rough measure of growth. Residential development in 1990 had reached this boundary everywhere but in the northwest. This gap is surprising at first inspection, for Interstate 29 provides good access to the quadrant and the Kansas City International

Airport provides a potential site for business. But these assets were not yet enough to overcome bottleneck bridges and the city's historical inertia toward the south. After the airport opened in the early 1970s, for instance, city officials were said to have "waited for a growth boom around it. And waited. And waited." Still, by 1990, the county's potential seemed close to realization, especially at KCI and the historical Missouri River community of Parkville. Parkville sits on scenic bluffs only 7 miles from downtown skyscrapers and is home to a small private school, Park University (then Park College). People had erected nice homes north of town around Riss Lake and to the west near the Windbrook Golf Course, but this latter territory had yet to be annexed. In fact, the town's official population of 2,402 was only slightly larger than it had been a decade before, and its median household income was a modest $35,496 (map 69). The level of affluence increased near the airport, but development was still modest. Wags referred to this area as South St. Joseph, and the only businesses of consequence were motels that catered to outstate residents who needed to catch early-morning flights.[46]

Clay County, closer to the urban core than Platte, grew steadily throughout the 1970s and 1980s until it approached Wyandotte in size. Its social geography mirrored that of Platte and was mostly predictable. Population stagnation and low incomes characterized relatively remote towns such as Excelsior Springs and Smithville as well as older industrial communities in the river bottoms: Birmingham, North Kansas City, Randolph, and adjacent Riverside in Platte County. Encircling the industrial sites was a slightly more prosperous zone—the 1950s suburb of Gladstone, the county seat of Liberty, and adjacent areas. Higher incomes were limited to newer suburban developments on the north side of Gladstone; sparsely populated rural areas (denoted by large census tracts on the map); and unexpectedly, a small section of the blufflands near the county's southwestern corner.

Proximity to downtown Kansas City was not the only reason Clay County attracted more people than Platte. Local jobs were significant, too, and many could be found in North Kansas City. Farmland Industries had its start there, to cite

Table 2. Population Characteristics of Counties in the Kansas City Metropolitan Area, 1970–2010

Characteristic	Clay	Jackson	Johnson	Platte	Wyandotte
Population:					
1970	123,323	654,558	220,073	32,081	186,845
1980	136,488	629,180	270,269	46,341	172,335
1990	153,411	633,232	355,054	57,867	161,933
2000	184,006	654,880	451,086	73,781	157,882
2010	221,939	674,158	544,179	89,322	157,505
Percent Change:					
1960–1970	+41	+5	+53	+37	+1
1970–1980	+10	-4	+24	+44	-8
1980–1990	+12	+1	+31	+25	-6
1990–2000	+20	+3	+27	+27	-2
2000–2010	+21	+3	+21	+21	0
Percent Racial Minority:					
1970	1	18	1	1	20
1980	4	24	5	5	33
1990	4	24	4	3	28
2000	7	30	9	10	42
2010	16	37	18	16	56
Median Family Income:					
1969	$10,429	$8,519	$12,763	$10,213	$8,127
1979	$21,029	$16,887	$25,173	$22,499	$15,454
1989	$34,370	$27,853	$42,741	$38,173	$23,780
1999	$48,347	$39,277	$61,455	$55,849	$33,784
2009	$71,191	$58,322	$89,112	$76,418	$44,224

Source: U.S. Census records.

one example, a giant cooperative involved with meatpacking, fertilizer manufacture, and grain marketing. Its headquarters were at 3315 North Oak Trafficway.[47]

Claycomo was another industrial center, home since 1952 to a large assembly plant of the Ford Motor Company. This plant, essentially at the intersection of Interstate Highways 35 and 435, made the area attractive to residential developers. Some housing came to Claycomo itself, but that community's small physical size forced most such activity to adjacent

Table 3. Population of Selected Cities in the Kansas City Metropolitan Area, 1980–2010

Missouri Communities	1980	1990	2000	2010	Kansas Communities	1980	1990	2000	2010
Kansas City	448,028	435,146	441,545	459,787	Kansas City	161,087	151,521	146,866	145,786
Belton	12,708	18,145	21,730	23,116	Bonner Springs	6,266	6,413	6,768	7,314
Blue Springs	25,936	40,153	48,080	52,575	Edwardsville	3,364	3,979	4,146	4,340
Claycomo	1,671	1,668	1,267	1,430	Fairway	4,619	4,173	3,952	3,882
Gladstone	24,990	26,243	26,365	25,410	Gardner	2,392	4,277	9,396	19,123
Grandview	24,561	24,967	24,881	24,475	Leawood	13,360	19,693	27,656	31,867
Greenwood	1,315	1,505	3,952	5,221	Lenexa	18,639	34,110	40,238	48,190
Independence	111,797	112,301	113,288	116,830	Merriam	10,794	11,819	11,008	11,003
Lee's Summit	28,741	46,418	70,700	91,364	Mission	8,643	9,504	9,727	9,323
Liberty	16,251	20,459	26,232	29,149	Mission Hills	3,904	3,446	3,593	3,498
North Kansas City	4,507	4,130	4,714	4,208	Olathe	37,258	63,402	92,962	125,872
Parkville	2,019	2,402	4,059	5,554	Overland Park	81,784	111,790	149,080	173,372
Raymore	3,154	5,592	11,146	19,206	Prairie Village	24,657	23,186	22,072	21,447
Raytown	31,831	30,601	30,388	29,526	Roeland Park	7,962	7,706	6,817	6,731
Riverside	3,206	3,010	2,979	2,937	Shawnee	29,653	37,962	47,996	62,209
Smithville	1,873	2,525	5,514	8,423					
Sugar Creek	4,305	3,982	3,839	3,345					

Source: U.S. Census records.

Liberty. This construction, plus Liberty's other assets—a small college (William Jewell) and a classic courthouse square—led to a doubling in population in the decade after Ford arrived. Steady growth has continued ever since. Residents say that the town's central square provides a community focus that is missing in most suburbs.[48]

One area stood apart from the 1990 stereotype of the Northland as middle-class suburbia. This was Briarcliff, a new bluffland development adjacent to North Kansas City whose 1,228 households had a median income of $64,342. Briarcliff can be compared to the Country Club Plaza, a large-scale luxury complex that integrates residences with retail and office centers. It also was the product of a single vision. Charles A. Garney, a lifelong resident of the Northland, believed that with a catalyst, Clay and Platte counties could rival the famous Country Club District as an upscale destination.

With some $11 million of his own money, Garney acquired and developed some 600 acres west of U.S. Highway 169 and north of Missouri Route 9. This was potentially scenic property with excellent access to downtown Kansas City, but it was badly neglected, with abandoned quarries, deep ravines, and a trailer slum. Garney transformed the site. Concentrating first on single-family residences, he laid out some 250 large lots with superb views, built a home for himself, and by 1990 had convinced many others to join him. In the years to follow, Garney would augment these homes with a corporate park and a 10-acre retail center—Briarcliff Village—that features high-end, locally owned stores. His work inspired others, too, and today, homeseekers do indeed judge this part of the Northland equal to the best of Johnson County.[49]

Just as the presence of the Missouri River creates a clear identity for Clay and Platte counties, the parallel valleys of the Blue and Little Blue provide similar distinctness east of the city (maps 2 and 3). The county seat of Independence, the industrial town of Sugar Creek, and the 1950s suburbs of Raytown, Hickman Mills, and Ruskin Heights occupy the divide between the two Blues. Beyond this arc of settlement,

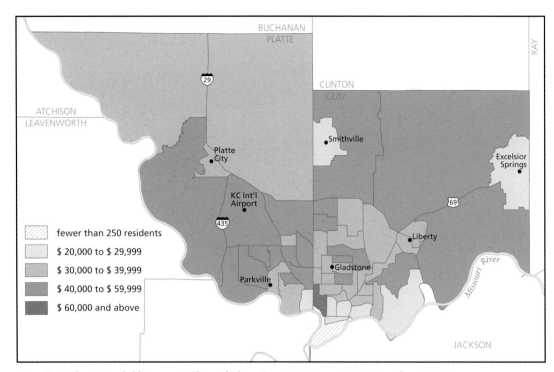

Map 69. Median Household Income in Clay and Platte Counties, Missouri, 1990. Data from U.S. Census.

rural Jackson County persisted late into the 1960s. Blue Springs, east of the Little Blue and Independence on U.S. 40, was home to only 2,555 residents in 1960. Lee's Summit, across the same river from Raytown on U.S. 50, was only slightly more populated, with 8,267 citizens. Straight south of the city, where the two streams are smaller, community separation was less apparent. Grandview abutted Belton (population 4,897 in 1960) across the Cass County line, with rural Raymore 4 miles to the south and east.

The communities between the Blue rivers, though united by the winding path of Blue Ridge Boulevard and a solidly middle-class lifestyle, faced varied challenges in the 1970s and 1980s. Two of them, Sugar Creek and Grandview, lost major employers. Three others, Hickman Mills, Raytown, and Ruskin Heights, coped with changing racial compositions, and venerable Independence saw political factionalism stymie hopes for economic expansion.

Sugar Creek, a small municipality carved from the north side of Independence, rivaled Claycomo as Kansas City's closest approximation to a company town. It was established shortly after 1900 to house workers at two new factories—a Standard Oil refinery and the Kansas City Portland Cement Company. Both operations expanded over time, becoming BP Amoco and Lafarge Cement, respectively, and the town's population grew accordingly. The peak population figure,

4,755, occurred in 1970. Then came rumors of closure for the increasingly antiquated Amoco plant, and finally, in 1982, the actual fact. Although a central location within the metropolitan area kept the town from collapse, its image suffered. The refinery was dismantled, but long-term contamination of soil and groundwater halted attempts to attract other industry. Litigation went on for years, and only in 2002 did the company agree to spend up to $30 million for restitution and to help establish a 300-acre business park. Lingering fears of environmental carcinogens, however, may limit even this success.[50]

At the south end of the Blue Ridge settlement arc, Grandview faced problems somewhat similar to those in Sugar Creek. Pollution was not an issue, but the scale of job losses was comparable when the giant Richards-Gebaur Air Force Base downsized in 1977 and then closed. Grandview, a sleepy railroad stop originally, had grown with the adjacent air base (table 3). Then came stagnation. During the boom years, military dollars had been nicely augmented by sales at the Truman Corners Shopping Center along U.S. 71 in northern Grandview. Started in 1957, this was one of the first suburban malls in the metropolitan area. But it suddenly looked small and outdated in 1980 when a new center, Bannister Mall, opened only 4 miles to the north. People in Grandview adapted to the economic disappointments. Some found work

151

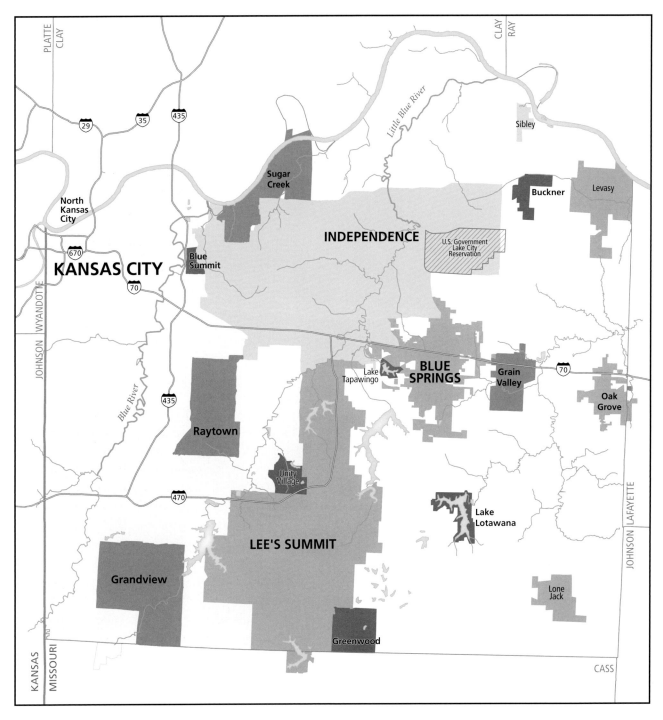

Map 70. Jackson County Suburbs, 1995. Modified from the "Highway Map of Jackson County Missouri," published in 1995 by the county's Department of Public Works.

at new factories recruited to town, and others became commuters. Overall, though, property values suffered, and so did community image. Rates of homeownership began to fall, and the town gradually slipped in status from middle class to lower middle class.[51]

A drift in social status during the 1970s and 1980s is practically a defining trait of American inner-ring suburbs. Sometimes, the cause was immediate and easy to identify, as in the cases of Sugar Creek and Grandview. The process was just as common in purely residential neighborhoods, however, including the Blue Ridge communities of Raytown, Hickman Mills, and Ruskin Heights. These places are classic 1950s suburbs with curving streets, small ranch houses, and strip malls. Social life centers on the local high schools—Raytown, Raytown South, Hickman Mills, and Ruskin as aligned from northeast to southwest (map 56). These schools, of course, were established as alternatives to the troubled Kansas City system, and minority students were scarce before the late 1980s.

In the 1960s and 1970s, Ruskin was known principally for a natural disaster—a 1957 tornado that destroyed hundreds of newly built homes and killed forty-four people, including my aunt Bessie Knorpp Smith, who had been picking strawberries in the area. By the 1980s, this memory had faded. As the housing stock aged here and in neighboring Hickman Mills and Raytown, boorishness became the new image. Raytown especially was labeled as "a backwoods mecca for rednecks, women with beehive hairdos and frequent UFO Hotline callers." Local residents naturally protested, but income levels had slipped compared to newer suburbs, and not all properties were well maintained.[52]

Accompanying the yokel stereotype (and in some ways causing it) was the reality of racism. Raytown again led the way. Its police department in the 1960s and 1970s under Marion Beeler openly practiced racial profiling, and other city officials refused a building permit for a new black church. It was a predictable pattern of behavior. The inner suburbs had been created by white flight a generation before. When middle-class African Americans began to move in during the 1980s, older white residents panicked. They recalled the fears of yesterday instead of recognizing these new home buyers as younger versions of themselves, seekers of the same safe haven.[53]

By 1990, black residents constituted a quarter of the population in the western and northern sections of Raytown (map 64). This number was lower, about 20 percent, in Hickman Mills and Ruskin Heights, but the social problems were greater. Nearly every contemporary report on that area notes a lack of community spirit despite the presence of an independent school district. Partly, this may have been a result of ongoing turmoil within the schools themselves, but most observers focused on a lack of homeownership. The houses there are modest ranchers built on slabs. As many of the original owners moved up to larger quarters, they often sold to speculators. These speculators, in turn, typically rented out the houses and neglected needed repairs. The practice led to falling property values and reduced the incentive for others to upgrade their homes. Distrust and fear increased as the cycle progressed. It did not slow until 2002 when, with the designation of Ruskin Heights as the city's first suburban renewal district, owners became eligible for financial assistance to make repairs.[54]

The story of Independence shares elements with that of Raytown and other inner-ring communities but is more complicated. The city's longer history and considerable population are part of this picture (tables 1 and 3). Its size, for instance, prevented encirclement via Kansas City annexations (as happened to Raytown) and allowed Independence officials to expand their city limit as far east as they chose. By exercising this option in 1963 to move the boundary east to the Little Blue River and then again in 1974 and 1975 to advance north to U.S. Route 24 and east beyond Missouri Route 7, the city effectively became both an inner-ring and an outer-ring suburb (map 70).

Although expansion to the east provided an opportunity for development, it also heightened already existing geographic tensions within the community. The courthouse square, for example, which had long been an important shopping district for eastern Jackson County, was dying, and many people blamed city officials. Critics said that, by blessing the construction of the Blue Ridge Mall in 1959 at the southwest corner of town (I-70 at the Blue Ridge Boulevard exit) and then, in 1974, the similar Independence Center in the southeast (I-70 at the I-470 junction), the city cannibalized itself. Retorts that malls would have materialized anyhow fell on deaf ears because the town's economic problems were severe except on the eastern and southern fringes (map 63). Houses were small, education levels low, and workers dependent on the rapidly declining industrial jobs in the Blue River valley and Sugar Creek.[55]

Distrust between the older and newer parts of town effectively paralyzed city government during the 1980s and early 1990s. Former mayor Ron Stewart recalled the chiding he would get when traveling to Jefferson City in search of grants: "Those state senators and representatives would say, 'why should we give you money when the City Council can't get four votes on anything?' It was humiliating." Such inaction was evident on the landscape. Despite the ambitious annexations, housing development in the early 1990s still ended at Missouri Route 291, no farther east than it had been twenty years before (table 3).[56]

The northwestern section of Independence was in the worst shape. Although establishment of the Truman National Historic Landmark District in 1971 provided funds for the restoration of homes along Delaware Street, continued downsizing of area industry hurt many families. The federal ammunition plant at Lake City east of town remained active, but Independence's signature manufacturer for seventy-five years, the Allis-Gleaner (AGCO) tractor plant in the heart of the city, closed in 2000. Because this followed so closely a similar shuttering of the Sugar Creek refinery, local people were in no mood for tax levies designed to help the new east side.[57]

Since the valley of the Little Blue River remained free of suburban development through most of the 1990s, the two small towns just to its east—Blue Springs and Lee's Summit—remained isolated from the city proper. The area had excellent access via Interstates 70 and 470 and U.S. Highways 40 and 50, however, and developers saw the physical separation as marketable. Translating isolation as seclusion, they began to erect relatively expensive houses and to promote the two communities as a Missouri alternative to burgeoning Johnson County across the state line.

The transformation from small town to smart suburb began about 1960. Both communities worked to build first-class school systems and were aggressive in annexation so as to block Kansas City's expansion. One might have expected Blue Springs to progress faster because of its direct access to Interstate 70, but Lee's Summit led the way. Extra tax dollars were the reason, most of them from a large Western Electric plant that came to town in 1960. Manufacturing telephone equipment for the Bell System, Western Electric employed 4,000 people with an annual payroll of $25 million. This financial cushion gave local planners confidence and ambition. With major annexations in 1959 and 1964, they extended the city west to the Kansas City border, north to Independence, and south to the Cass County line (map 70).[58]

Lee's Summit in the 1970s and 1980s was still a mixture of small town and suburb. Its core around the intersection of Douglas and Third streets featured small homes and locally owned stores (map 63). Several developments joined Western Electric as signs of the future, though, including John Knox Village, Kansas City's largest and most prestigious long-term care facility. Sponsored by Presbyterians but open to all, it housed a thousand residents soon after opening in 1970. Its 450-acre campus sits on the city's northwest side between U.S. 50 and Pryor Road. Another development, prestigious housing around Lakewood Lakes 4 miles north of downtown, was a primary reason for the big annexation of 1970. Median household incomes there exceeded $62,000 in 1990, one of the highest figures in the county (map 63). Finally, two more enterprises boded well for the future. Land at the intersection

of U.S. 50 with Interstate 470 was being assembled for major commercial development. Four miles to the west, Jackson County officials completed a dam on the Little Blue River in 1985 and were waiting for the new Longview Lake to fill. Besides water and views, amenities there included a new golf course and a community college.[59]

Growth in Blue Springs began in 1965 with the opening of Interstate 70. The pace was rapid—from 5,000 to 40,000 residents in twenty years (table 3)—but accompanied by little industry. This situation changed in 1990 when Mayor Greg Grounds promoted the conversion of a large dairy property a mile east of Missouri Route 7 into a lush corporate park called Adams Dairy Landing. Like Briarcliff in Clay County, the Adams complex was to be a direct imitation of Johnson County. Whereas Briarcliff concentrated on houses first, Blue Springs entrepreneurs went after business. Their $18 million parkway featured its own exit from I-70, artwork, water displays, a Marriott hotel, and the Adams Pointe Golf Course. Then, as a new decade began, the developers sat back to await corporate bids.[60]

In Kansas City's suburban world, Johnson County has always been the gold standard, a place openly envied in Missouri and Kansas City, Kansas, alike. Such icons do not always hold up well under scrutiny, of course, but this particular one seems blessed. Following a pattern begun just after World War II, its residential area expanded greatly in the 1970s and 1980s and did so with high-quality products. Even more impressive, these homes now were accompanied by a wealth-generating series of high-end office parks and retail centers. Taking Interstate 435 again as a rough measure of expansion from the urban core, it is obvious that Johnson County developers were the only ones in the city to breach this line by 1990. In fact, they were at the I-435 marker in Leawood and Overland Park when that roadway opened in the early 1970s. By 1990, the frontier lay another 3 miles farther south at 135th Street (Kansas Route 150), with scattered activity 3 miles beyond to 159th Street. No other part of the city came close to this pace, not even Shawnee on Johnson County's own west side.

How can one account for the spectacular success of Overland Park and its neighbors? The starting point, without question, is an image of prestige for the area established decades earlier by J. C. Nichols and the Kroh brothers. Newer builders extended the combination of luxurious homes, restricted deed covenants, and superior schools farther to the south. City managers supported the effort as well, led by Donald

Pipes in Overland Park. By annexing land far ahead of settlement, they ensured quality control (map 71). Overland Park also pioneered the use of a half-cent local sales tax, first approved by the Kansas legislature in 1977, to provide first-class services to the new housing tracts.[61]

The newer housing developments attracted affluent buyers from throughout the metropolitan area, including many from Johnson County itself. This pushed the 1990 median household income level as high as $93,000 around the Leawood South Country Club between 119th and 135th streets, but it drained money from older neighborhoods in Merriam, Mission, and the northern section of Overland Park (map 72). J. C. Nichols's developments, with their carefully coordinated planning, largely escaped such decline. Johnson County's wealthiest census tract remained in Mission Hills.

Residential expansion, although central to Johnson County growth at this time, was arguably not its most vital component. When Interstate 35 opened from downtown Kansas City to Ottawa in 1959 and then Interstate 435 across Lenexa, Overland Park, and Leawood in the early 1970s, at least some developers thought more about corporate offices and high-tech industry than about houses. This was no different from what was happening in Clay or Jackson counties, of course, but a strong tradition of upscale housing and quality schools gave Kansas entrepreneurs an edge. Executives knew they could recruit the best talent if the surrounding environment was genteel.

Given the opportunity to pursue commercial clients, local officials had several decisions to make. First was whether to participate at all. By tradition, suburbs were residential havens, and industry of any sort could threaten this serenity. Such a sentiment prevailed in Leawood through the 1980s. But a residential-only city inevitably had high property taxes, especially if its people demanded quality roads, parks, and other basic services. Leaders in Lenexa developed an alternative strategy. Realizing that their city possessed superb transportation at the junction of two interstate highways and controlled undeveloped land along these routes, they pursued distribution companies. Starting in 1965, they created a series of industrial parks, erected several buildings on speculation, and touted local amenities. Their early start and solid assets yielded success. By the 1990s, warehouses for J. C. Penney, United Parcel Service, Puritan-Bennett (medical gases), and similar companies employed over 3,000 local people.[62]

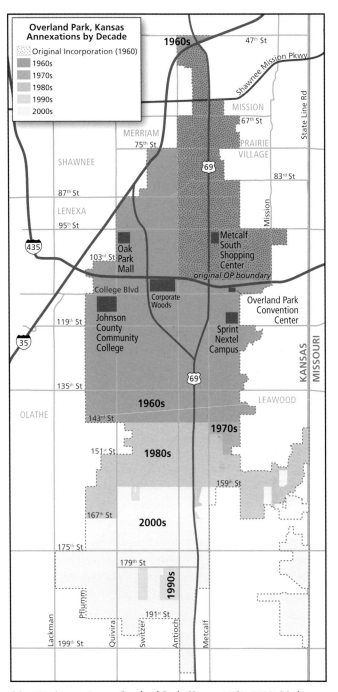

Map 71. Annexations to Overland Park, Kansas, 1960–2008. Modified from the map "Annexations by Decade" on the website of the City of Overland Park, available at http://www.opkansas.org/Doc/Annexation-by-Decade-Map.pdf (accessed March 2, 2009).

Although the development decisions made in Leawood and Lenexa were sound and produced prosperity, they paled in comparison to the magic touch on display in Overland Park. Activity there, in some ways, was a compromise between the conservatism of Leawood and the eagerness of

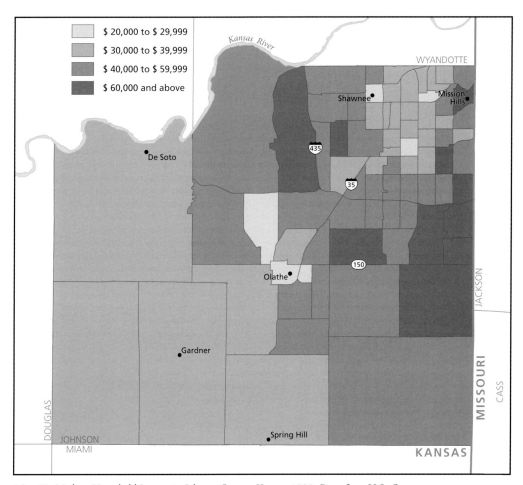

Map 72. Median Household Income in Johnson County, Kansas, 1990. Data from U.S. Census.

Lenexa. It began traditionally, with aggressive annexation and homebuilding combined with the pursuit of retail sales. Ninety-fifth Street soon thrived as a business corridor, with Metcalf South Shopping Center (1967) and Oak Park Mall (1974) as principal nodes (map 72).

Planning might well have progressed no further than malls had not a new opportunity presented itself in 1967. The state legislature had just approved the concept of community colleges, and a growth-minded city council saw such an institution as a way to assist business, promote a sense of place, and enhance quality of life. Johnson County Community College did this and more, starting a chain reaction. Location was key. Needing considerable space for a campus, the city rather innocently acquired 220 acres along 111th Street at Quivira Road. No sooner had classes begun there in 1972 than entrepreneurs decided that this quiet parkway at the fringe of settlement and parallel to Interstate 435 was an ideal site for corporate headquarters.[63]

College Boulevard (the new name for 111th Street) first blossomed as a business address in 1975. Overland Park officials promoted the idea, but one local developer—Tom Congleton—made it happen. Congleton envisioned a new kind of business environment, a campus of modest-sized buildings that blended into a parklike atmosphere of trees, waterways, walking trails, and picnic grounds. He and five partners assembled 294 acres for their Corporate Woods concept in the valley of Indian Creek (map 71). It was only 1.5 miles east of the new college and found immediate success. An initial five buildings filled with local firms, and as expansion went to seventeen buildings by 1981 and then to twenty-six, national companies came to dominate. Corporate Woods by the 1980s was Kansas City's largest and most prestigious office park, on its way to having some 250 tenants and 6,000 employees. It also served as a beacon for other entrepreneurs.[64]

By 1990, a trip along College Boulevard from Roe Avenue to Quivira Road provided a portrait of corporate America, with companies ensconced in parks named Executive Hills and Executive Centre. Several firms erected their own build-

Figure 42. Corporate Woods, circa 1990, Looking East. An office park that would combine a campuslike atmosphere with good interstate access and be set amid the quality housing of Johnson County was an inspired idea in 1975. Corporate Woods immediately became the city's most prestigious business address. This elevated view across Indian Creek shows some of the earlier buildings adjacent to College Boulevard. Management brags that 201 of their 294 acres are still open to nature. Lighton Tower, another corporate center near Metcalf, looms in the distance. (Courtesy Johnson County Museum)

ings, too, including the engineers Black and Veatch at 115th and Lamar and Yellow Freight (now YRC Worldwide) at 109th and Roe. The heart of the activity, at the intersection of College and Quivira and bounded by Highways 69, 169, and 435, became known as the Golden Triangle.[65]

Overland Park officials carefully observed the emerging corporate row and spared no expense to serve its needs. They saw the utility of a convention facility as early as the 1980s and put one together in stages. First came a big display building—the Overland Park International Trade Center—at 115th and Metcalf in 1985 and then, late in the 1990s, the 237,000-square-foot, $100 million Overland Park Convention Center just east of Lamar. Large hotels accompanied both enterprises. The capstone for the twenty-year boom came in 1997. Sprint Corporation, Kansas City's telecommunications giant, decided to build its own Corporate Woods–style campus. Two hundred and forty-seven acres between 115th and 119th streets east from Nall soon became the site of the largest construction project in metropolitan history. At a cost of some $700 million, workers erected eighteen environmentally friendly office buildings, planted 6,000 trees, and built

7 acres of lakes to accommodate some 14,000 employees in luxurious, naturalistic surroundings.[66]

Overland Park by the 1990s was the envy of every city in the nation. As Mid-America's "executive country," its corporate offices generated enough tax money to enhance its already excellent parks and schools and to attract first-class cultural events to its college. Moreover, the income allowed all these amenities without the usual companion of high property taxes. Much to the consternation of neighbors in Leawood and Prairie Village, in fact, the mill levy in Overland Park was one of the lowest in Greater Kansas City. Finally, the corporate presence enabled city officials to be highly selective in planning growth. High-end retail and housing developers were welcome. Manufacturers and other industrialists were politely directed to Lenexa and Olathe.[67]

Overland Park's neighboring communities displayed more conventional suburban behavior. Leawood planners continued to promote high-quality residential tracts as they annexed south of Interstate 435. Construction at Hallbrook, the former rural retreat of greeting card magnate Joyce C. Hall, epitomized this ideal in the 1980s. His estate stretched from College Boulevard to 119th Street. The exclusive Ironhorse Golf Club, which opened in 1995 near 151st Street and Mission Road, continued this pattern. Then, as Overland Park officials began to promote 119th Street as a retail corridor about 1990, Leawood people decided that such activity might be in their interest, too. They opened Town Center Plaza at the intersection of 119th with Roe Avenue in 1996. Again featuring quality, with merchants such as Bose electronics and Dean & DeLuca gourmet foods, the venture has been successful.[68]

Lenexa planners, after attaining a dependable revenue stream from their distribution centers, attempted to diversify. Retail was not an option, since Overland Park's Oak Park Mall was on their border. Instead, they pursued a share of the region's corporate business. Renner Road between Eighty-

seventh and 115th streets was the focus, a location similar to College Boulevard in being near and parallel to Interstate 435. They converted this road into a four-lane boulevard in 1990 at a cost of $10 million but then faced stiff competition. College Boulevard itself still had space available, and Overland Park people promoted it well. Consequently, Renner stood empty for nearly a decade.[69]

The situations at Shawnee and Olathe were less extreme. As long-existing communities, both had retail and manufacturing presences along with residential sectors. When suburbanization arrived, each town was aggressive with annexation and open to varied development, both in type and price. Shawnee features two retail corridors—Johnson Drive and Shawnee Mission Parkway—and a solidly middle-class image. Olathe, the next stop down Interstate 35 from Lenexa, began to match Overland Park in rate of expansion about 1990 (table 3). It was large enough by the mid-1990s to support its own shopping center—The Great Mall of the Great Plains—and to feature the most diverse economy in the county. Large employers included a federal air traffic control facility (started in 1962), MidAmerica Nazarene University (1968), and Garmin International (1996), a prominent manufacturer of global positioning systems.[70]

7 Toward a More Complete City, 1992–2011

When longtime observers of Kansas City looked at the census and traveled the town about 1990, they saw little that surprised them. The big events that had reconfigured local geography—such as Charles Adams's creation of blue-collar Armourdale in 1880, J. C. Nichols's move into Johnson County in 1913, and L. P. Cookingham's annexation of the Northland in the 1950s—were now decades in the past. In contrast, the pattern of recent development seemed almost inevitable. The rise of Corporate Woods in Overland Park and the economic adversity at Truman Corners and other older shopping centers, although certainly interesting, were basically continuations of past trends. Edge city, it seemed, would expand outward indefinitely. Similarly, downtown would remain a sterile zone of suits and skyscrapers and the area centered at Twenty-seventh Street and Prospect an island of poverty and frustration.

Still, urban developments sometimes surprise people, and this definitely has been the case for Kansas City. The biggest recent change, without question, has occurred in Wyandotte County. This perennially inward-looking, politically corrupt area had participated only marginally in the city's suburban expansion between 1950 and 1990. In 1991, however, leaders there became proactive, and by decade's end, the county image had been remade almost completely. In fact, Wyandotte's success was great enough to evoke envy even in perennially popular Johnson County.

Across the state line, renaissance also has come to two other sizable neighborhoods in recent years: the central business district and the African American East Side. Both renewals

began about 1992 and achieved widespread notice just after the turn of the century. Positive developments in these troubled locales, coupled with continued growth at other sites and several signs of cooperation across the barriers of race and state line, have breathed new life into Kansas City as a whole. In this chapter, I will first explore the three neighborhoods of unexpected change and then sketch recent developments elsewhere in the city.

Wyandotte County and the Speedway

In the eyes of at least one scholar, Kansas City, Kansas, had deteriorated beyond "the point of no return" by 1990. Serving for over a century as the principal dumping ground for the area's smokestack industries and the laborers who manned their dirtiest jobs, and evolving a local government known for cronyism and minimal planning, Wyandotte County after 1950 or so was the most isolated part of Greater Kansas City. Newcomers to the metropolitan area concentrated their home searches elsewhere, and if a "Dotte" (to use local shorthand) happened to acquire a particularly good job, he or she often relocated south to the superior schools and shopping malls of Johnson County. Lower home costs and stable neighborhoods compensated Kansas City Kansans to a degree, but the future looked dim. Manufacturing was on the decline locally and nationally, and a long-held image was hard to shed.[1]

Change for Wyandotte came first from within, stemming from a modest action by the county commissioners in 1991. To save money, they consolidated trash, police, and other services with the municipalities of Kansas City, Bonner Springs, and Edwardsville. This idea makes sense in many urban areas, and it was especially apt for Wyandotte because the county is compact and most of its acreage is developed. One powerful group was opposed, however—the county political machine. When this machine flexed its muscles at the next election, the progressives were out of office. Most observers then expected that business as usual would return, marked by patronage instead of efficiency.[2]

Machine politics did indeed reestablish itself, but the modest consolidations started a grassroots campaign for more radical reform. The movement surfaced in 1994 with speeches by local businesspeople who appreciated the new efficiency and wanted to expand the concept. They thought doing so also would improve the image of the city. To this end, they lobbied for a task force to explore complete unification of the city and county governments.[3]

The idea forced politicians to choose sides. Some said consolidation would be monopolistic and therefore bad, but both candidates for mayor—the incumbent Joseph E. Steineger, Jr., and Councilwoman Carol S. Marinovich—signed the "consolidation pledge." Officials collectively agreed to form the task force. From then on, the movement grew rapidly. Representatives from Athens, Georgia, and Indianapolis (where similar consolidation had occurred) spoke with enthusiasm about their experience, and local people embraced the dual benefits of efficiency and innovation. The task force approved consolidation in May 1995. Newly elected Carol Marinovich then pushed hard for state ratification, and once it came, Wyandotte County voters officially adopted the plan on April 1, 1997. Marinovich became chief executive officer of the new entity, presiding over a ten-member legislature. With this action, residents overcame decades of entrenched political behavior. They could hardly believe the accomplishment and immediately began to feel renewed pride in their Kansas City.[4]

While Wyandotte people were still debating consolidation, contractors throughout Greater Kansas City received pleasant news in December 1996. The International Speedway Corporation (ISC), the country's premier builder of automobile racetracks, was considering this area as the site for a world-class facility. Automobile racing, especially that sanctioned by the National Association for Stock Car Auto Racing (NASCAR), had become one of the most popular spectator sports in the country, and industry leaders wanted to expand venues beyond their traditional southern base. A new track in the Dallas–Fort Worth area had proved very profitable, and Kansas City was the next target community.[5]

With ISC already sold on the region, the task was essentially that of site selection. Several hundred acres were necessary, as well as good access to the interstate highway system. Kansas City, Kansas, could meet these criteria easily somewhere near the junction of Interstates 70 and 435, but local leaders initially showed little interest in the prospect since the matter of unified government was still unresolved. Soon, two competing sites emerged—along I-29 and I-435 in Platte County near the Kansas City International Airport and along I-35 near Gardner in Johnson County.

From the ISC perspective, a successful bid had to include basic utilities plus authorization for tax-increment financing (that is, construction costs were to be paid with retroactive tax dollars generated by the track) and the designation of a corporation-owned enterprise zone to house complementary businesses. These latter two demands were not allowed by Kansas state law, but Johnson County politicians promised to introduce remedial legislation as soon as possible. Within a month, however, the Gardner people dropped the entire campaign. They cited costs, but commentators noticed an abrupt decline in local enthusiasm after delegates visited Daytona, Florida, on a race day and returned with stories of noise pollution and traffic congestion.[6]

Platte County delegates visited Daytona, too, but came away impressed. They liked the excitement and said automobile noise would be no trouble at a site where airplane engines already roared. Their main problem was raising money from a small county tax base, and so they hoped for cooperation from Kansas City and the state. When such aid failed to materialize as much and as fast as was hoped, Platte's official bid to the Speedway Corporation was reported to be adequate but not overwhelming.[7]

Kansas City, Kansas, entered the speedway sweepstakes only after Gardner faltered in February 1997. Johnson and Wyandotte residents alike wanted to keep their state in contention, and the legislature was in the process of approving the tax incentives requested for the earlier proposal. Speedway officials liked both the state support and local demographics. While a Platte County supporter wondered, "Why would somebody buy into all the problems of Wyandotte County?" ISC people focused on the working-class similarities between their fan base and the residents of Kansas City, Kansas. Officials signed the paperwork in October 1997.[8]

Construction for the new Kansas International Speedway began in January 1999, and the initial races took place in July 2001. The crowds that first weekend totaled 175,000, and they have continued at high levels ever since. Season tickets sell out, and the fan base comes from an astonishing forty states. Still, the racetrack itself is no longer foremost in most residents' minds when they talk about the general speedway site. Instead, the focus is on even newer shopping and entertainment venues and how such facilities have transformed the overall feel of the county. In fact, one store in the complex—Cabela's outdoors outfitters—has become Kansas's number one tourist destination, with some 5 million visitors annually.[9]

The possibilities for the speedway as a base for more encompassing economic development became apparent in February 2001. Officials with the unified government, during earlier visits to the new ISC facility in Fort Worth, Texas, had noticed the popularity of a tourism district adjacent to the track. Without much fanfare, they then reserved 400 acres for a similar development in Kansas City. This land, just north and east of the track, was named Village West (map 73). Then, as the speedway proved itself a success, government promoters used this lure to attract other businesses. They wanted hotels and restaurants to keep the racing crowds close at hand, of course, but hoped for more. The strategy was to attract shoppers from the entire

Figure 43. Cabela's at Village West, 2010. The expansive stores of the "world's foremost outfitter" sell sporting goods and casual clothes in an atmosphere of aquariums and stuffed animals. Each outlet also features a unique bronze sculpture outside. Mountain Monarchs *by Fred Hoppe identifies the 180,000-square-foot Kansas City operation. Three mule deer, each based on actual record-book specimens, stand 19 feet tall and weigh about 5,000 pounds. (Photograph by Barbara Shortridge)*

metropolis by signing exclusive agreements with carefully selected, quality companies. Further, they wanted two or three of these to be gigantic in scale, true destination sites. This approach, which required a bravado that Wyandotte people might have lacked a decade before, worked.[10]

The two featured stores—Cabela's and Nebraska Furni-

ture Mart—opened in 2003. They were joined by a stadium for a minor-league baseball team called the Kansas City T-Bones and, two years later, by a more traditional shopping forum called The Legends. All drew big crowds. Together, they became the new standard for shopping and entertainment in Greater Kansas City and generated over $50 million

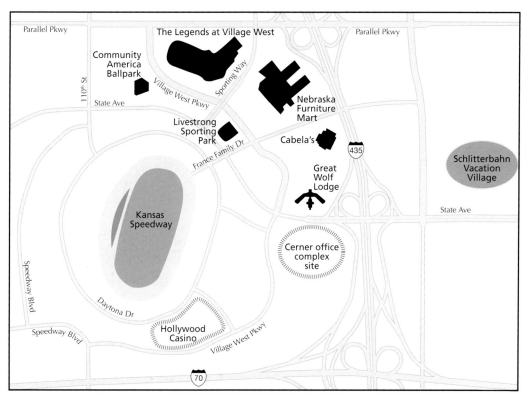

Map 73. *The Kansas International Speedway and Vicinity, 2010. Compiled from multiple sources.*

in annual tax revenue. Even more important, the development changed an entire community identity. Residents no longer had to go to another county to see a first-run movie or purchase a new sofa. Newcomers to the region began to ask realtors about houses in nearby neighborhoods. By late 2004, county property values had increased 40 percent, and officials reported issuing twice as many housing permits since 2000 as they had throughout the entire decade of the 1990s. Bob Marcusse, president of the Kansas City Area Development Council, called the progress profound, lifting "a veil that had fallen over KCK for many years, and suddenly a sense of optimism and prosperity is returning."[11]

If optimistic was the word to describe Wyandotte County people in 2004, the appropriate phrase for 2011 might be nearly overwhelmed. Good things just kept coming to the speedway intersection—first a $400 million water park, then a $700 million casino, and then a $400 million package for an office park and soccer stadium (map 73). Even though national economic turmoil in 2008 slowed implementation of these projects, tax money from the Village West stores still rolled in. Enough existed, in fact, to provide aid for the more disadvantaged parts of the city.

The water park proposal, called Schlitterbahn Vacation

Village, involved 300 acres on the east side of I-435 formerly used as the county fairgrounds. Government officials saw this development as complementary to Village West and especially liked the Texas company's plan to erect some 1,800 lodging units, a number that would double the county total as of 2006. The casino possibility drew even more interest. This came about in 2007 when the state announced that, should local voters approve, Wyandotte County would be awarded one of three state-owned casinos. Many Kansans had been frustrated to be losing gambling revenue to riverboats in adjacent Missouri, and therefore, Wyandotte people gave the idea enthusiastic approval. Bids came from seven prospective developers, all sited within 2 miles of the speedway. The one eventually selected, the $200 million Hollywood Casino, opened just southeast of the racetrack in February 2012.[12]

The capstone development to date, a new stadium for the city's major-league Sporting Kansas City soccer team, demonstrates the new, exalted status of the speedway district. The team's owners had agreed in 2007 to build in Missouri, where an aging Bannister Mall had recently been demolished. But economic recession the next year stalled this project, and when owners of the Nebraska Furniture Mart offered to sell land near their store, the soccer organization accepted. The decision naturally disappointed Jackson County people, but it made sense. It allowed a new stadium to be constructed faster, and it put this facility in an area with "a proven record of success." A related move adds to this latter point. Officials of the Cerner Corporation, a major manufacturer of medical software headquartered in North Kansas City, announced that, should the Sporting Kansas City offer be accepted, they would expand to this site themselves, bringing 4,000 new jobs. It was as though the Johnson County border magically had shifted 3 miles to the north.[13]

It is difficult to overstate the importance of speedway developments to Kansas City, Kansas, as a whole. Although not a complete panacea for decades of neglect, the tax dollars generated by Cabela's, Nebraska Furniture, and The Legends have enabled major public investments in the eastern part of the county and so raised general morale. Downtown, for example, the government built a convention center in the 500 block of Minnesota Avenue and then subsidized construction of adjacent office buildings and a Hilton Garden Inn. Similar aid has encouraged the conversion of the old city hall at Sixth and Ann into moderately priced condominiums and the construction of new townhouses in dilapidated blocks just to the north and south.[14]

Slightly west of downtown, two eyesore community centers are being revitalized. The I-70 exit at Eighteenth Street Expressway, which had become a haven for prostitution and drugs, is now home to a Sun Fresh Market, the first new urban grocery in the inner city for thirty years. At the intersection of State Avenue and I-635, the government has condemned the 1970s shopping center Indian Springs, which lost its last anchor store in 2001 after struggling against competition from Johnson County. A new mix of offices and big-box stores is planned. Finally, officials are using some of the new money to maintain the county's traditional manufacturing districts. In particular, aid is flowing into Armourdale, where DHL Delivery erected a new distribution center in 2005, and into the Argentine-Turner lowland, where Sara Lee has just opened a large meat-processing operation on Speaker Road.[15]

Downtown

Accounts of the central business district in Kansas City, Missouri, in the early 1990s echo the theme of neglect so commonly heard in reference to Wyandotte County. While civic efforts in Denver, Indianapolis, and similar metropolises were reviving their downtowns, Kansas City leaders failed to act. One observer thought that major retailers there were

"gone forever." Others cast an even broader net, acknowledging that downtown "hit perhaps its lowest point" at this time. Hope finally appeared on the horizon in 2002 when a new mayor, Kay Barnes, led a business coalition that promised to add life (the arts, entertainment, and loft apartments) to the existing starkness of skyscrapers and parking lots. This hope proved prescient, but the turnabout has featured infighting, chance, and lost opportunities as much as unified planning. Overall, far more dollars have been invested than in Wyandotte County. The results are spectacular, too, although not as transformative for local pride as those across the state line. In Missouri, residents viewed the achievements more with an inner smile, a reassertion of status rather than its invention from scratch. Still, the work has been monumental.[16]

The downtown renaissance stems from at least seven independent movements, several with roots in the 1980s and one reaching back even further. These include three on the fringes of the area: the restoration of Union Station, the grassroots emergence of an arts district near Nineteenth and Baltimore, and the relocation of the federal courthouse to 400 East Ninth Street. In the core proper, one action focused on hotels and the convention center, another on restoration of older buildings, a third on loft apartments, and a fourth on a cinema-based entertainment district. I will address these in turn and then discuss their coalescence starting about 2003.

Kansas City's massive Union Station, although obviously a railroad depot, has also served as the community's principal icon since its opening in 1914. Marking the southern limit of the business district, it is the classic framing device for photographs of the downtown skyline. The station remained functional into the 1960s, but drastically reduced passenger traffic soon made it obsolete and a financial liability. Its owners planned to raze the structure in the early 1970s and use the site for a mix of offices and apartments designed to blend in with nearby Crown Center.

The proposed demolition shocked many citizens. They promptly nominated the station for the National Register of Historic Places and otherwise foiled the owner's plans. Then came a stalemate. The building sat empty and subsequently deteriorated while various groups floated plans for its reuse as federal offices, an aquarium, a casino, a hotel, and even a theme park. Money was the principal problem, for the decay was extensive and the cost of modifying the huge structure too much for any private concern.[17]

The symbolic attachment Kansas City people felt for the depot was the only thing that saved it. After Jackson County

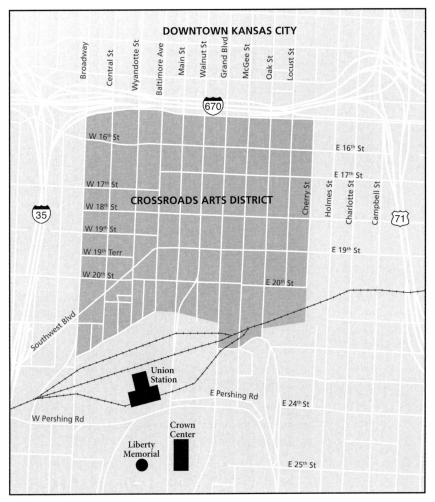

DOWNTOWN KANSAS CITY

CROSSROADS ARTS DISTRICT

Map 74. The Crossroads Arts District, 2010. Compiled from multiple sources.

the only chance they would have. The choice for salesperson was inspired—Steve Rose, publisher of a Johnson County newspaper and a frequent critic of Kansas City politics. After deciding for himself that the region's needs overrode local animosities, Rose was effective in convincing others.[19]

The ballot on November 6, 1996, asked voters in Clay, Jackson, Johnson, Platte, and Wyandotte counties to approve an additional eighth of a cent sales tax for six years. To take effect, the measure had to pass at least in Jackson and Johnson. The results, said to be more for Union Station than for the science exhibits, were positive everywhere except in relatively poor and highly taxed Wyandotte. Restoration work began immediately and was completed in 1999. Finances for the building remained tenuous for the next dozen years, but the icon was saved, a visual asset to the Crown Center neighborhood and a south end anchor for future downtown development projects.[20]

Just north of Union Station and the railroad tracks, a neighborhood of

voters refused to approve $35 million for restoration in 1988, the situation became desperate. Casting about for ideas, leaders hypothesized that local Kansans likely held the station in as high regard as did Missourians. If so, then a bistate taxing initiative might be the answer. The idea was unprecedented but logical, and it acknowledged the basic unfairness of Jackson County bearing total financial responsibility for cultural and other services enjoyed by the entire metropolitan area. If the cooperative concept could be made to work, it augured well for both Union Station and the future beyond.[18]

Groundwork for the initiative took several years, especially the identification of a suitable new use for the building and a salesperson to make the case in Kansas. The former solution was "science city," a longtime dream of officials at the Kansas City Museum. This project avoided high culture associations that might alienate voters, and museum leaders went along even though they found the cavernous space in Union Station less than ideal for their purposes. They knew this was likely

drab, multiple-story brick buildings extends six blocks to the beltway of Interstate 670. This area once was home to small transfer and storage companies, cabinetmakers, glove and sheet metal factories, upholsterers, and similar enterprises. Such businesses prospered until about 1960. Then, in a more mobile time, they dispersed to other parts of the city, leaving behind a derelict landscape that stretched from Broadway to Cherry Street and beyond (map 74).

The neighborhood sat nearly empty for fifteen years, decaying along with Union Station. Then, gradually, came revival. First, in 1977, the area acquired a name—Crossroads—as part of a citywide planning effort. Residents thought the label appropriate because this area was "in between everything. And we have a conglomeration of all businesses." In 1991, a reporter described this mixture in traditional terms—"wholesale, retail, light industrial, and graphic arts"—and as recently as 1995, Councilman Paul Danaher said the neighborhood was "neglected, taken for granted, by the city."[21]

The Crossroads changed rapidly after the mid-1990s, and through individual initiatives, it acquired a special identity. Jim and Sherry Leedy were pioneers. This couple had owned an art gallery in Westport in the early 1970s. Discouraged by gentrification in that area, they relocated to the Crossroads in 1985 at 1919 Wyandotte Street. The new space proved ideal for artists—a gallery at street level and studios above—and the price was right. They told friends at the Kansas City Art Institute, and by 1998, the neighborhood was home to some twelve galleries. The neglected warehouses now constituted the stylish new Crossroads Arts District.[22]

Art districts typically have short lives. Success brings higher property values and bigger operations, which eventually force the pioneers to alternate sites where they start the process anew. As the twelve galleries of 1988 grew to forty-two in 2004 and sixty-eight in 2007 and as "First Friday" exhibitions became the monthly social event in the city, prices did indeed rise. A high-end restaurant, Lidia's Cucina, opened in 1998, and the Kemper Museum of Contemporary Art purchased the Dolphin Gallery at 1901 Baltimore to use as a satellite site. Still, much of the original, informal flavor remains, largely because of a city initiative that keeps property taxes low for early investors. The remodeled Union Station definitely has contributed to the local boom, and, in turn, Crossroads activity helps the station's science museum. Synergy is building.[23]

Whereas the challenge on the southern fringe of downtown was to find new uses for solid, older buildings, the task on the eastern edge was reconstruction. The seven blocks there between Grand Avenue and the interstate loop had been largely residential in the 1920s, and these small houses had deteriorated over the years, with infill and urban renewal adding shops, cheap hotels, and poorly conceived apartment complexes. Islands of exception were few: the old public library building at Ninth and Locust, St. Patrick's Catholic Church at Eighth and Cherry, and the twin bastions of the Pendergast construction boom—the Jackson County Courthouse and the city hall across from one another on Twelfth Street.

Downtown planners knew about the decay on their eastern frontier but had ignored it over the years in light of more immediate problems. This policy changed when an outside player became involved and offered the prospect of a solution. This player was the national government. Beginning in the 1970s, Kansas City's federal judges had lobbied for a new courthouse to replace the stark 1939 building they shared

with the post office at 811 Grand Avenue. Politics slowed their efforts, but planning began in earnest in 1991. Specifications called for a 3.5-acre tract somewhere between downtown and Crown Center, but sentiment was strong to stay close to the original site if the city could guarantee safety for courthouse visitors. A few people argued for an area southeast of Twelfth and Grand, saying that construction there would link downtown with the existing city hall. The more popular choice, though, was just east of the old building, on the blocks bounded by Eighth and Ninth streets, McGee and Locust.[24]

Government officials approved the popular choice in August 1993. They wanted to stay downtown, and this land was reasonably priced (comprising mostly parking lots and older, small buildings). Mayor Emanuel Cleaver and other city leaders also had pushed hard for this site. The courthouse was part of a larger redevelopment project in their eyes. For them, the key would be a grand civic mall that could extend from the new federal structure on Ninth Street south to the city hall on Twelfth. Razing blighted buildings there between Oak and Locust obviously would make the area safer for courthouse patrons. But Cleaver envisioned much more than this, calling the mall "the greatest opportunity in this decade to regenerate Downtown." Such a public concourse could be lined by a new library and by stately buildings for the Internal Revenue Service, the Environmental Protection Agency, the Federal Aviation Administration, and the U.S. Department of Labor. As such, it would "stabilize and redefine the long-ignored northeast quadrant of Downtown."[25]

Construction of the $100 million, twelve-story courthouse went smoothly, starting in 1996. The mall was more of a challenge. Its acquisition was straightforward, with a coalition of local businesspeople providing the money. In exchange, Mayor Cleaver promised to spend $4 million to landscape the park itself and to purchase adjacent properties for the new public buildings. This money became an election year issue in 1995, and the city council delayed approval while candidates argued about which municipal needs were most pressing.[26]

Mayor Cleaver eventually prevailed, and in 2000, the city accepted bids for fountains, a reflecting pool, and similar beautification efforts at the newly christened Ilus W. Davis Park. The delays had robbed momentum from the rest of the project, however, causing officials with the public library and all the federal agencies save the Federal Aviation Administration to seek new sites elsewhere. An important opportunity had been lost. A visitor in 2001 or 2002 would have found the mall largely unused and the neighborhood blight pushed only a few blocks farther from the skyscrapers.[27]

The fiscal caution that stifled the potential of the civic mall was largely tied to competing, equally significant projects proposed for the downtown core. Although skyscraper construction there had gone on apace throughout the 1980s, it was obvious that law offices and banks alone formed an inadequate base for a vital urban center. Two interrelated ideas to expand this platform vied for attention in the 1990s. One vision promoted new hotel facilities to revive the city's once-vibrant convention business, the other a conversion of several moribund blocks into an entertainment district. Both would require major public spending, and in retrospect, it was perhaps foolish to propose the two simultaneously. The results—one partially completed and the other not at all—left downtown Kansas City far behind its peer communities at the time Kay Barnes assumed the mayor's office in 1999.

Probably because of their central location within the country, Kansas City people traditionally have seen their town as a convention city. The several national political conventions hosted locally fed this belief, and the construction of Municipal Auditorium in the 1930s provided one of the nation's finest meeting venues for that time. Yet starting in the 1960s, the city found itself in a game of catch-up. As the facilities at Municipal aged, leaders responded with the much larger Bartle Exhibition Hall next door to the west in 1976 and the Kemper Sports Arena in 1974. These were improvements, to be sure, but both had problems from the start. Kemper sat completely isolated in the West Bottoms and thereby was unable to contribute much to downtown foot traffic. The issue at Bartle was ambience rather than location. With long windowless walls facing Broadway and Central and ugly loading docks to the north and south, the building's exterior exuded "all the charm of the Berlin Wall." Equally as important, visitors found few restaurants, theaters, or other nighttime entertainments in the vicinity.[28]

Hotels were perhaps the city's most serious convention limitation in the early 1980s. The venerable Muehlebach was now considered small and outdated, and even though business leaders had augmented it in 1985 with the new Vista International Hotel (now Marriott) catercorner to Bartle on the north, promoters for big conventions were already demanding more rooms and exhibit space.

After considering their options, planners in 1990 delayed the hotel issue and pushed instead for a doubling of Bartle's floor space to nearly 400,000 square feet. This seemed coun-

terintuitive, but they knew voters would approve the hall's expansion because most of the cost (higher taxes on hotels and restaurants) would be borne by visitors. A bigger Bartle, in turn, might make it easier to attract private capital for a hotel. Things progressed as intended for the next two years. In January 1992, as work on the $144 million convention facility began, the city invited proposals to erect a first-class, thousand-room hotel at an adjacent location.[29]

Three developers responded: local entrepreneur Whitney E. Kerr in partnership with H. Ross Perot, Jr., of Texas; Californians Allan R. Carpenter and Dale E. Fredericks; and the Leo Eisenberg Company of Kansas City. The first two plans that were submitted fit the requirements exactly, calling for $135 million projects directly south and northwest of Bartle (map 75). The third proposed a cheaper renovation and expansion of the old Americana Hotel east of the center. Developers of the two big projects both enjoyed good political connections in Kansas City, but the Kerr-Perot bid appeared stronger. It involved a choice, 23-acre tract along Broadway and Central just south of Interstate 635. The developers had offered to donate 2 of these acres for Bartle if the city would expand the building south across the highway rather than west. When officials agreed, a hotel there seemed a logical next step. A southside location would complement the Marriott to the north and help to link downtown with Crown Center. Kerr and Perot also promised to develop the rest of their land (which they called Central Square) into an enclosed mall/office complex utilizing the theme of world trade.[30]

The Kerr-Perot plan won support from the city's Economic Development Corporation in July 1992 and the planning commission the following September. Then, momentum stopped. Interest rates had begun to rise, critics argued that the developers should invest more and the city less, and Mayor Cleaver tempered his words of support. Most talk about the project now occurred behind closed doors. What emerged, three years later, was a cheaper alternative. In July

Figure 44 (facing page). Ilus W. Davis Park, 2002, Looking North from Eleventh Street. Construction of the Charles Evans Whittaker Federal Courthouse in 1998 directly north of city hall created the opportunity for a civic mall between Oak and Locust streets that would define the eastern edge of downtown. Davis Park, with its signature reflecting pool, opened in 2001. It is beautiful but hardly used, partly because only one other government entity, the Federal Aviation Administration (upper right), has relocated to the area. Note also the diminutive twin steeples of St. Patrick's, the city's oldest church, at the corner of Eighth and Cherry. (Courtesy Missouri Valley Special Collections, Kansas City Public Library)

1995, Perot withdrew his plan just before the city council voted it down. Instead, officials endorsed a renovation of the stately (and by then closed) Muehlebach (map 75). A new 427-room tower would be added on its Wyandotte Street side, then a skywalk to connect this tower to the existing Marriott on Twelfth Street. The combined hotel, with nearly 1,000 new or renovated rooms, would be run by Marriott and cost only $35 million.[31]

Serious boosters of downtown were saddened by the hotel compromise, for they knew that the number of rooms available would still be inadequate to attract major conventions. Playing conservatively with city finances might be well and good from some perspectives, but it was not the way to revive a downtown or advance a city's self-image.

Kansas City leaders actually adopted one of the worst strategies imaginable in their 1990s game of core development, attempting three expensive projects simultaneously without adequate financing for any. Though the first two of these—the hotel and the civic mall—managed to yield partial results, the third failed completely. This final idea, for an entertainment district, had a potential equal to the other two, but it suffered from poor timing. Proposed slightly after the other projects, it ran directly into the wake of their political and financial tensions and lost support at a critical moment.

The use of entertainment as a vehicle for urban renaissance, a process now well established in the United States, held special potential for Kansas City. One of this movement's leaders, Stanley H. Durwood, was a native son. Durwood had become rich after inventing the multiple-screen movie theater (or multiplex) in 1963 and creating the locally based AMC chain of cinemas. His dream, though, was to utilize large theater complexes as anchors for downtown redevelopment in a way analogous to the role of big department stores in suburban malls. He proposed the innovative concept to the local city council in 1967 and did so on a grand scale. His Crosstown Center project called for the renovation of eighteen blocks between Wyandotte and Oak, Twelfth and

Figure 45 (facing page). Pylons and Sky Stations, 2012, Looking East from Fourteenth and Washington. When Bartle Hall opened in 1976 to replace Municipal Auditorium as a convention center, its exposed metal and concrete exterior lacked charm. An expansion south over Interstate 670 in 1994 added more bulk to the structure but also, indirectly, some beauty. Atop the four 335-foot pylons needed to support the new roof, sculptor R. M. Fischer added 25-foot aluminum creations he called sky stations to honor the Art Deco of Municipal Auditorium. People quickly adopted them as city icons. (Photograph by Barbara Shortridge)

Interstate 670. When the council approved this idea, including generous tax abatements, it looked as if Kansas City was about to become a leader in urban renewal.[32]

Crosstown Center never happened, of course. It fell victim to its pioneering nature. Opponents challenged the use of tax abatements for this type of activity, and although the courts eventually upheld the city's position, their ruling took seven years and the deal collapsed. But Durwood was persistent. In 1980, he reprised his idea as the Crosstown Galleria that would connect a new cinema complex to the existing Jones and Macy's stores. The city again endorsed the plan, but it fell through when debt problems hit AMC's developer, the Daon Corporation of Vancouver, British Columbia.[33]

Because his ideas garnered favorable publicity, other cities recruited Durwood in the late 1980s to help revive their downtowns. These efforts all proved successful, most notably the Third Street Promenade in Santa Monica and the Sundance District in Fort Worth. As a result, Durwood decided to try again in Kansas City. In October 1995, he unveiled plans for a development that would transform the eight blocks bounded by Wyandotte and Grand, Thirteenth and I-670. Although the project's name was odd—Power and Light District, honoring the skyscraper at Fourteenth and Baltimore that housed the AMC offices—the goal was breathtakingly ambitious. For $454 million, Durwood would build a bazaar the size of Oak Park Mall in Johnson County and elevate it all above street level. Municipal Auditorium would anchor one end, and a thirty-screen theater would command the other. In between, the Power and Light Building would become a grand hotel, and new construction would create space for several score restaurants, dance clubs, and concert venues.[34]

Durwood asked the city for $176 million in tax breaks, the largest such diversion in city history, and after debate, voters approved the deal in February 1998. Construction was to begin in late 1999, with a grand opening in late 2003. The plan, however, never came to pass. This time, the problem was Durwood himself. Sick with cancer during the campaign, he died in July 1999. Then, without his leadership, financing faltered. Demands for city money existed elsewhere, and increased competition for the public's entertainment dollar was coming from riverboat casinos and, ironically, Durwood's own theater complexes in the suburbs. The city council terminated the agreement in October 2000.[35]

The final two elements that underpinned Kansas City's downtown revival of 2004 were much more subtle than civic malls or grand hotels. Arguably, though, they were just as im-

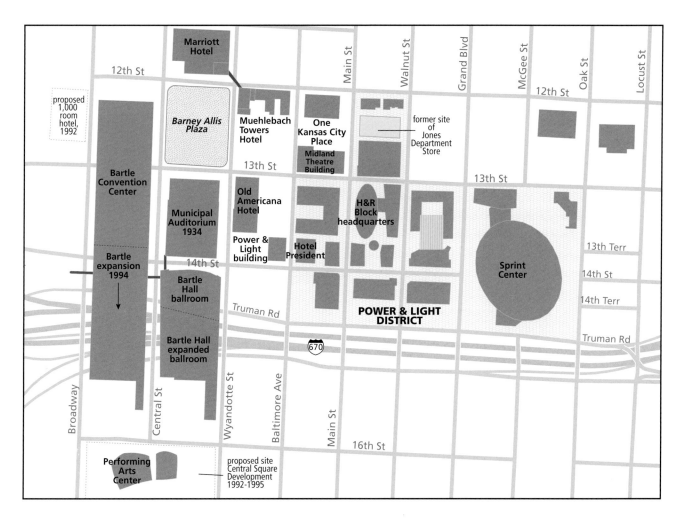

Map 75. *Development Proposals for Downtown Kansas City, Missouri, 1992–2006. Compiled from multiple sources.*

portant. Both involved the rehabilitation of older commercial buildings and owed much of their success to a 1998 Missouri law that authorized tax abatements to help improve blighted areas. Developers who converted historical structures to meet approved modern needs could have taxes frozen for ten years at the property's value before improvement and then pegged at only half the current market value for fifteen additional years. Many entrepreneurs saw the new ruling as a chance to create loft-style condominiums. Another company, DST Systems, which had been active in local conversion work since the 1980s, used the legislation to expand its operations from specific buildings and neighborhoods to the downtown district as a whole.[36]

The development of downtown loft apartments seemed a foolhardy goal at first glance, especially in Kansas City, which for the past several decades had epitomized the mass movement to the suburbs. Most people thought that if a re-

verse migration were ever to occur, the catalyst would have to be on a grand scale—a new sports facility, for example, or unique shopping opportunities. Countering such standard thinking was a trend seen in coastal cities where downtowns were becoming the preferred residential choice for a sophisticated younger generation, individuals who eschewed bluegrass lawns in favor of the art and music scene, nightlife, and diverse culture. Popular television shows of the time, such as *Frasier, Friends,* and *Sex and the City,* exposed such urban lifestyles across the land, and with the new Missouri tax abatements as a temptation, several local entrepreneurs took a chance.[37]

Loft development in Kansas City began slowly. On the one hand, buildings for conversion were easily available, and city leaders encouraged the process. If people remained downtown twenty-four hours a day instead of only eight, the reasoning went, new stores would open quickly to serve the growing clientele. Condominiums could spark redevelopment as a whole. Skeptics, naturally, saw this scenario in reverse. Why would anybody move to downtown Kansas City so long as it was nearly devoid of entertainment and other cultural venues? Moreover, where would such urban pioneers purchase groceries and other personal necessities?[38]

The actual process of loft conversion found a middle ground, partly encouraging other development and partly in response to it. Early units concentrated near the Missouri River where property was cheap, and the venerable city market at Fourth and Main provided a strong sense of neighborhood (map 76). The old Volker window-shade factory there at 200 Main became the Riverbend Lofts in 1999, for instance, and the Townley Metal and Hardware warehouse at 200 Walnut the Old Townley Lofts. In 2000, 185 new units came on the market, and in 2001, there were 303 more. These conversions were spread widely, including several in the Crossroads Arts District, some west of Broadway in old garment plants, and some in the downtown core itself.[39]

The pace of condominium construction crept upward to 389 units in 2003 and 455 in 2004 but then ballooned to 1,425 in 2005 as a new downtown entertainment district was becoming a reality (map 77). This year was a tipping point. City officials estimated that downtown now housed 9,000 residents, enough for a local grocer, Cosentino's, to announce a new store on Thirteenth Street between Main and Walnut. Larger-scale housing conversions came on the scene as well, including the old federal courts building at 811 Grand, the thirty-five–story Fidelity Bank and Trust building at 909 Walnut, and the eighteen-story BMA tower near Thirty-first and Broadway. Observers all praised this return of residential life to the central city. A few worried about an overemphasis on upscale projects.[40]

DST Systems, the single most prolific user of historical building tax abatements in the city, merits attention apart from other developers because it operates with a different mind-set. Its roots are with the Kansas City Southern Railway of the 1880s. As that original company prospered, it diversified, and DST emerged in 1969 as a data-management and software-service subsidiary using technology designed originally for tracking rail cars. DST became independent in 1995 and soon spawned its own subsidiary, DST Realty. The venture into property was not so much for profit as to honor the longtime commitment of Kansas City Southern executives to improve downtown, especially the area near their offices at Eleventh and Wyandotte.[41]

Under the leadership of Thomas McDonnell (DST) and J. Philip Kirk, Jr. (DST Realty), the company developed a

"west-side strategy" in the 1980s. It focused on the dwindling stock of Victorian buildings on Quality Hill. Buying them initially without a purpose beyond preservation, company officials conceived a plan for a philanthropic campus. DST restored the properties and then sold or leased them to the American Cancer Society, the YMCA of Greater Kansas City, the Heart of America United Way, and similar organizations. By sharing infrastructure in this way, the agencies saved dollars for their real work.[42]

With the area west of Broadway stabilized by the early 1990s (including a new building for Kansas City Southern Industries at 427 West Twelfth Street), DST announced a new initiative—the Eleventh Street Corridor Development Corporation. Again, the approach was at the neighborhood scale, using revenue generated from several quality buildings the company owned along the route west from Main Street to purchase and restore others. DST officials made their own offices there, at 333 West Eleventh, but viewed themselves as only temporary owners of the other structures.[43]

By 1994 or so, DST's "refreshingly bottoms-up approach to urban development" was garnering high praise from community leaders. By working "quietly but effectively" and delivering "more than they promise," McDonnell and Kirk became trusted advisers for even bigger projects. Thus, McDonnell helped coordinate the renovation of Union Station and cochaired the Downtown Development Authority with Mayor Kay Barnes starting in 2002. The company's most significant ongoing role, however, is in assembling urban land into units large enough for major new construction. In fact, having such land packages available has been critical to the success of the entire urban core renaissance since 2003. DST, with some 4,000 employees locally plus extensive real estate holdings, is the "quiet muscle" in downtown Kansas City today.[44]

In 2002, after a decade of mixed achievement in the central city, views on progress were divided. Optimists could point to new condominiums and a civic mall, the enlarged convention center, and the resurging Crossroads District, yet pessimists as easily could itemize lost opportunities and draw unfavorable comparisons to advances in Denver, Indianapolis, and other peer cities. Negativity seemed to be in the ascendancy late that year when the Kansas City Star published a six-part series that explored the community's "broken heart." Then, quite suddenly, a new spirit of cooperation emerged.[45]

The change, from big projects vying with one another for public attention to working toward a unified goal, had mixed

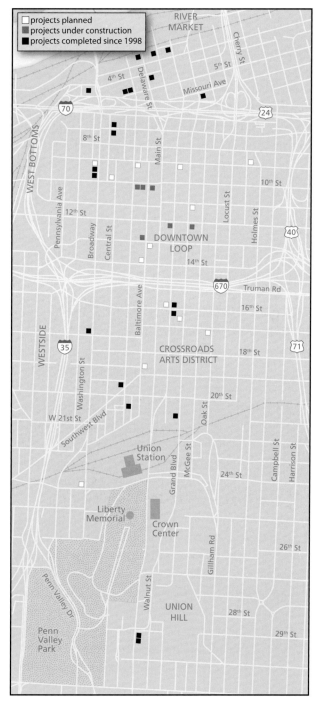

Map 76. *Loft Housing in Downtown Kansas City, Missouri, 2002. Modified from a map published in the* Kansas City Star, *September 29, 2002, p. A16.*

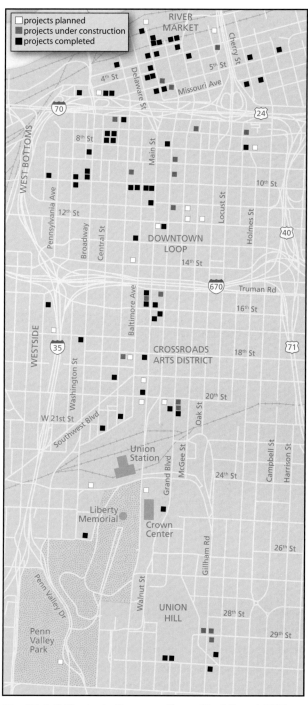

Map 77. *Loft Housing in Downtown Kansas City, Missouri, 2005. Modified from a map published in the* Kansas City Star, *September 18, 2005, p. A20.*

origins. The new mayor, Kay Barnes, was one ingredient, bringing an ability to forge consensus from her background in leadership consultation. The death of Stanley Durwood was arguably another, in that his absence freed downtown from a renovation that was possibly overreliant on a theater complex. A third part of the mix was the almost chance presence of a comprehensive development plan for downtown known as the Sasaki Report. This document, commissioned by the Civic Council of Greater Kansas City, was released in the summer of 2001. It could easily have been ignored.

Instead, coming as it did at a time when city troubles were severe and cooperation was essential, leaders embraced the report's ideas. Mayor Barnes made its agenda her own, and so did DST's McDonnell, the Kemper family, and other key businesspeople.[46]

The Sasaki planners opposed two common strategies for renewal. A push for big retailers would clash with existing activity at Crown Center, they reasoned, and mean possible failure for both places. Similarly, erection of a new baseball stadium downtown would force the abandonment of half of the still attractive Truman Sports Complex. Instead, they favored another expansion of the Bartle convention center, increased emphasis on the arts, and erection of a multipurpose arena to replace the poorly located Kemper facility. This mutually supportive triad would bring area residents downtown and promote tourism. The goal also seemed achievable. Funding for an arena would have to start from scratch, but a $74 million plan to modernize Bartle Hall had already been placed on the November 2002 ballot. In like manner, arts developments were currently in motion. From a base provided by the still-emerging Crossroads District, private entrepreneurship

Figure 46. Eleventh Street, 2005, Looking West from near Broadway. Investment by DST Realty and others has revitalized Quality Hill. Eleventh Street is its core. On the left is the Cathedral of the Immaculate Conception, a landmark since 1886. Its red-brick exterior has been duplicated on other area structures. On the right, a building called the Old Cathedral offers modern, one- and two-bedroom apartments in a vintage setting. A block ahead the headquarters of the Heart of America United Way have been retrofitted into the old Virginia Hotel. (Courtesy Wikipedia Commons)

in 1994 had added the possibility of a world-class performing arts center. The local Muriel McBrien Kauffman Foundation gave $105 million toward such a building in 1995 and four years later purchased a site for it near Sixteenth and Central, the same tract recently promoted by Ross Perot, Jr., for a grand hotel.[47]

The quality and potential of the performing arts center gave hope to all downtown enthusiasts. Its champion, Julia Kauffman, was widely respected within the city and had hired renowned architect Moshe Safdie to create a complex dominated by two elegant, shell-shaped bowls, one for the Kansas City Symphony and the other for opera and ballet. The cost was high—$326 million—but Kauffman's social and financial connections were impeccable. Following more fund-raising, a groundbreaking for this new civic icon was expected in 2006.[48]

Kay Barnes acted initially to solidify the growing consensus for major development. To that end, she assembled a thirteen-member advisory board that included DST's Tom McDonnell, banker Jonathan Kemper, developer Jon Copaken, and John Laney from the Hallmark Family Foundation. The board members met regularly in 2002 and 2003, sharing ideas for arena financing and complementary activities. Kemper, for example, assumed the lead in relocating the Kansas City Public Library from inadequate, leased quarters to the former First National Bank building at Tenth and Baltimore. This $30 million project, completed in 2004, restored a magnificent 1906 structure and sparked condominium and other development in surrounding blocks.[49]

Barnes and her advisers decided to concentrate on what they called the South Loop area between Twelfth Street and I-670. These blocks were in relatively poor condition, yet they occupied vital territory east of Bartle, south of the office skyscrapers, and west of city hall (map 75). Members of the group agreed on the importance of a new arena but thought even more development was necessary if the downtown were truly to revive. Rather than taking an incremental approach where risk would be high for the initial business to commit, they worked behind the scenes to secure simultaneous pacts with developers for the arena and an adjacent entertainment district together with at least one major corporate headquarters. The plan was more than ambitious, but it all came together early in 2004.[50]

Each of the South Loop pieces depended on personal connections. The first announcement came from H&R Block, a local firm that had become the nation's largest tax preparation company. More out of loyalty to his hometown than real need, Henry Bloch agreed to relocate from the Plaza area and erect a landmark oval office tower in the middle of the new district. Financing for the arena was hamstrung initially by the mayor's pledge not to raise taxes, but two more personal contacts saved the project. First, the highly respected Anschutz Entertainment Group contributed $50 million and agreed to manage the facility. Anschutz, though California based, is owned by Kansas native Philip Anschutz and operated by Timothy J. Leiweke, a former general manager of a local soccer team. A second financial boost came from Sprint Corporation, the city's largest company. This contribution gave the building its name—the Sprint Center.[51]

The decision to add an entertainment focus as the final element in the "spectacular new district" downtown was popular but controversial. The city council had rejected Stanley Durwood's concept in this regard a few years earlier, and so had the Sasaki consultants. Nonetheless, a center for nightlife would complement events at both the convention center and the arena. A good developer could make it work. Kay Barnes pushed the project because she had such a firm in mind—the Cordish Company of Baltimore. Its owner, David Cordish, was interested because of past ties to Andi Udris, the president of Kansas City's Economic Development Corporation.[52]

The grand announcement for the arena and entertainment center in May 2004 left Kansas City people giddy. The total investment was overwhelming—some $1.6 billion—but since most of this was to come from private corporations or tax-incremental financing, it seemed like a gift. Mayor Barnes, like her counterpart Carol Marinovich in Wyandotte County, became a culture hero, and citizens sat back to watch the transformation begin. Blake Cordish, David's son and now the company head, even smoothed over the possibility of resentment from Durwood admirers. With the permission of AMC, he revived the Power and Light name for the entire new district and restricted his own KC Live label to a smaller plaza area adjacent to Sprint Center. Cordish also partnered with the AMC people to restore the Empire and Midland theaters downtown as part of the entertainment package.[53]

Not enough time has passed to fully judge whether the downtown renaissance has been successful. Still, so far so good. The H&R Block building opened in 2006, the Sprint Center in late 2007, and the Power and Light District the following March. An anticipated professional basketball or hockey franchise has yet to materialize as an anchor tenant, but the arena is nevertheless doing well. Attendance exceeded expectations in the first year. The same is true for the surrounding restaurants and other businesses. People praise the district's design, especially its wide sidewalks, a pedestrian mall midblock between Thirteenth and Fourteenth streets,

Figure 47. H&R Block World Headquarters, 2012, Looking North on Main Street from the 1400 Block. Henry Bloch's decision to move his company downtown gave credibility to the city's larger redevelopment plan of 2004. His distinctive elliptical building, sheathed in green glass, opened in 2006. It includes five levels of parking underground and a 300-seat stage used by the Kansas City Repertory Theater. A portion of the KC Live entertainment district appears in the foreground. The Commerce Tower, the AT&T Town Pavilion, and the 1201 Walnut Building mark the skyline. (Photograph by Barbara Shortridge)

and the "living-room" atmosphere of its KC Live plaza. Economic recession starting in late 2007 has hurt traffic some but not severely.[54]

Anybody who knew Kansas City at the turn of the twenty-first century has to be elated at the revival of its downtown core. Nevertheless, as the glow of opening nights has ebbed, several concerns remain. With so much money dedicated to a single enterprise, other efforts have been shortchanged. One potential victim, ironically, was the performing arts center that had inspired other area investments. Julia Kauffman's group had hoped for funding from a bistate tax proposal in 2004, similar to the one that had saved Union Station. Voters, however, turned it down. Talk then turned to the possibility of a less expensive center in and around the Lyric Theater at Eleventh and Central. In the end, a desire to create a spectacular building that might draw larger attention to the arts produced additional private donations and a return to the original site and plan. Construction was delayed, but the $326 million Kauffman Center opened to national praise in September 2011.[55]

A second awkwardness involves Kemper Arena in the West Bottoms. Its inadequacies had promoted the construction of the Sprint Center, of course, and since this project was completed, the older site has struggled to find events. Razing would seem a logical step, but this is impossible because of a fifty-year lease officials signed with the American Royal in 1995 to hold stock shows there. Kemper currently costs the city $4 million annually in subsidy and debt payments. More rodeos, barbecue contests, and similar agriculture-related events may slow this drain but likely not enough.[56]

Finally, the hesitancy to spend more money has interrupted progress on two needed downtown projects—a second convention hotel and a resuscitation of the area east of the civic mall. Although nobody argues that these concerns are of greater merit than the ones Mayor Barnes chose to emphasize, they surfaced again once the rest of the urban core began to glow. The hotel dominates discussions.

Promoters of major conventions say that, to be competitive, a city needs not only an adequate meeting facility but also an active restaurant/entertainment district nearby and at least 3,000 hotel rooms within walking distance. Kansas City before 2007 offered only the first of these three ingredients, and so it competed poorly. But with the opening of the Power and Light area, success seemed near. Studies commissioned by the city agree with this thinking but note that current room-occupancy rates—about 55 percent—are too low to at-

tract a privately funded grand hotel. Major bond issues and tax incentives would have to be added.[57]

The city council feels that a new hotel justifies the expense, but Kay Barnes's successor as mayor, Mark Funkhouser, was skeptical. Stalemate has resulted. Proponents have identified four potential sites just east or south of Bartle, and they stress the millions of dollars lost with the recent departure of the city's three biggest regular conventions (Sam's Club, SkillsUSA, and Walmart managers). Opponents stress fiscal responsibility and the possibility of specializing in medium-sized conventions.[58]

The long-neglected eastern side of the downtown loop, which gained the imposing Charles Evans Whittaker Federal Courthouse in 1998 but then saw support for its adjoining civic mall atrophy after Mayor Cleaver left office, again claimed the spotlight in 2005. Following a suggestion in the Sasaki Report, the city endorsed a twelve-block redevelopment called East Village. This area from Locust (the eastern edge of the civic mall) to Charlotte and from Eighth to Twelfth would be largely cleared and then given over to three projects: an anchor corporate headquarters for and by the city's largest construction firm, J. E. Dunn; additional commercial space via another local developer; and 1,200 moderately priced housing units built by a Minnesota corporation. It was a big ($350 million) but awkward arrangement. Dunn already was based in the neighborhood and agreed to stay if the city cleaned up the environs. The other developers hoped for generous city financing (like that given to the Power and Light District) plus state and federal funds in support of low-income housing and a contract to erect a new federal office building.[59]

The results were perhaps predictable. Although Dunn completed an impressive, six-story building adjacent to the civic mall for its 500 employees, the other projects foundered. City money was provided but not as generously as for the downtown core. The Minnesota developer pulled out, the local firm missed a deadline to obtain financing, and federal officials have yet to fund their long-promised office building. Fifty apartment units and a parking garage opened late in 2011, but for the near future at least, the view east from the J. E. Dunn building is mostly parking lots.[60]

The East Side

The story of recent, unexpected progress that unites the speedway and downtown areas applies as well to Kansas City's residential East Side. The transformation of this traditionally poor, African American district has not attracted nearly as many dollars or as much publicity as the other two sites. Still, considering its starting point and continuing obstacles, the modest achievements there are equally noteworthy.

The dynamics of modern life on the East Side are underappreciated. Everybody knows about white flight in the 1950s and 1960s, but less is known about the large and equally disruptive exodus of middle-class African Americans that followed soon after. A surplus of houses resulted, most of which were purchased by outsiders as speculative investments. Block after block thereby became rental property. Although some of the new owners were responsible landlords, the majority did little maintenance. Rent money accumulated in suburban bank accounts while roofs on Prospect and Indiana avenues began to sag and paint began to peel.

Decay was widespread by 1990, and owners simply abandoned some of the worst properties. Such spaces naturally became invitations to crime. Drug dealers, crack cocaine producers, and prostitutes all utilized these havens, and their presence led to more abandonment. By 2006, officials counted some 5,000 vacant and deteriorating houses in the city, almost all of them east of Troost Avenue (map 78). People too poor or too old to move were the only ones who remained, and Curtis Walker, who delivered mail near Prospect Avenue and Twenty-sixth Street at the time, saw "a sense of hopelessness here . . . like nobody cares."[61]

As city agencies worked to transfer property to individuals and organizations for attempts at rehabilitation, a national recession made things worse. Abandonments grew to 7,500 by 2009 and to 10,900 by 2010, including a group of larger homes south of Brush Creek (map 79). The situation became so bad that one could find blocks with no more than one occupied home left. In fact, prices dropped so low in 2009 that rehabilitation work essentially stopped, with no way to recoup the money invested.[62]

Although it is hard to consider abandonment as a part of progress, in some ways it is. Having fewer houses makes property acquisition for development simpler, for instance, and a smaller population is easier to aid and educate. Dire conditions also primed residents to accept new ideas. So, as census reports for the year 2000 revealed a loss of 40,000 people since 1950 in an eight-block corridor along Prospect Avenue between Eighteenth Street and Brush Creek, planners began to unveil ideas for renewal (map 80). Changing social attitudes aided the process. The presence of a middle-class black population in the suburbs, to take one example, helped

the general public see the East Side problem in economic rather than racial terms. This change in perspective, in turn, helped to attract development dollars.[63]

The increased ability of Kansas City people in recent years to separate race from poverty is partly a product of national events, but it has been aided locally by the presence of three transcendent African American men: a politician, a businessman/philanthropist, and a charismatic public ambassador. The politician, Emanuel Cleaver II, arrived in the area in the 1970s to serve as a minister. His leadership abilities not only produced congregation growth, but also earned him three terms on the city council, starting in 1979. Between 1991 and 1999, he served as the city's first African American mayor. By doing his job well, Cleaver has built lasting bridges across the community and still serves the area as a member of the U.S. House of Representatives.

Whereas Cleaver's role in the community has largely been defined by his occupations, Kansas City's public ambassador extraordinaire, John "Buck" O'Neil, came to his calling by chance at age eighty-three. O'Neil was a baseball player with the Kansas City Monarchs who, after retirement, worked to establish a local museum for the old Negro Leagues. He was a gifted storyteller and a generous soul, a person who saw life clearly but without bitterness. When filmmaker Ken Burns observed these traits in 1993, he made O'Neil the star of his PBS documentary *Baseball*. Buck then became a celebrity. What started with sports quickly grew to bigger things. Buck loved people and was generous with his time. Never preachy, he was amazingly effective at bringing disparate groups together. When he died in 2006, the *Kansas City Star* published an eight-page special section in his honor. As a friend put it, in the last twelve years of his life, O'Neil served as "an ambassador and a personal friend to all Kansas Citians, period."[64]

Finally, a man named Ollie Gates occupies a pragmatic position between Cleaver and O'Neil. Gates, an octogenarian, serves several roles in the city. Most obviously, he symbolizes barbecue as the owner of a large and highly respected chain of restaurants. Barbecue, in turn, through its expansion from a limited position within the black community to an enthusiastic embracement by the city as a whole, has played a powerful role in bridging racial divides. Although fellow restaurateur Arthur Bryant certainly deserves much credit for introducing white Kansas City to the charms of smoked meat (the aromas wafting across Brooklyn Avenue from his "grease shack" proved irresistible to crowds at nearby Municipal Stadium where the Athletics and Chiefs played), it is Gates who

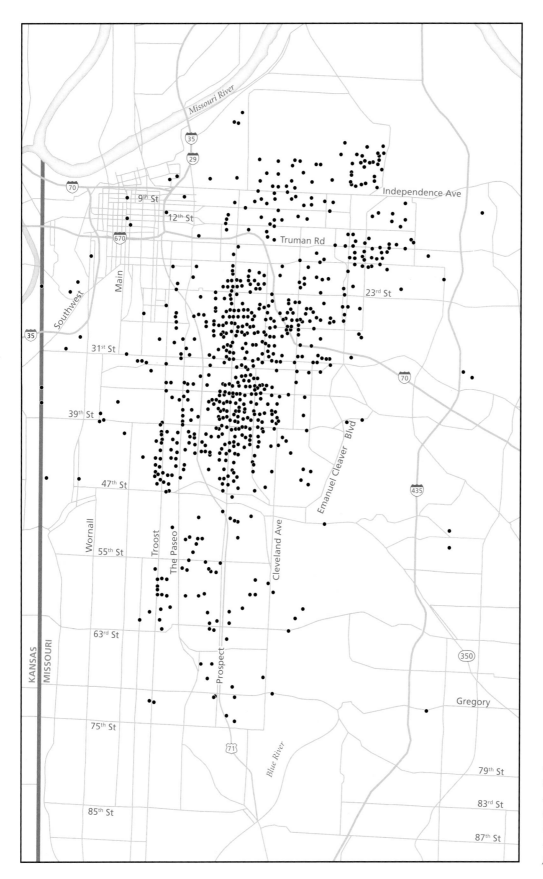

Map 78. Vacant Structures in Kansas City, Missouri, 2006. Modified from a map published in the Kansas City Star, February 12, 2006, p. A10.

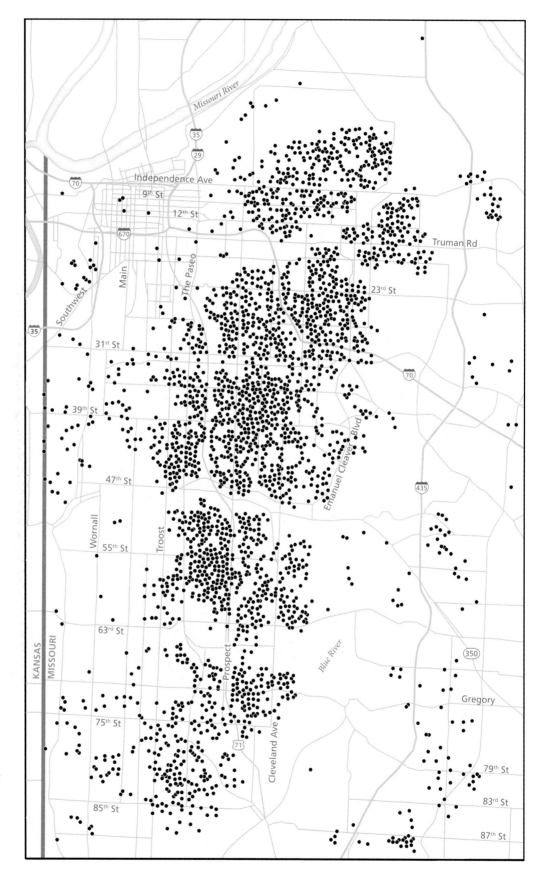

*Map 79. Vacant Structures
in Kansas City, Missouri,
2009. Modified from a
map published in the
Kansas City Star,
October 6, 2009, p. A9.*

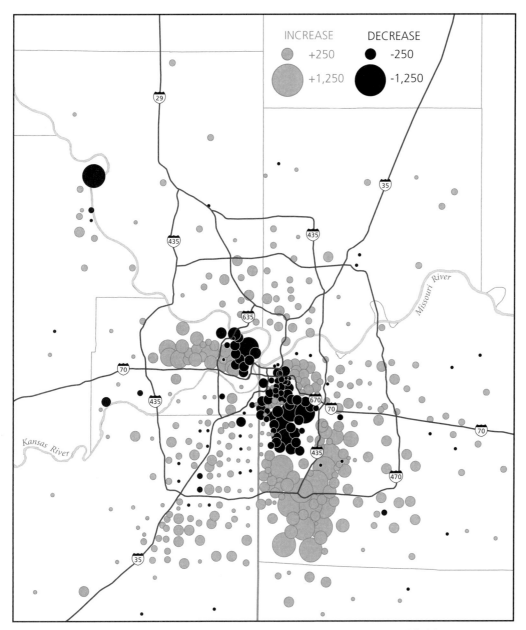

Map 80. Change in African American Population in Greater Kansas City, 1990–2000. Modified from a map compiled from U.S. Census data by the Mid-America Regional Council, available at http://www.marc.org (accessed February 25, 2009).

has used his money and status to enhance the city. As I will detail, he has been active in several major initiatives on the East Side and has been the leader in work near Twelfth Street and The Paseo.[65]

Development on the East Side since the early 1990s has been anything but smooth. Every achievement has been marred by setbacks, and some initiatives have failed completely. The progress also has been uneven spatially, with successes more common near the Troost and Paseo corridors than farther to the east. Some people attribute this pattern to

larger and better-built original housing along The Paseo, others to this area's relative proximity to white Kansas City's investment dollars, and still others to the presence there of the old African American business district at Eighteenth and Vine. All three arguments contain elements of truth.

Schools are the most challenging development issue. I detailed the extraordinary troubles of the city district in the last chapter, and these issues remained largely uncontested until 2010. Despite massive infusions of money to create first-class buildings, raise salaries, and implement new programs, test

scores remain low. Outside observers have seen little account-ability from administrators and a school board more con-cerned with job numbers and maintenance contracts than with education itself. As a result, parents sought alternative educational environments, and enrollments plummeted from 28,000 students in 2001–2002 to 17,000 in 2009–2010. Many buildings operated at less than half capacity.[66]

The nadir was reached in 2007. People living in western Independence, an area that had been served by the Kansas City school district for a century, vowed to secede and attach themselves to the Independence system instead (map 56). Kansas City leaders called the movement a "hostile takeover" and doubted it would succeed, since approval would be re-quired from voters in both districts. The election results that November were shocking. Independence people approved, of course, but so did those in Kansas City. It was a public ad-mission of the district's failings. Van Horn High School and its feeder institutions, with some 3,100 students, moved the next year to a new administration.[67]

The combination of falling student numbers and the In-dependence rebellion served as a call to action. When a new

Figure 48. Emanuel Cleaver II and Ollie W. Gates, 1991. Politician Cleaver and businessman Gates are leaders in easing racial tensions within the city. Besides championing redevelopment on the black East Side, they have worked equally hard for citywide progress. The cer-emony here, for example, is on Ward Parkway at Sixty-seventh Street, where a large Japanese-made statue of an eagle had been refurbished. Mayor Cleaver is at the podium next to philanthropist Sheila Kemper Dietrich. Gates is at left center next to the city's park commissioner, Anita Gorman. (Courtesy Missouri Valley Special Collections, Kansas City Public Library)

superintendent, John Covington, arrived in the city in 2009, the public and the school board were ready to support his plan to close almost half of the district's buildings. This move has saved money, allowed a winnowing out of poor teachers, and provided a real chance for educational improvement.[68]

Covington's plan was to build on several successful schools that are already present, particularly Lincoln College Prepara-tory Academy at 2111 Woodland Avenue, where test scores are on a par with those in suburban schools. The Paseo Visual and Performing Arts Academy at 4747 Flora Avenue also shows promise, as does the Afrikan Centered Education Collegium Campus at the former Southeast High School (3500 Meyer

Boulevard). When these programs are combined with those at three highly regarded independent high schools—Alta Vista Charter School at 1720 Holly Street serving the Hispanic West Side, University Leadership Charter Academy at 6801 Holmes Road underwritten by philanthropists Barnett and Shirley Helzberg, and Christo Rey Catholic High School at 211 Linwood Boulevard where study is combined with work at local businesses—a solid foundation is in place. Kansas City high schools are now small enough that they participate in sports at the 3A level instead of their former 6A, but they are finally positioned for substantial academic growth.[69]

Recent economic development on the East Side began in 1989 with a $114 million city initiative pushed by then councilman Emanuel Cleaver. This effort had three parts: a new American Royal arena in the West Bottoms; flood control on Brush Creek; and improvements to the Eighteenth and Vine area, including a jazz hall of fame and a Negro Leagues baseball museum. Two of these three projects became stimuli for East Side business revival.[70]

The possibility of creating national centers in Kansas City to honor jazz and the Negro Leagues had been contemplated for some time before 1989, with the Liberty Memorial mall seen as a likely site for the former and the Truman Sports Complex for the latter. Cleaver argued, though, that if these two potential tourist destinations were positioned together in the Eighteenth and Vine district where jazz music was once king, they might transform the entire neighborhood. In theory, public seed money would attract private investment, new businesses and apartment houses would arise, and the movement then would expand far beyond the original intersection.[71]

The initial stages went smoothly. A renovation of the Gem Theater as a cultural center was completed in 1993, the same year that construction began across the street for the two museums. They opened in 1997 to widespread acclaim, attracting some 350,000 visitors the first year. Work then began on the neighborhood, with $37 million raised for a series of retail and office buildings and more than that for housing. Problems arose as this construction neared completion. The new apartments filled easily, but attendance fell at the museums and few businesses leased space. The reason—one everybody worried about but nobody expressed publicly—was fear. White residents and visitors were reluctant to linger in a black neighborhood even though the deputy police chief insisted that crime there was "nonexistent." Promoters hoped that a little more effort and time would solve the problem, but it persists to a degree. The Peachtree Restaurant, selling

upscale soul food, was successful after opening in 2002, but its owners relocated to the more trafficked Power and Light District in 2008.[72]

Cleaver's other East Side initiative, the Brush Creek corridor, began with less fanfare than the jazz district, but it has advanced faster. Its first phase, from 1992 to 1994, entailed basic engineering—a deepening and widening of the creek's channel by the U.S. Corps of Engineers to lessen flooding. Then, while this work was under way, Mayor Cleaver and others pushed to enhance the area with better roads, new parks, and development sites. The idea was to use the cachet of commercial and cultural institutions upstream on Brush Creek (the Country Club Plaza, the Nelson-Atkins Museum of Art, and the University of Missouri–Kansas City) to encourage expansion eastward. Such an opportunity would serve business well, they argued, and also bring jobs into and across the East Side.[73]

Two cooperative efforts have brought the plan to life. First came the East Side Initiative, put together by officials at the city-owned Swope Parkway Health Center, which had operated since 1978 in an old bank building near Cleveland Avenue. When the center wanted to erect a drug abuse facility in 1990, neighbors objected, worried about its effect on property values. This dilemma prompted innovation. In exchange for obtaining permission to build, people at the center promised to assist neighborhood revitalization. They created the Community Builders of Kansas City, a nonprofit group that, in turn, developed a 40-acre site on the southeast corner of Cleveland. The end product was The Shops on Blue Parkway, a $37 million project that includes a badly needed grocery (Sun Fresh), two shoe stores, a salon, and two fast-food franchises. Across the street on the north, the Community Builders worked with the H&R Block Company to create a new call center that has 200 permanent and 600 seasonal employees.[74]

The second cooperative started at the corridor's western end near Troost. Here, the University of Missouri–Kansas City served as instigator, and its officials recruited area hospitals,

Figure 49 (facing page). The Museums at Eighteenth and Vine, 2012. City officials placed proposals for jazz and Negro Leagues baseball museums in the city's historical black center on Vine Street in the hope of revitalizing that neighborhood. A public bond issue augmented by private funds led to a successful opening in 1997, along with adjacent shops, a jazz club, a theater, and new housing. Recent business has been less than anticipated, however, a product of a poor economy, lingering racial distrust, and the death of unofficial host Buck O'Neil. (Photograph by Barbara Shortridge)

the J. C. Nichols Company, and others to form Brush Creek Partners. They then convinced the Ewing Marion Kauffman Foundation to purchase 37 acres on the north side of the creek for a combination park and foundation headquarters. Next, they arranged a site where another local philanthropist, James Stowers, Jr., of American Century Investments, could construct a $300 million cancer research center. This facility opened in 2000 across Blue Parkway from the Kauffman Foundation. As these projects neared completion, the new roadway on Brush Creek's north side was appropriately christened Emanuel Cleaver II Boulevard.[75]

Two additional East Side developments in the 1990s complemented Mayor Cleaver's initiatives. The first, proposed by Councilman Jim Glover in 1992, was to bring major retailers to the midtown area. This was a needed and ambitious project, involving four square blocks on the southeast corner of Main Street at Linwood Boulevard. The city made overtures to Kmart, Payless Cashways (building supplies), and Price Chopper (groceries), but negotiations went slowly. These companies were used to suburban environments, not the inner city, and the first two of them were struggling nationally at the time. The site was still sitting empty in 2000 when an infusion of $48 million in city revenue bonds ended the impasse. The two primary tenants at the end—Costco and Home Depot—opened in 2001 to widespread applause, and they continue to attract black and white customers from a large area. This was the first Kansas City store for the popular Costco chain.[76]

The final big push on the East Side in recent years has been residential, not commercial, and therefore a complement to the others. Its focus is the Beacon Hill neighborhood, extending from Troost to The Paseo and from Twenty-fourth to Thirty-first Street. This area is nicely situated between the museums at Eighteenth and Vine and the new Costco and is accessible to jobs in the downtown core. For these reasons and because Beacon Hill residents themselves have been active in neighborhood preservation since the 1970s, planners saw it as an ideal poster project for renewal. Public and private financiers were excited and contributed $66 million to the cause in 1999.[77]

Beacon Hill developers wisely adopted blocks as their working units (instead of individual houses) and planned to erect new homes where needed while repairing and upgrading others. This approach would create a blight-free but pleasantly heterogeneous living environment. Some 300 to 400 homes would be involved. Despite this solid and well-financed plan, Beacon Hill progressed slowly. By 2003, work had begun on

only three houses, and the next year, reporters found that two of these restorations had consumed $600,000. Investigation revealed that the process of property condemnation was a major problem, with people trying to overcharge the city. Lack of a master developer hurt progress, too. Authorities finally resolved these issues by 2008, and the project is now nearly complete.[78]

Economic development east of Troost has not been easy. Even the best-conceived and best-financed plans have faced delays, some because of lingering racial fears, some because of greed, and some because of overoptimism. Still, success has come, and the work at Beacon Hill, Brush Creek, and elsewhere has helped adjacent neighborhoods with their own, more grassroots rehabilitations. The Ivanhoe district is a good example. In this area, stretching from Troost to Prospect between Thirty-first Street and Brush Creek, residents secured a small private grant and used it to help restore a park and bring citizen pressure against local drug houses and vandalism. Similarly, the revitalization of Eighteenth and Vine inspired a private group headed by restaurateur Ollie Gates to create a park at the city's other fabled jazz corner at Twelfth and Vine. Gates further envisions a restoration of The Paseo that connects the two music hearths, perhaps with trolley service to better showcase the boulevard's fountains and statuary.[79]

Not all East Side stories are positive, of course. Meiner's Thriftway grocery, in the Linwood Shopping Center at 3110 Prospect, closed in 2007. This minimall had opened in 1986 to considerable enthusiasm, but it fell victim to population losses in that area plus competition from the new Sun Fresh store on Blue Parkway. The area's biggest failure has been the $100 million Citadel Plaza development northwest of Sixty-third Street and Prospect. This 35-acre project was conceived by people at the adjacent Research Medical Center. They assembled the tract and razed over a hundred blighted homes and businesses preparatory to construction of a mixed retail, office, and residential complex. The hospital transferred development rights to the nonprofit Community Development Corporation of Kansas City in 2005, but there, progress stopped. Accusations of waste and corruption abounded, and city officials finally called the project "failed" in 2010.[80]

Expansion and Division

In 1990, Interstates 435 and 470 had encircled nearly all the residents of Greater Kansas City. Such packaging was tidy but ephemeral. By 2000, this ring had been breached in many places, and the expansion continues. A map of the city's white population outlines this perimeter well and also depicts the numerous internal separations created and maintained by stream valleys (map 81). The "island" of Kansas City, Kansas, is easy to distinguish, for example, as is the Northland. Less stark but still significant divisions can be seen at Mill Creek just west of I-435 in Johnson County; at the Blue River just west of I-435 between Kansas City and Independence; and at the Little Blue farther east that separates Grandview, Raytown, and Independence from Lee's Summit and Blue Springs. The East Fork of the Little Blue (Lake Jacomo) then isolates Lee's Summit from Blue Springs. In striking contrast to these natural divides, the more widely discussed political borders between Johnson County and its neighbors to the east and north are invisible.

African American and Hispanic residents have been vital parts of the city's recent expansion. Although their numbers outside the interstate loop are still moderate, both groups now have a sizable presence in Olathe and along the southern U.S. 71 corridor in and near Grandview (maps 82 and 83). Suburbanization, in fact, has arguably been the biggest geographic change for these peoples in recent years. Inside the city proper, the most important Hispanic expansion since 1990 has come in the venerable Northeast neighborhood. Census tracts north of Truman Road and east of Prospect are now a quarter Latin, a doubling of the earlier fraction. Business signs along Independence Avenue today are as likely to be in Spanish as in English.

For African Americans, recent migration has taken two main forms. Johnson County, with its quality public schools, has attracted many people from Wyandotte and Jackson counties. For those of lesser means, the best alternative has been moving south into aging suburban housing. Since 1990, census tracts with black percentages exceeding 90 have expanded from Seventy-ninth to Ninety-fifth street in the wedge of land between Troost and the Blue River. The map also reveals a second gore across that stream between Raytown and Grandview. Besides moderately priced homes, these areas all feature school systems other than the troubled one of the city proper (map 56). Black percentages in the trans-Blue district ranged between 20 and 50 percent in 2000.

To better understand the current cultural geography of Kansas City, racial maps should be paired with a map of household income. Although the old stereotypes of rich Johnson County, poor Wyandotte, and middle-class Northland continue to apply, several significant but more subtle patterns are present as well (map 84). The long-asserted separation across the Jackson-Wyandotte county line, for example, no longer

exists. The depopulated, industrial, and semivacant West Bottoms in the northwestern corner of Jackson faces a similar landscape across the Kaw in Armourdale. Just to the south, the Hispanic West Side of Kansas City, Missouri, is matched by the equally Latin Argentine and Central Avenue corridor. Finally, the ever-expanding University of Kansas Hospital obscures the county line in the working-class Rosedale-Westport neighborhood at Thirty-ninth Street.

Distinctions remain real along the Wyandotte-Johnson border. Housing prices change there, for instance, producing buyers from different economic strata or, in the words of a local state representative, a separation of "the serfs from the landowners" (maps 82 and 83). This difference is now blurring, however. As Johnson County suburbs such as Merriam and Mission age, they become more affordable for Wyandotte buyers who seek better schools and/or shopping opportunities. The process is creating a transition zone.[81]

On the north, the new frontier begins on the uplands south of Argentine and west of Rosedale, a region of suburban homes and curved streets that looks very much like Johnson County. Residents here resent the entrenched political power they see north of the Kansas River and how their home neighborhood receives a disproportionately small share of city-county tax money, including the new dollars generated at the speedway complex. As for the Johnson County portion of this transition area, State Representative Judy Morrison said in 2007 that she regarded her district in Merriam and Shawnee as "Wyandotte County South," a place that was "blue collar" and "union heavy." The county attorney at that time, Phill Kline, implied essentially the same thing when he called Shawnee the "stepchild of Johnson County. It's beer and pickups; the rest of the county is wine and SUVs." How far south does this borderland extend? One state representative placed the line at Seventy-fifth Street, and the income map generally supports this view. Quivira and Mission roads mark its western and eastern boundaries, respectively.[82]

Comparisons across the line between Johnson and Jackson counties also are revealing. The Country Club District of J. C. Nichols, though now a century old, remains as prestigious as ever. Wealth still spans the state border, and the highest median household income for the entire city—$192,718 in 2000—can be found in its core census tract of Mission Hills. In a change from previous decades, however, the high-income portion of this district has shrunk in size and become increasingly isolated from other well-to-do neighborhoods. Only the grandest homes proximate to exclusive golf courses and the

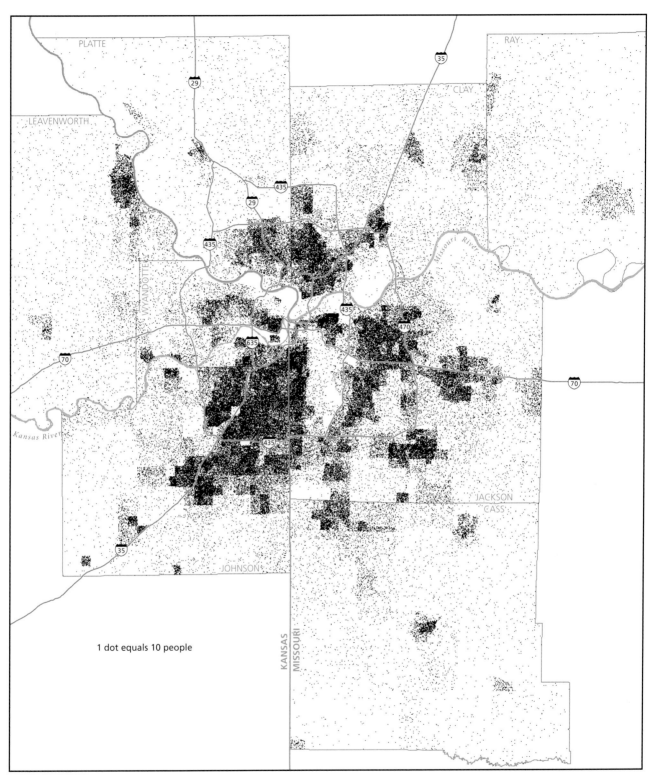

PLATTE

RAY

LEAVENWORTH

CLAY

WYANDOTTE

Missouri River

JACKSON

CASS

Kansas River

JOHNSON

1 dot equals 10 people

KANSAS MISSOURI

*Map 81. White, Non-Hispanic Population in Greater Kansas City,
2000. Modified from a map compiled from U.S. Census data by the
Mid-America Regional Council, available at http://www.marc.org
(accessed February 25, 2009).*

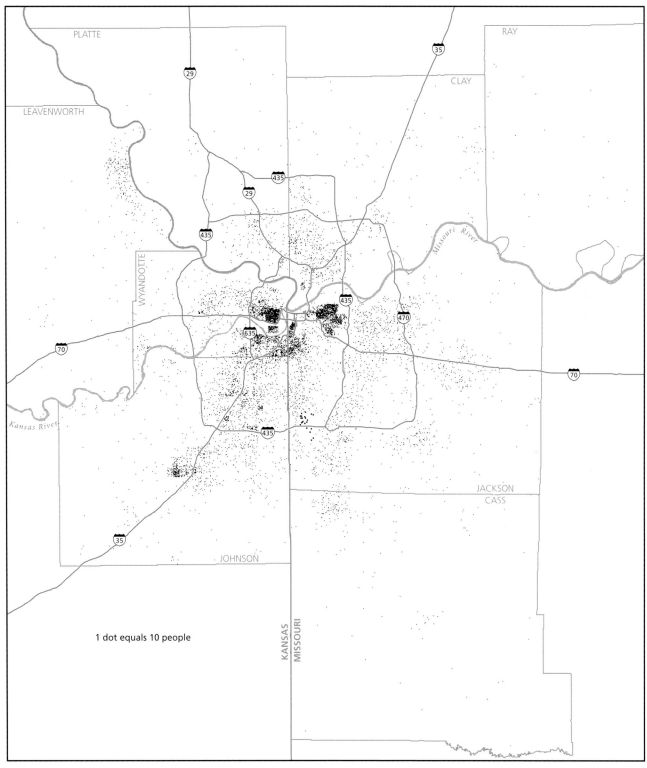

1 dot equals 10 people

Map 82. Hispanic Population in Greater Kansas City, 2000. Modified from a map compiled from U.S. Census data by the Mid-America Regional Council, available at http://www.marc.org (accessed February 25, 2009).

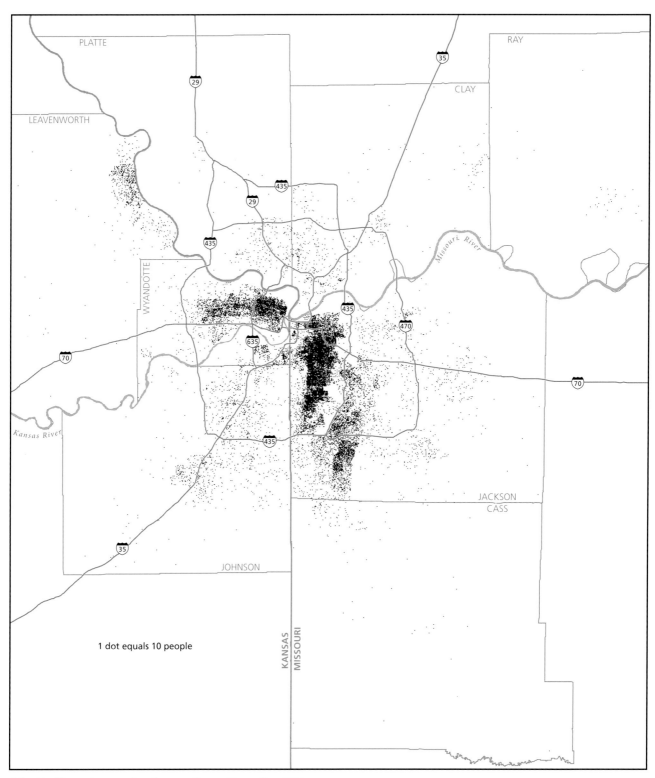

PLATTE

RAY

CLAY

LEAVENWORTH

WYANDOTTE

JACKSON

CASS

Missouri River

Kansas River

KANSAS

MISSOURI

JOHNSON

1 dot equals 10 people

Map 83. African American Population in Greater Kansas City, 2000.
Modified from a map compiled from U.S. Census data by the Mid-
America Regional Council, available at http://www.marc.org (accessed
February 25, 2009).

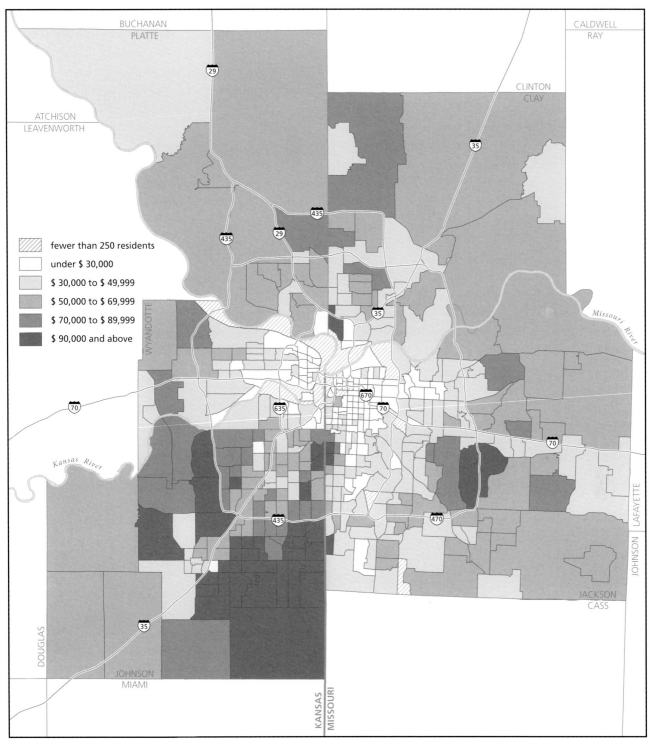

BUCHANAN
PLATTE

CALDWELL
RAY

ATCHISON
LEAVENWORTH

CLINTON
CLAY

fewer than 250 residents

under $ 30,000

$ 30,000 to $ 49,999

$ 50,000 to $ 69,999

$ 70,000 to $ 89,999

$ 90,000 and above

WYANDOTTE

Missouri River

Kansas River

LAFAYETTE

DOUGLAS

JOHNSON
MIAMI

JOHNSON
CASS

JACKSON
CASS

KANSAS
MISSOURI

*Map 84. Median Household Income in Greater Kansas City, 2000.
Data from U.S. Census.*

Plaza stores have been able to maintain top value. The immediate surrounding area is in transition. Age and income levels of residents vary widely, and many older lots have been cleared to allow for construction of larger houses.

In the heyday of J. C. Nichols, his Country Club District created prestige on the Missouri side east beyond The Paseo and south to the Red Bridge neighborhood at 111th Street. This glory has faded considerably. First, when the school board designated Troost as a racial boundary in the 1950s, home values fell in part of this area. The 2000 map shows an additional westward retreat to Wornall Road north of Gregory Boulevard (Seventy-first Street) and all the way to the state line farther south. This change, too, is school (and race) driven. Southwest High School, the pride of the Country Club District, first enrolled significant numbers of African American students in 1974, about the time when district policies began to spiral out of control. The wealthiest families, who could easily afford private education at the nearby Sunset Hill and Pembroke Country Day schools, stayed where they were. But middle-income people saw their best option as a short migration to Kansas and its quality Shawnee Mission School District. The Center School District, south of Eighty-fifth Street in Missouri, was another possibility, but its reputation was only moderate. If a person had to move, why not select the better option?[83]

Schools, together with at least some residual racism, made the state line south from Gregory Boulevard much more culturally significant in 2010 than it was in 1970 or 1980. This demarcation has only two exceptions, both on the Missouri side. In the vicinity of 125th Street, the Blue Hills Country Club between State Line Road and Wornall is girded by expensive homes. Similarly, builders of the Loch Loyd Country Club at about 167th Street in extreme northwestern Cass County have incorporated a small gated community around their creation. In spirit, Blue Hills and Loch Loyd belong in Kansas. They are part of a vast complex of exclusive country clubs and luxurious new homes that today encompasses the entire southeastern quarter of Johnson County. Median household incomes there exceed $90,000 everywhere except in downtown Olathe. The school district du jour is now Blue Valley instead of Shawnee Mission, but the result is the same.

The Northland

Although the stereotype of middle-class suburbia fits present-day Clay and Platte counties well, it misses reality in the area's Missouri River bottomlands, where the communi-

ties of North Kansas City and Riverside have long embraced an industrial, blue-collar existence. One might expect a grim fate for these two cities in the twenty-first century. Heavy industry is decreasing nationwide, and no physical expansion is possible because Kansas City has already annexed the adjacent land. Still, despite all this, both places have prospered since 1994 at a level equivalent to the rest of the Northland. The reason is casino gambling.

Casinos typically are discussed in moral terms, but they can be powerful economic engines for small communities. People in North Kansas City, Parkville, Riverside, and Sugar Creek all realized this fact early on when the Missouri state legislature first approved riverboat gambling in 1992. Each city submitted bids to the state licensing commission, and largely because they were first on the scene, North Kansas City and Riverside received approval for two of the five operations granted to the metropolitan area. With licenses in hand, the two city governments then partnered with established Las Vegas companies, and the Argosy Riverside and Harrah's North Kansas City casinos both opened in 1994.[84]

The economic promise of gambling lies less with direct casino employment and more with the state-regulated distribution of profits. In Missouri, almost 28 percent of gross revenue goes to state and local governments. Of this amount, 79 percent is allotted to public schools, but most of the rest goes back to the host cities. This small percentage equals big dollars, some $11 million annually for Riverside and somewhat more for North Kansas City. Although these totals are smaller than the amount received by Kansas City proper, the impact is much larger. In fact, casino money has been a godsend for the two communities. North Kansas City's 4,208 people enjoy one of the area's best hospitals because of this, as well as superior schools and a $20 million community center. They also have been able to finance an ambitious, $100 million housing project, starting in 2004. Northgate Village, at the north edge of town, has replaced some thirteen blocks of old apartment buildings with over 200 quality homes designed in an integrated, new urbanist mode. At Riverside, population 2,937, gambling finances 65 percent of the city budget. It is responsible for funding a new city hall and civic center, improved sewers, and immaculate streets. It also provided nearly half the money for an $80 million reconstruction of the Missouri River levee that protects a new, 900-acre business park called Horizons.[85]

North of the two casino communities, the Northland today has two faces. The 1950s and 1960s suburban tracts in Gladstone and near Vivion Road have lost prestige and need major infrastructure improvements if they are to avoid sinking further. But north of Gladstone, where a newly widened Missouri Route 152 forms a high-speed, east-west corridor across the area, a dream environment awaits developers (map 85). Projects here are almost all post 2000, too recent to be reflected yet in detailed census figures (map 84), but they are transforming Kansas City.[86]

The potential of the Northland has long been appreciated, but other than the creation of Briarcliff by Charles Garney (discussed in the previous chapter), actual progress was slowed by competition from Johnson County and eastern Jackson County. A lack of local jobs hurt as well, plus a nagging neglect by the city in terms of new parks, boulevards, and similar amenities. This situation all began to change about 1991. The first victory was political, when a redrawing of district boundaries for the city council in Kansas City doubled the Northland's representation. A fairer share of tax money soon appeared and, with it, ideas for major new subdivisions and retail centers.[87]

Because nearly all residential developers want to foster an air of distinction in their properties, it was perhaps predictable that a gated, golf course com-

Figure 50. Argosy Casino, 2010. The small community of Riverside and the new Argosy Gaming Company from Alton, Illinois, took chances on one another in 1994 to open the metropolitan area's first casino. The partnership has been immensely successful, pumping some $11 million annually into Riverside's budget. Here, the use of Moroccan tile and terrazzo floors helps to enhance a sense of escaping from the ordinary, something most casino operators try to convey to their patrons. The Argosy tries to re-create "a Mediterranean village with charming streetscapes and the warmth of old-world architecture." (Photograph by Barbara Shortridge)

munity would initiate the boom. Choosing Parkville as the site also made sense given that town's collegiate amenities and quality homes around Riss Lake. Somewhat surprisingly, however, the money came from outsiders. Investors from the

Pinehurst National Management Company judged the rolling Missouri River blufflands northwest of town an ideal setting for a midwestern version of their famous Pinehurst Resort in North Carolina. They purchased 800 acres in 1998 and

191

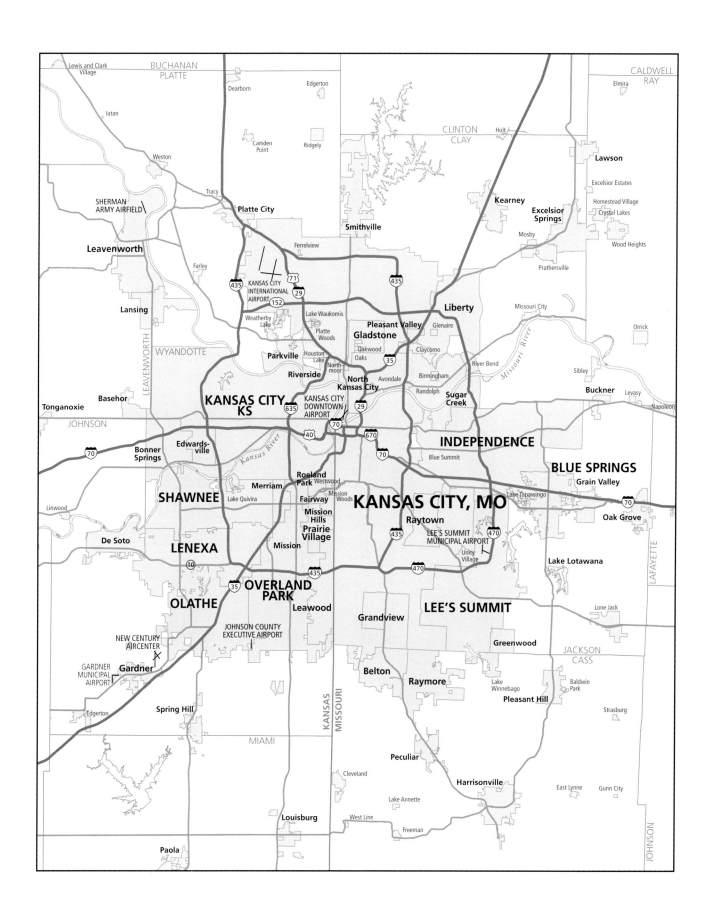

hired the distinguished local golfer Tom Watson to design the course. Everything progressed smoothly at the National Golf Club of Kansas City. Missouri Highway 45 was widened west from I-29 to serve as the principal access route, and about 850 homes sold at prices ranging upward from $250,000. In 2005, four years after the development's opening, the magazine *Travel and Leisure Golf* recognized the National as one of America's "top 100" golf communities.[88]

If Briarcliff and the National Golf Club mark the beginning of upscale development in the Northland, the Zona Rosa Shopping Center supplied its focal point. This impressive project was locally inspired, the idea of LaVonne C. "Bonnie" Poteet, whose family had owned for decades a 94-acre tract at the intersection of Interstate 29 and Missouri 152. As this land emerged as the most desirable business site in the region, she decided to do something special. Poteet, a professor at Bucknell University in Pennsylvania, had become inspired by the pedestrian-friendly designs known as new urbanism. Wanting to create a large shopping center in this style, she interviewed some eighty developers until she found Yaromir Steiner in Columbus, Ohio. Steiner was the recognized leader for such projects, having built CocoWalk in Miami and Easton Town Center in Columbus. Poteet christened her project Zona Rosa after an elegant district in Mexico City and named Steiner as master developer.[89]

Zona Rosa broke ground in 2002 and opened the first of its two phases in 2004. It emphasizes retail but also includes office and residential space plus two parking garages and lots of open space intended for farmer's markets, jazz concerts, and the like. The scope is enormous—a million square feet costing $200 million—and the quality of stores high enough to attract shoppers from afar. All is open air in design, looking something like a Main Street town from a century ago. Narrow streets and short blocks enhance the mood.[90]

When Steiner began work, he said that he hoped to create "the Country Club Plaza of the Northland." This descriptor has been much repeated. Although a cynic could argue that Zona Rosa lacks the neighborhood ambience of the original Plaza, since it is surrounded by urban sprawl, no one can deny that it is now the economic and social hub for Clay and Platte counties.[91]

The successful completion of the National Golf Club and

Map 85 (facing page). The Greater Kansas City Area, 2007. Modified from the map "Counties and Cities," published by the Mid-America Regional Council, available at http://www.marc.org (accessed February 25, 2009).

Zona Rosa has inspired two types of new development. The first takes advantage of opportunities in their immediate neighborhoods. No sooner had Route 45 been improved for the National, for example, than George and Pamela Gunter created Tuileries Plaza on 50 acres where that road joins I-29. It is an upscale retail and office complex with a design inspired by the gardens at the Louvre in Paris. Similarly, Zona Rosa's presence on the southwest corner of its major junction prompted a big-box complex called MarketCenter catercorner to the northeast. Zona Rosa also has forced the venerable Metro North Shopping Center 3 miles to the east to either reinvent itself or go bankrupt.[92]

The second face of the new Northland is a series of huge, mostly high-end residential developments planned for the still nearly vacant land between Route 152 and I-435 to its north. The scope here can perhaps best be seen via the parkway system designed as its skeleton (map 86). With increased funding from the city after the council redistricting of 1991 and much more since 2002 when new legislation required housing developers to help fund connector roads, this work is now ongoing. Tiffany Springs Parkway will open up the area just south of Kansas City International Airport, and Line Creek and Shoal Creek parkways will do the same farther east.[93]

At the airport end, the big players are Hunt Midwest Real Estate and Kansas City itself. Hunt controls 296 acres adjacent to Route 152 and broke ground for the $320 million Riverstone project there in 2007. It will include commercial and office space plus some 1,250 homes and apartments. This project, although huge, pales compared to the 8,000 acres the city government owns just south of the airport. In 2006, officials hired the Trammel Crow Company of Dallas to develop 640 acres of this next to I-29 and the Tiffany Springs Parkway. Houses are part of the plan, but there will also be buildings suitable for distributors, logistics firms, and other companies with significant air transport needs. The first big success, a distribution center for the cutting-equipment manufacturer Blount International, was announced in July 2011.[94]

Moving east, two additional massive operations are under way. The first, Shoal Creek Valley, involves 1,700 acres between Interstates 435 and 35. Highway 152 bisects the tract east and west. The landowner here, the Church of Jesus Christ of Latter-day Saints, works with four builders and plans to open ten subdivisions over the course of twenty years, incorporating some 2,500 homes. All will feature the new urbanist

Creek, the developer has adopted a new urbanist approach and will spread the process over two decades. Groundbreaking occurred early in 2008.[95]

Jackson and Cass Counties

Although expansion on the east and south sides of Kansas City has been considerable in recent years, both the scale of projects and the value of individual structures are more modest than in the Northland. Why such a discrepancy should exist is not clear. To some degree, it is because of chance, having a Bonnie Poteet grow up near I-29 instead of I-470. Proximity to Kansas City International Airport is a factor, too, and perhaps also the fact that Northland property offers a "clean slate" where few small towns exist to lower property values. Finally, any Jackson County developer, no matter how far beyond the city's political limits, has to cope with image issues related to poor people and poorer schools.

From the perspective of retailers and homebuilders alike, the I-70 and I-470 corridors offered Jackson County's best potential for development at the turn of the twenty-first century. The ideal spot, of course, would be the roads' junction point in southeastern Independence (map 85). Like

Figure 51. Zona Rosa, 2010, Looking Northwest across Dixon Avenue. Yaromir Steiner's new urbanist creation rivals the Country Club Plaza in scale, opulence, and skillful blend of retail, residential, and office space. It is the pride of Kansas City's Northland. This view epitomizes intimacy and mixed use. A large Dillard's store sits at the end of the block, but the immediate focus is a small Village Market that serves residential apartments in the Dixon Building. To bolster local connections, the developer has reinstituted two lost city traditions: oversized crowns that hang during the Christmas season and an Easter parade. (Photograph by Barbara Shortridge)

design. Two areas are now complete, with The Preserve on Route 152 at Shoal Creek Parkway drawing comparisons to Mission Hills. The final big project, New Town at Liberty, will unfold on 939 acres just west of Interstate 35. As at Shoal

Village West and Zona Rosa at equivalent locations on the city's western and northern fringes, respectively, a business there could hope to attract customers from several counties. Such enterprises, in turn, would spur house construction

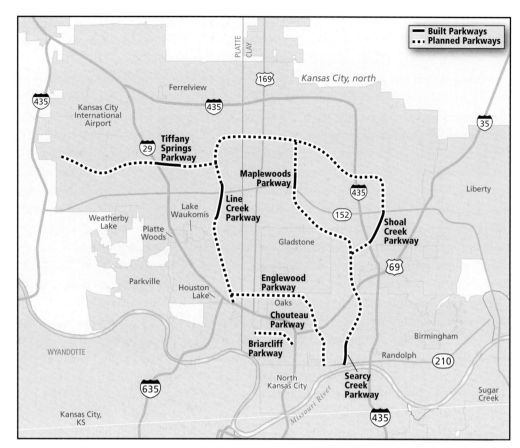

Map 86. The Planned Parkway System in the Northland, 2005. Modified from a map published in the Kansas City Star, *January 9, 2005, p. B3.*

farther east and south in Blue Springs, Lee's Summit, and smaller communities.

Actual experience has matched the model, with only a few exceptions. Development due east of Independence is blocked by the massive presence of the federal government's Lake City Army Ammunition Plant. Its 4,000 acres adjacent to Missouri Route 7 lie only 3.5 miles north of I-70, and so, people and businesses are funneled down the interstate route to Blue Springs, Grain Valley, and now Oak Grove. These three towns have now essentially coalesced. For the same reason, southward expansion is also strong, much of it along Route 7.

Surprisingly, major development at the 70–470 interstate junction did not occur until 2007. The Independence Center mall had been there since 1974, of course, but it encountered only halfhearted local support early on out of fear that its stores would steal business away from established retailers on Noland Road and at the Blue Ridge Mall. But people were more aware by 2004. The older mall was dead, and residents now realized that new development offered the best hope for

the future. Their planners essentially replicated the strategy that had worked in Wyandotte County. Looking for a retailer that could pull customers citywide, they identified Bass Pro Shops, builders of the highly successful Outdoor World Adventure Stores. Looking for a similar but purely entertainment draw, they decided on minor-league hockey.[96]

Both plans are working. Bass Pro anchors The Falls, a $174 million development that opened in 2008. Across I-470 in the Eastland Center sits the $68 million, city-owned Independence Events Center. This facility seats 5,800 people and opened in the fall of 2009 for the Missouri Mavericks of the Central Hockey League. Independence entrepreneurs even surpassed their Kansas model in at least one respect. Reasoning that a new hospital would augment traffic flow even more, they bid successfully for the Centerpoint Medical Center. Joining Menorah and Research hospitals as the core of the HCA Midwest Health System, its site is just north of I-70, immediately east of the Independence Center mall.[97]

People in Blue Springs, realizing that the Independence projects would hurt their prospects for major retailing, pursued instead the corporate office market. I described their ambitious plan for Adams Dairy Landing and Parkway off of I-70 in the last chapter. They began early enough (in 1990) to avoid many competitors and invested heavily in a golf course and similar amenities, but they ultimately failed. Walmart, Target, and Home Depot are now the principal local businesses along with two corporate headquarters (Durvet and Haldex) that relocated from other Blue Springs sites. Why did this strategy go wrong? Consultants said part of the reason was poor timing, given the saturated market that also slowed Lenexa's plans for an office cluster along Renner Boulevard. But more fundamentally, Blue Springs could not offer the volume and tradition of luxury homes that corporate executives demanded. A community of Kansas City's size can support only one Johnson County.[98]

Housing as an explanation for the struggles at Adams Dairy Landing is supported by the nature of two major residential developments in Jackson County. In 2006, three years after Blue Springs annexed land to its south, investors announced an 820-acre project called Chapman Farms. It flanks Highway 7 at Colbern Road. The plan called for 4,000 homes and up to 13,000 residents, but significantly, the designs are conventional (not new urbanist), the prices moderate (starting at $160,000), and the principal amenities a bank and a Walmart Supercenter. As these homes are constructed over the years ahead, they will reinforce the middle-class image of Jackson County, not transform it.[99]

The second housing project, Harmony, is the largest in the entire metropolitan area. It involves 2,300 acres in the Little Blue valley just north of Interstate 70, with a potential of 14,000 homes. The Community of Christ Church is the landowner here, but the key to development is a new, federally subsidized road that will link I-70 with U.S. Route 24, 7 miles to the north. Four miles of this Little Blue Parkway are now open, and home construction commenced in 2007. As in Chapman Farms, the prices will be moderate and the pace of building slow.[100]

Traveling around the southeastern and southern periphery of Kansas City, the pattern of middle-class housing repeats itself from Lee's Summit and Greenwood to Raymore and Belton before meeting the small gated enclave of Loch Loyd, as noted earlier. Of these communities, Lee's Summit was the first to boom (in the 1970s and 1980s) and Raymore the most recent (table 3). Their growth has been aided by the presence of U.S. Highways 50 and 71, which carry commuters to the 435–470 loop road. Still, the extent of development is more

than one might expect. At Belton, subdivisions are common south to 181st Street and at Raymore to 188th. These limits are twenty blocks farther south than in adjacent Johnson County and are not supported by sizable local employers.

To a degree, the exceptional growth to the south and southeast is the latest manifestation of a trend started in the 1880s when the developers of Hyde Park and then William R. Nelson and J. C. Nichols first pushed the city in this direction. The current situation is aided by a similar southward trajectory for the area's African American population, as discussed previously. Whether via a lingering racism or a more justified concern for school quality and property values, a large group of middle-class whites has been migrating one community ahead of the blacks. Lee's Summit today is to some extent the Raytown of the 1950s; Raymore is Grandview reincarnated. A third factor applies only to Belton and Raymore. They are in relatively rural Cass County, where property taxes are lower than in Jackson.[101]

Though the southern periphery cities share similarities, differences also exist. Lee's Summit incomes are somewhat higher than those in Raymore, and Raymore's, in turn, exceed those in Belton. As discussed in the last chapter, officials in Lee's Summit utilized tax revenue from their big (but now closed) Western Electric plant to fund a top-rated school system and to establish a similar level of parks and other civic amenities. This made the area attractive to retailers and higher-end homebuilders. An elegant, lakeside residential district in the northern part of town was joined in 2004 by a similar development in the southwest. Called New Longview, it occupies 260 acres of the old utopian farm of lumber baron Robert A. Long. The developer's homes, which purposefully echo the styles of the Hyde Park and Brookside neighborhoods, sell for between $240,000 and $800,000.[102]

Lee's Summit also claims the only substantial retail center on the Missouri south side. This development began in 2001 with Summit Woods Crossing at the intersection of U.S. 50 and I-470. The same developer returned in 2007 to build Summit Fair on an adjacent corner, with Macy's as an anchor. The company wanted to add two entertainment venues as well: a Sea Life aquarium and the nation's second Legoland children's theme park. These projects fell through in late 2007, however, when anticipated state funds did not materialize.[103]

Belton and Raymore were founded in 1871 as stations on a short-lived railroad that connected Lawrence, Kansas, with Pleasant Hill, Missouri. Both remained small places until 1960, when Belton began to attract workers at the nearby

Richards-Gebaur Air Force Base. Today, with the base closed for decades and a plan to transform it into an intermodal railroad and trucking port moving slowly, residents have had to look elsewhere for jobs. Some have found spots at several small manufacturing firms that Grandview leaders have recruited recently. Others drive a little farther to the nuclear weapons parts plant at the federal center on Bannister Road at Troost. This operation is currently the talk of the two towns because it will soon relocate, bringing 2,000 high-paying jobs to a site on Missouri Route 150 at Botts Road, only 1 mile north of the Belton city limit.[104]

Still, local Missouri employers support only a small portion of the 45,000 or so people who now call Belton and Raymore home. Most workers, about 6,700, commute west to the offices and retail centers of Johnson County. This edge-city phenomenon has prompted two related transportation initiatives. In 2007, engineers suggested a $91 million "south metro connector" road for Johnson County. This route would run from U.S. 69 at 179th Street east to Holmes Road, a mile inside Missouri. There, the pavement would link with another new creation, the North Cass Parkway, that would intersect U.S. 71 at 187th Street and extend on eastward to Raymore and Pleasant Hill. Predictably, Cass County commuters have greeted the project with enthusiasm, and construction there is under way. Johnson County people, by contrast, saw the road more as an intrusion. Their county commission killed the idea in 2008.[105]

Johnson County

Despite challenges from Blue Springs, the Northland, the speedway area, and elsewhere, Johnson County remains Kansas City's nirvana for developers. This success has come with seeming ease, and it attracts most of the companies new to the metropolitan area, together with a stream of relocations from Jackson County. Between 1990 and 2008, Johnson County saw a net gain of 118,323 private-sector jobs, an increase of 7 percent to an already large base. When this number is compared to 39,388 new jobs for the four other urbanized counties combined, it is no surprise that Johnson is now poised to surpass Jackson as the employment center of the region.[106]

I have explored reasons for the county's success in earlier chapters, and these continue: a large stock of quality housing, a tradition of good schools, intelligent planning, and (because of these things) a substantial presence of retail centers and corporate headquarters that keeps homeowner taxes low. By 1990 or so, city and county planners had become so famil-

iar with expansion that they could execute the process with military precision. If movement to the south was not quite as far as in adjacent Belton, its path was far broader. From the state line 13 miles west to Kansas Route 7, its mile-spaced collector roads became familiar to shoppers all across the city: Mission, Nall, Metcalf, Antioch, Switzer, Quivira, Pflumm, and Renner, plus, more recently, Ridgeview, Woodland, Lone Elm, and K-7 itself.

An absence of large stream valleys has aided planners in the creation of an efficient traffic grid. Joining the north-south arteries noted previously is a similar series of east-west collectors, every other one of which is zoned for major retail development. The series begins a mile south of corporate College Boulevard with 119th Street. Two miles beyond is 135th Street; 2 more beyond that is 151st; and then come 167th, 183rd, and 199th near the Miami County line. The process of adding substance to this skeleton is similarly ordered. Parks and schools are laid out first, ahead of housing. Planners established the 1,120-acre Heritage Park southwest of 159th and Pflumm in 2004, for example, about the same time that they built Blue Valley West High School on Antioch at 161st and Olathe Northwest on College Boulevard near Lone Elm. Then comes housing and, some twenty blocks behind, commerce. Shopping centers arrived on 119th Street about 1995 when housing was at 135th Street. In 2005, when new dwellings had advanced to 159th, stores came to 135th.[107]

Three communities have led the southward expansion: Leawood, Overland Park, and Olathe. Of these, Leawood has been least involved, since its city limits extend south only to 155th Street (map 85). More aggressive Overland Park annexed the land directly south of Leawood in the 1980s and then added acreage south to 191st Street and beyond in 2008. Despite these actions, however, Olathe is now Johnson County's biggest power player. Its planners have annexed extensive acreage to the south, matching Overland Park, and to the northwest all the way to Highway 10. This new land (all convenient to Interstate 35) gives the city two development frontiers: first, shared space along 135th and 151st streets with Overland Park and, second, the western ends of 119th Street and College Boulevard (plus K-10). Local entrepreneurs thereby are positioned to tap into several adjacent specialties—the corporate and retail world of Overland Park, the distributorships of Lenexa, and even the intellectual capital of the University of Kansas, only 20 miles to the west in Lawrence. About 1990, they decided to pursue all three.[108]

Perhaps the best way to understand recent events in Olathe is by an anthropomorphic comparison between aristocrats and social climbers. Leaders in elite Leawood and Overland Park reason correctly that companies will want to come to them. They therefore can be selective and not have to cut special deals. Up-and-coming Olathe people, in contrast, see opportunity—but only if they pursue it forcefully. In practice, the issue has hinged on major tax breaks for new companies. Overland Park officials have chosen to grant these only four times since 1990. Olathe leaders, however, have used a "fairly aggressive set of development incentives" to become the fastest-growing city in the entire metropolitan area.[109]

People in Leawood, who had broadened their tax base in 1996 via genteel shopping at the Town Center Plaza, decided to stay with this approach to planning. They therefore approved similar projects at three additional sites. First, to participate in the southward population movement, came The Cornerstone at Leawood. This is an 8-acre retail and office complex on 135th Street at Nall. The other two efforts are physically closer to Town Center Plaza. Developers saw an opportunity there to convert an already prosperous shopping node into the county's premier high-end destination. Mayor Peggy Dunn described their goal as re-creating "the atmosphere of the [Country Club] Plaza."[110]

One group focused on the southeastern flank of Town Center. There, at the southwest corner of 119th and Roe, they added Hawthorne Plaza with its signature Talbots clothing store. Next, across the street to the east, they created space for Crate and Barrel. This Chicago-based seller of quality housewares is a perfect fit for Johnson County tastes, and it anchors a center called One Nineteen. The third big Leawood development, Park Place, occupies 30 coveted acres west of Town Center Plaza and east of the Sprint corporate campus. This is a $250 million, new urbanist project conceived by Jeffrey Alpert and Melanie Mann. They want to bring "city-style living" to the suburbs, and as with Zona Rosa, they have arrayed stores along a Main Street with offices on the second floors. Three hundred condominiums in five-story buildings, a hotel, a 4-acre park, and a garage complete the package. After recession-induced delays, the first half of the project opened to high praise in 2009.[111]

While Leawood people have sought to create a new Country Club Plaza, their colleagues in Overland Park are orchestrating a more complex series of goals. Because their city's portions of College Boulevard and 119th Street were largely full by the late 1990s (Pflumm is the city's western border), new efforts have been concentrated on two other corridors. For corporate clients, planners reserved a north-south strip adjacent to interstate-quality U.S. 69. For retailers, the choice was 135th Street. The Deer Creek Commons office park on Highway 69 has seen only modest development because of the country's recent economic troubles. Its biggest tenant was Capital One Financial Corporation, which opened a new five-story building in 2006 for its home loan division. Capital One fell victim to the recession two years later, but Overland Park's strong reputation attracted a U.S. Bank service center as a replacement. This facility now employs 1,100 people. Economic difficulties also have caused a now downsized Sprint Nextel Corporation to lease out increasing amounts of its vast campus to other companies at favorable rates. This practice helps Overland Park as a whole but hurts the newer corporate parks.[112]

To provide focus for the strip malls along 135th Street, planners are emphasizing three projects: a county-sponsored youth soccer complex, an upscale new urbanist "village," and a million-square-foot regional shopping center. All of these began construction in 2007, just in time to face a major economic recession. Only the publicly funded soccer park was able to proceed as scheduled.

The three new developments are close together. Farthest west is the $75 million soccer complex, featuring twenty-four lighted fields just west of Antioch Road. It opened in August 2009. A mile and a half east, at the southeast corner of Metcalf Avenue, lies the 96-acre Corbin Park shopping center. Ambitions here were huge: a $225 million, open-air development assembled by the respected Cormac Company of Omaha and anchored by a fashionably upscale Von Maur department store. With immense amounts of money invested, work continued into the recession. Von Maur opened, but not many ancillary stores did. When the developer filed for bankruptcy in 2010, investors suffered, but the area's housing density should ensure long-term success.[113]

The final large project, Prairiefire at Lionsgate, is Overland Park's version of Zona Rosa. It enjoys a perfect setting, 60 acres a half mile east of Corbin Park and adjacent on the south to a Jack Nicklaus–designed golf course. Prairiefire's developers, led by Fred Merrill, Jr., planned offices, condominiums, hotels, and even a natural history museum, all surrounded by tasteful greenery. They had $30 million invested in basic infrastructure by 2009 but then wisely suspended work. They plan to start afresh in 2012.[114]

Recent development in Olathe has been widespread but with a concentration in the north along 119th Street, College Boulevard, and Highway 10. Land is open there, close to the interstate loop, and easily assembled into large tracts. This stands in contrast to 135th Street near the city's historical center, which was filled piecemeal with stores several decades ago. Farther south, newer development resumes at 151st Street near its intersection with I-35.

The retail focus in the north, appropriately called Olathe Gateway Center, is on 119th Street at Renner Road, adjacent to I-35. Following the successful model of Village West, developers there wanted to combine standard retailers with several rarer attractions. Bass Pro Shops agreed to build (seeing their Independence store as too far away to be a competitor), but plans to pair its outdoor theme with a new natural history museum faltered in the recent recession. The museum's bond issue defaulted in September 2011.[115]

Planners are being careful with the Olathe Gateway because they had erred seriously a decade earlier with The Great Mall of the Great Plains, their first regional shopping center. Located on 151st Street at I-35, it enjoyed good access and an even better selection of stores (160 in all), but it was too far south at that time to attract adequate customer flow. Population is no longer an issue, of course, but a weak start led to the departure of all its anchor stores by 2009. The entire venture was facing bankruptcy when local investors recently purchased it for renovation.[116]

The pursuit of corporate headquarters is a second important development strategy in Olathe. Planners have laid out four new office parks and recruited aggressively, but curiously, they have dispersed their locations. The first of the four, across I-35 from the Great Mall on 151st Street, houses Olathe's homegrown corporate giant, Garmin International. This manufacturer of global positioning systems grew rapidly in the 1990s and now has 2,000 employees. The company expanded its previously modest campus in 2004 with an eight-story office tower and large warehouse.[117]

The other three office parks lie in the north and are still under development. Across the road from the Gateway Center is 119th Street Technical Park. It is home to 800 workers of the Farmers Insurance Group, a company spirited away from Overland Park. Two miles to the northwest, along the increasingly busy Highway 10 corridor, planners have laid out the 110-acre Corporate Ridge park at Ridgeview Road. Only one major structure has been completed there so far—a $10 million home for the National Board of Respiratory Care, the credentialing body for respiratory therapists. The last corporate venture is the most innovative—the Kansas Bioscience Park at the junction of College Boulevard with Highway 7. This joint investment of the city with Kansas State University features a 92-acre site, and with this development, planners hope to capitalize on the growing public concern for food safety. The facility's first building, a $28 million structure dedicated to animal health, opened in 2011.[118]

The idea for distribution centers, Olathe's third specialization, was borrowed from Lenexa to the north, but these are concentrated on the far south side of town. Pacific Sunwear, for instance, announced a $65 million facility there in 2006, at 167th Street and Lone Elm Road, and the Coleman camping supplies company has an even larger warehouse nearby. The southside preference is partly a response to cheaper land, but it also anticipates a huge rail and truck intermodal center. The main line of the Burlington Northern Santa Fe Railway parallels the highway in this area, and the railroad company is in the process of acquiring 1,300 acres for the new shipping facility. A potential exists for some 7,500 jobs, but public opinion in the adjacent town of Gardner is mixed. Some people fear the increased noise and traffic, others growth in general. But since growth is a way of life in Johnson County, these fears likely will be short lived.[119]

8 Conclusion

The U.S. Census Bureau recently reported that Greater Kansas City now contains 2,035,334 people. This is an impressive total and represents a solid 10.8 percent gain over the 2000–2010 period. Yet the number is deflating in another sense because many competing cities have grown even faster. Kansas City, the nation's twenty-sixth-largest metropolis a decade ago, is now number twenty-nine. These numbers and rankings present local residents with a familiar dilemma. Should they stress the positive and feel good about themselves, or should they obsess over the negative and feel despondent? The city is now bigger than Milwaukee and New Orleans and gaining on Cleveland and St. Louis. But previously unpretentious places such as Orlando, Portland, and San Diego have left the heartland capital in their dust.[1]

Reflecting their core position within the modest American Midwest, Kansas City people have long been unsure how to perceive themselves. They are proud of their history of cattle marketing and grain milling yet afraid of appearing unsophisticated if they let these rural roots show. A longtime observer of the local scene, Calvin Trillin, has called this reaction rubophobia. Writing in the 1980s, he saw the condition leading to pretension and overcompensation. Officials started a "glamour city" promotion and claimed that their city had more boulevards than Paris and more fountains than Rome. Another native writer, Richard Rhodes, observed the same tendency. To hide any unrefined tastes that a visiting Rockefeller might see, Kansas City people sought sanctuary in blandness and conformity. Touring performers all received standing ovations, not critical evaluation. Everybody went to

church. Nobody read serious books. Rhodes traced the phenomenon back at least to the 1930s, citing *Mrs. Bridge,* Evan Connell's classic portrayal of sterile, outer-directed life along Ward Parkway.[2]

What is reality in Kansas City today? Is rubophobia still alive and well, or are citizens finally learning to embrace their particular place in the sun? Trillin saw progress when he wrote in 1983 and even more when he revisited the subject in 2001. He reasoned that residents have become more secure as their farm background recedes and more appreciative of the work ethic and ecological consciousness they have inherited. One measure, he suggested, is a renewed local appreciation for the oversized statue of a Hereford bull that gazes over the West Bottoms from atop Quality Hill.[3]

If residents choose to emphasize positive aspects of their city, the list is long. George Kessler's system of boulevards is an amazing legacy, for example, one that can inspire both neighborhood renewal (in the case of The Paseo) and solid planning for the future (the parkways of the Northland). Much the same can be said for parks and fountains; other cities have long been jealous of Kansas City in this regard. The value of J. C. Nichols is also difficult to overstate. Though all cities had ambitious suburban developers early in the twentieth century, no one can match Nichols for sustained, high-quality work; integration of retail and residential land use; and sheer volume. His Country Club Plaza is indeed world famous. His Mission Hills and Sunset Hills districts were so well planned that they remain the city's premier addresses a hundred years later. Even Johnson County as a whole, whose reputation for superior housing, schools, and planning is the envy of city officials everywhere, also can be laid largely at the feet of Mr. Nichols.

Partnering with Kessler and Nichols in the creation of a positive legacy for Kansas City were people such as August Meyer, William R. Nelson, and William Volker from a century ago; the Bloch, Hall, Helzberg, Kauffman, and Kemper families continuing to the present; and modern individuals such as L. P. Cookingham, Ollie Gates, Thomas McDonnell, John "Buck" O'Neil, and James Stowers, Jr. If their visions and philanthropies are not as unique on the American scene as those of Kessler or Nichols, they are just as important. Where would the city be financially were it not for Cookingham's bold annexations during the 1950s? Where would downtown redevelopment be without the behind-the-scenes efforts of Tom McDonnell?

Beyond the work of individuals, Kansas City has been fortunate in its economic and social history. Because of the community's inland location and relatively late industrial development, it did not receive immigrant workers in the variety and volume found in many other large cities. This is a loss in many ways, of course, but having sizable, foreign-born populations only from Croatia, Germany, Ireland, Italy, Russia, and more recently Mexico has made acceptance and assimilation easier than in other locales. Rarely did immigrant numbers exceed job openings in the packing plants and rail yards. Rarely was housing so scarce as to spark violent protest. Timing was fortunate, too, with German and Irish assimilation largely complete before the Croatian, Italian, and Russian arrivals and these, in turn, before the Mexican influx.

Particular industries can be a source of urban pride. One thinks of banking in Charlotte, beer in Milwaukee, and computer software in Seattle. But overspecialization in this way can easily lead to disaster, as Detroit found out with automobiles and Pittsburgh with steel. Kansas City luckily has avoided this roller coaster. Several of its nineteenth-century specialties—grain milling, wholesale distribution, and railroads—have proved enduring and find current form in the big rail/truck intermodal centers now under construction near Gardner and Grandview. The closest equivalent to Pittsburgh's steel industry was meatpacking. Although the decline in this sector was rapid, the city felt little economic pain because of the simultaneous rise of a more diversified job base via the innovative Fairfax Industrial Park, Trans World Airlines, and the various World War II defense industries.

Kansas City's past is not completely a source of pride, of course. The two biggest failures concern relationships between black and white residents and a series of internal, regional jealousies driven partly by race and partly by physical and political barriers. Local racial relations actually have a mixed history. Despite being one of America's most segregated cities in the 1960s and 1970s, for instance, Kansas City experienced no large-scale riots. Writers explain this paradox via the area's relative openness to black commercial and political activity. Though commerce was more in evidence on the Kansas side and politics in Missouri, it all was opportunity and acted to keep anger in check. A political club called Freedom, Inc., arose in 1962 to campaign for voter registration. It is credited with producing Missouri-side mayoral victories for Ilus Davis in 1963 and Charles Wheeler in 1971. African American Bruce Watkins narrowly lost a bid for mayor there in 1978, and progress was similarly apparent in city council and school board elections.[4]

Still, as I have detailed earlier, segregation persisted in both Jackson and Wyandotte counties, and the school district in Missouri became a disaster. Given the intertwined fears over race and property values during the 1950s and 1960s, some problems would have been inescapable even with the best of political leaders. The biggest issue was geographic. Had the state line and the Missouri River been farther away from the original urban focus, the school district likely would have expanded west and north and incorporated suburbs there into the whole. If this were the case, then the entire metropolitan area would have acquired a vested interest in solving the school district's issues, and the money to do so would have been at hand. As it happened, an array of separate municipalities and school districts divided the larger urban area against itself. While the suburban ring prospered, the city core suffered. And since this core was home to so much local history and iconography, Greater Kansas City began to lose its sense of unity and pride.

Although racial fears certainly have exacerbated sectionalism within the metropolis, basic physical and political geography suggest that divisions were inevitable. Everybody in the area knows the resultant labels and can attach descriptive adjectives to each. Jackson County, the city's birthplace, is the most complex unit and the one most often compared to others. Its first pairing, with Wyandotte County, developed in the nineteenth century. Jackson County people made the decisions then and kept the department stores and elite housing districts for themselves while assigning smoky industry and new immigrant workers to Kansas. No wonder resentments began to build. No wonder the story arose that residents "from the Missouri side invariably state that they are from Kansas City, Missouri, while persons living on the Kansas side report they are from Kansas City. The implication is clear."[5]

Surprisingly to some people, a competition between Jackson and Johnson counties dates not to the initial suburbanization in Kansas before World War II or even to the first decade postwar. Instead, its timing correlates with the forced integration of public schools. White flight to the west created resentment in Jackson County—and also envy. This rivalry intensified in the 1970s and 1980s. Race receded as a factor to some degree, but it was replaced by ever-growing differentials in income level and school quality. By 1990, commerce was a factor, too. On average, Johnson County jobs paid more than those in Jackson, and they now began to rival the latter in total numbers. Today, one can argue that Johnson County has become the city's economic heart.

Johnson County people rarely think about life across the state border except for the sliver of land west of Troost Avenue that contains the Plaza, Crown Center, and downtown. Their world is serene and comfortable. They just want to be left alone. Jackson County people, in contrast, think often about Johnson County. Partly, this is jealousy, of course, but an element of righteous indignation is present, too. One can still hear the argument that since Johnson County residents caused the Missouri school problems by moving away, they should help to fix the situation. More recently, a similar economic logic has been applied to the downtown area and the Truman Sports Complex. These facilities serve the entire metropolitan region, but they are financed entirely by Missourians. Why should Kansans get a free pass (so to speak) to watch the Royals or attend a Sprint Center concert?

An informed Kansan could point out that the Jackson County complaint is overstated. Since 1970, nonresidents who work in Kansas City, Missouri, have been paying 1 percent of their earnings to the city as a special tax. This totaled some $200 million in 2009, comprising 40 percent of the general fund. Johnson County people also supported a special bistate tax in the 1990s to restore Union Station. Still, resentment remains. Every movement of a company from Jackson to Johnson hits a nerve. So did the construction of the Overland Park Convention Center on I-435 as at least a partial rival to Bartle Hall. Smaller insults may hurt even more. Consider three past actions by Leawood officials, the eastern gatekeepers to the promised land. When laying out their city, planners opted to minimize parks for fear that "nonresidents"

might frequent them. When a bridge on their Eighty-ninth Street link to Missouri flooded out, they elected to blockade the road one block short of the state line rather than rebuild. When Ninety-fifth Street was designated a major east-west collector across the urban area, they restricted their portion to two lanes. Nobody in Kansas particularly noticed these actions; many Missourians did.[6]

The remaining primary divisions in Kansas City repeat the familiar arguments in slightly different context. The one between Johnson and Wyandotte, for example, is essentially central city versus suburb, with all its expected components—class, ethnicity, and income. This division is now ebbing somewhat. The aging of northern Johnson County creates a blurred border. More profoundly, the success of the speedway complex has raised Wyandotte County pride to levels unimaginable in 1990. The commonplace sight of Wyandotte license plates in Johnson's Oak Park Mall is now matched by an equal number of Johnson plates at Village West. Such renewed pride also has prompted new housing developments, giving Kansas City, Kansas, a broader demographic and income profile.

The final geographic division, Jackson County versus the Northland, is the least discussed. This relative silence stems from the fact that a single municipal government embraces much of the two areas and cooperation is essential. The Northland needs the job base and cultural amenities found south of the Missouri River, whereas Jackson County people rely heavily on the residential tax base in Clay and Platte counties. Still, the Northland is as much a product of white flight as is Johnson County. Residents there wanted no part of the Kansas City school district and instead willingly accepted expansions from neighboring towns (map 56). In this way, the once tiny North Kansas City district now sponsors four high schools and Park Hill (from Parkville) two. The Northland and Johnson County are similar in more ways than either group would like to admit—the schools, the golf courses, the elite shopping districts. They differ in their amounts of

Figure 52 (facing page). Bryant's Barbecue, 1727 Brooklyn Avenue, 2012. After occupying two earlier locations on the city's East Side, Arthur Bryant moved his "grease shack" to this site in 1958. His fame first moved beyond the African American community when smoky aromas wafted in the air above nearby Municipal Stadium. It spread further in the 1970s when writer Calvin Trillin enthusiastically and repeatedly claimed this restaurant to be the best in the world. Bryant died in 1982, but his operation has been carried on by Gary Berbiglia and Bill Rauschelbach. (Photograph by Barbara Shortridge)

high-end housing and, of course, in the corporate business that allies itself to this amenity.

Given Kansas City's unique historical legacy, its unavoidable geographic divisions, and its midwestern mind-set, what can one forecast about the future? From my perspective, I see mostly positive trends. The school district has just survived its crisis point and is poised to rebuild. With this prospect comes hope for the inner city, especially as race recedes as a societal issue. The recent economic revivals in Wyandotte County and in downtown Kansas City, Missouri, are equally remarkable. The former has transformed the area's most regressive county into a healthy, active part of the whole. The latter allows the core of the city to once again function as a unifying symbol and a countering force to the centrifugal tendencies of suburbanization. When one adds in a local economy that is diversified and seemingly well suited to twenty-first-century reality, the package is impressive.

Similar feelings come at the regional level. People on the coasts are growing more appreciative of midwestern life. They see it as a touchstone to traditional values at a time when standards are needed. They like the diversified economy; they admire contact with the land. Such attitudes have a reciprocal effect as well; local rubophobia eases when outsiders begin to compliment regional culture.[7]

The rise of barbecue as Kansas City's most symbolic food over the last generation is a case in point. This cuisine clearly possesses roots in folk culture, not the kitchens of Milan or Paris. It also links the city with the rural South, not the sophisticated Northeast or West Coast. Furthermore, barbecue honors both the meatpacking and the mixed racial heritages of Kansas City. Its wide embrace is a healthy and long-awaited sign that Kansas City people are accepting themselves for what they are and taking pride in that uniqueness.

Barbecue's strength as a city symbol comes from its popularity on both sides of the state line and across the big rivers. Even as the original restaurants of Arthur Bryant and Ollie Gates on the black East Side attract pilgrims from across the metropolitan area and far beyond, Wyandotte County people are equally passionate about their Rosedale Barbecue on Southwest Boulevard and Oklahoma Joe's on Forty-seventh Avenue. Northlanders head to Smokehouses at Zona Rosa and on North Oak Trafficway, and Johnson County people praise KC Masterpiece and Fiorella's Jack Stack. Wily Ollie Gates, with six locations, now sells citywide.

A community split by rivers, a state line, and race needs as many unifying agents as it can find. Barbecue certainly is one, the revived downtown another. A strong local university might play a similar role if one existed, but instead, Kansas City must cope with partisan fans, some loyal to the University of Kansas in nearby Lawrence and others to the University of Missouri in Columbia. Luckily, this division is at least partially countered by two major professional teams: the Chiefs and the Royals. In fact, I would suggest that many of the city's most positive steps toward unity and pride might not have occurred without the presence of these teams. Their primary role today is not to prove that Kansas City is "big league" or to satisfy the needs of sports zealots. Many, perhaps most, neighborhood gatherings on Chiefs Sundays are hosted and attended by people who do not really like football all that much. The games are an excuse to meet with friends and to celebrate life in America's heartland city.

Notes

Chapter 1 Introduction

1. Bill Graham, "A Piece of KC's Past Is Rediscovered," *Kansas City Star,* November 27, 2003, p. A1.

2. Richard J. Gentile, "Geology and Utilization of Underground Space in Metropolitan Kansas City Area, USA," *Environmental Geology* 29 (1997): 11–16. Details of local rock structure are available in John M. Jewett and Norman D. Newell, *The Geology of Wyandotte County, Kansas,* Bulletin 21, pt. 2 (Lawrence: State Geological Survey of Kansas, 1935); Walter E. McCourt, assisted by Maurice M. Albertson and John W. Bennett, *The Geology of Jackson County,* 2nd ser., vol. 14 (Rolla: Missouri Bureau of Geology and Mines, 1917); Howard G. O'Connor, *Geology and Ground-Water Resources of Johnson County, Northeastern Kansas,* Bulletin 203 (Lawrence: State Geological Survey of Kansas, 1971).

3. Howard G. O'Connor and Lowell W. Fowler, "Pleistocene Geology in a Part of the Kansas City Area," *Transactions of the Kansas Academy of Science* 66 (1963): 622–631; Eldon J. Parizek, "Kansas City: Its Geologic Setting," *Geotimes* 10 (October 1965): 9–13.

4. *Western Journal of Commerce,* August 7, 1863.

5. Jewett and Newell, *Geology of Wyandotte County,* pp. 185–188; McCourt, Albertson, and Bennett, *Geology of Jackson County,* pp. 70–72.

6. Charles C. Spalding, *Annals of the City of Kansas and the Great Western Plains* (Kansas City, Mo.: Van Horn and Abeel, 1858), p. 26.

7. Walter A. Schroeder, "The Presettlement Prairie in the Kansas City Region," *Missouri Prairie Journal* 7 (December 1985): 3–12.

8. Two recent examples are Shirley Christian, "Kansas City Could Flourish by Erasing Its State Line Mode," *Kansas City Star,* February 19, 2005, p. B7; and Mike Hendricks, "State Line Mentality Shackles Us," *Kansas City Star,* March 4, 2005, p. B1.

9. Perry McCandless, *A History of Missouri,* vol. 2, *1820–1860* (Columbia: University of Missouri Press, 1972), p. 12; Franklin K. Van Zandt, *Boundaries of the United States and the Several States,* Bulletin 1212 (Washington, D.C.: U. S. Geological Survey, 1966), pp. 188–190; Milton D. Rafferty, *Historical Atlas of Missouri* (Norman: University of Oklahoma Press, 1982), pl. 2. The quotation is cited in Rick Montgomery and Shirl Kasper, *Kansas City: An American Story* (Kansas City, Mo.: Kansas City Star Books, 1999), p. 19.

10. George W. Martin, "The Boundary Lines of Kansas," *Kansas Historical Collections* 11 (1909–1910): 72–74; Henry C. Haskell, Jr., and Richard B. Fowler, "The Attempted Annexation of Kansas City to the State of Kansas," *Missouri Historical Review* 44 (1950): 221–224; Walter H. Schoewe, "The Geography of Kansas, Part 1, Political Geography," *Transactions of the Kansas Academy of Science* 51 (1948): 265–267; Robert W. Patrick, "When Kansas City, Mo., Came Close to Being a City in Kansas," *Kansas History* 1 (1978): 266–277.

11. Quotations cited in Haskell and Fowler, "Attempted Annexation," pp. 223–224.

12. William G. Cutler, ed., *History of the State of Kansas,* vol. 1 (Chicago: A. T. Andreas, 1883), pp. 417, 624.

Chapter 2 River Towns and Trailheads, 1822–1860

1. Charles E. Hoffhaus, *Chez Les Canses: Three Centuries at Kawsmouth* (Kansas City, Mo.: Lowell Press, 1984), pp. 53–58, 115, 135.

2. Ibid., p. 171.

3. Dorothy B. Marra, *Cher Oncle, Cher Papa: The Letters of François and Berenice Chouteau* (Kansas City, Mo.: Western Historical Manuscript Collection—Kansas City, 2001), pp. 23–26, 196–200.

4. Ibid., pp. 202–203.

5. Ibid., pp. 77, 148–149, 174; Hoffhaus, *Chez Les Canses,* pp. 151–154, 164.

6. Hoffhaus, *Chez Les Canses,* pp. 157–162; Marra, *Cher Oncle, Cher Papa,* pp. 4–5, 66, 148–149.

7. William J. Dalton, *Pioneer Priest: The Life of Father Bernard Donnelley* (Kansas City, Mo.: Grimes-Joyce Printing, 1921), pp. 64–66, 133; Hoffhaus, *Chez Les Canses,* pp. 163–168; Marra, *Cher Oncle, Cher Papa,* pp. 123, 179–180.

8. William L. Webb, *The Centennial History of Independence, Mo.* (Independence, Mo.: William L. Webb, 1927), pp. 51–54.

9. Quoted in ibid., pp. 99, 96.

10. Daniel Fitzgerald, "Town Booming: An Economic History of Steamboat Towns along the Kansas-Missouri Border, 1840–1860" (master's thesis, Department of History, University of Kansas, 1983), p. 7.

11. Eugene T. Wells, "The Growth of Independence, Missouri, 1827–1850," *Bulletin of the Missouri Historical Society* 16 (October 1959): 34–35. A recent overview of the Mexican trade is available in David Dary, *The Santa Fe Trail: Its History, Legends, and Lore* (New York: Alfred A. Knopf, 2000).

12. Dary, *Santa Fe Trail,* pp. 108–110; Wells, "Growth of Independence," pp. 35–38; William McCoy to Ellen Waddle, undated letter, William McCoy Papers, Missouri Historical Society, St. Louis.

13. Wells, "Growth of Independence," pp. 39–41.

14. For introductions to Gilpin, see Henry N. Smith, *Virgin Land: The American West as Symbol and Myth* (Cambridge, Mass.: Harvard University Press, 1950), pp. 35–43, and Webb, *Centennial History,* pp. 158–168.

15. William Gilpin, "The Cities of Missouri," *Western Journal and Civilian* 11 (1853): 32, 37.

16. Ibid., p. 37.

17. Webb, *Centennial History,* pp. 71, 237–239; Wells, "Growth of Independence," pp. 40, 45.

18. Wells, "Growth of Independence," p. 42.

19. Ibid., p. 38; Fitzgerald, "Town Booming," pp. 14–67.

20. Gilpin, "Cities of Missouri," p. 31; Wells, "Growth of Independence," pp. 44, 46; *Westport Border Star,* November 10, 1859; *Missouri Republican,* May 13, 1859.

21. Joseph B. Herring, *The Enduring Indians of Kansas: A Century and a Half of Acculturation* (Lawrence: University Press of Kansas, 1990), pp. 13–28.

22. Louise Barry, ed., *The Beginning of the West: Annals of the Kansas Gateway to the American West, 1540–1854* (Topeka: Kansas State Historical Society, 1972), pp. 234, 268, 544. The Baptist mission stood near the modern intersection of 55th Street and Walmer Avenue in Mission, Kansas.

23. Patricia C. Miller, *Westport: Missouri's Port of Many Returns* (Kansas City, Mo.: Lowell Press, 1983), p. 35; Sherry L. Schirmer and Richard D. McKinzie, *At the River's Bend: An Illustrated History of Kansas City, Independence, and Jackson County* (Woodland Hills, Calif.: Windsor Publications, 1982), p. 26.

24. Nellie M. Harris, "Memories of Old Westport," *Annals of Kansas City* 1 (1921–1924): 466; William R. Bernard, "Westport and the Santa Fe Trade," *Kansas Historical Collections, 1905–1906* 9 (1906): 552. Detailed maps of the Osage trace, the Santa Fe Trail, and other early routes in the Kansas City area are in Gregory M. Franzwa, *Maps of the Oregon Trail* (Gerald, Mo.: Patrice Press, 1982).

25. Union Historical Company, *The History of Jackson County, Missouri* (Kansas City, Mo.: Birdsall, Williams, 1881), p. 380; Charles C. Spalding, *Annals of the City of Kansas and the Great Western Plains* (Kansas City, Mo.: Van Horn and Abeel, 1858), p. 26.

26. Harris, "Memories of Old Westport," pp. 471–472. Harris was the daughter of John C. McCoy. Daniel Geary, "Looking Backward," *Annals of Kansas City* 1 (1921–1924): 226.

27. Lewis H. Garrard, *Wah-To-Yah and the Taos Trail,* ed. Walter S. Campbell (1850; repr., Oklahoma City, Okla.: Harlow Publishing, 1927), p. 4. Historian Francis Parkman recorded similar observations that same year. See Parkman, *The Oregon Trail,* ed. E. N. Feltskog (1849; repr., Madison: University of Wisconsin Press, 1969), p. 4.

28. Union Historical Company, *History of Jackson County,* pp. 388–393; Bernard, "Westport," pp. 556–558; Miller, *Westport,* p. 46.

29. A. Theodore Brown, *Frontier Community: Kansas City to 1870* (Columbia: University of Missouri Press, 1963), p. 31; Union Historical Company, *History of Jackson County,* pp. 395–396.

30. Union Historical Company, *History of Jackson County,* pp. 380–381; Brown, *Frontier Community,* pp. 31–38.

31. Brown, *Frontier Community,* pp. 38–42; *Kansas City Daily Journal,* March 18, 1882.

32. Brown, *Frontier Community,* p. 42; Spalding, *Annals of the City,* pp. 19–20; Washington H. Chick, "A Journey to Missouri," *Annals of Kansas City* 1 (1921–1924): 99; Union Historical Company, *History of Jackson County,* pp. 405–406.

33. Union Historical Company, *History of Jackson County,* pp. 405–406; Washington H. Chick, "The Vicissitudes of Pioneer Life," *Annals of Kansas City* 1 (1921–1924): 208–210.

34. Union Historical Company, *History of Jackson County,* p. 384; Brown, *Frontier Community,* p. 43.

35. Brown, *Frontier Community,* p. 43; Union Historical Company, *History of Jackson County,* p. 408; Eugene T. Wells, "St. Louis and Cities West, 1820–1880: A Study in History and Geography" (Ph.D. diss., Department of History, University of Kansas, 1951), p. 361; Spalding, *Annals of the City,* p. 17; *St. Louis Union,* February 26, 1848.

36. The spelling *Wyandott* appears not only on McCoy's plat but also as the original name for the community that forms the core of today's Kansas City, Kansas. Tribal members usually spelled their name *Wyandot,* however, whereas the French used *Wyandotte.* The French form soon became dominant and was used on street maps of Kansas City, Missouri, as early as 1860. See William G. Cutler, ed., *History of the State of Kansas,* vol. 2 (Chicago: A. T. Andreas, 1883), p. 1227, and George Ehrlich, *Kansas City, Missouri: An Architectural History, 1826–1976* (Kansas City, Mo.: Historic Kansas City Foundation, 1979), p. 10. Union Historical Company, *History of Jackson County,* p. 407. I explain the composition and origin of the river bluffs in chapter 1.

37. Union Historical Company, *History of Jackson County,* pp. 133, 419.

38. William L. Campbell, "Fashionable Pearl Street," *Annals of Kansas City* 1 (1921–1924): 109–113; Marra, *Cher Oncle, Cher Papa,* pp. 180–183.

39. Parkman, *Oregon Trail,* p. 8; Garrard, *Wah-To-Yah,* p. 2; McCoy Scrapbook, p. 39, Native Sons Archives, Western Historical Manuscript Collection, University of Missouri–Kansas City.

40. Spalding, *Annals of the City,* pp. 25–27.

41. Union Cemetery, on the upland overlooking Union Station, is generally bounded by 27th, 30th, Walnut, and McGee streets. It now encompasses 34 acres and can be accessed at the intersection of Warwick Boulevard and 28th Terrace. See Landmarks Commission of Kansas City, Missouri, *Kansas City: A Place in Time* (Kansas City, Mo.: Landmarks Commission of Kansas City, Missouri, 1977), p. 158.

42. Charles N. Glaab, "Business Patterns in the Growth of a Midwestern City: The Kansas City Business Community before the Civil War," *Business History Review* 33 (1959): 156–174; Union Historical Company, *History of Jackson County,* pp. 427–430.

43. Union Historical Company, *History of Jackson County,* p. 433. The politics involved in the creation of Kansas Territory are described in H. Craig Miner and William E. Unrau, *The End of Indian Kansas: A Study of Cultural Revolution, 1854–1871* (Lawrence: Regents Press of Kansas, 1978).

44. *Western Journal of Commerce,* May 7, 1859; Union Historical Company, *History of Jackson County,* p. 419.

45. *Western Journal of Commerce,* May 7, 1859; Wells, "St. Louis and Cities West," pp. 404–420; Chamber of Commerce of Kansas City, *Where These Rocky Bluffs Meet: Including the Story of the Kansas City Ten-Year Plan* (Kansas City, Mo.: Kansas City Chamber of Commerce, 1938), p. 13; Albert D. Richardson, *Beyond the Mississippi* (Hartford, Conn.: American Publishing, 1867), p. 26.

46. *Kansas City Enterprise,* May 23, 1857; Union Historical Company, *History of Jackson County,* pp. 439–440.

47. Wells, "St. Louis and Cities West," p. 410.

48. R. Richard Wohl, "Three Generations of Business Enterprise in a Midwestern City: The McGees of Kansas City," *Journal of Economic History* 16 (1956): 514–528; James Sutherland, comp., *Kansas City Directory and Business Mirror for 1860–61* (Indianapolis, Ind.: James Sutherland, 1860), p. 18; Union Historical Company, *History of Jackson County,* pp. 432–433.

49. Spalding, *Annals of the City,* p. 39; Sutherland, *Kansas City Directory,* p. 18; Dory DeAngelo and Jane F. Flynn, *Kansas City Style: A Social and Cultural History of Kansas City as Seen through Its Lost Architecture* (Kansas City, Mo.: Harrow Books, 1990), p. 129; *Western Journal of Commerce,* May 24, 1860.

50. Sutherland, *Kansas City Directory,* pp. 14, 23; DeAngelo and Flynn, *Kansas City Style,* p. 129; Spalding, *Annals of the City,* p. 39.

51. William C. Lobenstine, *Extracts from the Diary of William C. Lobenstine, December 31, 1851–1858* (New York: William C. Lobenstine, 1920); Sutherland, *Kansas City Directory,* p. 20.

52. Laura C. Reed, ed., *In Memoriam, Sarah Walter Chandler Coates* (Kansas City, Mo.: Hudson-Kimberly, 1897), pp. 164–172; Spalding, *Annals of the City,* p. 47; DeAngelo and Flynn, *Kansas City Style,* p. 51.

53. DeAngelo and Flynn, *Kansas City Style,* pp. 50–51; Spalding, *Annals of the City,* p. 47.

54. *Kansas City Enterprise,* December 22, 1855; Wells, "St. Louis and Cities West," pp. 411–412. Remnants of the Broadway route west survive in the Rosedale and Argentine neighborhoods in Kansas as Shawnee Road. Turkey Creek now has a new channel, and the old link in Missouri between Shawnee Road and Broadway was gradually relocated to Southwest Boulevard.

55. Spalding, *Annals of the City,* pp. 47–48. Construction on the Broadway Hotel began in 1857, but wartime troubles delayed completion until 1868. The Coates House building that stands on its site today (1005 Broadway) is a reconstruction done between 1889 and 1891.

56. Union Historical Company, *History of Jackson County,* pp. 433, 437, 442.

57. Sutherland, *Kansas City Directory;* Hattie E. Poppino, *Census of 1860: Population Schedules for Jackson County, Missouri* (Kansas City, Mo.: H. E. Poppino, 1964).

58. Spalding, *Annals of the City,* pp. 53–55.

59. Poppino, *Census of 1860,* p. xii; Paul C. Nagel, *Missouri: A History* (New York: W. W. Norton, 1977), pp. 95–98. The ethnic percentages are calculated from the heads of households I was able to locate in both the census and the city directory. The German total includes natives of Austria and Switzerland. The Yankee total includes natives of the New England states plus Delaware, Michigan, New Jersey, New York, Pennsylvania, and Wisconsin.

60. Poppino, *Census of 1860,* p. xii. The percentage is calculated from the number of households I was able to locate in both the census and the city directory.

61. Dalton, *Pioneer Priest,* pp. 48–49.

62. Pat O'Neill, *From the Bottom Up: The Story of the Irish in Kansas City* (Kansas City, Mo.: Seat o' the Pants Publishing, 2000), pp. 13–14; Dalton, *Pioneer Priest,* pp. 57–60. According to Dalton, the Irish still dominated Kansas City's construction business at the time of Donnelly's death in 1880 (p. 173). John Campbell, although Irish born, relocated to Kansas City from St. Louis to manage the substantial investments of his uncle, Robert Campbell. As a developer of the eastern section of the original town, John named adjacent streets after himself (Campbell) and his wife (Charlotte). He lived on Second Street, just east of Campbell.

63. Dalton, *Pioneer Priest,* pp. 49, 54; Poppino, *Census of 1860.*

64. Reed, *In Memoriam,* pp. 121–123.

Chapter 3 The Rise of a Metropolis, 1867–1889

1. Charles N. Glaab, *Kansas City and the Railroads: Community Policy in the Growth of a Regional Metropolis* (Madison: State Historical Society of Wisconsin, 1962), p. 64; Robert E. Riegel, "The Missouri Pacific Railroad to 1879," *Missouri Historical Review* 18 (1923–1924): 3–26. The Pacific Railroad of Missouri was renamed the Missouri Pacific in 1876 as part of a company reorganization.

2. Patricia C. Miller, *Westport: Missouri's Port of Many Returns* (Kansas City, Mo.: Lowell Press, 1983), pp. 46, 59.

3. Glaab, *Kansas City and the Railroads,* pp. 68–77, 125; James R. Shortridge, "Edward Miller's Town: The Reconceptualization of Pleasant Hill by the Pacific Railroad of Missouri," *Missouri Historical Review* 101 (2007): 205–225.

4. A. Theodore Brown, *Frontier Community: Kansas City to 1870* (Columbia: University of Missouri Press, 1963), pp. 93, 97; Dory DeAngelo and Jane F. Flynn, *Kansas City Style: A Social and Cultural History of Kansas City as Seen through Its Lost Architecture* (Kansas City, Mo.: Harrow Books, 1990), p. 129.

5. Charles N. Glaab, "Business Patterns in the Growth of a Midwestern City: The Kansas City Business Community before the Civil War," *Business History Review* 33 (1959): 156–174; A. Theodore Brown, "Business 'Neutralism' on the Missouri-Kansas Border: Kansas City 1854–1857," *Journal of Southern History* 29 (1963): 229–240.

6. Alan W. Farley, "Samuel Hallett and the Union Pacific Railway Company in Kansas," *Kansas Historical Quarterly* 25 (1959): 1–16.

7. Ibid.

8. William G. Cutler, ed. *History of the State of Kansas,* vol. 2 (Chicago: A. T. Andreas, 1883), p. 1231.

9. Ibid. The avenue names honor the four federal territories that existed in 1857. Kansas Avenue was renamed State in 1886 as part of a consolidation agreement when Wyandotte united with four other communities to create Kansas City, Kansas. One of these four cities, Armourdale, also had a Kansas Avenue.

10. Ibid.

11. The word *Lee* in Lee's Summit refers to a local resident, Pleasant Lea, but railroad officials spelled his name incorrectly. In a reverse situation that psychically balances this error, Oscar Lee is the namesake of the newer Kansas City suburb of Leawood.

12. Development strategies are thoroughly explored in Glaab, *Kansas City and the Railroads.*

13. The stories of James Joy and the Hannibal Bridge are nicely summarized by Glaab, *Kansas City and the Railroads,* pp. 138–160; Brown, *Frontier Community,* pp. 197–217; and Daniel Serda, *Boston Investors and the Early Development of Kansas City, Missouri* (Kansas City, Mo.: Midwest Research Institute, 1992). Joy's name once was found on two different West Bottoms streets. The one on the Missouri side later became Thirteenth Terrace; the Kansas one, which paralleled James Street two blocks to the east, has simply disappeared.

14. Joseph G. McCoy, *Historic Sketches of the Cattle Trade of the West and Southwest* (1874; repr., Glendale, Calif.: A. H. Clark, 1940), pp. 116–120. This McCoy is not related to the Isaac and John McCoy of an earlier-day Westport and Kansas City.

15. Serda, *Boston Investors,* p. 12; Edward C. Kirkland, *Charles Francis Adams, Jr.: 1835–1915—The Patrician at Bay* (Cambridge, Mass.: Harvard University Press), pp. 69–72; Arthur Charvat, "Growth and Development of the Kansas City Stock Yards: A History, 1871–1947" (master's thesis, Department of History, University of Kansas City, 1948), p. 5; G. K. Renner, "The Kansas City Meat Packing Industry before 1900," *Missouri Historical Review* 55 (1960): 21–23; Edwin D. Shutt, "The Saga of the Armour Family in Kansas City, 1870–1900," *Heritage of the Great Plains* 23 (Fall 1990): 28–30.

16. The Kansas City, Kansas, in the West Bottoms existed as an independent community from 1868 until 1886, when it merged with Wyandotte, Armourdale, Armstrong, and Riverview to create a new entity also called Kansas City. To limit confusion, the original Kansas City, Kansas, is sometimes referred to as "old" Kansas City. Members of the 1868 town company led by David E. James (the eponym of today's James Street) were mostly Kansans. They were pragmatic enough, however, to negotiate with their only accessible neighbor—Kansas City, Missouri—for fire protection and postal services. See Cutler, *History of the State,* p. 1240.

17. The population of Kansas City, Missouri, was estimated at 40,740 in 1873 and at 41,786 in 1877. See Union Historical Company, *The History of Jackson County, Missouri* (Kansas City, Mo.: Birdsall, Williams, 1881), p. 547, and Renner, "Kansas City Meat Packing Industry," pp. 23–26.

18. Quoted in Kirkland, *Charles Francis Adams, Jr.,* p. 69. Although he traveled and invested extensively throughout the West, Adams saw the region as unsophisticated and was always eager to return home to Massachusetts (pp. 74–75).

19. Shutt, "Saga of the Armour Family," pp. 31–33; *Kansas City Star,* May 27, 1892, p. 1.

20. Kirkland, *Charles Francis Adams, Jr.,* pp. 66–69; Charles F. Morse, *A Sketch of My Life Written for My Children and a Buffalo Hunt in Nebraska in 1871* (Cambridge, Mass.: Riverside Press, 1927), pp. 35–42.

21. A. Theodore Brown and Lyle W. Dorsett, *K.C.: A History of Kansas City, Missouri* (Boulder, Colo.: Pruett Publishing, 1978), p. 166; Morse, *Sketch of My Life,* pp. 50–52.

22. Renner, "Kansas City Meat Packing Industry," pp. 27–28; City Plan Commission, *Locational Costs in Industrial Districts: Greater Kansas City* (Kansas City, Mo.: City Plan Commission, 1950), pp. 14–15; Cutler, *History of the State,* p. 1243; Morse, *Sketch of My Life,* p. 53.

23. Charvat, "Growth and Development," pp. 7, 15–16; *Fifth Biennial Report of the Kansas State Board of Agriculture for the Years 1885–86* (Topeka: Kansas Publishing House, 1887), p. 594.

24. *Fifth Biennial Report,* p. 36.

25. Charvat, "Growth and Development," p. 18.

26. *Fifth Biennial Report,* p. 37; *Sixth Biennial Report of the Kansas State Board of Agriculture for the Years 1887–88* (Topeka: Kansas Publishing House, 1889), p. 536; Cutler, *History of the State,* p. 1243.

27. Cutler, *History of the State,* p.1246.

28. Donald H. Simmons, ed., *Centennial History of Argentine, Kansas City, Kansas, 1880–1980* (Kansas City, Kans.: Simmons Funeral Home, 1980), pp. 4–5; Kirkland, *Charles Francis Adams, Jr.,* pp. 78, 180–181.

29. Cutler, *History of the State,* p. 1246; Simmons, *Centennial History,* pp. 4–5; *Fifth Biennial Report,* pp. 37, 593.

30. Glaab, *Kansas City and the Railroads,* pp. 147–148, 158, 163, 168–169. Officials of the Pacific Railroad of Missouri changed the company name to Missouri Pacific in 1876.

31. Union Historical Company, *History of Jackson County,* pp. 510, 545; William M. Reddig, *Tom's Town: Kansas City and the Pendergast Legend* (Philadelphia: J. B. Lippincott, 1947), p. 26.

32. Dwayne R. Martin, "The Hidden Community: The Black Community of Kansas City, Missouri, during the 1870s and 1880s" (master's thesis, Department of History, University of Missouri–Kansas City, 1982), pp. 11, 32, 60; Sherry L. Schirmer, *A City Divided: The Racial Landscape of Kansas City, 1900–1960* (Columbia: University of Missouri Press, 2002), pp. 34–35.

33. Charles D. Warner, "Studies of the Great West: St. Louis and Kansas City," *Harper's New Monthly Magazine* 77 (1888): 760; Frederic Trautmann, ed., "Across Kansas by Train in 1877: The Travels of Ernest von Hesse-Wartegg," *Kansas History* 6 (1983): 145.

34. Roy E. King, "The Great South," *Scribner's Monthly* 8 (1874): 281; Union Historical Company, *History of Jackson County,* p. 605; William J. Dalton, *Pioneer Priest: The Life of Father Bernard Donnelly* (Kansas City, Mo.: Grimes-Joyce Printing, 1921), p. 165.

35. Cutler, *History of the State,* p. 1245; Margaret Landis, *The Winding Valley and the Craggy Hillside: A History of the City of Rosedale, Kansas* (Kansas City, Kans.: Margaret Landis, 1976), pp. 11–15.

36. H. James Maxwell and Bob Sullivan, Jr., *Hometown Beer: A History of Kansas City's Breweries* (Kansas City, Mo.: Omega Innovative Marketing, 1999), pp. 123–124. The main Heim building still stands, remodeled for the needs of the Empire Storage and Ice Company.

37. Octave Chanute and George Morison, *The Kansas City Bridge, with an Account of the Regimen of the Missouri River, and a Description of Methods Used for Founding in That River* (New York: D. Van Nostrand, 1870).

38. Union Historical Company, *History of Jackson County,* p. 493.

39. Ibid., pp. 493, 512.

40. Ibid., pp. 529-31; DeAngelo and Flynn, *Kansas City Style,* pp. 29, 85; George Ehrlich, *Kansas City, Missouri: An Architectural History, 1826-1976* (Kansas City, Mo.: Historic Kansas City Foundation, 1979), p. 36.

41. Union Historical Company, *History of Jackson County,* p. 488; Lawrence H. Larsen and Nancy J. Hulston, "Through the Eyes of a Medical Student: A Window on Frontier Life in Kansas City, 1870-1871," *Missouri Historical Review* 88 (1994): 432.

42. Jane F. Flynn, *Kansas City Women of Independent Minds* (Kansas City, Mo.: Fifield Publishing, 1992), pp. 26-27; DeAngelo and Flynn, *Kansas City Style,* pp. 104-105.

43. Monroe Dodd, *A Splendid Ride: The Streetcars of Kansas City, 1870-1957* (Kansas City, Mo.: Kansas City Star Books, 2002), pp. 39-40.

44. Ibid., pp. 40-45.

45. Ibid.

46. Ibid., pp. 42-49.

47. Warner, "Studies of the Great West," p. 761.

48. Henry C. Haskell, Jr., and Richard B. Fowler, *City of the Future: A Narrative History of Kansas City, 1850-1950* (Kansas City, Mo.: Frank Glenn, 1950), p. 62.

49. DeAngelo and Flynn, *Kansas City Style,* pp. 80-81; Ehrlich, *Kansas City, Missouri,* pp. 50-51.

50. Dodd, *Splendid Ride,* pp. 56-57.

51. Ibid.

52. DeAngelo and Flynn, *Kansas City Style,* pp. 28-29, 132-133; Ehrlich, *Kansas City, Missouri,* pp. 44-45.

53. Dodd, *Splendid Ride,* pp. 51-56; Morse, *Sketch of My Life,* pp. 61-62.

54. Ehrlich, *Kansas City, Missouri,* pp. 46-50; DeAngelo and Flynn, *Kansas City Style,* pp. 76-77.

55. DeAngelo and Flynn, *Kansas City Style,* pp. 36-37, 46-47, 104-105. The courthouse in Kansas City, although officially a branch of the one in Independence, actually conducted most of the county's business by this time.

56. Morse, *Sketch of My Life,* p. 44; Shutt, "Saga of the Armour Family," p. 39; Brown, "Business 'Neutralism,'" pp. 229-240; Pierre R. Porter, "Quality Hill: A Study in Heredity," *Missouri Historical Review* 35 (1941): 562-563. The most complete account of the area is Clifford Naysmith, *Quality Hill: The History of a Neighborhood,* Missouri Valley Series No. 1 (Kansas City, Mo.: Kansas City Public Library, 1962).

57. Union Historical Company, *History of Jackson County,* p. 838; Dory DeAngelo, *Passages through Time: Stories about Kansas City, Missouri and Its Northeast Neighborhood* (Kansas City, Mo.: Tapestry Publications, 1992), pp. 85-88.

58. DeAngelo, *Passages through Time,* pp. 2-4, 44-50; DeAngelo and Flynn, *Kansas City Style,* pp. 102-103.

59. DeAngelo and Flynn, *Kansas City Style,* pp. 134-135.

60. Ernest Ingersoll, "Kansas City," *Cosmopolitan* 8 (1889): 144-145.

61. Schirmer, *City Divided,* pp. 28-32.

62. Union Historical Company, *History of Jackson County,* p.

439; Charles C. Spalding, *Annals of the City of Kansas and the Great Western Plains* (Kansas City, Mo.: Van Horn and Abeel, 1858), p. 41; Charles P. Deatherage, *Early History of Greater Kansas City, Missouri and Kansas: The Prophetic City at the Mouth of the Kaw* (Kansas City, Mo.: Interstate Publishing, 1927), p. 558; Schirmer, *City Divided,* pp. 36-37.

63. Union Historical Company, *History of Jackson County,* p. 593; Schirmer, *City Divided,* pp. 37-39. The most complete analysis of local black life for this time is Martin, "The Hidden Community." The smallest houses at Belvidere clustered in and near a steep ravine bisected by Lydia Avenue. Those at Hick's Hollow correspond to a subdivision built by Albert Marty.

64. U.S. Bureau of the Census, *Statistics of the Population of the United States at the Tenth Census* (Washington, D.C.: Government Printing Office, 1883), p. 540; U.S. Bureau of the Census, *Report on Population of the United States at the Eleventh Census* (Washington, D.C.: Government Printing Office, 1895), p. 671; Pat O'Neill, *From the Bottom Up: The Story of the Irish in Kansas City* (Kansas City, Mo.: Seat o' the Pants Publishing, 2000), pp. 65, 76.

65. O'Neill, *From the Bottom Up,* pp. 54-56, 113; *Kansas City Star,* February 22, 1893, p. 1.

66. *Kansas City Star,* February 22, 1893, p. 1; *Kansas City Star,* July 23, 1884, p. 2; O'Neill, *From the Bottom Up,* p. 51.

67. O'Neill, *From the Bottom Up,* pp. 74, 101.

68. U.S. Bureau of the Census, *Statistics of Population, Ninth Census of the United States* (Washington, D.C.: Government Printing Office, 1872), pp. 386-391; U.S. Bureau of the Census, *Population at the Tenth Census,* p. 539; U.S. Bureau of the Census, *Population at the Eleventh Census,* p. 671.

69. Rose G. Kingsley, *South by West, or Winter in the Rocky Mountains and Spring in Mexico* (London: W. Isbister, 1874), p. 34; Spalding, *Annals of the City,* p. 39.

70. Warner, "Studies of the Great West," p. 760; Union Historical Company, *History of Jackson County,* p. 697.

71. Grant W. Harrington, *Historic Spots or Mile-Stones in the Progress of Wyandotte County* (Merriam, Kans.: Mission Press, 1935), p. 241; Cutler, *History of the State,* p. 1235.

72. U.S. Bureau of the Census, *Population at the Tenth Census,* p. 184; U.S. Bureau of the Census, *Population at the Eleventh Census,* p. 156; Union Historical Company, *History of Jackson County,* p. 690. The population estimate for 1890 comes from summing the totals for Wards Two and Three of the newly agglomerated Kansas City, Kansas.

73. Susan D. Greenburg, *Strawberry Hill: A Neighborhood Study* (Kansas City, Kans.: City of Kansas City, Kansas, 1978), pp. 1-5; Cutler, *History of the State,* p. 1233.

74. Harrington, *Historic Spots,* pp. 205-210; Dunbar PTA, comp., *In Commemoration of the Dunbar Elementary School* (Kansas City, Kans.: n.p., 1971), pp. 81-82; *Fifth Biennial Report,* pp. 36, 593. For context, see Nell I. Painter, *Exodusters: Black Migration to Kansas after Reconstruction* (New York: Alfred A. Knopf, 1977).

75. Charles M. Chase, *The Editor's Run in New Mexico and Colorado* (Lyndon: Vermont Union, 1882), p. 220; Harrington, *Historic*

Spots, pp. 244–247; Larry K. Hancks and Meredith Roberts, *Roots: The Historic and Architectural Heritage of Kansas City, Kansas* (Kansas City, Kans.: City of Kansas City, Kansas, 1976), pp. 19–20. Almost no landscape evidence remains of old Armstrong because of the construction of Interstates 70 and 670. The name Perry Square, honoring railroad president John D. Perry survives but as a short street instead of the town center it was originally. Riverview also has been modified drastically. Riverview, Simpson, and Sumner avenues remain in their original positions, but several curving connector streets are gone, as is a large park that once stretched south from the corner of Sixth Street and Reynolds Avenue.

76. *Fifth Biennial Report,* p. 593.

77. Dodd, *Splendid Ride,* p. 75.

78. U.S. Bureau of the Census, *Statistics of Population, Ninth Census,* p. 190; U.S. Bureau of the Census, *Population at the Tenth Census,* p. 242. The newspaper article is reprinted in Union Historical Company, *History of Jackson Country,* pp. 666–667.

79. Union Historical Company, *History of Jackson Country,* pp. 647–649.

80. The feel of the boom and Winner's role in it is captured well in S. Ferdinand Howe's *The Commerce of Kansas City in 1886; with a General Review of Its Business Progress* (Kansas City, Mo.: S. F. Howe, 1886), esp. pp. 80–82. See also Brown and Dorsett, *K.C.: A History,* pp. 55–59.

81. Bernd Foerster, *Independence, Missouri* (Independence, Mo.: Independence Press, 1978), pp. 53–88; U.S. Bureau of the Census, *Population at the Eleventh Census,* p. 216. At 219 North Delaware Street sits another large home, built in 1865 for miller George P. Gates. It passed to his daughter and then to his granddaughter and her husband, Bess and Harry Truman. The site is now operated by the National Park Service.

82. Union Historical Company, *History of Jackson County,* p. 395; *Weekly Western Journal of Commerce,* March 13, 1858, p. 2. One exception existed to the transfer of Kansas City street names north. Perhaps as a joke, Grand Avenue in Harlem became Short Street. The ferry port on the Kansas City side moved from Grand Avenue to Main Street after the construction of the Pacific Railroad.

83. Mildred Fulton, ed., *Bridge to the Past: A Personal History of North Kansas City* (Marceline, Mo.: Walsworth Publishing, 1983), pp. 13–18; Brown and Dorsett, *K.C.: A History,* pp. 57–59.

Chapter 4 Maturity in a Railroad Mode, 1893–1933

1. U.S. Bureau of the Census, *Report on Population of the United States at the Eleventh Census* (Washington, D.C.: Government Printing Office, 1895), p. 580.

2. The quotation is from Hugh O'Neill and John M. Steele, "Kansas City: A City That Is Finding Itself," *World To-day* 11 (1906): 1156. The mood of the time is also captured well in Henry Allaway, "Kansas City's Race with St. Louis for Supremacy," *New York Times,* February 15, 1903, p. 32; Charles S. Gleed, "The Central City of the West," *Cosmopolitan* 29 (1900): 297–304; and Poultney Bigelow, "What I Saw at Kansas City," *Contemporary Review* 78 (1900): 442–456.

3. The quotation is from Uriah S. Epperson, head of the Kansas City Commercial Club, as cited in Rick Montgomery and Shirl Kasper, *Kansas City: An American Story* (Kansas City, Mo.: Kansas City Star Books, 1999), p. 149. Montgomery and Kasper provide a good summary of convention events on pp. 144–154.

4. George F. Damon, "The Kansas City Flood in Retrospect," *Charities* 11 (1903): 574–576; William R. Hill, *The Great Flood of 1903* (Kansas City, Mo.: Enterprise Publishing, 1903). Good daily reports on the disaster appear in the *New York Times* for June 1, 1903, p. 2; June 2, p. 1; June 3, p. 1; and June 5, p. 1.

5. Rose G. Kingsley, *South by West, or Winter in the Rocky Mountains and Spring in Mexico* (London: W. Isbister, 1874), p. 33; Henry Holt, "A Foreign Tour at Home," *Putnam's Monthly and The Reader* 3 (1908): 648.

6. William H. Wilson, *The City Beautiful Movement in Kansas City* (Columbia: University of Missouri Press, 1964).

7. Ibid., pp. 1–44; Harry Haskell, *Boss-Busters and Sin Hounds: Kansas City and Its Star* (Columbia: University of Missouri Press, 2007), pp. 42–50.

8. Haskell, *Boss-Busters and Sin Hounds,* p. 44.

9. Ibid., pp. 50–52; Ray F. Weirick, "The Park and Boulevard System of Kansas City, Mo.," *American City* 3 (1910): 211–218, quotation on p. 214. Other early tributes to Kessler's creation include: Frederick W. Coburn, "Public Parks in Kansas City," *Brush and Pencil* 13 (1903): 288–290, and Henry Schott, "A City's Fight for Beauty," *World's Work* 11 (1906): 7191–7205. The name Paseo is adapted from the Paseo de la Reforma, a major thoroughfare in Mexico City.

10. Wilson, *City Beautiful Movement,* pp. 61–66; *Kansas City Star,* June 25, 1896, p. 1, and June 26, 1896, p. 1. Discussion of city expansion is in A. Theodore Brown and Lyle W. Dorsett, *K.C.: A History of Kansas City, Missouri* (Boulder, Colo.: Pruett Publishing, 1978), pp. 55–60. Monroe Dodd's *A Splendid Ride: The Streetcars of Kansas City—1870–1957* (Kansas City, Mo.: Kansas City Star Books, 2002), contains a trolley map for 1880 on p. 41.

11. Wilson, *City Beautiful Movement,* pp. 122–123.

12. Jeffrey Spivak, *Union Station: Kansas City* (Kansas City, Mo.: Kansas City Star Books, 1999).

13. Ibid., pp. 4–11.

14. Ibid., pp. 11–12; Chamber of Commerce of Kansas City, *Where These Rocky Bluffs Meet: Including the Story of the Kansas City Ten-Year Plan* (Kansas City, Mo.: Kansas City Chamber of Commerce, 1938), p. 62; "Crash at Kansas City," *Chicago Daily Tribune,* April 17, 1891, p. 1.

15. Charles F. Morse, *A Sketch of My Life Written for My Children and a Buffalo Hunt in Nebraska in 1871* (Cambridge, Mass.: Riverside Press, 1927), pp. 53–60.

16. Spivak, *Union Station,* pp. 4–5, 14.

17. Ibid., pp. 12–14; Wilson, *City Beautiful Movement,* p. 99; *New York Times,* February 19, 1906, p. 10.

18. Spivak, *Union Station,* pp. 14–20, quotation on p. 20.

19. Ibid., pp. 60–89.

20. Ibid., pp. 34, 66; William M. Reddig, *Tom's Town: Kansas*

City and the Pendergast Legend (Philadelphia: J. B. Lippincott, 1947), p. 176.

21. Chamber of Commerce, *Where These Rocky Bluffs Meet*, p. 62.

22. Wilson, *City Beautiful Movement*, p. 101.

23. Ibid.

24. Ibid., p. 107.

25. *Kansas City Star*, March 2, 1914, p. 2; Jane F. Flynn, *Kansas City Women of Independent Minds* (Kansas City, Mo.: Fifield Publishing, 1992), pp. 4–6.

26. Wilson, *City Beautiful Movement*, pp. 111–114; *Kansas City Star*, June 23, 1907, p. 1, November 25, 1909, p. 8, August 3, 1910, pp. 8–9; *Kansas City Times*, November 25, 1909, p. 3.

27. Wilson, *City Beautiful Movement*, pp. 111–114.

28. Ibid., pp. 115–116; Henry J. Haskell, "A Notable Memorial," *World's Work* 42 (1921): 488–490; George Marvin, "'K.C.': The City Where Trails Begin," *Outlook* 144 (1926): 533–535; H. I. Brock, "East and West Meet in Peace Memorial," *New York Times*, August 22, 1926, p. SM18.

29. Herbert C. Cornuelle, *"Mr. Anonymous": The Story of William Volker* (Caldwell, Idaho: Caxton Printers, 1951), pp. 110–111; Haskell, "Notable Memorial," p. 489.

30. Chamber of Commerce, *Where These Rocky Bluffs Meet*, p. 104.

31. Ibid., p. 105; *Chicago Tribune*, August 9, 1925, p. 10; *New York Times*, September 18, 1925, p. 15; *Kansas City Star*, December 16, 1930, p. 1.

32. *New York Times*, February 28, 1926, p. 7, and March 4, 1926, p. 34.

33. Henry J. Haskell, "Kansas City: Where the Frontier Lingers," *American Review of Reviews* 77 (1928): 622–623.

34. *Kansas City Star*, December 16, 1930, p. 1; Cornuelle, *"Mr. Anonymous,"* pp. 146–148; *New York Times*, December 8, 1933, p. 28, and December 11, 1933, p. 24. Volker essentially created the university. His gifts between 1930 and 1944 totaled more than $2,600,000 and included funds to construct the library, liberal arts building, and science laboratory.

35. "Art in a Mid-West Center," *Outlook* 148 (1928): 369; Flynn, *Kansas City Women*, pp. 52–53; Michael Coleman, *This Far by Faith: A Popular History of the Catholic People of West and Northwest Missouri*, vol. 2, *The Facts* (Marceline, Mo.: Walsworth Publishing, 1992), pp. 555–557; Bella E. Schultz, "The Highest Degree of *Tzedakah*: Jewish Philanthropy in Kansas City, 1870–1933," in *Mid-America's Promise: A Profile of Kansas City Jewry*, ed. Joseph P. Schultz (Kansas City, Mo.: Jewish Community Foundation of Greater Kansas City, 1982), pp. 228–232. The Jesuits wanted to name their school Rockhill to honor the *Kansas City Star*'s publisher, who had platted their land. Another college already bore that name, however, and so they selected a close approximation.

36. *New York Times*, February 5, 1928, p. 1, February 6, 1928, p. 1, May 27, 1928, p. 74.

37. *New York Times*, June 16, 1928, p. 2; Chamber of Commerce, *Where These Rocky Bluffs Meet*, p. 109.

38. Chamber of Commerce, *Where These Rocky Bluffs Meet*, pp. 109–165, quotation on p. 165. Less altruistic motives also helped the plan to pass, especially an anticipation of construction jobs that would be important during depression times. The city's increasingly influential Democratic political boss, Tom Pendergast, endorsed the measure partly for this reason. Pendergast also expected to (and did) profit personally, since he owned a large cement company. See Lawrence H. Larsen and Nancy J. Hulston, *Pendergast!* (Columbia: University of Missouri Press, 1997), pp. 88–89.

39. Chamber of Commerce, *Where These Rocky Bluffs Meet*, p. 160.

40. "Kansas City's New Municipal Auditorium," *American City* 51 (June 1936): 103.

41. Chamber of Commerce, *Where These Rocky Bluffs Meet*, pp. 134–136.

42. Ibid., p. 136.

43. Ibid.

44. George Ehrlich, *Kansas City, Missouri: An Architectural History, 1826–1976* (Kansas City, Mo.: Historic Kansas City Foundation, 1979), pp. 104–105.

45. Charles P. Deatherage, *The Early History of the Lumber Trade of Kansas City* (Kansas City, Mo.: Retail Lumberman, 1924), p. 8. Workers for the Kansas City, Fort Scott and Gulf Railroad had laid a spur partway up OK Creek about 1880 to serve a tract of land owned by Charles Adams. This spur was what attracted lumberman Merrill to the neighborhood in 1881; see Morse, *Sketch of my Life*, pp. 53–54.

46. Coleman, *This Far by Faith*, pp. 109–110.

47. William S. Worley, *Development of Industrial Districts in the Kansas City Region: From the Close of the Civil War to World War II* (Kansas City, Mo.: Midwest Research Institute, 1993), pp. 4–6.

48. Brown and Dorsett, *K.C.: A History*, p. 57.

49. Arthur Charvat, "Growth and Development of the Kansas City Stock Yards: A History, 1871–1947" (master's thesis, Department of History, University of Kansas City, 1948), pp. 33–34; *Kansas City Star*, November 7, 1912, p. 1.

50. John Q. Adams, "The North Kansas City Urban District," *Economic Geography* 8 (1932): 409–412. The creation of North Kansas City effectively blocked expansion of Kansas City, Missouri, into Clay and Platte counties except for tiny Harlem and the land just outside the levee that became Municipal Airport in 1928. Not until 1950 did Kansas City first leapfrog over North Kansas City to annex the area near Vivion Road.

51. Ibid., pp. 417–419; Mildred Fulton, ed., *Bridge to the Past: A Personal History of North Kansas City* (Marceline, Mo.: Walsworth Publishing, 1983), p. 32.

52. Adams, "North Kansas City," pp. 416–417, 419–420.

53. Ibid., pp. 412, 415, 422–424.

54. Joseph H. McDowell, *Building a City: A Detailed History of Kansas City, Kansas* (Kansas City, Kans.: Kansas City Kansan, 1969), pp. 31–33.

55. Ibid., pp. 33, 49–50.

56. Campbell Gibson, *Population of the 100 Largest Cities and Other Urban Places in the United States: 1790 to 1990*, Working Paper

No. 27 (Washington, D.C.: Population Division, U.S. Bureau of the Census, 1998). For evidence of city pride at the time, see Haskell, "Kansas City," and Shaemas O'Sheel, "Kansas City: The Crossroads of a Continent," *New Republic* 54 (1928): 375–378.

57. Clifford Naysmith, *Quality Hill: The History of a Neighborhood,* Missouri Valley Series No. 1 (Kansas City, Mo.: Kansas City Public Library, 1962), p. 24.

58. S. Ferdinand Howe, *The Commerce of Kansas City in 1886; with a General Review of Its Business Progress* (Kansas City, Mo.: S. F. Howe, 1886), pp. 82–83; Ehrlich, *Kansas City, Missouri,* p. 43; Brown and Dorsett, *K.C.: A History,* p. 161; Morse, *Sketch of My Life,* p. 46.

59. William S. Worley, *J. C. Nichols and the Shaping of Kansas City: Innovation in Planned Residential Communities* (Columbia: University of Missouri Press, 1990), p. 52; Patricia C. Miller, *Westport: Missouri's Port of Many Returns* (Kansas City, Mo.: Lowell Press, 1983), pp. 69, 75; Naysmith, *Quality Hill,* pp. 16–22; Richard P. Coleman, *The Kansas City Establishment: Leadership through Two Centuries in a Midwestern Metropolis* (Manhattan, Kans.: KS Publishing, 2006), pp. 265–266.

60. Miller, *Westport,* pp. 74–75; Keith L. Bryant, Jr., *Arthur Stilwell: Promoter with a Hunch* (Nashville, Tenn.: Vanderbilt University Press, 1971), pp. 117–118. Although the name Hyde Park has its ultimate origin in London, Chicago was the immediate source for Kansas City. This connection is made clear by another name. In both Chicago and Kansas City, a Kenwood Addition adjoins Hyde Park.

61. Haskell, *Boss-Busters and Sin Hounds,* pp. 37, 46; Worley, *J. C. Nichols,* pp. 59–60; Miller, *Westport,* p. 75; Janice Lee, David Boutros, Charlotte R. White, and Dean Wolfenbarger, eds., *A Legacy of Design: An Historical Survey of the Kansas City, Missouri, Parks and Boulevards System, 1893–1940* (Kansas City, Mo.: Kansas City Center for Design and Research, 1995), pp. 89–90, 259–260.

62. Coleman, *Kansas City Establishment,* p. 266.

63. Morse, *Sketch of My Life,* pp. 62–64.

64. Worley, *J. C. Nichols,* pp. 60–66; Robert Pearson and Brad Pearson, *The J. C. Nichols Chronicle* (Kansas City, Mo.: Country Club Plaza Press, 1994), pp. 34, 51–52; Coleman, *Kansas City Establishment,* p. 37.

65. Worley, *J. C. Nichols,* pp. 67–88; Pearson and Pearson, *J. C. Nichols Chronicle,* pp. 41–51.

66. Pearson and Pearson, *J. C. Nichols Chronicle,* p. 52; Worley, *J. C. Nichols,* pp. 80, 103–104.

67. Worley, *J. C. Nichols,* pp. 70–123; Pearson and Pearson, *J. C. Nichols Chronicle,* pp. 43–87. In order to fit Nichols's short north-south blocks into the preexisting nomenclature for Kansas City streets, each numbered roadway had to assume two forms. Fifty-seventh Terrace, for example, was sandwiched between Fifty-seventh and Fifty-eighth streets. This system still marks Nichols's imprint on the modern landscape. Regarding the golf courses, the Kansas City Country Club relocated just west of Mission Hills in 1926 to what had been the Community Golf Club. Nichols then constructed the Indian Hills Country Club just to the south for former Community members.

68. Pearson and Pearson, *J. C. Nichols Chronicle,* pp. 28–60; Worley, *J. C. Nichols,* pp. 90, 124–155. Nichols's work attracted a national audience by the early 1920s. See Henry J. Haskell, "What Kind of Pittsburgh Is Kansas City?" *World's Work* 41 (1921): 289–298; A. B. McDonald, "A Home District Beautiful," *Ladies' Home Journal* 38 (February 1921): 12–13, 80, 82; James H. McCullough, "He Makes Homes Grow in Waste Places," *American Magazine* 95 (March 1923): 50–51, 157–159; J. C. Nichols, "Suburban Subdivisions with Community Features," *American City* 31 (1924): 335–338.

69. Worley, *J. C. Nichols,* pp. 72–73, 232–240; J. C. Nichols Company, *Map of the Country Club District* (Kansas City, Mo.: J. C. Nichols, 1917); Pearson and Pearson, *J. C. Nichols Chronicle,* pp. 65–66.

70. Pearson and Pearson, *J. C. Nichols Chronicle,* pp. 91–106; Worley, *J. C. Nichols,* pp. 241–259; Kenneth T. Jackson, *Crabgrass Frontier: The Suburbanization of the United States* (New York: Oxford University Press, 1985), p. 258; Coleman, *Kansas City Establishment,* p. 266.

71. Sherry L. Schirmer, *A City Divided: The Racial Landscape of Kansas City, 1900–1960* (Columbia: University of Missouri Press, 2002), pp. 39–49.

72. Charles E. Coulter, *"Take Up the Black Man's Burden": Kansas City's African American Communities, 1865–1939* (Columbia: University of Missouri Press, 2006), pp. 66–67.

73. Schirmer, *City Divided,* pp. 14, 39, 50–54.

74. Ibid., p. 55; Kevin F. Gotham, *Race, Real Estate, and Uneven Development: The Kansas City Experience, 1900–1920* (Albany: State University of New York Press, 2002), p. 33.

75. Coulter, *"Take Up the Black Man's Burden,"* p. 182; Schirmer, *City Divided,* p. 41.

76. Coulter, *"Take Up the Black Man's Burden,"* pp. 135–140, 260–262; Schirmer, *City Divided,* pp. 122–131, 166–173.

77. Schirmer, *City Divided,* pp. 160–173. The best treatment of this music scene is Frank Driggs and Charles Haddix, *Kansas City Jazz: From Ragtime to Bebop—A History* (New York: Oxford University Press, 2005).

78. Schirmer, *City Divided,* pp. 122–124, 166.

79. Gotham, *Race, Real Estate,* p. 17; Schirmer, *City Divided,* p. 100.

80. Gotham, *Race, Real Estate,* pp. 1–26.

81. Ibid., pp. 27–69.

82. Schirmer, *City Divided,* pp. 99–107.

83. Ibid., pp. 112–114; Lee et al., *Legacy of Design,* pp. 17, 93; Coulter, *"Take Up the Black Man's Burden,"* pp. 99–107.

84. U.S. Bureau of the Census, *Fifteenth Census of the United States: 1930; Population,* vol. 3, pt. 1, *Reports by States* (Washington, D.C.: Government Printing Office, 1932), p. 1388; U.S. Bureau of the Census, *Fourteenth Census of the United States Taken in the Year 1920,* vol. 3, *Population 1920: Composition and Characteristics of the Population by States* (Washington, D.C.: Government Printing Office, 1923), pp. 360, 567.

85. Frank J. Adler, *Roots in a Moving Stream: Centennial History of Congregation B'nai Jedudah of Kansas City, 1870–1970* (Kansas City, Mo.: B'nai Jedudah, 1972), pp. 86, 129.

86. Schirmer, *City Divided*, pp. 44–45; *Kansas City Star*, February 21, 1893, p. 1. The other slums noted in parallel articles on February 20, 22, and 23 were the "Patch" in the West Bottoms, the West Bluff, and "Little Italy" in the North End. McClure Flats was razed in 1911. See Henry Oyen, "The Awakening of Cities," third article, "Making Better Citizens," *World's Work* 22 (August 1911): 14725–14726.

87. Coleman, *This Far by Faith*, p. 157; *Kansas City Star*, February 20, 1893, p. 1.

88. *Kansas City Star*, February 20, 1893, p. 1; Coleman, *This Far by Faith*, pp. 157–158; John W. Briggs, *An Italian Passage: Immigrants to Three American Cities, 1890–1930* (New Haven, Conn.: Yale University Press, 1978), pp. 76–77, 101–103; Lee et al., *Legacy of Design*, pp. 15–16; "Mamma Mia, That's a Lawn Bowling Court," *Kansas City Star*, August 21, 2008, p. B2. Columbus Square, a block west of Holy Rosary Church, was bounded originally by Missouri Avenue and Pacific, Holmes, and Charlotte streets.

89. U.S. Bureau of the Census, *Twelfth Census of the United States, Taken in the Year 1900: Population, Part 1* (Washington, D.C.: Government Printing Office, 1901), p. 798; U.S. Bureau of the Census, *Thirteenth Census of the United States Taken in the Year 1910*, vol. 1, *General Report and Analysis* (Washington, D.C.: Government Printing Office, 1914), pp. 855, 861; Judith F. Laird, "Argentine, Kansas: The Evolution of a Mexican-American Community, 1905–1940" (Ph.D. diss., Department of History, University of Kansas, 1975), p. 44; Coleman, *This Far by Faith*, pp. 179–81.

90. Coleman, *This Far By Faith*, pp. 275, 277; U.S. Bureau of the Census, *Fourteenth Census*, p. 360.

91. Coleman, *This Far by Faith*, pp. 400–402.

92. *Facts Concerning Kansas City Kansas* (Kansas City: Kansas City Kansas Chamber of Commerce, circa 1935).

93. Julian Street, "Kansas City: The Beginning of the West," *Collier's* 54 (September 19, 1914): 12; John McDermott, "'Our Town': A Sketch of Kansas City, Kansas," *Haldeman-Julius Monthly* 7 (1927): 103–107, quotations on p. 104; Larry K. Hancks and Meredith Roberts, *Roots: The Historic and Architectural Heritage of Kansas City, Kansas* (Kansas City, Kans.: City of Kansas City, Kansas, 1976), p. 166.

94. McDermott, "Our Town," p. 104.

95. U.S. Bureau of the Census, *Fifteenth Census*, p. 889.

96. Susan D. Greenbaum, "The Historical, Institutional and Ecological Parameters of Social Cohesiveness in Four Urban Neighborhoods" (Ph.D. diss., Department of Anthropology, University of Kansas, 1981), pp. 120–123, 142.

97. Junius J. N. Gray, ed., *Who's Who in Kansas City, 1921: Authoritative Rating of People of Color Engaged in the Various Professions, Business Enterprises and Industries of Kansas City* (Kansas City, Kans.: Gray Printing, 1921), pp. 35–39, 46–49.

98. Joseph T. Manzo, "Strawberry Hill: An Urban Ethnic Neighborhood" (master's thesis, Department of Geography, University of Kansas, 1975), pp. 11–26; Susan D. Greenbaum, *Strawberry Hill: A Neighborhood Study* (Kansas City, Kans.: City of Kansas City, Kansas, 1978), pp. 1–12.

99. Laird, "Argentine," pp. 70–172.

Chapter 5 The City in the Gray Flannel Suit, 1940–1967

1. Three good studies exist for the Pendergast period: William M. Reddig, *Tom's Town: Kansas City and the Pendergast Legend* (Philadelphia: J. B. Lippincott, 1947); Lyle W. Dorsett, *The Pendergast Machine* (New York: Oxford University Press, 1968); and Lawrence H. Larsen and Nancy J. Hulston, *Pendergast!* (Columbia: University of Missouri Press, 1997).

2. A. Theodore Brown and Lyle W. Dorsett, *K.C.: A History of Kansas City, Missouri* (Boulder, Colo.: Pruett Publishing, 1978), pp. 217–232; Bill Gilbert, *This City, This Man: The Cookingham Era in Kansas City* (Washington, D.C.: International City Management Association, 1978); "Reform in Kansas City," *New York Times*, November 28, 1940, p. 22; William L. McCorkle, "Annexation: The Way Kansas City Has Continued to Grow," *Kansas City Times*, August 13, 1970, p. A5.

3. "The State of Missouri," *Fortune* 32 (July 1945): 112–119, 212–218; "Kansas City: Factories Can't Conceal a Cowtown," *Business Week* (February 21, 1953): 110–124; L. P. Cookingham, "The Kansas City Story," *American City* 73 (September 1958): 170–174; "Ten Lessons Kansas City Can Teach the Nation," *Coronet* 39 (November 1955): 79–84.

4. "Why Everything's Up to Date in Kansas City," *Business Week* (April 18, 1967): 102–106, quotation on p. 105; Homer Bigart, "U.S. Helps Poor to Rent Own Homes," *New York Times*, July 9, 1972, pp. 1, 32; Sloan Wilson, *The Man in the Gray Flannel Suit* (New York: Simon & Schuster, 1955). A 1956 movie with this same title, starring Gregory Peck, was even more popular than the book.

5. H. Craig Miner, *Kansas: The History of the Sunflower State, 1854–2000* (Lawrence: University Press of Kansas, 2002), pp. 303–307; Robert Pearson and Brad Pearson, *The J. C. Nichols Chronicle* (Kansas City, Mo.: Country Club Plaza Press, 1994), pp. 151–157; Margaret Whittemore, "The Combines Are Humming in Kansas," *Christian Science Monitor Weekly Magazine* (July 26, 1941): 8–9, quotation on p. 9.

6. Rick Montgomery and Shirl Kasper, *Kansas City: An American Story* (Kansas City, Mo.: Kansas City Star Books, 1999), p. 242; Pearson and Pearson, *J. C. Nichols Chronicle*, p. 156; Henry C. Haskell, Jr., and Richard B. Fowler, *City of the Future: A Narrative History of Kansas City, 1850–1950* (Kansas City, Mo.: Frank Glenn, 1950), pp. 167–169; James R. Shortridge, *Kaw Valley Landscapes: A Traveler's Guide to Northeastern Kansas*, 2nd ed. (Lawrence: University Press of Kansas, 1988), pp. 195–196; Miner, *Kansas: The History*, p. 311; "Goal in the Clouds," *Business Week* (April 22, 1944): 34–36; Rhonda Cornelius, ed., *The Best of Remember When: 100 Warm Tastes of Life as We Lived It* (Kansas City, Mo.: Kansas City Star Books, 2001), p. 131.

7. *Official Guide and Map of Greater Kansas City* (Kansas City, Mo.: Gallup Map and Stationery, 1944), p. 15; "Kansas City: Factories," pp. 110–124.

8. W. G. Clugston, "Kansas City: Gateway to What?" in *Our Fair City*, ed. Robert S. Allen (New York: Vanguard Press, 1947), p. 261; "State of Missouri," p. 117.

9. "Cattle City Branches Out," *Business Week* (November 1, 1947): 36–41; Sherry L. Schirmer and Richard D. McKinzie, *At*

the River's Bend: An Illustrated History of Kansas City, Independence, and Jackson County (Woodland Hills, Calif.: Windsor Publications, 1982), p. 231.

10. "Cattle City," p. 40; "N.Y. Interests Get Industrial Center Near Kansas City," *New York Times,* June 8, 1947, p. R1; "Gas Problem Solved, Kansas City Gets Ford," *Business Week* (December 16, 1950), p. 26; William S. Worley, *Kansas City: Rise of a Regional Metropolis* (Carlsbad, Calif.: Heritage Media, 2002), p. 162.

11. Haskell and Fowler, *City of the Future,* pp. 174–175; Charles N. Kimball, *Midwest Research Institute: Some Recollections of the First 30 Years, 1945–1975* (Kansas City, Mo.: Midwest Research Institute, 1985).

12. "Everything's Up to Date in Kansas City," *Business Week* (February 4, 1950): 66–70; "Kansas City Store Reopens as Macy's," *New York Times,* October 16, 1949, p. F1. The centennial celebration included a special exposition to honor the city's "billion dollar manufacturing industry." See William M. Blair, "Kansas City's 100th Birthday," *New York Times,* May 14, 1950, p. 131, and *Kansas City Centennial Souvenir Program* (Kansas City, Mo.: Kansas City Centennial Association, 1950).

13. U.S. Geological Survey, Water Resources Division, *Kansas-Missouri Floods of July 1951,* Water-Supply Paper 1139 (Washington, D.C.: Government Printing Office, 1952); U.S. Department of Commerce, Weather Bureau, *Kansas-Missouri Floods of June–July 1951,* Technical Paper 17 (Washington, D.C.: Government Printing Office, 1952); "Flood Emergency Declared as Disaster Hits Kansas City," *New York Times,* July 14, 1951, p. 1; "Kansas City Area Fights Flood, Fire; River Is Receding," *New York Times,* July 16, 1951, p. 1. The north-bank levees of the Missouri River held, saving North Kansas City and Municipal Airport.

14. U.S. Geological Survey, *Kansas-Missouri Floods,* p. 42; Montgomery and Kasper, *Kansas City,* p. 264; Brian Burnes, *High and Rising: The 1951 Kansas City Flood* (Kansas City, Mo.: Kansas City Star Books, 2001).

15. "Kansas City Plans Offer for Yankee Park There," *New York Times,* August 9, 1953, p. S3; "Kansas City Votes Big Bond Program," *New York Times,* August 5, 1954, p. 32; "Kansas City Is Certain Athletics Will Attract 1,000,000 Yearly," *New York Times,* November 7, 1954, p. S1; "Kansas City Welcomes Its Team in Major League Fashion," *New York Times,* April 12, 1955, p. 34; quotation in Montgomery and Kasper, *Kansas City,* p. 258.

16. James N. Primm, *Lion of the Valley: St. Louis, Missouri* (Boulder, Colo.: Pruett Publishing, 1981), pp. 316–325; Brown and Dorsett, *K.C.: A History,* p. 244; Gilbert, *This City, This Man,* pp. 125–126.

17. Gilbert, *This City, This Man,* pp. 125–128.

18. Brown and Dorsett, *K.C.: A History,* pp. 245–246.

19. Ibid., pp. 246–250; Gilbert, *This City, This Man,* pp. 127–137.

20. Gilbert, *This City, This Man,* pp. 127–137; Brown and Dorsett, *K.C.: A History,* pp. 246–250; "New Bridges Spur Kansas City Gains," *New York Times,* June 5, 1955, p. 118.

21. Roberta L. Bonnewitz and Lois T. Allen, *Raytown Remembers: The Story of a Santa Fe Trail Town* (Raytown, Mo.: Raytown Historical Society, 1975), pp. 108–109; "Gladstone History," available at http://www.gladstoneonline.com/history.html (accessed February 15, 2004). Gladstone as a creation to resist incorporation into the larger Kansas City produced an interesting chain reaction. Five neighborhoods in the area abhorred affiliation with either Kansas City or Gladstone and so formed their own set of local governments. Lined up on or near North Oak Trafficway, they were Oaks, Oakwood, Oakwood Manor, Oakwood Park, and Oakview. Oakwood Manor merged with Gladstone in 1987, but the others persist, tolerating a lack of storm drains and curbs in exchange for low property taxes. Many people think change is needed, but so far, these small remnants of 1950s politics remain part of the Clay County landscape.

22. McCorkle, "Annexation," p. A5. The 484-acre Blue Summit neighborhood between Kansas City and Independence has never been annexed by either city (map 48). Bounded by Truman Road and Twenty-third Street, Blue Ridge Boulevard and Interstate 435, this area was already a slum by 1950. Both cities shun it because of potential financial burdens. See Gromer Jeffers, Jr., "Blue Summit: A Rural Slum," *Kansas City Star,* February 28, 1993, p. A15; Joe Robertson, "Leadership Void Threatens Blue Summit Community," *Kansas City Star,* April 4, 2005, pp. B1, B3.

23. McCorkle, "Annexation," p. A5.

24. Gilbert, *This City, This Man,* p. 155.

25. Murrel Bland, *The 50s in Wyandotte County* (Kansas City, Kans.: Kansas Colloquies, 2005), p. 7; Shortridge, *Kaw Valley Landscapes,* p. 19.

26. Bland, *50s in Wyandotte County,* pp. 7–9.

27. Chamber of Commerce of Kansas City, *Where These Rocky Bluffs Meet: Including the Story of the Kansas City Ten-Year Plan* (Kansas City, Mo.: Kansas City Chamber of Commerce, 1938), pp. 88, 94–95; George R. Bauer, *A Century of Kansas City Aviation History* (Olathe, Kans.: Historic Preservation Press, 1999), pp. 34–36; Julius A. Karash and Rick Montgomery, *TWA: Kansas City's Hometown Airline* (Kansas City, Mo.: Kansas City Star Books, 2001).

28. Bauer, *Century of Kansas City Aviation,* p. 131.

29. Earle K. Radford, "Downtown Air Terminal—Fantastic?" *American City* 58 (August 1943): 49–50; "Kansas City Airports Look to the Future," *American City* 58 (November 1943): 13; George Scullin, "But Spirit Was Undampened," *Nation's Business* 39 (November 1951): 32.

30. Grandview Historical Society, *History of Grandview, Missouri: 1844–1994* (Grandview, Mo.: Grandview Historical Society, 1995), p. 44; "Air Field near Truman Family Farm Wins O.K.," *Chicago Tribune,* October 11, 1951, p. W8; Brown and Dorsett, *K.C.: A History,* p. 261.

31. "Air Field near Truman," p. W8.

32. Grandview Historical Society, *History of Grandview,* p. 44; Bauer, *Century of Kansas City Aviation,* p. 128.

33. Carol A. Mickett, *History Speaks: Visions and Voices of Kansas City's Past* (Kansas City, Mo.: Midwest Research Institute, 2002), p. 9; Bill Graham, "Booster of KC Region Is Dead," *Kansas City Star,* August 15, 2007, pp. B1, B4.

34. "Million for Air Aid Goes to Kansas City," *New York Times,* February 19, 1956, p. S10; Bauer, *Century of Kansas City Aviation,* pp. 41, 128–129. The Mid-Continent label ultimately refers to an oil field centered in eastern Oklahoma. Mid-Continent Airlines primarily served cities in that region before its merger with Braniff International Airlines in 1952.

35. Bauer, *Century of Kansas City Aviation,* pp. 41, 128–129; Tania Long, "Kansas City Sets Superjet Airport," *New York Times,* December 22, 1966, p. 49.

36. Chamber of Commerce, *Where These Rocky Bluffs Meet,* pp. 142–144.

37. Cookingham, "Kansas City Story," pp. 170–174; Debs Myers, "Kansas City," *Holiday* 7 (March 1950): 48.

38. Philip E. Geissal, "Kansas City Sees Expressways Preventing 1970 Traffic Jams," *American City* 67 (March 1952): 141–143; Clayton Knowles, "Politics Clouds Redevelopment in Kansas City," *New York Times,* July 5, 1959, p. 28.

39. W. G. Roeseler, "Kansas City's Downtown Story," *American City* 71 (April 1956): 123–124, quotation on p. 123.

40. Kevin F. Gotham, *Race, Real Estate, and Uneven Development: The Kansas City Experience, 1900–2000* (Albany: State University of New York Press, 2002), p. 77; "Kansas City Wars on Blighted Area," *New York Times,* August 7, 1955, p. R1.

41. Al Bohling, "Kansas City Boom Paced by Building," *New York Times,* January 3, 1956, p. F22; Knowles, "Politics Clouds Redevelopment," p. 28. Time-series photographs of "The Junction" at Ninth and Main are in Monroe Dodd's *Kansas City Then and Now* (Kansas City, Mo.: Kansas City Star Books, 2000), pp. x–xi.

42. Roeseler, "Kansas City's Downtown," pp. 123–124; Cookingham, "Kansas City Story," pp. 170–174; Knowles, "Politics Clouds Redevelopment," p. 28.

43. Knowles, "Politics Clouds Redevelopment," p. 28. See also Cookingham, "Kansas City Story," pp. 170–174.

44. Gotham, *Race, Real Estate,* pp. 80–82.

45. Ibid. The names of both black housing projects honored local African Americans. Wayne Minor was the final American soldier killed in World War I; Theron B. Watkins was a business and political leader.

46. Cookingham, "Kansas City Story," p. 173; "Kansas City Envisions a Complex," *New York Times,* March 13, 1966, p. 157; Jeremy Main, "The Kempers of Kansas City," *Fortune* 75 (April 1967): 170–172, 194, 196, 200, 202, quotation on p. 171; "Why Everything's Up to Date," p. 105; "Kansas City Sets Mark for Convention Attendance," *New York Times,* February 11, 1968, p. F17.

47. Knowles, "Politics Clouds Redevelopment," p. 28; Gilbert, *This City, This Man,* pp. 210–211.

48. "Kansas City Envisions," p. 157.

49. "Dallas Texans's Transfer to Kansas City Due Today," *New York Times,* March 29, 1963, p. 8; "Texans Give Kansas City More Time to Sell Tickets," *New York Times,* May 13, 1963, p. 54; "Hunt Is Offering $52-Million to Rule Kansas City Sports," *New York Times,* November 1, 1967, p. 60.

50. "Kansas City Envisions," p. 157; Montgomery and Kasper, *Kansas City,* pp. 315–316.

51. Montgomery and Kasper, *Kansas City,* pp. 315–316; "Kansas City Envisions," p. 157.

52. Gotham, *Race, Real Estate,* pp. 81–89.

53. Ibid., pp. 53–58.

54. Ibid., pp. 103–116.

55. Ibid., p. 101.

56. Ibid., pp. 99–103. Westport High, at 315 East Thirty-ninth Street, was integrated on paper in the late 1960s under pressure from federal authorities. This was accomplished via busing rather than new neighborhood boundaries, however, and the school remained segregated by classroom. Lincoln High at 2111 Woodland Avenue, the city's designated school for African Americans before 1955, stayed nearly all black throughout the 1960s and 1970s.

57. "District Annexations," Kansas City, Missouri, School District, available at http://www2.kcmsd.net/Pages/DistrictAnnex ations.aspx (accessed October 4, 2008).

58. "Center History," Center School District, available at http://www.center.k12.mo.us/gen/center_generated_pages/Center_His tory_m13.html (accessed November 21, 2008).

59. U.S. Bureau of the Census, *United States Census of Population: 1950,* vol. 3, *Census Tract Statistics,* chap. 27, *Kansas City, Missouri, and Adjacent Area* (Washington, D.C.: Government Printing Office, 1952), p. 9.

60. Ibid., p. 7.

61. A good account of life in the Northeast neighborhood in the 1940s and 1950s is Bruce Clayton's *Praying for Base Hits: An American Boyhood* (Columbia: University of Missouri Press, 1998). Sheffield Steel took over the Kansas City Bolt and Nut Company in 1925 and, in turn, became a division of the ARMCO Corporation in 1930. Montgomery Ward operated a warehouse and retail store at Belmont Boulevard near St. John Avenue from 1913 until 1977. See Dory DeAngelo, *Passages through Time: Stories about Kansas City, Missouri, and Its Northeast Neighborhood* (Kansas City, Mo.: Tapestry Publications, 1992), pp. 65–66, 91–93.

62. George Creel, "Independence Makes a President," *Collier's* 116 (August 18, 1945): 14–15, 26; Cabell Phillips, "Truman's Home Town Is 'Smalltown, U.S.A.,'" *New York Times Magazine* (July 1, 1945): 13, 37–38; "Summer White House," *Newsweek* 25 (June 18, 1945): 34–36.

63. "200-Million Renewal Projects on Kansas City Drawing Boards," *New York Times,* February 5, 1967, p. R1.

64. Edward Dahlberg, "Return to Kansas City," *Holiday* 41 (June 1967): 20.

65. George S. Perry, "The Cities of America: Kansas City," *Saturday Evening Post* 218 (August 25, 1945): 15. The University of Kansas City joined the state education system in 1963 and was renamed the University of Missouri–Kansas City.

66. Bonnewitz and Allen, *Raytown Remembers,* pp. 108–111.

67. Grandview Historical Society, *History of Grandview,* pp. 9, 26, 39.

68. Calvin Trillin, "U.S. Journal: Kansas City—I Got Nothing against the Colored," *New Yorker* 44 (May 11, 1968): 110. The populations quoted are for the Clay and Platte county portion of Kansas City plus Claycomo, Gladstone, North Kansas City, Parkville, and Riverside.

69. Perry, "Cities of America," p. 39; Myers, "Kansas City," p. 48; "Kansas City: Factories," p. 112.

70. Bland, *50s in Wyandotte,* pp. 7–10.

71. Ibid., pp. 12, 17; U.S. Department of Commerce, *Kansas-Missouri Floods,* p. 74; U.S. Geological Survey, *Kansas-Missouri Floods,* p. 11; Burnes, *High and Rising.*

72. Bland, *50s in Wyandotte,* pp. 7, 53.

73. Ibid., p. 8; U.S. Bureau of the Census, *United States Census of Population and Housing: 1960, Census Tracts,* Final Report PHC (1)-70, *Kansas City, Missouri-Kansas* (Washington, D.C.: Government Printing Office, 1962), pp. 14–15. Indian Springs Shopping Center, at Forty-fifth and State Avenue, opened in 1972.

74. U.S. Bureau of the Census, *United States Census of Population and Housing: 1960,* p. 98; Susan D. Greenbaum, "The Historical, Institutional and Ecological Parameters of Social Cohesiveness in Four Urban Neighborhoods" (Ph.D. diss., Department of Anthropology, University of Kansas, 1981), p. 142; Joseph H. McDowell, *Building a City: A Detailed History of Kansas City, Kansas* (Kansas City, Kans.: Kansas City Kansan, 1969), pp. 58–65.

75. Mindi C. Love, ed., *Johnson County, Kansas: A Pictorial History, 1825–2005* (Shawnee, Kans.: Johnson County Museum, 2006), p. 170.

76. Pearson and Pearson, *J. C. Nichols Chronicle,* pp. 131–133, 198; Prairie Village Book Committee and Dawn Grubb, *Prairie Village: Our Story* (Prairie Village, Kans.: City of Prairie Village, 2002). Nichols's Johnson County developments are the subject of a recent novel: Whitney Terrell's *The King of Kings County* (New York: Viking Penguin, 2005).

77. William G. Cutler, ed., *History of the State of Kansas,* vol. 1 (Chicago: A. T. Andreas, 1883), pp. 636–637; Kendall Bailes, *From Hunting Ground to Suburb: A History of Merriam, Kansas* (Merriam, Kans.: Kendall Bailes, 1956), pp. 17–20.

78. Love, *Johnson County, Kansas,* pp. 79, 93, 109–110; Norman Keech and Florent W. Wagner, eds., *Historic Overland Park: An Illustrated History* (San Antonio, Tex.: Historical Publishing Network, 2005), pp. 22–31.

79. Keech and Wagner, *Historic Overland Park,* pp. 22–31; Love, *Johnson County, Kansas,* pp. 93, 109–110.

80. Love, *Johnson County, Kansas,* pp. 80, 98–99, 125; City of Mission, Kansas, *The City of Mission, Kansas: 50 Years of Progress* (Prairie Village, Kans.: Joe Vaughn Associates, 2003), p. 6; Ann Morris, *Leawood: A Portrait in Time* (Leawood, Kans.: Leawood Historic Commission, 1997), pp. 11, 20–24.

81. Love, *Johnson County, Kansas,* pp. 157–158.

82. Ibid., pp. 143, 148, 158; Keech and Wagner, *Historic Overland Park,* pp. 63–64.

83. Love, *Johnson County, Kansas,* pp. 161–169.

84. Ibid.

Chapter 6 Geography in Black and White, 1968–1991

1. Joel Garreau, *Edge City: Life on the New Frontier* (New York: Doubleday, 1991).

2. For background and a national overview of these patterns, see Robert M. Fogelson, *Downtown: Its Rise and Fall, 1880–1950* (New Haven, Conn.: Yale University Press, 2001).

3. Calvin Trillin, "U.S. Journal: Kansas City, Missouri—Reflections of Someone Whose Home Town Has Become a Glamour City," *New Yorker* 50 (April 8, 1974): 94–101.

4. Campbell Gibson, *Population of the 100 Largest Cities and Other Urban Places in the United States: 1790 to 1990,* Working Paper Number 27 (Washington, D.C.: Population Division, U.S. Bureau of the Census, 1998); B. Drummond Ayres, Jr., "Kansas City Says Its Time Is Here," *New York Times,* March 23, 1973, p. 39; Pamela Bayless, "What's Doing in Kansas City," *New York Times,* December 24, 1978, p. XX7. See also "Why Everything's Up to Date in Kansas City," *Business Week* (April 18, 1967): 102.

5. Rick Montgomery and Shirl Kasper, *Kansas City: An American Story* (Kansas City, Mo.: Kansas City Star Books, 1999), pp. 306–308; Ayres, "Kansas City Says," p. 39; B. Drummond Ayres, Jr., "Kansas City," *New York Times,* January 6, 1974, p. 155; Harper Barnes, "Kansas City Modern," *Atlantic Monthly* 233 (February 1974): 60–67; Richard Rhodes, "Convention Fever in Kansas City," *Harper's Magazine* 252 (May 1976): 28, 30.

6. Ayres, "Kansas City Says," p. 39; Rhodes, "Convention Fever," p. 28; Calvin Trillin, "A Reporter at Large: American Royal," *New Yorker* 59 (September 26, 1983): 57–125; Richard Rhodes, "Cupcake Land: Requiem for the Midwest in the Key of Vanilla," *Harper's Magazine* 275 (November 1987): 51–57.

7. Dory DeAngelo and Jane F. Flynn, *Kansas City Style: A Social and Cultural History of Kansas City as Seen through Its Lost Architecture* (Kansas City, Mo.: Harrow Books, 1990), pp. 76–77.

8. "Where the Delegates Are Gathering: Good Food, Jazz—and Even Culture," *New York Times,* August 16, 1976, p. 48; Jeanne A. Fox, "In Kansas City Missouri," *Black Enterprise* 8 (March 1978): 45; Arthur Brisbane, *Arthur Brisbane's Kansas City* (n. p.: Rosalindajones Enterprises, 1982), pp. 26–27, 30–33; Arthur W. Lamb, *Sanderson's Lunch* (Leawood, Kans.: Leathers Publishing, 1998).

9. Jeremy Main, "The Kempers of Kansas City," *Fortune* 75 (April 1975): 196; "Why Everything's Up to Date," p. 106.

10. Main, "Kempers," p. 196; Diane Stafford, "Robert Ingram Dies at 80," *Kansas City Star,* October 22, 1997, p. A1.

11. Thomas W. Ennis, "News in the Field of Real Estate: Company to Help Cities Rebuild," *New York Times,* May 18, 1965, p. 62; "U.S. Business: Kansas City Center Advances," *New York Times,* December 26, 1965, p. F13; "$200-Million Renewal Projects on Kansas City Drawing Boards," *New York Times,* February 5, 1967, p. R1.

12. "A Midwest Hotel Enhances Luster," *New York Times,* October 9, 1966, p. R13; Montgomery and Kasper, *Kansas City,* p. 332. The Vista International Hotel is now the Kansas City Marriott.

13. Main, "Kempers," p. 196; "$200-Million Renewal Projects," pp. R1, R10.

14. "Lifting the Face of Kansas City," *Business Week,* May 20,

1972, p. 96; Mildred F. Schmertz, "Crown Center: Urban Renewal for a Kansas City Grey Area," *Architectural Record* 154 (October 1973): 113–126; Denise Otis, "A New Town Comes to Life in Downtown Kansas City," *House and Garden* 145 (March 1974): 39–40, 162.

15. "Lifting the Face," p. 96; Walter McQuade, "Two Cities, New and Old, Show the Way to Urban Amenity," *Fortune* 92 (July 1975): 92–99; Lisa Gross, "The Project That Grew and Grew," *Forbes* 126 (August 4, 1980): 63.

16. Trillin, "Reporter at Large: American Royal," p. 68; "A Gracious Town in the Heartland," *Time* 108 (August 16, 1976): 11. A severe rainstorm in 1979 collapsed the roof of Kemper Arena, but the damage was promptly repaired with no consideration given to a building relocation.

17. Carter B. Horsley, "Kansas City Office Tower Recruiting Here," *New York Times,* July 2, 1978, p. R4; Bayless, "What's Doing," p. XX7; Chris Lester, "City Center Square Gets Anchor," *Kansas City Star,* August 30, 1992, p. F13.

18. William Robbins, "Inner City Promoting a Revival," *New York Times,* March 30, 1987, p. A10; Joseph Rebello, "Town Pavilion Catalyst for Downtown Growth," *Kansas City Star,* July 26, 1991, p. A13.

19. Chris Lester, "No Renaissance at Town Pavilion," *Kansas City Star,* July 28, 1991, p. E9. AT&T sold its share of the building in 1987 and reduced its presence there. Another tenant—Transamerica—then placed its sign atop the tower.

20. Montgomery and Kasper, *Kansas City,* pp. 332–333; "One Kansas City Place," *Kansas City Star,* January 31, 1988, p. J19; Chris Lester, "Developer, Banker Dies," *Kansas City Star,* October 25, 1993, p. A1. Before his downtown projects, Morgan financed many of the community's biggest suburban shopping malls, including Indian Springs, Metcalf South, Metro North, and Oak Park.

21. Montgomery and Kasper, *Kansas City,* pp. 316–318; Patricia C. Miller, *Westport: Missouri's Port of Many Returns* (Kansas City, Mo.: Lowell Press, 1983), pp. 100–106.

22. Marion A. Trozzolo, *Tales of River Quay: A New Old Towne,* ed. Judy Goodman (Kansas City, Mo.: Bimbi Publications, 1974); Paul Delaney, "Violence Destroys a Boom in Kansas City's Old Section," *New York Times,* April 19, 1977, p. 16.

23. Delaney, "Violence," p. 16; John Bayliss, "Kansas City, Ain't She Pretty!" *Holiday* 55 (January 1974): 83.

24. William Robbins, "Kansas City 'Doorstep' Facing a Major Cleanup," *New York Times,* December 16, 1986, p. A20; Scott Cantrell, "Renaissance at River Market: Renovations Reverse Decades of Sad Neglect," *Kansas City Star,* September 1, 1991, p. F1; Kevin Collison, "River Market Builder Steps Up Pace," *Kansas City Star,* July 12, 2005, p. D4.

25. James R. Shortridge, *Kaw Valley Landscapes: A Traveler's Guide to Northeastern Kansas,* 2nd ed. (Lawrence: University Press of Kansas, 1988), p. 9.

26. Ibid., pp. 9–11; Joseph H. McDowell, *Building a City: A Detailed History of Kansas City, Kansas* (Kansas City, Kans.: Kansas City Kansan, 1969), pp. 61–62.

27. McDowell, *Building a City,* p. 62; Shortridge, *Kaw Valley Landscapes,* pp. 9–10; Mark Wiebe, "Downtown's Lessons Are Profound," *Kansas City Star,* June 28, 2006, p. 2 of photo section.

28. Shortridge, *Kaw Valley Landscapes,* p. 10; Rich Hood, "New EPA Building Will Bolster KCK," *Kansas City Star,* November 26, 1998, p. 2 of Wyandotte County Zone section. The EPA's stay in downtown Kansas City proved only temporary. In April 2011, federal officials announced a move to the Renner Road corridor in suburban Lenexa. The new building features state-of-the-art environmental design. See Kevin Collison, "Decision on EPA Office Seems Flawed," *Kansas City Star,* April 12, 2011, p. C4.

29. "Kansas City Opens 90 Schools to All," *New York Times,* September 8, 1955, p. 16; Benjamin Fine, "Kansas City Makes Big Strides in Integration Despite Tensions," *New York Times,* May 20, 1957, p. 1.

30. Kevin F. Gotham, *Race, Real Estate, and Uneven Development: The Kansas City Experience, 1900–2000* (Albany: State University of New York Press, 2002), pp. 100–103; "Everything's Up to Date in Kansas City," *Time* 78 (June 28, 1961): 38; Martin Mayer, "The Good Slum Schools," *Harper's Magazine* 222 (April 1961): 46–48.

31. Paul Ciotti, *Money and School Performance: Lessons from the Kansas City Desegregation Experiment,* Cato Policy Analysis No. 298 (Washington, D.C.: Cato Institute, 1998), pp. 3–4.

32. "A Moderate Busing Plan Is Adopted in Kansas City," *New York Times,* December 7, 1976, p. 32; Paul Delaney, "Teacher Strike in Kansas City Tests New Chief," *New York Times,* April 12, 1977, p. 11.

33. Paul Delaney, "Integration Suit by Kansas City Board Could Open Way to Interstate Schools," *New York Times,* May 28, 1977, p. 8.

34. "Suburban Districts Dropped in Kansas City School Case," *New York Times,* April 3, 1984, p. A26; William Robbins, "Kansas City Holds Hope for Schools," *New York Times,* March 23, 1986, p. 34.

35. "Federal Judge Bars Kansas City's Plan for Desegregation," *New York Times,* January 29, 1985, p. A19; Ciotti, *Money and School Performance,* pp. 7–12.

36. Ciotti, *Money and School Performance,* pp. 7–8, 19; William Robbins, "Kansas City Tries to Revive School, But the Cost Is Criticized," *New York Times,* October 10, 1989, p. A25.

37. Ciotti, *Money and School Performance,* pp. 7–8, 17–18; Dirk Johnson, "'F' for Kansas City Schools Adds to District's Woes," *New York Times,* May 30, 2000, p. A16.

38. Ciotti, *Money and School Performance,* pp. 15–29.

39. Accounts of four of these schools can be found in Michael Coleman, *This Far by Faith: A Popular History of the Catholic People of West and Northwest Missouri,* vol. 2, *The Facts* (Marceline, Mo.: Walsworth Publishing, 1992), pp. 523–525, 562–563, 582–586; Mary P. Eckels and Roselee K. Ennis, *Listen to the Echoes Ring: A History of the Sunset Hill School* (Kansas City, Mo.: Pembroke Hill School Alumni Association, 1985); and Carl R. Schulkin, *In Pursuit of Greatness: A History of the Pembroke-Country Day School* (Kansas City, Mo.: Pembroke Hill School Alumni Association, 1985).

40. Good overviews of this area's recent history are Jeffrey Spivak, "Movers, Shakers Dwelt There before Time Took its Toll," *Kansas City Star,* May 18, 1998, p. A1; Dan Margolies and Randolph

Heaster, "Shutdown Is End of an Era," *Kansas City Star,* February 8, 2001, p. A1.

41. Montgomery and Kasper, *Kansas City,* pp. 289–291; Joseph J. Kerski, "The Impact of the Bruce R. Watkins Roadway Project on Neighborhoods in Kansas City, Missouri" (master's thesis, Department of Geography, University of Kansas, 1993).

42. Gibson, *Population of the 100 Largest Cities;* Gotham, *Race, Real Estate,* p. 17; Information and Research Department, *Kansas City, Kansas Factbook* (Kansas City, Kans.: City of Kansas City, Kansas, 1995), p. 4.

43. Rowe Findley, "Kansas City: Heartland U.S.A.," *National Geographic* 150 (July 1976): 114; Barnes, "Kansas City Modern," p. 61; Robert W. Butler, "Kansas City," *Travel/Holiday* 174 (June 1991): 32; Information and Research Department, *Kansas City, Kansas Factbook,* p. 6.

44. Susan D. Greenbaum, "The Historical, Institutional and Ecological Parameters of Social Cohesiveness in Four Urban Neighborhoods" (Ph.D. diss., Department of Anthropology, University of Kansas, 1981), pp. 195–199.

45. Montgomery and Kasper, *Kansas City,* p. 269.

46. Lynn Horsley and Jeffrey Spivak, "Rating Our Neighborhoods: KCI Cluster Is the Best in the Outer Northland Section," *Kansas City Star,* December 8, 2006, p. A16.

47. Gilbert C. Fite, *Beyond the Fence Rows: A History of Farmland Industries, Inc.: 1929–1978* (Columbia: University of Missouri Press, 1978). This company declared bankruptcy in 2002 and liquidated in 2003. See David Barboza, "Facing Huge Debt, Large Farm Co-op Is Closing Down," *New York Times,* September 16, 2003, pp. C1–C2.

48. Jeffrey Spivak, "All Squared Away," *Kansas City Star,* November 15, 2005, pp. A1, A6.

49. Chris Lester, "Developer's View Begins to Take Shape: Briarcliff West May Help Northland and Downtown," *Kansas City Star,* January 8, 1991, p. D1; Kady McMaster, "Briarcliff Parkway Opens to Praise," *Kansas City Star,* March 21, 1991, p. A1; Nathaniel Hagedorn, "Kansas City Is Reaping the Benefits of Briarcliff," *Kansas City Star,* March 9, 2007, p. B8.

50. Brian Burnes, "Deal Viewed as a 'New Beginning'—Business Park Set for Old Refinery Site," *Kansas City Star,* August 19, 2002, p. B1; Karen Dillon, "2 Person Law Firm Wrestles Oil Giant," *Kansas City Star,* November 26, 2005, pp. A1, A7.

51. Sherry Schirmer and Richard D. McKinzie, *At the River's Bend: An Illustrated History of Kansas City, Independence, and Jackson County* (Woodland Hills, Calif.: Windsor Publications, 1982), p. 268; Eyobong Ita, "Grandview Turns Big Loss into Industry Incubator," *Kansas City Star,* September 7, 2004, pp. B1, B6; Mary Sanchez, "Lessons for All 'First Ring Suburbs,'" *Kansas City Star,* December 18, 2008, pp. B1, B4.

52. Mike Rice, "Raytown Target of Hayseed Humor," *Kansas City Star,* March 25, 1997, p. B1.

53. Ibid.; Eyobong Ita, "Newest Official Looks to the Future," *Kansas City Star,* December 7, 2007, pp. B1, B2.

54. Donald Bradley, "Criticisms Turn Up in Hickman Mills Survey," *Kansas City Star,* June 5, 1997, p. B1; Joe Robertson, "Ruskin

Battles Suburban Decline," *Kansas City Star,* July 20, 2003, p. B1; Mike Sherry, "District Grapples with Internal Troubles," *Kansas City Star,* April 24, 2006, pp. B1, B2; Karen Uhlenhuth, "Resident Envisions a Renewal," *Kansas City Star,* October 23, 2006, p. B12.

55. Schirmer and McKinzie, *At the River's Bend,* pp. 262–263.

56. Brian Burnes, "Independence Reaches an Important Juncture," *Kansas City Star,* August 13, 2007, pp. A1, A10.

57. Brian Burnes, "Plan Would Expand Truman District," *Kansas City Star,* August 29, 2005, p. B6; Randolph Heaster, "Plant's Closing to Cost 500 Jobs," *Kansas City Star,* May 4, 2000, p. A1.

58. Schirmer and McKinzie, *At the River's Bend,* pp. 267–268. The annexation of 1959 placed Lee's Summit adjacent to an unusual suburban community called Unity Village. Unity is a Christian school devoted to the healing power of prayer. Its roots are local and date back to 1889. After prospering through donations, its leaders purchased 1,400 acres along U.S. Highway 50 and constructed a beautiful Mediterranean-styled campus in the 1920s. Neighbors have long admired its grounds replete with fountains, rose garden, and restaurant. They also appreciate the boost its 500 employees give to the local economy. To ensure independence from the expanding city, Unity's residents incorporated as a separate city in 1953. See *Unity: 100 Years of Faith and Vision* (Unity Village, Mo.: Unity Books, 1988), and Brian Burnes, "Village Marks 50 Years since Incorporation," *Kansas City Star,* April 14, 2003, p. B1.

59. Schirmer and McKinzie, *At the River's Bend,* pp. 267–268; Russ Pulley, "Economic Consultant Shares Findings of Lee's Summit Survey," *Kansas City Star,* October 30, 1999, p. B1; Julius A. Karash, "John Knox Village Expansion Planned," *Kansas City Star,* October 11, 2006, pp. C1, C8; Russ Pulley, "Project to Ease Traffic Flow," *Kansas City Star,* July 16, 2006, pp. B1, B5.

60. Schirmer and McKinzie, *At the River's Bend,* pp. 263–265; Eyobong Ita, "Fifteen Years On, Parkway Hasn't Reached Destination," *Kansas City Star,* July 10, 2005, p. B2.

61. Turner Lake, "Is There No End to this Boom?" *Kansas Business News* 5 (August 1984): 28–32; Mindi C. Love, ed., *Johnson County, Kansas: A Pictorial History, 1825–2005* (Shawnee, Kans.: Johnson County Museum, 2006), p. 194.

62. *Community Profile for Lenexa in Johnson County* (Topeka: Kansas Department of Commerce and Housing, 2002); Dan Bearth, "Business Moves to the Suburbs," *Kansas Business News* 2 (June 1981): 34–39.

63. Norman Keech and Florent W. Wagner, eds, *Historic Overland Park: An Illustrated History* (San Antonio, Tex.: Historical Publishing Network, 2005), pp. 69–70.

64. Ibid., pp. 68, 114; Bearth, "Business Moves," pp. 34–39; Love, *Johnson County, Kansas,* pp. 184–185.

65. Love, *Johnson County, Kansas,* p. 181.

66. Keech and Wagner, *Historic Overland Park,* pp. 74–77; Associated Press, "Sprint Headquarters to Display Company's Wealth," *Lawrence Journal-World,* December 8, 1997, p. D3; Shirley Christian, "Sprint Is Building Huge Headquarters in Kansas," *New York Times,* July 12, 1998, p. RE5.

67. The term *executive country* was first employed in a 1975

brochure from the Overland Park Chamber of Commerce according to Tim McKee, a former official with that chamber; Brent J. Piepergerdes, interview with author, August 1998. McKee also supplied the other information in this paragraph.

68. Ann Morris, *Leawood: A Portrait in Time* (Leawood, Kans.: Leawood Historic Commission, 1997), pp. 79–80.

69. Love, *Johnson County, Kansas,* p. 190; Ita, "Fifteen Years On," p. B2.

70. George R. Bauer, *Trails, Rails, and Tales: Olathe's First 150 Years* (Kansas City, Mo.: Kansas City Star Books, 2006), pp. 42, 46–47, 58–59.

Chapter 7 Toward a More Complete City, 1992–2011

1. Michael Pacione, *Urban Geography: A Global Perspective* (London: Routledge, 2001), p. 304.

2. The arguments in this section draw heavily on Nathan W. Brinson, "Political, Economic, and Cultural Revival in Kansas City, Kansas" (master's thesis, Department of Geography, University of Kansas, 2006). See also Mark Bocchetti, "Commitment to Change in County Urged," *Kansas City Star,* January 17, 1991, p. B2; Phillip O'Connor, "Service Will Merge in Wyandotte County," *Kansas City Star,* December 7, 1991, p. C3; Robert P. Sigman, "KCK Moves Ahead," *Kansas City Star,* December 28, 1991, p. C6; and Steve Nicely, "Bad News for a Reform Movement," *Kansas City Star,* August 6, 1992, p. A1.

3. Steve Nicely, "Two Try to Throw Wyandotte County a Lifeline," *Kansas City Star,* October 11, 1994, p. A1.

4. Steve Nicely, "Task Force to Tackle Consolidation," *Kansas City Star,* December 31, 1994, p. C5; Nicely, "Forum Explores Merging," *Kansas City Star,* February 21, 1995, p. B1; Nicely, "Wyandotte Merger with KCK Proposed," *Kansas City Star,* May 18, 1995, p. C2; Nicely, "KCK-County Merger Passes," *Kansas City Star,* April 2, 1997, p. A1; Nicely, "Reformers Win Big," *Kansas City Star,* September 10, 1997, p. A1.

5. Joe Gose, "Fast Cars, Big Crowds: Promoters Hope to Bring a Big-League Stock Car Track to Area," *Kansas City Star,* December 13, 1996, p. A1.

6. Jim Sullinger, "Gardner Seeks Help from Lawmakers in Landing Racetrack," *Kansas City Star,* January 16, 1977, p. C2; Sullinger and Regina Akers, "Gardner Decides It Can Do without NASCAR Track," *Kansas City Star,* February 19, 1997, p. A1.

7. Sullinger and Akers, "Gardner Decides"; Joe Gose, "Missouri Still Seeks Racetrack," *Kansas City Star,* May 22, 1997, p. B1; Gose, "Missouri's Bid In, Kansas Group to Make NASCAR Pitch," *Kansas City Star,* July 31, 1997, p. D1.

8. Cindy Eberting, "Racetrack News Is Greeted with Relief, Disappointment," *Kansas City Star,* August 14, 1997, p. C4; Steve Nicely, "Questions about Track Aired," *Kansas City Star,* October 16, 1997, p. C8.

9. Randy Covitz, "A Great Day for Race Fans," *Kansas City Star,* July 9, 2001, p. A1; Brinson, "Political, Economic, and Cultural Revival," p. 56; Covitz, "Track Is a Green Light for County," *Kansas City Star,* October 9, 2004, pp. A1, A8.

10. Mark P. Couch and Mark Wiebe, "On Track for a Bright Retail Future," *Kansas City Star,* February 9, 2001, p. C1; Rick Alm, "KCK Seeks a Texas-Size Economic Benefit from Car Track," *Kansas City Star,* July 13, 1999, p. D1; Joyce Smith, "Breaking Ground for the Future," *Kansas City Star,* October 13, 2004, p. C3.

11. Covitz, "Track Is a Green Light"; Loey Lockerby, "KCK Ready for Its Theater Legend," *Kansas City Star,* October 15, 2004, p. E8; Jennifer A. Claybrook, "Evolution of an Urban Fringe Landscape: The Case of Piper, Kansas" (master's thesis, Department of Geography, University of Kansas, 2002).

12. Mark Wiebe, "KCK Sets Sights on Waterpark," *Kansas City Star,* September 15, 2005, pp. A1, A8; Wiebe, "A Lot More Lodging for WyCo," *Kansas City Star,* October 17, 2006, pp. A1, A6; Wiebe and Rick Alm, "Wyandotte Countians Back Casino and Slots," *Kansas City Star,* June 27, 2007, pp. A1, A14; Alm and Wiebe, "Dreamers Line Up for KCK Casino," *Kansas City Star,* September 25, 2007, pp. A1, A6; Steve Rosen, "Opening Planned for Feb. 3," *Kansas City Star,* January 3, 2012, p. C3.

13. Kevin Collison and Lynn Horsley, "Wyandotte Moves ahead on Stadium as KC Fumes," *Kansas City Star,* September 10, 2009, pp. A1, A17; Mike Hendricks, "For Cerner, an Offer They Can't Refuse," *Kansas City Star,* September 11, 2009, p. A4; Kevin Collison, "Cerner Unveils Plans for Two KCK Office Towers," *Kansas City Star,* August 25, 2011, pp. A1, A16. The moves of the soccer team and Cerner are related, since the cofounders of Cerner, Clifford Illig and Neal Patterson, are also part owners of Sporting Kansas City.

14. Mark Wiebe, "KCK Loft Developers Aim for Allies," *Kansas City Star,* June 17, 2005, pp. B1, B6; Wiebe, "KCK Condo Sales Slow to Take Off," *Kansas City Star,* February 1, 2006, p. B4; Wiebe, "Planning a New Flavor for Strawberry Hill," *Kansas City Star,* November 25, 2006, pp. B1, B5; Wiebe, "Downtown KCK Project Unveiled," *Kansas City Star,* June 26, 2008, pp. C1, C5.

15. Mark Wiebe, "'Epitome of Blight' in KCK Could See Revival," *Kansas City Star,* October 12, 2005, p. B4; Mike Hendricks, "Modest KCK Development Kindles Some Big Hopes," *Kansas City Star,* March 31, 2008, pp. B1, B2; Wiebe, "New Vision for KCK Mall," *Kansas City Star,* November 15, 2006, pp. A1, A14; Wiebe, "Mall Site Talks to Continue," *Kansas City Star,* March 20, 2009, p. B2; Mike Hendricks, "One KCK Site Still Stagnates," *Kansas City Star,* September 6, 2011, pp. A1, A3; Kevin Collison, "DHL Set to Open Facility in KCK," *Kansas City Star,* September 9, 2005, pp. C1, C5; Wiebe, "Sara Lee Plant Latest Uptick for KCK," *Kansas City Star,* May 29, 2009, p. A16. DHL closed its local operation in 2009. The building is now operated by the Sealy Mattress and Faultless Starch companies.

16. Scott Cantrell, "Boom and Bust Kansas City Enjoys Construction Surge," *Kansas City Star,* November 8, 1998, p. J1; Jeffrey Spivak and Kevin Collison, "City's Ailing Center in Search of Revival," *Kansas City Star,* September 22, 2002, p. A15.

17. Jeffrey Spivak, *Union Station: Kansas City* (Kansas City, Mo.: Kansas City Star Books, 1999), pp. 163–186.

18. Ibid., p. 188.

19. Ibid., pp. 174, 182–183, 196–204, 213–214.

20. Ibid., pp. 208, 248. Financial stability came via the relocation here of offices for the Greater Kansas City Chamber of Commerce, the Kansas City Area Development Council, and the regional branch of the National Archives plus the Todd Bolender Ballet Center in Union Station's former power plant. See Kevin Collison, "Union Station Tactics Pay Off," *Kansas City Star,* October 4, 2011, p. C3.

21. Judy Thomas, "Crossroads: 'This Is the Very Heart of our City,'" *Kansas City Star,* November 2, 1995, p. A8; Diane Stafford, "Crossroads Area Asks for More Street Lights," *Kansas City Star,* November 21, 1991, p. B1.

22. Alice Thorson, "Leedys Pioneered District that Continues to Grow," *Kansas City Star,* August 2, 1998, p. J3.

23. Mindie Paget, "First Fridays Create Crossroads Carnival," *Lawrence Journal-World,* August 29, 2004, pp. D1, D6; Joyce Smith, "Area Gains a Foothold as Downtown Seeks New Life," *Kansas City Star,* June 24, 2007, pp. A1, A6; Steve Paul, "Kemper Museum Ready to Expand into Downtown," *Kansas City Star,* December 8, 2007, pp. A1, A8; Kevin Collison, "A Plan to Protect Crossroads Artists," *Kansas City Star,* August 8, 2006, p. D14.

24. Andrew C. Miller and Tom Jackman, "Courthouse Isn't Part of 1994 Budget," *Kansas City Star,* April 2, 1993, p. C1; John T. Dauner, "Courthouse Will Not Be Torn Down," *Kansas City Star,* April 11, 1991, p. A14; Chris Lester, "Designers Chosen, Location Sought for Federal Courthouse," *Kansas City Star,* April 14, 1992, p. D3; Lester, "Downtown to Be Reshaped," *Kansas City Star,* April 19, 1992, p. D13; John T. Dauner, "Project Is Key, Says Cleaver," *Kansas City Star,* July 10, 1992, p. C8.

25. Dauner, "Project is Key"; Yael T. Abouhalkah, "Tantalizing Civic Mall Idea," *Kansas City Star,* March 10, 1994, p. C5; Lester, "Downtown to Be Reshaped."

26. John T. Dauner, "Business to Finance Civic Mall," *Kansas City Star,* January 9, 1993, p. C1; Tom Jackman, "Design Plan Revealed for Courthouse," *Kansas City Star,* August 31, 1993, p. B1; James C. Fitzpatrick, "Cleaver Plans Citywide Uses for Tax Money," *Kansas City Star,* September 1, 1994, p. C1, Mark Morris, "Plan for Civic Mall a Campaign Issue," *Kansas City Star,* February 22, 1995, p. C2; Yael T. Abouhalkah, "Civic Mall Creeps Ahead," *Kansas City Star,* June 27, 1995, p. B6.

27. Lynn Horsley, "Downtown Park Nears Fruition," *Kansas City Star,* March 3, 2000, p. B3. Ilus Winfield Davis was Kansas City's mayor from 1963 until 1971.

28. Kevin Klinkenberg, "Remake Bartle from the Street Up," *Kansas City Star,* June 5, 2005, p. B7.

29. Chris Lester, "Hotel Builder Sought for KC," *Kansas City Star,* January 25, 1992, p. B7.

30. Jennifer Greer, "Food World Mall Tourist Plan Studied," *Kansas City Star,* February 2, 1991, p. B1; Chris Lester, "Plans for Hotel Unveiled," *Kansas City Star,* April 11, 1992, p. B1; Lester, "Perot's Plan Puts Hotel outside Loop," *Kansas City Star,* May 10, 1992, p. K21; James C. Fitzpatrick and Lester, "Politics, Power and a KC Hotel," *Kansas City Star,* May 24, 1992, p. A1.

31. Chris Lester, "Fourth Hotel Plan Enters Picture," *Kansas City Star,* May 22, 1992, p. E9; Lester, "Perot Gets Nod for Hotel," *Kan-sas City Star,* July 22, 1992, p. A1; Lester, "KC Plan Commission Endorses Hotel Plans," *Kansas City Star,* September 16, 1992, p. B1; Yael T. Abouhalkah, "The Perot Hotel Deal Will Not Die Quietly," *Kansas City Star,* July 2, 1994, p. C7; Charles R. T. Crumpley, "Perot Hotel Plan Still On, but On Hold," *Kansas City Star,* March 9, 1995, p. B1; Julius A. Karash, "Perot Hotel Plans Killed," *Kansas City Star,* July 13, 1995, p. A1.

32. Jennifer Mann Fuller, "Multiplex Pioneer Due for Big Hollywood Salute," *Kansas City Star,* March 5, 1996, p. A1; Joe Gose, "Can the Proposed AMC Entertainment Center Revitalize Downtown?" *Kansas City Star,* January 12, 1997, p. A1.

33. Gose, "Can the Proposed."

34. Ibid.; Hearne Christopher, Jr., "One Possible Downtown 'Reality' Is a Power & Light Hotel," *Kansas City Star,* September 16, 1995, p. E2; Joe Gose, "A Vision of Downtown's South Edge," *Kansas City Star,* October 14, 1995, p. A1; Rich Hood, "Visionaries Help City to Grow and Thrive," *Kansas City Star,* December 17, 1997, p. L1; Arthur S. Brisbane, Laura M. Shultz, and Suzanne Robinson, *Celebrating Greater Kansas City* (Memphis: Towery Publishing, 1998), p. 378.

35. Chris Lester, "The Risk of Revival," *Kansas City Star,* January 18, 1998, p. A1; Hearne Christopher, Jr., "His Illness Hasn't Put a Stop to His Ideas," *Kansas City Star,* June 4, 1999, p. F5; Lester, "Durwood's Legacy Is Unfinished," *Kansas City Star,* July 20, 1999, p. D16.

36. Gregory S. Reeves, "Downtown Becomes Home of the Tax Breaks," *Kansas City Star,* May 29, 2005, pp. A1, A8; Chris Lester, "Agencies' Move Helping 'Rebuild City,'" *Kansas City Star,* June 14, 1992, p. F13.

37. Larry R. Ford, *America's New Downtowns: Revitalization or Reinvention?* (Baltimore, Md.: Johns Hopkins University Press, 2003); Curtis Johnson and Neal Pierce, "An Urban Pulse to Lure Fresh Talent," *Kansas City Star,* January 13, 2002, pp. B5–B6; Jeffrey Spivak and Kevin Collison, "Downtown Revival Hinges on Housing," *Kansas City Star,* September 29, 2002, pp. A1, A16.

38. Spivak and Collison, "Downtown Revival," pp. A1, A6.

39. Ibid.; "Downtown KC Comes Alive" (special section), *Kansas City Star,* June 26, 2005, p. 12.

40. "Downtown KC Comes Alive"; Joyce Smith and Kevin Collison, "Cosentino's Set to Be Downtown's Grocer," *Kansas City Star,* September 8, 2005, pp. A1, A6; Eric Adler, "A Can-Do Mood in Condo Market," *Kansas City Star,* September 18, 2005, pp. A1, A20.

41. Sherry L. Schirmer and Richard D. McKinzie, *At the River's Bend: An Illustrated History of Kansas City, Independence, and Jackson County* (Woodland Hills, Calif.: Windsor Publications, 1982), pp. 312–313; Mark Davis, "Southern Comfort, Technology with a Twist," *Kansas City Star,* September 19, 2000, p. E19.

42. Chris Lester, "Agencies' Move Helping 'Rebuild City.'"

43. Chris Lester, "DST Plan Would Fund Urban Projects," *Kansas City Star,* November 15, 1992, p. F15; E. Thomas McClanahan, "A Welcome Addition Downtown," *Kansas City Star,* February 3, 1997, p. B4.

44. Chris Lester, "Working West Side Wonders," *Kansas City*

Star, January 15, 1994, p. B1; Charles R. T. Crumpley, "Quiet Muscle Flexed Downtown," *Kansas City Star,* February 25, 1995, p. A1; Yael T. Abouhalkah, "We Need More Take-Charge Civic Leaders," *Kansas City Star,* May 10, 1998, p. L3; Kevin Collison, "Downtown Revival Authority Selected," *Kansas City Star,* January 18, 2002, p. C1; Kevin Collison and Jeffrey Spivak, "Land Grab Could Lead to Clash of Visions," *Kansas City Star,* July 28, 2003, p. A1; Mark Downs, "DST To Lay Off 700 Workers," *Kansas City Star,* February 2, 2010, pp. D3, D16.

45. The series, "Downtown KC: Mending Our Broken Heart," by Jeffrey Spivak, Kevin Collison, and Steve Paul, ran on the front page of the *Kansas City Star* for six consecutive Sundays beginning September 22, 2002. It compared progress in the city with that in sixteen similar communities: Buffalo, Charlotte, Cincinnati, Cleveland, Columbus, Denver, Indianapolis, Louisville, Memphis, Milwaukee, Minneapolis, Nashville, Oklahoma City, Pittsburgh, St. Louis, and Salt Lake City.

46. Kevin Collison, "Rewards Rising for Barnes as She Sees Downtown Grow," *Kansas City Star,* February, 1, 2005, p. D18; Curtis Johnson and Neal Pierce, "Designing a Better Downtown for Kansas City," *Kansas City Star,* January 13, 2002, p. B6.

47. Jeffrey Spivak and Kevin Collison, "Downtown Needs Diversions to Thrive," *Kansas City Star,* October 6, 2002, pp. A1, A24–A25.

48. Ibid.

49. Kevin Collison, "Downtown Group Is Needed Again," *Kansas City Star,* November 16, 2004, pp. D16, D21; Yael T. Abouhalkah, "A New Anchor for Downtown?" *Kansas City Star,* September 3, 2000, p. B8; Eric Adler, "Vision Turns a Bank into a Grand Library," *Kansas City Star,* January 4, 2004, p. A1.

50. Jeffrey Spivak and Lynn Horsley, "Downtown Arena Proposal Envisions Opening in 2007," *Kansas City Star,* May 13, 2004, pp. A1, A8.

51. "H&R Block Chooses Downtown for Offices," *Lawrence Journal-World,* December 19, 2003, p. D1; Spivak and Horsley, "Downtown Arena."

52. Spivak and Horsley, "Downtown Arena"; Collison, "Rewards Rising."

53. Spivak and Horsley, "Downtown Arena"; Kevin Collison, "Downtown Vision: A Sight to Behold, by Day and by Night," *Kansas City Star,* November 28, 2004, pp. A1, A19; Collison, "AMC to Revive Empire," *Kansas City Star,* July 15, 2005, pp. A1, A6; Collison, "Empire to Transform from Eyesore to Eye-Catcher," *Kansas City Star,* July 15, 2006, pp. A1, A6.

54. E. Thomas McClanahan, "Power & Light an Urban-Design Standout," *Kansas City Star,* May 18, 2008, p. B9.

55. Jeffrey Spivak, "Downtown KC's Long Road Back," *Kansas City Star,* May 18, 2008, pp. A1, A12–A13; Spivak, "Rivals Upping the Ante," *Kansas City Star,* May 19, 2008, pp. A1, A4; Kevin Collison and Spivak, "Critical Work Ahead for KC," *Kansas City Star,* May 20, 2008, pp. A1, A6; Kevin Murphy and Finn Bullers, "Arts Tax Is in Eyes of Beholders," *Kansas City Star,* October 10, 2004, pp. A1, A8; Spivak, "Arts Center Mulls a Shift to Lyric Site," *Kansas City Star,* April 16, 2005, pp. A1, A6; Collison and Paul Horsley, "Plans Revive Arts Center's Original Site," *Kansas City Star,* September 18, 2005, pp. A1, A22; Collison and Horsley, "PAC to Become Reality," *Kansas City Star,* April 14, 2006, pp. A1, A6; Steve Paul, "An Artistic Gem, Inside and Out," *Kansas City Star,* September 15, 2011, pp. A1, A12; A. G. Sulzberger, "In Kansas City, an Arts Center Makes a Debut," *New York Times,* September 16, 2011, p. A11.

56. Lynn Horsley and Matt Campbell, "Trickle-Down Economics," *Kansas City Star,* March 16, 2009, pp. A1, A5; Horsley and Sara Shepherd, "An Unfulfilled Kemper," *Kansas City Star,* August 15, 2009, pp. A1, A12; Aleese Kopf, "What to Do about Kemper?" *Kansas City Star,* July 19, 2011, pp. A1, A6.

57. Kevin Collison, "Report Sees Need for Hotel," *Kansas City Star,* January 26, 2007, pp. C1, C6; Rick Alm, "Little Hotels, Big Problem," *Kansas City Star,* July 17, 2007, pp. D1, D18–D19.

58. Kevin Collison, "Next Step: 1,000 Rooms," *Kansas City Star,* April 3, 2008, pp. A1, A4; Yael T. Abouhalkah, "Think Twice before Subsidizing a Huge Hotel," *Kansas City Star,* July 10, 2008, p. B9; Collison, "Hotel Push Gains Backing," *Kansas City Star,* May 22, 2009, pp. A1, A19; Collison, "KC Has Lost Its Top Three Conventions," *Kansas City Star,* October 1, 2009, pp. A1, A18.

59. Kevin Collison, "Developers Eye Site East of City Hall," *Kansas City Star,* August 17, 2005, pp. A1, A6; Collison, "Dunn, Swope Unite for Plan," *Kansas City Star,* January 7, 2006, pp. C1, C6.

60. Kevin Collison, "Dispute with City Puts East Village in Doubt," *Kansas City Star,* February 14, 2006, pp. D4, D7; Collison, "Progress Slow on Building East Village," *Kansas City Star,* March 4, 2008, p. D14; Collison, "East Village Project Loses One Developer," *Kansas City Star,* August 1, 2008, pp. C1, C5; Collison, "East Village Project Faces New Setbacks," *Kansas City Star,* March 19, 2009, pp. C1, C2; Collison, "Gleaming New Project Opens Downtown," *Kansas City Star,* September 15, 2009, pp. D12–D13; "Swope Community Builders Moves into East Village's Second Phase," *Kansas City Business Journal,* February 11, 2011, p. 1.

61. Michael Mansur and Lynn Horsley, "Prospect Corridor: Analysis of Block Points Up Depth of Area's Neglect," *Kansas City Star,* September 12, 2004, pp. A1, A8; Malcolm Garcia, "Prospect Corridor: Many Hold Hope for Turnaround in Community," *Kansas City Star,* September 12, 2004, pp. A1, A9; Mansur and Matt Campbell, "It's a Place They Call Home," *Kansas City Star,* September 25, 2004, pp. A1, A6; Horsley, "Desperate Homes," *Kansas City Star,* February 12, 2006, pp. A1, A10.

62. Michael Mansur, "A 'Staggering' Problem," *Kansas City Star,* October 6, 2009, pp. A1, A9; Mansur, "More Houses Sit Empty," *Kansas City Star,* April 20, 2011, pp. A1, A8.

63. Mansur and Horsley, "Prospect Corridor."

64. Barry Garron, "Hitter-Fielder Will Find Real Fame in 'Baseball,'" *Kansas City Star,* March 23, 1993, p. E1; Joe Posnanski, "A KC Legend Dies," *Kansas City Star,* October 7, 2006, p. A1; Steve Penn, "How Blessed Our Community Was to Know Buck," *Kansas City Star,* October 8, 2006, p. A4.

65. Cathy Gripka, "Ollie Gates: Barbecue King Is a Community Builder," *Kansas City Star,* June 19, 2005, p. A9. For general background, see Doug Worgul, *The Grand Barbecue: A Celebration of the*

History, Places, Personalities, and Techniques of Kansas City Barbecue (Kansas City, Mo.: Kansas City Star Books, 2001).

66. Joe Robertson, "KC School District's Enrollment Declines," *Kansas City Star,* October 25, 2005, pp. B1, B6.

67. Joe Robertson, "Plans to Annex Schools Move Ahead," *Kansas City Star,* February 5, 2006, pp. B1–B2; Mike Sherry, "KC's Amato Takes Aim at Motives," *Kansas City Star,* September 7, 2007, pp. B1, B5; Joe Robertson, "KC School District Feeling Besieged," *Kansas City Star,* November 8, 2007, pp. B1, B5.

68. Joe Robertson, "Half of Schools Could Close," *Kansas City Star,* February 14, 2010, pp. A1, A20; Robertson, "They've All Fought This Battle Before," *Kansas City Star,* February 20, 2010, pp. A1, A11.

69. Deann Smith, "District Officials Ponder Changes at Paseo Academy," *Kansas City Star,* October 26, 2004, p. B3; Steve Penn, "Education Priceless to Helzbergs," *Kansas City Star,* October 4, 2005, p. B1; Penn, "Christo Rey Benefits Students, Businesses," *Kansas City Star,* December 18, 2008, pp. B1, B4; Meredith Rodriguez, "Halls of Progress, Promise," *Kansas City Star,* January 5, 2009, pp. A1, A4; Candace Buckner, "Missouri Moves Teams," *Kansas City Star,* January 31, 2010, p. C11.

70. Yael Abouhalkah, "Two Years Old," *Kansas City Star,* November 26, 1991, p. B6.

71. Jennifer Greer, "Jazz Hall of Fame Could Energize Community, Some Say," *Kansas City Star,* June 9, 1991, p. E8.

72. Kevin Q. Murphy, "Timetable Presented for Jazz Hall, Black Museums," *Kansas City Star,* September 3, 1992, p. B1; Steve Penn, "Second Phase of 18th Street Plan to Start," *Kansas City Star,* October 26, 1999, p. B2; Glenn E. Rice, "Figures Show Dip in Attendance at the 18th and Vine District," *Kansas City Star,* September 16, 2000, p. B1; Penn, "Crime at 18th and Vine Is Only a Tall Tale," *Kansas City Star,* February 23, 2000, p. B2; Penn, "Rebirth Has Been Slow but Steady," *Kansas City Star,* September 13, 2007, pp. B1, B12; Joyce Smith, "Peachtree to Leave KC's Jazz District," *Kansas City Star,* December 14, 2007, pp. A1, A16. The Peachtree now has closed altogether. See Smith, "Peachtree Seeks Chapter 11," *Kansas City Star,* June 29, 2010, p. C3.

73. Christine Riccelli, "Brush Creek Face-Lift Plan Is a Boost to City's Amenities," *Kansas City Star,* March 12, 1991, p. D22.

74. J. D. Moore, Jr., "Health Center Will Rebuild Community," *Kansas City Star,* April 16, 1993, p. A1; E. Frank Ellis, "Health Center Boosts Neighborhoods," *Kansas City Star,* June 24, 1999, p. B2; Joyce Smith, "With New Center, Suburbs Come to City," *Kansas City Star,* August 23, 2005, pp. A1, A6.

75. Chris Lester, "Progress as Promised," *Kansas City Star,* April 16, 1998, p. A12; Mark P. Couch, "A Plan for Area East of Troost," *Kansas City Star,* December 9, 1999, p. A1; Kevin Collison, "Gates Retail Plan Rolling Again," *Kansas City Star,* September 8, 2011, p. A9.

76. Joe Gose, "Glover Plan Unfolds in Midtown," *Kansas City Star,* March 28, 1996, p. B1; Julius A. Karash, "Racing the Clock," *Kansas City Star,* November 17, 1998, p. D1; Lynn Horsley and Mark P. Couch, "KC Council Approves Bonds for Glover Plan," *Kansas*

City Star, March 24, 2000, p. C1; Joyce Smith, "Marketplace Location Now Beckons Shoppers," *Kansas City Star,* January 12, 2001, p. A1.

77. Yael T. Abouhalkah, "Inspiration for Neighbors," *Kansas City Star,* May 16, 1997, p. C8; Jeffrey Spivak, "Beacon Hill Plan Breaks Tradition in Funding, Scope," *Kansas City Star,* February 8, 1999, p. A1.

78. Lynn Horsley, "Urban Rebirth a Slow Process," *Kansas City Star,* May 27, 2003, p. A1; Michael Mansur, "Was It Worth the Cost?" *Kansas City Star,* October 13, 2004, pp. A1, A6; Horsley, "Back to Being a Beacon," *Kansas City Star,* July 31, 2006, pp. A1, A4; Horsley and Kevin Collison, "$11 Million Later, Vision Unfulfilled," *Kansas City Star,* July 23, 2008, pp. A1, A4.

79. Ron Knox, "Neighbors Tackle Drug Houses Together," *Kansas City Star,* May 15, 2005, p. B3; Jeffrey Spivak and Adjoa Adofo, "Rehabbers Raise This Urban Area," *Kansas City Star,* December 5, 2006, pp. A1, A6; Matt Campbell, "Once-Hot Corner Now a Cool Park," *Kansas City Star,* September 11, 2005, pp. B1, B4; Steve Penn, "12th Street Poised for Big Things," *Kansas City Star,* March 2, 2006, p. B1; Matt Campbell, "Oldest Fountain Is Now a Fountain Again," *Kansas City Star,* June 3, 2009, p. A5.

80. Joyce Smith, "Longtime Grocery Is Calling It Quits," *Kansas City Star,* February 24, 2007, pp. C1, C6; Karen Dillon and Lynn Horsley, "Asbestos Concern Delays Project," *Kansas City Star,* June 14, 2006, pp. A1, A4; Horsley, "Kansas City Is at Crossroads on Citadel Plaza," *Kansas City Star,* October 13, 2007, pp. A1, A6; Kevin Collison, "City Weighs Advancing Millions to Citadel Plaza," *Kansas City Star,* December 18, 2008, pp. C1, C5; Michael Mansur, "Developer of Citadel Plaza Sues City," *Kansas City Star,* February 6, 2010, p. A11.

81. Quoted in Henry A. Way, "The Chimera of Kansas: An Exploration of Place, Politics, and Culture" (Ph.D. diss., Department of Geography, University of Kansas, 2008), p. 344.

82. Ibid., pp. 340–344, 350–353.

83. Kevin F. Gotham, *Race, Real Estate, and Uneven Development: The Kansas City Experience, 1900–2000* (Albany: State University of New York Press, 2002), p. 101. The Sunset Hill and Pembroke Country Day schools merged in 1984 to create the present-day Pembroke Hill School.

84. John A. Dvorak, "Casino Companies Spinning Dreams," *Kansas City Star,* December 28, 1993, p. A1.

85. Rick Alm, "Public Gains, Personal Losses," *Kansas City Star,* June 20, 2004, p. A1; Mike Rice, "Northgate Has 'Changed the Face' of North Kansas City," *Kansas City Star,* December 19, 2004, p. B1, B3; Laura Quinn, "Unique Benefits Draw Businesses and Residents to North Kansas City," *Kansas City Star,* March 21, 2007 (special advertising section), pp. 6, 14; Mike Sherry, "Riverside Hopes Levee Brings Boost," *Kansas City Star,* April 4, 2005, p. B2.

86. Joyce Smith, "Total Remake Proposal for Antioch Center," *Kansas City Star,* September 11, 2004, pp. C1–C2; Mike Rice, "Property Tax Hike Would Go toward Upgrades," *Kansas City Star,* January 30, 2005, pp. B1–B2; Tanya Fogg Young, "Plan Seeks to Improve North Oak," *Kansas City Star,* September 19, 2005, pp. B1–B2; Lynn

Horsley, "Council to Vote Today on $51 Million Project," *Kansas City Star,* July 20, 2006, p. B5.

87. Matt Campbell and Mike Rice, "Push for Parkways Picks Up Speed in the Northland," *Kansas City Star,* January 9, 2005, pp. B1, B3.

88. Bill Graham, "Parkville to Hear National Golf Club's Plan," *Kansas City Star,* October 3, 1997, p. C4; Graham, "At National Golf Club, Watson Builds Excitement," *Kansas City Star,* March 22, 2000 (Progress 2000 section), p. 14; "The National Golf Club of Kansas City," *Kansas City Star,* June 8, 2008, p. I1.

89. Kevin Collison, "'Country Club Plaza of Northland' Proposed," *Kansas City Star,* October 17, 2001, p. A1; Mike Rice, "In the Zona," *Kansas City Star,* May 23, 2004, p. B1.

90. Mike Rice, "North Star: Ceremony Marks the Official Kick Off for 93-Acre Zona-Rosa Development," *Kansas City Star,* May 16, 2002, p. C1; Rice and Joyce Smith, "Zona Rosa Set to Debut as 'A City unto Itself,'" *Kansas City Star,* May 16, 2004, p. A1.

91. Collison, "'Country Club Plaza'"; David Greusel, "New Urbanist Island in the Sprawl," *Kansas City Star,* July 24, 2005, p. G3.

92. Joyce Smith, "Worth Waiting For," *Kansas City Star,* August 12, 2006, pp. C1, C6; Smith, "Two Malls Scheduled for Facelifts," *Kansas City Star,* October 13, 2006, pp. A1, A6; Glenn E. Rice, "Metro North Plan Suffers Setback," *Kansas City Star,* September 23, 2010, p. A15. The recent recession forced change on the Tuileries Plaza in 2011. Now called the Village at Burlington, its stores currently focus more on the local neighborhood and less on destination shopping. See Kevin Collison, "Briarcliff Realty Purchases Tuileries Plaza," *Kansas City Star,* December 29, 2011, p. A10.

93. Campbell and Rice, "Push for Parkways."

94. Mike Rice, "Development Planned near Zona Rosa," *Kansas City Star,* November 27, 2006, p. B4; Kevin Collison, "Increasing the Buzz at KCI," *Kansas City Star,* March 11, 2006, pp. C1, C2; Rice, "Firm Is Hired to Develop near KCI," *Kansas City Star,* August 5, 2006, pp. C1, C6; Collison, "KC Is Called 'Predatory,'" *Kansas City Star,* September 27, 2011, pp. D1, D8–D9.

95. Craig S. Campbell, *Images of the New Jerusalem: Latter Day Saint Faction Interpretations of Independence, Missouri* (Knoxville: University of Tennessee Press, 2004), pp. 184–189; Mike Rice, "Shoal Creek Offers Newest 'Old' Homes," *Kansas City Star,* October 10, 2004, p. B2; Jason Noble, "Liberty Betting Big on Small-Town Ideal," *Kansas City Star,* February 1, 2007, pp. C1, C6.

96. Brian Burnes, "Independence Puts Big Tax Incentives to Work on Developments," *Kansas City Star,* November 2, 2004, p. B2; Burnes, "Independence Reaches an Important Juncture," *Kansas City Star,* August 13, 2007, pp. A1, A10.

97. Kevin Collison, "Finding Right Lure to Reel in Tenants," *Kansas City Star,* October 24, 2007, pp. C1, C7; Collison, "Come Fall, the Puck Stops Here," *Kansas City Star,* June 2, 2009, pp. C1, C10–C11; Brian Burnes, "Independence's Big Event," *Kansas City Star,* November 2, 2009, pp. A1, A10.

98. Eyobong Ita, "15 Years on, Parkway Hasn't Reached Destination," *Kansas City Star,* July 10, 2005, p. B2; "Adams Dairy Development Files Bankruptcy," *Kansas City Business Journal,* October 1, 2009, p. 1. Similar corporate hopes existed in Independence but

were dashed before people made big investments. See Brian Burnes, "Report Suggests New Plan for Independence Tract," *Kansas City Star,* October 9, 2005, p. B2.

99. Eyobong Ita, "A Suburb from Scratch," *Kansas City Star,* August 13, 2006, pp. B1, B12.

100. Brian Burnes, "Church Plans Huge Housing Development," *Kansas City Star,* May 29, 2007, pp. B1, B9; Jeff Fox, "Developer Bringing New Business to Empty Building," *Independence Examiner,* May 14, 2011, p. 1.

101. Mary Sanchez, "Lessons for All 'First Ring Suburbs,'" *Kansas City Star,* December 18, 2008, p. B1.

102. "Signs of Progress at Lee's Summit Community," *Kansas City Star,* September 12, 2004, pp. K1, K8.

103. Kevin Collison, "Macy's to Grow in Area," *Kansas City Star,* November 20, 2007, pp. D5, D36; Collison, "Theme Park Makes a Play for Missouri," *Kansas City Star,* January 19, 2007, pp. A1, A12; Jim Davis, "Legoland Plans Could Tumble after State's Modesta Denial," *Kansas City Business Journal,* November 16, 2007, p. 1. The Legoland and Sea Life projects were revived at Crown Center in Kansas City's midtown area. Groundbreaking for both $15 million projects occurred in late 2011, with openings planned for May 2012. See Joyce Smith, "A New Crown Center Evolving," *Kansas City Star,* September 28, 2011, p. A11.

104. Rick Alm, "June Close Eyed for Richards-Gebaur Sale," *Kansas City Star,* May 30, 2007, p. C3; Randolph Heaster, "Rail-Truck Center to Open Soon," *Kansas City Star,* January 19, 2008, p. C1; Kevin Collison, "Weapons Plant Location Picked," *Kansas City Star,* April 18, 2007, pp. A1, A4; Collison, "KC Council Gets $673 Million Plan to Replace Honeywell Plant," *Kansas City Star,* January 8, 2010, p. A10; Collison, "Farmland Readied for Nuclear Crop," *Kansas City Star,* September 5, 2010, pp. A1, A8–A9.

105. Brad Cooper and Finn Bullers, "Proposed Parkway Offers a New Commute," *Kansas City Star,* May 17, 2007, pp. A1, A4; Cooper, "Proposed Parkway That Would Have Linked Johnson, Cass Counties Dies," *Kansas City Star,* June 6, 2008, p. B5.

106. Diane Stafford, "Trend Drives Jobs toward JoCo," *Kansas City Star,* October 1, 2009, pp. A1, A12.

107. A similar expansion process can be seen west from Interstate 435 in Lenexa and Shawnee. This one, however, is limited largely to residences because of the proximity of Oak Park Mall on Ninety-fifth Street and the new Village West stores in Wyandotte County.

108. Finn Buller, "County Approves Partial Annexation," *Kansas City Star,* February 22, 2008, pp. B1–B2.

109. Brad Cooper, "Capital One Plants Overland Park Center," *Kansas City Star,* September 22, 2005, pp. B1–B2; Kevin Collison, "Olathe Basks in a Development Glow," *Kansas City Star,* November 27, 2007, pp. D10, D15.

110. Henry C. Jackson, "Beckoning Urbanites to Suburbia," *Kansas City Star,* November 3, 2005, pp. B1, B3.

111. Ibid.; Kevin Collison, "City Living in the Country," *Kansas City Star,* February 5, 2005, pp. C1, C6; Joyce Smith, "Rolling Out in Leawood," *Kansas City Star,* May 21, 2005, pp. C1, C6.

112. Cooper, "Capital One"; Kevin Collison, "JPMorgan Site

Frustrates KC Leaders," *Kansas City Star,* December 16, 2009, pp. A1, A18; Collison, "U.S. Bank's Good News: 1,100 Jobs for Area," *Kansas City Star,* December 17, 2009, pp. A1, A18; Collison, "Mighty Magnet for Tenants," *Kansas City Star,* October 5, 2010, pp. E1, E8–E9.

113. Finn Bullers, "Soccer Complex Is Step Closer to Its Goal," *Kansas City Star,* August 26, 2006, pp. A1, A4; Joyce Smith and Kevin Collison, "Overland Park Snags Von Maur," *Kansas City Star,* February 3, 2006, pp. C1, C5; Smith, "Corbin Park Project Has Tenants Lining Up," *Kansas City Star,* March 8, 2007, pp. C1, C6; Smith, "Corbin Park Work Slowing to a Crawl," *Kansas City Star,* September 19, 2009, p. A11; Collison, "Corbin Park Is Renamed Aspen Square to Give Project a 'Fresh Start,'" *Kansas City Star,* December 10, 2011, p. A15.

114. Kevin Collison, "Developer Plans a 60-Acre Complex," *Kansas City Star,* September 20, 2006, pp. C1–C2; Brad Cooper, "Museum Project Moves Forward," *Kansas City Star,* August 18, 2009, pp. A1, A8.

115. Brad Cooper, "Olathe's Big Catch," *Kansas City Star,* June 11, 2005, pp. C1–C2; Mike Ekey, "Learning Mixes with Shopping," *Kansas City Star,* May 19, 2007, pp. C1, C4; "Olathe Gateway's Bond Issue Defaults, Even with Bass Pro," *Kansas City Business Journal,* September 16, 2011, p. 1.

116. Joyce Smith, "Local Investors Acquire Great Mall in Olathe," *Kansas City Star,* January 6, 2009, pp. A1, A4.

117. Katie Weeks, "City OKs Garmin Expansion," *Kansas City Star,* May 7, 2003 (*Olathe Star* section), p. 1; Kevin Collison, "Olathe Basks in a Development Glow," *Kansas City Star,* November 27, 2007, pp. D10, D15.

118. Brandon Babcock, "Olathe Grants Record Tax Break," *Kansas City Star,* September 21, 2005, pp. C1, C8; Kevin Collison, "Office Park to Get First Office Building," *Kansas City Star,* September 9, 2005, pp. C1, C5; Brad Cooper and Jason Gertzen, "K-State Plans Olathe Site," *Kansas City Star,* July 14, 2006, pp. A1, A6; Collison,

"Olathe Basks"; Joe Lambe, "Innovation Goes on Display," *Kansas City Star,* April 23, 2011, pp. A4, A6.

119. Kevin Collison, "Pacific Sunwear Coming to Olathe," *Kansas City Star,* June 2, 2006, pp. C1, C5; Collison, "Distribution Center Will Employ 200," *Kansas City Star,* December 16, 2008, pp. D3, D5; Collison, "Gardner on Short List for Intermodal Hub," *Kansas City Star,* May 12, 2005, pp. C1, C8; Collison, "Gardner at Critical Juncture," *Kansas City Star,* April 27, 2006, pp. C1, C5; Brad Cooper, "Freight Plan Puzzles Gardner: Development or Disruption?" *Kansas City Star,* May 22, 2006, pp. A1, A8.

Chapter 8 Conclusion

1. Kevin Collison, "More People, Lower Ranking," *Kansas City Star,* March 25, 2010, pp. A1, A3.

2. Calvin Trillin, "A Reporter at Large: American Royal," *New Yorker* 59 (September 26, 1983): 57–125; Richard Rhodes, "Cupcake Land: Requiem for the Midwest in the Key of Vanilla," *Harper's Magazine* 275 (November 1987): 51–57; Evan S. Connell, Jr., *Mrs. Bridge* (New York: Viking Press, 1959).

3. Calvin Trillin, "Letter from Kansas City: The Bull Vanishes," *New Yorker* 77 (June 11, 2001): 36–41.

4. Jeanne A. Fox, "In Kansas City Missouri," *Black Enterprise* 8 (March 1978): 43–46, 54; Ronald Harris, "Kansas City: It Calls Itself One of the Few Livable Cities Left," *Ebony* 36 (November 1980): 80–90.

5. William P. Bracke, *Wheat Country* (New York: Duell, Sloan & Pearce, 1950), p. 273.

6. Michael Mansur and Lynn Horsley, "Possible Demise of Earnings Tax Alarming for KC," *Kansas City Star,* January 17, 2010, pp. A1, A14; Jeffrey Spivak, "The Security Zone," *Kansas City Star,* November 19, 2005, pp. A1, A10.

7. James R. Shortridge, "Regional Image and Sense of Place in Kansas," *Kansas History* 28 (2005): 202–219.

Bibliography

Adams, John Q. "The North Kansas City Urban District." *Economic Geography* 8 (1932): 409–425.

Adler, Frank J. *Roots in a Moving Stream: Centennial History of Congregation B'nai Jedudah of Kansas City, 1870–1970.* Kansas City, Mo.: B'nai Jedudah, 1972.

Adler, Jeffrey. *Yankee Merchants and the Making of the Urban West: The Rise and Fall of Antebellum St. Louis.* Cambridge: Cambridge University Press, 1991.

Allaway, Henry. "Kansas City's Race with St. Louis for Supremacy." *New York Times,* February 15, 1903, p. 32.

"Art in a Mid-West Center." *Outlook* 148 (1928): 369.

Bailes, Kendall. *From Hunting Ground to Suburb: A History of Merriam, Kansas.* Merriam, Kans.: Kendall Bailes, 1956.

Barnes, Elizabeth E. *Historic Johnson County: A Bird's Eye View of the Development of the Area.* Shawnee Mission, Kans.: Neff Printing, 1969.

Barnes, Harper. "Kansas City Modern." *Atlantic Monthly* 233 (February 1974): 60–67.

———. *Blue Monday.* St. Louis, Mo.: Patrice Press, 1991.

Barnes, Lela, ed. "An Editor Looks at Early-Day Kansas: Letters of Charles Monroe Chase." *Kansas Historical Quarterly* 26 (1960): 113–151, 267–301.

Barry, Louise, ed. *The Beginning of the West: Annals of the Kansas Gateway to the American West, 1540–1854.* Topeka: Kansas State Historical Society, 1972.

Bauer, George R. *A Century of Kansas City Aviation History.* Olathe, Kans.: Historic Preservation Press, 1999.

———. *Trails, Rails, and Tales: Olathe's First 150 Years.* Kansas City, Mo.: Kansas City Star Books, 2006.

Bayliss, John. "Kansas City, Ain't She Pretty!" *Holiday* 55 (January 1974): 38–39, 82–83.

Bearth, Dan. "Business Moves to the Suburbs." *Kansas Business News* 2 (June 1981): 34–39.

———. "Kansas City, Kansas, Ushers in New Political and Business Climate." *Kansas Business News* 5 (January 1984): 42–45.

Bernard, William R. "Westport and the Santa Fe Trade." *Kansas Historical Collections, 1905–1906* 9 (1906): 552–565.

Betton, Frank H. "The Genesis of the State's Metropolis." *Kansas Historical Collections, 1901–1902* 7 (1902): 114–120.

Biennial Report of the Kansas State Board of Agriculture. Topeka: Kansas Publishing House, various years.

Bigelow, Poultney. "What I Saw at Kansas City." *Contemporary Review* 78 (1900): 442–456.

Birmingham, Frederic A. "Kansas City: Cosmopolis of the Heartland." *Saturday Evening Post* 247 (September 1975): 54–72.

Bland, Murrel. *The 50s in Wyandotte County..* Kansas City, Kans.: Kansas Colloquies, 2005.

Bodine, Walt. *What Do You Say to That?* Kansas City, Mo.: Westport Publishers, 1988.

———. *My Times, My Town.* Kansas City: Kansas City Star Books, 2003.

Bonnewitz, Roberta L., and Lois T. Allen. *Raytown Remembers: The Story of a Santa Fe Trail Town.* Raytown, Mo.: Raytown Historical Society, 1975.

Bracke, William P. *Wheat Country.* New York: Duell, Sloan & Pearce, 1950.

Briggs, John W. *An Italian Passage: Immigrants to Three American Cities, 1890–1930.* New Haven, Conn.: Yale University Press, 1978.

Brink, McDonough and Company. *Illustrated Historical Atlas of Jackson County, Missouri.* Philadelphia: Brink, McDonough, 1877.

Brinson, Nathan W. "Political, Economic, and Cultural Revival in Kansas City, Kansas." Master's thesis, Department of Geography, University of Kansas, 2006.

Brisbane, Arthur S. *Arthur Brisbane's Kansas City.* N.p.: Rosalindajones Enterprises, 1982.

Brisbane, Arthur S., Laura M. Shultz, and Suzanne Robinson. *Celebrating Greater Kansas City.* Memphis, Tenn.: Towery Publishing, 1998.

Brown, A. Theodore. "Robert Thompson Van Horn and the Growth of One Frontier." *Trail Guide* 6 (October 1961): 1–15.

———. "Business 'Neutralism' on the Missouri-Kansas Border: Kansas City, 1854–1857." *Journal of Southern History* 29 (1963): 229–240.

———. *Frontier Community: Kansas City to 1870.* Columbia: University of Missouri Press, 1963.

Brown, A. Theodore, and Lyle W. Dorsett. *K.C.: A History of Kansas City, Missouri.* Boulder, Colo.: Pruett Publishing, 1978.

Bruce, Janet. *The Kansas City Monarchs: Champions of Black Baseball.* Lawrence: University Press of Kansas, 1985.

Bryant, Girard, Richard McKinzie, and George Griffin. *The Spirit of Freedom: A Profile of the History of Blacks in Kansas City, Missouri.* Kansas City, Mo.: Office of Housing and Community Development, 1978.

Bryant, Keith L., Jr. *Arthur Stilwell: Promoter with a Hunch.* Nashville, Tenn.: Vanderbilt University Press, 1971.

Burnes, Brian. *High and Rising: The 1951 Kansas City Flood.* Kansas City, Mo.: Kansas City Star Books, 2001.

Burrus, Anna P., Betty M. Fullerton, Mary P. S. Hare, Margaret W. Izzard, and Jane F. Saunders. *Historic Independence.* Independence: Junior Service League of Independence, Missouri, 1946.

Butler, Robert W. "Kansas City." *Travel/Holiday* 174 (June 1991): 32, 34.

Campbell, Craig S. *Images of the New Jerusalem: Latter Day Saint Faction Interpretations of Independence, Missouri.* Knoxville: University of Tennessee Press, 2004.

Campbell, William L. "Fashionable Pearl Street." *Annals of Kansas City* 1 (1921–1924): 109–113.

Case, Theodore S., ed. *History of Kansas City, Missouri.* Syracuse, N.Y.: D. Mason, 1888.

"Cattle City Branches Out." *Business Week* (November 1, 1947): 36–41.

Chamber of Commerce of Kansas City. *Where These Rocky Bluffs Meet: Including the Story of the Kansas City Ten-Year Plan.* Kansas City, Mo.: Kansas City Chamber of Commerce, 1938.

Chanute, Octave, and George Morison. *The Kansas City Bridge, with an Account of the Regimen on the Missouri River, and a Description of Methods Used for Founding in That River.* New York: D. Van Nostrand, 1870.

Charvat, Arthur. "Growth and Development of the Kansas City Stock Yards: A History, 1871–1947." Master's thesis, Department of History, University of Kansas, 1948.

Chase, Charles M. *The Editor's Run in New Mexico and Colorado.* Lyndon: Vermont Union, 1882.

Chick, Washington H. "A Journey to Missouri." *Annals of Kansas City* 1 (1921–1924): 96–103.

———. "The Vicissitudes of Pioneer Life." *Annals of Kansas City* 1 (1921–1924): 207–218.

Ciotti, Paul. *Money and School Performance: Lessons from the Kansas City Desegregation Experiment.* Cato Policy Analysis No. 298. Washington, D.C.: Cato Institute, 1998.

City of Mission, Kansas. *The City of Mission, Kansas: 50 Years of Progress.* Prairie Village, Kans.: Joe Vaughn Associates, 2003.

City Plan Commission. *Locational Costs in Industrial Districts: Greater Kansas City.* Kansas City, Mo.: City Plan Commission, 1950.

Claybrook, Jennifer A. "Evolution of an Urban Landscape: The Case of Piper, Kansas." Master's thesis, Department of Geography, University of Kansas, 2004.

Clayton, Bruce. *Praying for Base Hits: An American Boyhood.* Columbia: University of Missouri Press, 1998.

Clendening, E. M. "The Development of Kansas City." *Harper's Weekly* 49 (October 28, 1905): 1570–1572.

Clugston, W. G. "Kansas City: Gateway to What?" In *Our Fair City,* ed. Robert S. Allen. New York: Vanguard Press, 1947, pp. 256–726.

Coburn, Frederick W. "Public Parks in Kansas City." *Brush and Pencil* 13 (1903): 288–290.

Coleman, Michael. *This Far by Faith: A Popular History of the Catholic People of West and Northwest Missouri,* vol. 2, *The Facts.* Marceline, Mo.: Walsworth Publishing, 1992.

Coleman, Richard P. *The Kansas City Establishment: Leadership through Two Centuries in a Midwestern Metropolis.* Manhattan, Kans.: KS Publishing, 2006.

Community Profile (various cities). Topeka: Kansas Department of Commerce and Housing, various years.

Connell, Evan S., Jr. *Mrs. Bridge.* New York: Viking Press, 1959.

———. *Mr. Bridge.* New York: Alfred A. Knopf, 1969.

Connelley, William E. "Kansas City, Kansas: Its Place in the History of the State." *Kansas Historical Collections, 1919–1922* 15 (1922): 181–191.

Cookingham, L. P. "The Kansas City Story." *American City* 73 (September 1958): 170–174.

Copeland, Laura. *Historic Photos of Kansas City.* Nashville, Tenn.: Turner Publishing, 2006.

Copely, Josiah. *Kansas and the Country Beyond on the Line of the Union Pacific Railway, Eastern Division.* Philadelphia: J. B. Lippincott, 1867.

Cornelius, Ronda, ed. *The Best of Remember When: 100 Warm Tales of Life as We Lived It.* Kansas City, Mo.: Kansas City Star Books, 2001.

Cornuelle, Herbert C. *"Mr. Anonymous": The Story of William Volker.* Caldwell, Idaho: Caxton Printers, 1951.

Coulter, Charles E. *"Take Up the Black Man's Burden": Kansas City's African American Communities, 1865–1939.* Columbia: University of Missouri Press, 2006.

"The Country Clubber." *Time* 50 (December 1, 1947): 94–96.

Cravens, Jacqueline, and Dorothea F. Hyde. "Conference Tips." *Library Journal* 63 (1938): 456–459.

Creel, George. "Independence Makes a President." *Collier's* 116 (August 18, 1945): 14–15, 26.

Creel, George, and John Slavens, comps. *Men Who Are Making Kansas City: A Biographical Directory.* Kansas City, Mo.: Hudson-Kimberly, 1902.

Cronon, William. *Nature's Metropolis: Chicago and the Great West.* New York: W. W. Norton, 1991.

Cutler, William G., ed. *History of the State of Kansas.* 2 vols. Chicago: A. D. Andreas, 1883.

Dahlberg, Edward. "Return to Kansas City." *Holiday* 41 (June 1967): 16, 18, 20, 24, 27.

Dalton, William J. *Pioneer Priest: The Life of Father Bernard Donnelly.* Kansas City, Mo.: Grimes-Joyce Printing, 1921.

Damon, George F. "The Kansas City Flood in Retrospect." *Charities* 11 (1903): 574–576.

Dary, David. *The Santa Fe Trail: Its History, Legends, and Lore.* New York: Alfred A. Knopf, 2000.

Davidson, Bill. "Untangling the Traffic Snarl." *Collier's* 126 (July 1, 1950): 32–33, 71–72.

Davies, Oscar G., ed. *Social Directory of Kansas City* (titles vary by year). Kansas City, Mo.: Kansas City Social Directory Company, 1923–1949.

DeAngelo, Dory. *Voices across Time: Profiles of Kansas City's Early Residents.* Kansas City, Mo.: Tapestry Publications, 1987.

———. *Passages through Time: Stories about Kansas City, Missouri, and Its Northeast Neighborhood.* Kansas City, Mo.: Tapestry Publications, 1992.

———. *What about Kansas City! A Historical Handbook*. Kansas City, Mo.: Two Lane Press, 1995.

DeAngelo, Dory, and Jane F. Flynn. *Kansas City Style: A Social and Cultural History of Kansas City as Seen through Its Lost Architecture*. Kansas City, Mo.: Harrow Books, 1990.

Deatherage, Charles P. *The Early History of the Lumber Trade of Kansas City*. Kansas City, Mo.: Retail Lumberman, 1924.

———. *Early History of Greater Kansas City, Missouri and Kansas: The Prophetic City at the Mouth of the Kaw*. Kansas City, Mo.: Interstate Publishing, 1927.

DeLaurier, Nancy. *Eastwood Hills: The Changing Face of a Kansas City Neighborhood*. Kansas City, Mo.: Eastwood Hills Community Association, 2005.

Dellinger, Harold, ed. *The Lykins Neighborhood Guidebook*. Kansas City, Mo.: Lykins Neighborhood Association, 2000.

Detzer, Karl. "What's the Score in Kansas City?" *Reader's Digest* 55 (September 1949): 114–117.

Dodd, Monroe. *Kansas City Then and Now*. Kansas City, Mo.: Kansas City Star Books, 2000.

———. *A Splendid Ride: The Streetcars of Kansas City, 1870–1957*. Kansas City, Mo.: Kansas City Star Books, 2002.

———. *Kansas City Then and Now 2*. Kansas City, Mo.: Kansas City Star Books, 2003.

———. *Kansas City Then and Now 3*. Kansas City, Mo.: Kansas City Star Books, 2007.

Dorsett, Lyle W. "Slaveholding in Jackson County, Missouri." *Bulletin of the Missouri Historical Society* 20 (October 1963): 25–37.

———. *The Pendergast Machine*. New York: Oxford University Press, 1968.

Dougherty, Laura. "Fiestas in Kansas City." *Recreation* 40 (1947): 527, 559.

Driggs, Frank, and Chuck Haddix. *Kansas City Jazz: From Ragtime to Bebop—A History*. New York: Oxford University Press, 2005.

Dunbar PTA, comp. *In Commemoration of the Dunbar Elementary School*. Kansas City, Kans.: n. p., 1971.

Duncan, John T., and Severiano Alonzo. *Guadalupe Center: Fifty Years of Service*. Kansas City, Mo.: Guadalupe Center, 1972.

Eames, E. L. "Kansas City and Manifest Destiny." *Magazine of Western History* 9 (1888): 698–702, and 10 (1889): 61–65, 221–224.

Eckels, Mary P., and Roselee K. Ennis. *Listen to the Echoes Ring: A History of the Sunset Hill School*. Kansas City, Mo.: Pembroke Hill School Alumni Association, 1985.

Ehrlich, George. *Kansas City, Missouri: An Architectural History, 1826–1976*. Kansas City, Mo.: Historic Kansas City Foundation, 1979.

Ek, Hildur. *Growing Up in Kansas City*. Lindsborg, Kans.: Hildur Ek, 1985.

Ellis, Roy. *A Civic History of Kansas City*. Springfield, Mo.: Elkins-Sawyer, 1930.

"Everything's Up to Date in Kansas City." *Business Week* (February 4, 1950): 66–70.

"Everything's Up to Date in Kansas City." *Time* 78 (July 28, 1961): 38.

Facts Concerning Kansas City, Kansas. Kansas City: Kansas City, Kansas, Chamber of Commerce, circa 1935.

"Fairfax District Getting More Industrial Activity." *Kansas Business Magazine* 22 (November 1954): 8–9, 60–61.

"Fairfax Gains New Industry." *Midwest Industry Magazine* 27 (January 1959): 42.

"Fairfax Industrial District Gains New Plants, Warehouses." *Kansas Business Magazine* 21 (January 1953): 7, 77.

"Fairfax Industrial District: One of Finest in Nation." *Kansas Business Magazine* 15 (January 1947): 6, 64–66.

Farley, Alan W. "Samuel Hallett and the Union Pacific Railway Company in Kansas." *Kansas Historical Quarterly* 25 (1959): 1–16.

Fellman, Michael. *Inside War: The Guerrilla Conflict in Missouri during the American Civil War*. New York: Oxford University Press, 1989.

Fiftieth Anniversary Committee. *The City of Mission, Kansas: 50 Years of Progress*. Prairie Village, Kans.: Joe Vaughn Associates, 2003.

"Fight over Terminals." *Business Week* (December 16, 1939): 20, 23.

Findley, Rowe. "Kansas City: Heartland U. S. A." *National Geographic* 150 (July 1976): 112–139.

Fite, Gilbert C. *Beyond the Fence Rows: A History of Farmland Industries, Inc.: 1929–1978*. Columbia: University of Missouri Press, 1978.

Fitzgerald, Daniel. "Town Booming: An Economic History of Steamboat Towns along the Kansas-Missouri Border, 1840–1860." Master's thesis, Department of History, University of Kansas, 1983.

Flynn, Jane F. *Kansas City Women of Independent Minds*. Kansas City, Mo.: Fifield Publishing, 1992.

Foerster, Bernd. *Independence, Missouri*. Independence, Mo.: Independence Press, 1978.

Fogelson, Robert M. *Downtown: Its Rise and Fall, 1880–1950*. New Haven, Conn.: Yale University Press, 2001.

"Food Mart Unloaded." *Business Week* (September 21, 1940): 18.

"Ford Closing Stirs Kansas City." *Business Week* (October 30, 1937): 24–25.

Ford, George B. "The Park System of Kansas City, Mo." *Architectural Record* 40 (1916): 498–504.

Ford, Larry R. *America's New Downtowns: Revitalization or Reinvention?* Baltimore, Md.: Johns Hopkins University Press, 2003.

Fowler, Richard B. *Leaders in Our Town*. Kansas City, Mo.: Burd and Fletcher, 1952.

Fox, Jeanne A. "In Kansas City Missouri." *Black Enterprise* 8 (March 1978): 43–46, 54.

Franzwa, Gregory M. *Maps of the Oregon Trail*. Gerald, Mo.: Patrice Press, 1982.

Fritz, Leslie. "The Development of the Milling Industry in Kansas." *Kansas Historical Collections, 1911–1912* 12 (1912): 53–59.

Fulton, Mildred, ed. *Bridge to the Past: A Personal History of North Kansas City*. Marceline, Mo.: Walsworth Publishing, 1983.

Garraghan, Gilbert J. *Catholic Beginnings in Kansas City, Missouri*. Chicago: Loyala University Press, 1920.

Garrard, Lewis H. *Wah-To-Yah and the Taos Trail*, 1850. Reprint, edited by Walter S. Campbell, Oklahoma City: Harlow Publishing, 1927.

Garreau, Joel. *Edge City: Life on the New Frontier.* New York: Doubleday, 1991.

Garwood, Darrell. *Crossroads of America: The Story of Kansas City.* New York: W. W. Norton, 1948.

"Gas Problem Solved, Kansas City Gets Ford." *Business Week* (December 16, 1950): 26.

Geary, Daniel. "Looking Backward." *Annals of Kansas City* 1 (1921–1924): 224–235.

Geissal, Philip E. "Kansas City Sees Expressways Preventing 1970 Traffic Jams." *American City* 67 (March 1952): 141–143.

Gentile, Richard J. "Geology and Utilization of Underground Space in Metropolitan Kansas City Area, USA." *Environmental Geology* 29 (1997): 11–16.

Gibson, Campbell. *Population of the 100 Largest Cities and Other Urban Places in the United States: 1790 to 1990.* Working Paper No. 27. Washington, D.C.: Population Division, U. S. Bureau of the Census, 1998.

Gilbert, Bill. *This City, This Man: The Cookingham Era in Kansas City.* Washington, D.C.: International City Management Association, 1978.

Gilpin, William. "The Cities of Missouri." *Western Journal and Civilian* 11 (1853): 31–40.

Glaab, Charles N. "Business Patterns in the Growth of a Midwestern City: The Kansas City Business Community before the Civil War." *Business History Review* 33 (1959): 156–174.

———. *Kansas City and the Railroads: Community Policy in the Growth of a Regional Metropolis.* Madison: State Historical Society of Wisconsin, 1962.

Gleed, Charles S. "The Central City of the West." *Cosmopolitan* 29 (1900): 297–304.

———. "Kansas City: The Central City." In *Historic Towns of the Western States,* ed. Lyman P. Powell.. New York: G. P. Putnam's Sons, 1901, pp. 375–399.

"Goal in the Clouds." *Business Week* (April 22, 1944): 34–36.

Goodspeed Publishing Company. *Wyandotte County and Kansas City, Kansas: Historical and Biographical.* Chicago: Goodspeed, 1890.

Gotham, Kevin F. *Race, Real Estate, and Uneven Development: The Kansas City Experience, 1900–2000.* Albany: State University of New York Press, 2002.

"A Gracious Town in the Heartland." *Time* 108 (August 16, 1976): 11–12.

Grandview Historical Society. *History of Grandview, Missouri: 1844–1994.* Grandview, Mo.: Grandview Historical Society, 1995.

Gray, Junius J. N., ed. *Who's Who in Kansas City, 1921: Authoritative Rating of People of Color Engaged in the Various Professions, Business Enterprises and Industry of Kansas City.* Kansas City, Kans.: Gray Printing, 1921.

Green, George F. *A Condensed History of the Kansas City Era: Its Mayors and Some V.I.P.s.* Kansas City, Mo.: Lowell Press, 1968.

Greenbaum, Susan D. *Strawberry Hill: A Neighborhood Study.* Kansas City, Kans.: City of Kansas City, Kansas, 1978.

———. "The Historical, Institutional and Ecological Parameters of Social Cohesiveness in Four Urban Neighborhoods." Ph.D. diss., Department of Anthropology, University of Kansas, 1981.

———. *The Afro-American Community in Kansas City, Kansas: A History.* Kansas City, Kans.: City of Kansas City, Kansas, 1982.

———. "The Preservation of Strawberry Hill: Continuity and Adaptation in an Urban Ethnic Neighborhood." *Ethnic Groups* 6 (1985): 275–292.

Greenwood, James M. "Colonel Robert T. Van Horn: His Life and Public Service." *Annals of Kansas City* 1 (1921–1924): 417–433.

Gross, Lisa. "The Project That Grew and Grew." *Forbes* 126 (August 4, 1980): 63.

Hager, Gerald F. "'Getting It Done' in Kansas City." *American City* 24 (1921): 513–515.

Haines, Adelbert S. "Reminiscences of Adelbert S. Haines." *Annals of Kansas City* 1 (1921–1924): 196–202.

Hall, Joyce C., with Curtiss Anderson. *When You Care Enough.* Kansas City, Mo.: Hallmark Cards, 1992.

Hancks, Larry K., and Meredith Roberts. *Roots: The Historic and Architectural Heritage of Kansas City, Kansas.* Kansas City, Kans.: City of Kansas City, Kansas, 1976.

Harrington, Grant W. *Historic Spots or Mile-stones in the Progress of Wyandotte County.* Merriam, Kans.: Mission Press, 1935.

Harris, Nellie M. "Memories of Old Westport." *Annals of Kansas City* 1 (1921–1924): 465–475.

Harris, Ronald. "Kansas City: It Calls Itself One of the Few Livable Cities Left." *Ebony* 36 (November 1980): 80–90.

Haskell, Harry. *Boss-Busters and Sin Hounds: Kansas City and Its Star.* Columbia: University of Missouri Press, 2007.

Haskell, Henry C., Jr., and Richard B. Fowler. "The Attempted Annexation of Kansas City to the State of Kansas." *Missouri Historical Review* 44 (1950): 221–224.

———. *City of the Future: A Narrative History of Kansas City, 1850–1950.* Kansas City, Mo.: Frank Glenn, 1950.

Haskell, Henry J. "A Notable Memorial." *World's Work* 42 (1921): 488–490.

———. "What Kind of a Pittsburgh Is Kansas City?" *World's Work* 41 (1921): 289–298.

———. "Kansas City: Houn'dawg vs. Art." In *The Taming of the Frontier: El Paso, Ogden, Denver, St. Paul, San Francisco, Portland, Kansas City, Cheyenne, San Antonio, Los Angeles,* ed. Duncan Aikman. New York: Minton, Balch, 1925, pp. 199–233.

———. "Kansas City: Where the Frontier Lingers." *American Review of Reviews* 77 (1928): 616–624.

Herring, Joseph B. *The Enduring Indians of Kansas: A Century and a Half of Acculturation.* Lawrence: University Press of Kansas, 1990.

Hickman, William Z. *History of Jackson County, Missouri.* Topeka, Kans.: Historical Publishing, 1920.

Hill, William R. *The Great Flood of 1903.* Kansas City, Mo.: Enterprise Publishing, 1903.

Hoffhaus, Charles E. *Chez les Canses: Three Centuries at Kawsmouth.* Kansas City, Mo.: Lowell Press, 1984.

Holliday, Cyrus K. "The Cities of Kansas." *Kansas Historical Collections, 1883–1885* 3 (1885): 396–401.

Holt, Henry. "A Foreign Tour at Home." *Putnam's Monthly and The Reader* 3 (1908): 645–654.

Howe, Frank M. "The Development of Architecture in Kansas City, Missouri." *Architectural Record* 15 (1904): 134–157.

Howe, S. Ferdinand. *The Commerce of Kansas City in 1886; with a General Review of Its Business Progress.* Kansas City, Mo.: S. F. Howe, 1886.

Hoye's Kansas City Blue Book (titles vary by year). Kansas City, Mo.: Hoye Directory, 1890–1922.

Hudson, David S. *The Plaza: Kansas City's World-Famous Shopping District.* Prairie Village, Kans.: Harrow Books, 1989.

Hughes, T. "A Railroad Centre and the Kansas Valley." *Month* 69 (1889): 167–178.

Information and Research Department. *Kansas City, Kansas Factbook.* Kansas City, Kans.: City of Kansas City, Kansas, 1995.

Ingersoll, Ernest. "Kansas City." *Cosmopolitan* 8 (1889): 141–152.

Insurance Maps of Kansas City, Kansas. New York: Sanborn Map and Publishing, 1889.

Insurance Maps of Kansas City, Missouri. New York: Sanborn-Perris Map, 1895.

Insurance Maps of Kansas City, Missouri. New York: Sanborn Map, 1909.

Insurance Maps of Kansas City, Rosedale and Argentine, Kansas. New York: Sanborn Map, 1907–1908.

Isaacson, Darlene. *Kansas City: Then and Now.* San Diego, Calif.: Thunder Bay Press, 2006.

Isaacson, Darlene, and Elizabeth Wallace. *Kansas City in Vintage Postcards.* Charleston, S. C.: Arcadia Publishing, 2003.

Jackson, Kenneth T. *Crabgrass Frontier: The Suburbanization of the United States.* New York: Oxford University Press, 1985.

J. C. Nichols Company. *Map of the Country Club District.* Kansas City, Mo.: J. C. Nichols, 1917.

Jewett, John M., and Norman D. Newell. *The Geology of Wyandotte County, Kansas.* Bulletin 21, pt. 2. Lawrence: State Geological Survey of Kansas, 1935.

Johnson, Arthur M., and Barry E. Supple. *Boston Capitalists and Western Railroads.* Cambridge, Mass.: Harvard University Press, 1967.

"Joseph Chick." *Magazine of Western History* 10 (1889): 224–226.

"Kansas City." In *Union Pacific Sketchbook: A Brief Description of Prominent Places of Interest along the Line of the Union Pacific Railway.* Omaha: D. C. Dunbar, 1887, pp. 51–67.

"Kansas City Aims to Prove Everything's Up to Date." *U.S. News & World Report* 81 (August 16, 1976): 18–19.

"Kansas City Airports Look to the Future." *American City* 58 (November 1943): 13.

"Kansas City and St. Louis." *Life* 36 (March 29, 1954): 106–115.

"Kansas City Cable Railway." *Kansas City Review of Science and Industry* 8 (1885): 541–548.

Kansas City Centennial Souvenir Program. Kansas City, Mo.: Kansas City Centennial Association, 1950.

"Kansas City: Factories Can't Conceal a Cowtown." *Business Week* (February 21, 1953): 110–124.

"Kansas City: In the Heart of North America." *Bulletin of the Pan American Union* 50 (February 1920): 140–159.

"Kansas City Invites You." *American Journal of Public Health* 28 (1938): 670–676.

"Kansas City Itself." *Journal of Home Economics* 29 (1937): 102–104.

"Kansas City, Kansas." *Kansas Business* 3 (December 1935): 5, 7, 12–14, 26.

"Kansas City, Kansas: Great Industrial Center." *Kansas Business* 6 (June 1938): 5, 19–22.

Kansas City, Kansas, Mercantile Club. *The Story of Three Years' Progress in Kansas City, Kansas.* Kansas City, Kans.: Meseraull, 1909.

"Kansas City Portfolio of American Home Readers' Homes." *American Home* 18 (June 1937): 46–55.

"Kansas City Shows Missouri." *Independent* 120 (1928): 107–110.

"Kansas City's New Art Gallery." *Art and Archaeology* 35 (January 1934): 39–42.

"Kansas City's New Municipal Auditorium." *American City* 51 (June 1936): 103.

"Kansas City's New Museum." *American Magazine of Art* 26 (1933): 523–530.

Kansas City Stock Yards Commission. *75 Years of Kansas City Livestock Market History: 1871–1946.* Kansas City, Mo.: Kansas City Stock Yards Commission, 1946.

Karash, Julius A., and Rick Montgomery. *TWA: Kansas City's Hometown Airline.* Kansas City, Mo.: Kansas City Star Books, 2001.

Keech, Norman, and Florent W. Wagner, eds. *Historic Overland Park: An Illustrated History.* San Antonio, Tex.: Historical Publishing Network, 2005.

Kellogg, Clara, and Katherine Baxter, eds. *Kansas City Blue Book and Club Directory* (titles vary by year). Kansas City, Mo.: Kellogg-Baxter Directory, 1901–1923.

Kemper, James M. *A Bank and Its Community: The Story of Commerce Trust Company.* New York: Newcomen Society in North America, 1966.

Kerski, Joseph J. "The Impact of the Bruce R. Watkins Roadway Project on Neighborhoods in Kansas City, Missouri." Master's thesis, Department of Geography, University of Kansas, 1993.

Kimball, Charles N. *Midwest Research Institute: Some Recollections of the First 30 Years, 1945–1975.* Kansas City, Mo.: Midwest Research Institute, 1985.

King, Roy E. "The Great South." *Scribner's Monthly* 8 (1874): 257–284.

Kingsley, Rose G. *South by West, or Winter in the Rocky Mountains and Spring in Mexico.* London: W. Isbister, 1874.

Kirkland, Edward C. *Charles Francis Adams, Jr.: 1835–1915—The Patrician at Bay.* Cambridge, Mass.: Harvard University Press, 1965.

Kohr, Harry F. "Huge Railroad Station That Can Expand." *Technical World Magazine* 20 (September 1913): 80–83.

Koues, Helen. "Beauty in Community Planning." *Good Housekeeping* 104 (April 1937): 50–53, 235–236.

Laird, Judith F. "Argentine, Kansas: The Evolution of a Mexican-American Community, 1905–1940." Ph.D. diss., Department of History, University of Kansas, 1975.

Lake, Turner. "Is There No End to This Boom?" *Kansas Business News* 5 (August 1984): 28–32.

Lamb, Arthur W. *Sanderson's Lunch*. Leawood, Kans.: Leathers Publishing, 1998.

Landis, Margaret. *The Winding Valley and the Craggy Hillside: A History of the City of Rosedale, Kansas*. Kansas City, Kans.: Margaret Landis, 1976.

Landmarks Commission of Kansas City, Missouri. *Kansas City: A Place in Time*. Kansas City, Mo.: Landmarks Commission of Kansas City, Missouri, 1977.

Lanterman, Alice. "The Development of Kansas City as a Grain and Milling Center." *Missouri Historical Review* 42 (1947): 20–33.

Larsen, Lawrence H., and Nancy J. Hulston. "Through the Eyes of a Medical Student: A Window on Frontier Life in Kansas City, 1870–1871." *Missouri Historical Review* 88 (1994): 430–445.

———. *Pendergast!* Columbia: University of Missouri Press, 1997.

Lee, Janice, David Boutros, Charlotte R. White, and Dean Wolfenbarger, eds. *A Legacy of Design: An Historical Survey of the Kansas City, Missouri, Parks and Boulevards System, 1893–1940*. Kansas City, Mo.: Kansas City Center for Design Education and Research, 1995.

"Lifting the Face of Kansas City." *Business Week* (May 20, 1972): 96.

Lobenstine, William C. *Extracts from the Diary of William C. Lobenstine, December 31, 1851–1858*. New York: William C. Lobenstine, 1920.

Love, Mindi C., ed. *Johnson County, Kansas: A Pictorial History, 1825–2005*. Shawnee, Kans.: Johnson County Museum, 2006.

Macias, Richard. "'We All Had a Cause': Kansas City's Bomber Plant, 1941–1945." *Kansas History* 28 (2005–2006): 244–261.

Main, Jeremy. "The Kempers of Kansas City." *Fortune* 75 (April 1967): 170–172, 194, 196, 200, 202.

Manheim, Ernest. *Kansas City and Its Neighborhoods: Facts and Figures*. Kansas City, Mo.: Kansas City Council of Churches and Department of Sociology at the University of Kansas City, 1943.

Manzo, Joseph T. "Strawberry Hill: An Urban Ethnic Neighborhood." Master's thesis, Department of Geography, University of Kansas, 1975.

———. "The Role of External Factors in the Decline of the Strawberry Hill Neighborhood." *Ethnicity* 7 (1980): 47–55.

———. "Sequent Occupance in Kansas City, Kansas: A Historical Geography of Strawberry Hill." *Kansas History* 4 (1981): 20–29.

Marra, Dorothy B. *Cher Oncle, Cher Papa: The Letters of François and Berenice Chouteau*. Kansas City, Mo.: Western Historical Manuscript Collection—Kansas City, 2001.

Martin, Asa E. *Our Negro Population: A Sociological Study of the Negroes of Kansas City, Missouri*. Kansas City, Mo.: Franklin Hudson, 1913.

Martin, Dwayne R. "The Hidden Community: The Black Community of Kansas City, Missouri, during the 1870s and 1880s." Master's thesis, Department of History, University of Missouri–Kansas City, 1982.

Martin, George W. "The Boundary Lines of Kansas." *Kansas Historical Collections, 1909–1910* 11 (1910): 53–74.

Marvin, George. "'K.C.': The City Where Trails Begin." *Outlook* 144 (1926): 533–535.

Maurois, André. Translated by Joan Charles. *From My Journal*. New York: Harper & Brothers, 1948.

Maxwell, H. James, and Bob Sullivan, Jr. *Hometown Beer: A History of Kansas City's Breweries*. Kansas City, Mo.: Omega Innovative Marketing, 1999.

Mayer, Michael. "The Good Slum Schools." *Harper's Magazine* 222 (April 1961): 46–52.

McCandless, Perry. *A History of Missouri*, vol. 2, *1820–1860*. Columbia: University of Missouri Press, 1972.

McCourt, Walter E., assisted by Maurice M. Albertson and John W. Bennett. *The Geology of Jackson County*. 2nd ser., vol. 14. Rolla: Missouri Bureau of Geology and Mines, 1917.

McCoy, John C. Scrapbook. Native Sons Archives, Western Historical Manuscript Collection, University of Missouri–Kansas City.

McCoy, Joseph G. *Historic Sketches of the Cattle Trade of the West and Southwest*. 1874. Reprint, Glendale, Calif.: A. H. Clark, 1940.

McCoy, William. Papers. Missouri Historical Society, St. Louis.

McCullough, James H. "He Makes Homes Grow in Waste Places." *American Magazine* 95 (March 1923): 50–51, 157–159.

McDermott, John. "'Our Town': A Sketch of Kansas City, Kansas." *Haldeman-Julius Monthly* 7 (1927): 103–107.

McDonald, A. B. "A Home District Beautiful." *Ladies' Home Journal* 38 (February 1921): 12–13, 80, 82.

McDougal, Henry C. "Historical Sketch of Kansas City, Mo. from the Beginning to 1909." *Kansas Historical Collections, 1909–1910* 11 (1910): 581–589.

McDowell, Joseph H. *Building a City: A Detailed History of Kansas City, Kansas*. Kansas City, Kans.: Kansas City Kansan, 1969.

McKenna, Joseph M. *The Growth and Problems of Metropolitan Wyandotte County*. Citizen's Pamphlet 32. Lawrence: Governmental Research Center, University of Kansas, 1963.

McQuade, Walter. "Two Cities, New and Old, Show the Way to Urban Amenity." *Fortune* 92 (July 1975): 92–99.

Mendoza, Valerie Marie. "The Creation of a Mexican Immigrant Community in Kansas City, 1890–1930." Ph.D. diss., Department of History, University of California–Berkeley, 1997.

Mickett, Carol A. *History Speaks: Visions and Voices of Kansas City's Past*. Kansas City, Mo.: Midwest Research Institute, 2002.

Miller, Merle. "Mr. Truman's Hometown." *Holiday* 47 (May 1970): 40–45, 86, 88.

Miller, Patricia C. *Westport: Missouri's Port of Many Returns*. Kansas City, Mo.: Lowell Press, 1983.

Miller, William H. *The History of Kansas City*. Kansas City, Mo.: Birdsall and Miller, 1881.

Miner, H. Craig. "The Kansas and Neosho Valley: Kansas City's Drive for the Gulf." *Journal of the West* 17 (October 1978): 75–85.

———. *Kansas: The History of the Sunflower State, 1854–2000.* Lawrence: University Press of Kansas, 2002.

Miner, H. Craig, and William E. Unrau. *The End of Indian Kansas: A Study of Cultural Revolution, 1854–1871.* Lawrence: Regents Press of Kansas, 1978.

Mitchell, Giles C. *There Is No Limit: Architecture and Sculpture in Kansas City.* Kansas City, Mo.: Brown-White, 1934.

Mobley, Jane, and Shifra Stein. *Kansas City: Heart of America.* Montgomery, Ala.: Community Communications, 1994.

Montgomery, Rick, and Shirl Kasper. *Kansas City: An American Story.* Kansas City, Mo.: Kansas City Star Books, 1999.

Morgan, Perl W., ed. *History of Wyandotte County, Kansas and Its People.* 2 vols. Chicago: Lewis Publishing, 1911.

Morris, Ann. *Leawood: A Portrait in Time.* Leawood, Kans.: Leawood Historic Commission, 1997.

Morse, Charles F. *A Sketch of My Life Written for My Children and a Buffalo Hunt in Nebraska in 1871.* Cambridge, Mass.: Riverside Press, 1927.

"The Murders and Mysteries of Kansas City's 'Little Italy.'" *Literary Digest* 61 (April 5, 1919): 51–55.

Myers, Debs. "Kansas City." *Holiday* 7 (March 1950): 46–55, 119–122.

Nagel, Paul C. *Missouri: A History.* New York: W. W. Norton, 1977.

Naylor, Lois A. "Kansas City, Missouri." *Better Homes and Gardens* 68 (October 1990): 166.

Naysmith, Clifford. *Quality Hill: The History of a Neighborhood.* Missouri Valley Series No. 1. Kansas City, Mo.: Kansas City Public Library, 1962.

Negro Business and Professional Directory of Greater Kansas City, 1928–1929, Kansas City, Kans.: Booster Advertising, 1928.

"The New West." *Saint Louis Magazine* 20 (1880): 371–405.

Nichols, J. C. "Suburban Subdivisions with Community Features." *American City* 31 (1924): 335–338.

———. "Developing Outlying Shopping Centers." *American City* 41 (1929): 98–101.

"Not for Sale." *Time* 65 (May 16, 1955): 85–86.

O'Connor, Howard G. *Geology and Ground-Water Resources of Johnson County, Kansas.* Bulletin 203. Lawrence: State Geological Survey of Kansas, 1971.

O'Connor, Howard G., and Lowell W. Fowler. "Pleistocene Geology in a Part of the Kansas City Area." *Transactions of the Kansas Academy of Science* 66 (1963): 622–631.

Official Guide and Map of Greater Kansas City. Kansas City, Mo.: Gallup Map and Stationery, various years.

O'Gara, Geoffrey. *A Long Road Home: Journeys through America's Present in Search of America's Past.* New York: W. W. Norton, 1989.

O'Neill, Hugh, and John M. Steele. "Kansas City: A City That Is Finding Itself." *World To-day* 11 (1906): 1155–1162.

O'Neill, Pat. *From the Bottom Up: The Story of the Irish in Kansas City.* Kansas City, Mo.: Seat o' the Pants Publishing, 2000.

O'Sheel, Shaemas. "Kansas City: The Crossroads of a Continent." *New Republic* 54 (1928): 375–378.

Oster, Donald B. "Community Image in the History of Saint Louis and Kansas City." Ph.D diss., Department of History, University of Missouri–Columbia, 1969.

Otis, Denise. "A New Town Comes to Life in Downtown Kansas City." *House and Garden* 145 (March 1974): 39–40, 162.

Oyen, Henry. "The Awakening of the Cities," third article, "Making Better Citizens." *World's Week* 22 (August 1911): 14725–14733.

Pacione, Michael. *Urban Geography: A Global Perspective.* London: Routledge, 2001.

Painter, Nell I. *Exodusters: Black Migration to Kansas after Reconstruction.* New York: Alfred A. Knopf, 1977.

Parizek, Eldon J. "Kansas City: Its Geologic Setting." *Geotimes* 10 (October 1965): 9–13.

Parkman, Francis. *The Oregon Trail.* 1849. Reprint, edited by E. N. Feltskog, Madison: University of Wisconsin Press, 1969.

"Parks as a Commercial Asset." *Outlook* 96 (1910): 806–807.

Patrick, Robert W. "When Kansas City, Mo., Came Close to Being a City in Kansas." *Kansas History* 1 (1978): 266–277.

Paxton, Heather N. *The American Royal: 1899–1999.* Kansas City, Mo.: BkMk Press, University of Missouri–Kansas City, 1999.

Pearman, Robert. "Black Crime, Black Victims." *Nation* 208 (April 21, 1969): 500–503.

Pearson, Nathan W., Jr. *Goin' to Kansas City.* Urbana: University of Illinois Press, 1994.

Pearson, Robert, and Brad Pearson. *The J. C. Nichols Chronicle.* Kansas City, Mo.: Country Club Plaza Press, 1994.

Pen and Sunlight Sketches of Greater Kansas City: America's Most Progressive Metropolis. Kansas City, Mo.: American Illustrating, 1912.

Perry, George S. "The Cities of America: Kansas City." *Saturday Evening Post* 218 (August 25, 1945): 14–15, 37–39.

———. "Independence, Missouri." *Saturday Evening Post* 223 (September 2, 1950): 22–23, 70–71, 74.

Phillips, Cabell. "Truman's Home Town Is 'Smalltown, U.S.A.'" *New York Times Magazine* (July 1, 1945): 13, 37–38.

Polvay, Marina. "Kansas City." *Travel/Holiday* 153 (April 1980): 64–66.

Poppino, Hattie E. *Census of 1860: Population Schedules for Jackson County, Missouri.* Kansas City, Mo.: H. E. Poppino, 1964.

Porter, Pierre R. "Quality Hill: A Study in Heredity." *Missouri Historical Review* 35 (1941): 562–569.

Powell, Cuthbert. *Kansas City: Queen of the Southwest.* Kansas City, Mo.: H. P. Wright Investment, 1910.

Prairie Village History Book Committee and Dawn Grubb. *Prairie Village: Our Story.* Prairie Village, Kans.: City of Prairie Village, 2002.

Primm, James N. *Lion of the Valley: St. Louis, Missouri.* Boulder, Colo.: Pruett Publishing, 1981.

"Prizewinning Arena Collapses." *Time* 113 (June 18, 1979): 74.

Radford, Earle K. "Downtown Air Terminal—Fantastic?" *American City* 58 (August 1943): 49–50.

Rafferty, Milton D. *Historical Atlas of Missouri.* Norman: University of Oklahoma Press, 1982.

Ray, Mrs. Sam [Mildred]. *Postcards from Old Kansas City.* Kansas City, Mo.: Historic Kansas City Foundation, 1980.

———. *Postcards from Old Kansas City II.* Kansas City, Mo.: Historic Kansas City Foundation, 1987.

Raymond, Robert S. "The Economic History of a Midwestern Retail Store, 1911–1934." *Kansas Historical Quarterly* 42 (1976): 308–328.

Reddig, William M. *Tom's Town: Kansas City and the Pendergast Legend.* Philadelphia: J. B. Lippincott, 1947.

Reed, Laura C., ed. *In Memoriam, Sarah Walter Chandler Coates.* Kansas City, Mo.: Hudson-Kimberly, 1897.

Renner, G. K. "The Kansas City Meat Packing Industry before 1900." *Missouri Historical Review* 55 (1960): 18–29.

Rhodes, Richard. "Harry's Last Hurrah." *Harper's Magazine* 240 (January 1970): 48–58.

———. "Convention Fever in Kansas City." *Harper's Magazine* 252 (May 1976): 28, 30.

———. "Cupcake Land: Requiem for the Midwest in the Key of Vanilla." *Harper's Magazine* 275 (November 1987): 51–57.

———. *The Inland Ground: An Evocation of the American Middle West.* Rev. ed. Lawrence: University Press of Kansas, 1991.

Richardson, Albert D. *Beyond the Mississippi.* Hartford, Conn.: American Publishing, 1867.

Riegel, Robert E. "The Missouri Pacific Railroad to 1879." *Missouri Historical Review* 18 (1923–1924): 3–26.

Rodgers, Justine. "A Young City Will Greet You." *Independent Woman.* 18 (February 1939): 49–50.

Roeseler, W. G. "Kansas City's Downtown Story." *American City* 71 (April 1956): 123–124.

Rose, William W. "My Fight against the Ring." *Independent* 61 (1906): 681–684.

Sachs, Howard F. "Development of the Jewish Community of Kansas City, 1864–1908." *Missouri Historical Review* 60 (1966): 350–360.

Sandy, Wilda. *Here Lies Kansas City: A Collection of Our City's Notables and Their Final Resting Places.* Kansas City, Mo.: Bennett Schneider, 1984.

Sasaki Associates, Inc. *Kansas City Downtown Corridor Strategy.* Kansas City, Mo.: Civic Council of Greater Kansas City, 2005.

Scarritt, W. C. "'Park and Plan Week' Arouses Much Interest." *American City* 27 (1922): 327–328.

Schiavo, Giovanni E. *The Italians in Missouri.* New York: Italian-American Publishing, 1929.

Schirmer, Sherry L. *Historical Overview of the Ethnic Communities in Kansas City.* Kansas City, Mo.: Pan-educational Institute, 1976.

———. *A City Divided: The Racial Landscape of Kansas City, 1900–1960.* Columbia: University of Missouri Press, 2002.

Schirmer, Sherry L., and Richard D. McKinzie. *At the River's Bend: An Illustrated History of Kansas City, Independence, and Jackson County.* Woodland Hills, Calif.: Windsor Publications, 1982.

Schmertz, Mildred F. "Crown Center: Urban Renewal for a Kansas City Grey Area." *Architectural Record* 154 (October 1973): 113–126.

Schoewe, Walter H. "The Geography of Kansas, Part I, Political Geography." *Transactions of the Kansas Academy of Science* 51 (1948): 253–288.

Schott, Henry. "A City's Fight for Beauty." *World's Work* 11 (1906): 7191–7205.

Schroeder, Walter A. "The Presettlement Prairie in the Kansas City Region." *Missouri Prairie Journal* 7 (December 1985): 3–12.

Schulkin, Carl. *Pursuit of Greatness: A History of the Pembroke–Country Day School.* Kansas City, Mo.: Pembroke Hill School Alumni Association, 1985.

Schultz, Joseph P., ed. *Mid-America's Promise: A Profile of Kansas City Jewry.* Kansas City, Mo.: Jewish Community Foundation of Greater Kansas City, 1982.

Schwendemann, Glenn. "Wyandotte and the First 'Exodusters' of 1879." *Kansas Historical Quarterly* 26 (1960): 233–249.

Scullin, George. "But Spirit Was Undampened." *Nation's Business* 39 (November 1951): 30–32, 166–169.

Serda, Daniel. *Boston Investors and the Early Development of Kansas City, Missouri.* Kansas City, Mo.: Midwest Research Institute, 1992.

———. *An Intentional Community: History and Local Identity.* Kansas City, Mo.: Midwest Research Institute, 1992.

———. *A Blow to the Spirit: The Kaw River Flood of 1951 in Perspective.* Kansas City, Mo.: Midwest Research Institute, 1993.

Serling, Robert. *Howard Hughes' Airline: An Informal History of TWA.* New York: St. Martin's Marek, 1983.

Shortridge, James R. *Kaw Valley Landscapes: A Traveler's Guide to Northeastern Kansas.* 2nd ed. Lawrence: University Press of Kansas, 1988.

———. *Cities on the Plains: The Evolution of Urban Kansas.* Lawrence: University Press of Kansas, 2004.

———. "Regional Image and Sense of Place in Kansas." *Kansas History* 28 (2005): 202–219.

———. "Edward Miller's Town: The Reconceptualization of Pleasant Hill by the Pacific Railroad of Missouri." *Missouri Historical Review* 101 (2007): 205–225.

Shultz, G. P. *Gully Town: A Novel of Kansas City.* Bonner Springs, Kans.: Shadow Mountain Press, 1990.

Shutt, Edwin D. "'Silver City': A History of the Argentine Community of Kansas City, Kansas." Master's thesis, Department of History, Emporia State College, 1976.

———. "The Saga of the Armour Family in Kansas City, 1870–1900." *Heritage of the Great Plains* 23 (Fall 1990): 25–42.

Simmons, Donald H., ed. *Centennial History of Argentine, Kansas City, Kansas, 1880–1980.* Kansas City, Kans.: Simmons Funeral Home, 1980.

Smith, Henry N. *Virgin Land: The American West as Symbol and Myth.* Cambridge, Mass.: Harvard University Press, 1950.

Soward, James L. *Hospital Hill: An Illustrated Account of Public Healthcare Institutions in Kansas City, Missouri.* Kansas City, Mo.: Truman Medical Center Charitable Foundation, 1995.

Spalding, Charles C. *Annals of the City of Kansas and the Great Western Plains.* Kansas City, Mo.: Van Horn and Abeel, 1858.

Spence, Hartzell. "The Colossal Mayor of Kansas City." *Saturday Evening Post* 228 (January 28, 1956): 17–19, 79–80.

Spivak, Jeffrey. *Union Station: Kansas City.* Kansas City, Mo.: Kansas City Star Books, 1999.

Spletstoser, Fredrick M. "A City at War: The Impact of World War II on Kansas City." Master's thesis, Department of History, University of Missouri–Kansas City, 1971.

Spletstoser, Fredrick M., and Lawrence H. Larsen. *Kansas City: 100 Years of Business.* Kansas City, Mo.: Kansas City Business Journal, 1987.

"The State of Missouri." *Fortune* 32 (July 1945): 112–119, 212–218.

Stauffer, Truman P. *Guidebook to the Occupance and Use of Underground Space in the Greater Kansas City Area.* Publication No. 1. Kansas City, Mo.: University of Missouri–Kansas City, Department of Geology-Geography, 1972.

Stevens, Walter B. "One Hundred Years on the Missouri River." *Annals of Kansas City* 1 (1921–1924): 20–38.

Stote, Amos. "The Ideal American City." *McBride's Magazine* 97 (April 1916): 89–99.

Street, Julian. "Kansas City: The Beginning of the West." *Collier's* 54 (September 19, 1914): 11–12, 28–32.

"Summer White House." *Newsweek* 25 (June 18, 1945): 34–36.

Sutherland, James, comp. *Kansas City Directory and Business Mirror for 1860–61.* Indianapolis, Ind.: James Sutherland, 1860.

Sutton, Horace. "Kansas City: Better Than a Magic Lantern Show." *Saturday Review* 3 (June 26, 1976): 14–16.

Swain, Virginia. *The Dollar Gold Piece.* New York: Farrar and Rinehart, 1942.

Sweet, A. T., Henry H. Krusekopf, and J. E. Dunn. *Soil Survey of Jackson County, Missouri.* Washington, D.C.: Government Printing Office, 1910.

Taylor, Jon E. *A President, a Church, and Trails West: Competing Histories in Independence, Missouri.* Columbia: University of Missouri Press, 2008.

Taylor, Loren L. *The Consolidated Ethnic History of Wyandotte County.* Kansas City, Kans.: Ethnic Council, 2000.

"Ten Lessons Kansas City Can Teach the Nation." *Coronet* 39 (November 1955): 79–84.

Terrell, Whitney. *The Huntsman.* New York: Viking Penguin, 2001.

———. *The King of Kings County.* New York: Viking Penguin, 2005.

Thomas, John Clayton. "Kansas City: A City in the Middle." In *Snowbelt Cities: Metropolitan Politics in the Northeast and Midwest since World War II,* ed. Richard M. Bernard. Bloomington: Indiana University Press, 1990, pp. 158–169.

Thomas, Tracy, and Walt Bodine. *Right Here in River City.* Garden City, N.Y.: Doubleday, 1976.

Thruston, Ethylene B. *Echoes of the Past: A Nostalgic Look at Early Raytown and Jackson County.* Kansas City, Mo.: Lowell Press, 1973.

"A Touch of Class in the Heartland." *Time* 108 (August 30, 1976): 38, 41.

Tracy, Walter P. *Kansas City and Its One Hundred Foremost Men.* Kansas City, Mo.: Walter P. Tracy, 1924.

Trillin, Calvin. "U.S. Journal: Kansas City—I Got Nothing against the Colored." *New Yorker* 44 (May 11, 1968): 107–114.

———. *American Fried: Adventures of a Happy Eater.* New York: Doubleday, 1974.

———. "U.S. Journal: Kansas City, Missouri—Reflections of Someone Whose Home Town Has Become a Glamour City." *New Yorker* 50 (April 8, 1974): 94–101.

———. U.S. Journal: St. Louis, Mo.—Regional Thoughts from atop the Gateway Arch." *New Yorker* 56 (June 16, 1980): 104–109.

———. "A Reporter at Large: American Royal." *New Yorker* 59 (September 26, 1983): 57–125.

———. *Messages from My Father.* New York: Farrar, Straus and Giroux, 1996.

———. "Letter from Kansas City: The Bull Vanishes." *New Yorker* 77 (June 11, 2001): 36–41.

———. *Feeding a Yen: Savoring Local Specialties, from Kansas City to Cuzco.* New York: Random House, 2004.

Troutmann, Frederic, ed. "Across Kansas by Train in 1877: The Travels of Ernst von Hesse-Wartegg." *Kansas History* 6 (1983): 142–163.

Trozzolo, Marion A. *Tales of River Quay: A New Old Towne.* Edited by Judy Goodman. Kansas City, Mo.: Bimbi Publications, 1974.

Tuttle and Pike. *Atlas of Kansas City, USA and Vicinity.* Kansas City, Mo.: Tuttle and Pike, 1900.

Tuttle-Ayers-Woodward. *Atlas of Kansas City, Mo. and Environs.* Kansas City, Mo.: Tuttle-Ayers-Woodward, 1925.

Union Historical Company. *The History of Jackson County, Missouri.* Kansas City, Mo.: Birdsall, Williams, 1881.

Unity: 100 Years of Faith and Vision. Unity Village, Mo.: Unity Books, 1988.

U.S. Bureau of the Census. *Report on Population of the United States* (titles vary by year). Washington, D.C.: Government Printing Office, various years.

———. *Urban Atlas: Kansas City, Mo.-Kans. SMSA.* Washington, D.C.: Government Printing Office, 1974.

U.S. Department of Commerce, Weather Bureau. *Kansas-Missouri Floods of June–July 1951.* Technical Paper 17. Washington, D.C.: Government Printing Office, 1952.

U.S. Geological Survey, Water Resources Division. *Kansas-Missouri Floods of July 1951.* Water-Supply Paper 1139. Washington, D.C.: Government Printing Office, 1952.

Van Zandt, Franklin K. *Boundaries of the United States and the Several States.* Bulletin 1212. Washington, D.C.: U.S. Geological Survey, 1966.

Warner, Charles D. "Studies of the Great West: St. Louis and Kansas City." *Harper's New Monthly Magazine* 77 (1888): 748–762.

Way, Henry A. "The Chimera of Kansas: An Exploration of Place, Politics, and Culture." Ph.D. diss., Department of Geography, University of Kansas, 2008.

Webb, William L. *The Centennial History of Independence, Mo.* Independence, Mo.: William L. Webb, 1927.

Weirick, Ray F. "The Park and Boulevard System of Kansas City, Mo." *American City* 3 (1910): 211–218.

Wells, Eugene T. "St. Louis and Cities West, 1820–1880: A Study in Historical Geography." Ph.D. diss., Department of History, University of Kansas, 1951.

———. "The Growth of Independence, Missouri, 1827–1850." *Bulletin of the Missouri Historical Society* 16 (October 1959): 33–46.

"Where Beauty Is Profitable." *Outlook* 98 (1911): 919.

Whitney, Carrie W. *Kansas City, Missouri: Its History and Its People, 1808–1908.* 3 vols. Chicago: S. J. Clarke, 1908.

Whittemore, Margaret. "The Combines Are Humming in Kansas." *Christian Science Monitor Weekly Magazine* (July 26, 1941): 8–9.

"Why Everything's Up to Date in Kansas City." *Business Week* (April 8, 1967): 102–106.

Wilcox, Charles F. "Kansas City as a Musical Center." *Midland Monthly Magazine* 11 (1899): 65–81.

Wild, Edward O., comp. *Kansas City as It Is.* Kansas City, Mo.: Union Bank Note, 1906.

Wilson, Sloan. *The Man in the Gray Flannel Suit.* New York: Simon & Schuster, 1955.

Wilson, William H. "Beginning of the Park and Boulevard Movement in Frontier Kansas City, 1872–1882." *Missouri Historical Review* 56 (1962): 255–273.

———, ed. "The Diary of a Kansas City Merchant, 1874–1880." *Bulletin of the Missouri Historical Society* 19 (1963): 247–259.

———. *The City Beautiful Movement in Kansas City.* Columbia: University of Missouri Press, 1964.

Wohl, R. Richard. "Urbanism, Urbanity, and the Historian." *University of Kansas City Review* 22 (1955): 53–61.

———. "Three Generations of Business Enterprise in a Midwestern City: The McGees of Kansas City. *Journal of Economic History* 16 (1956): 514–528.

Wohl, R. Richard, and A. Theodore Brown. "The Usable Past: A Study of Historical Traditions in Kansas City." *Huntington Library Quarterly* 23 (1960): 237–259.

Woods, Jason M. "A Historical Geography of Kansas City's Jazz District." Master's thesis, Department of Geography, University of Kansas, 2006.

Worgul, Doug. *The Grand Barbecue: A Celebration of the History, Places, Personalities, and Techniques of Kansas City Barbecue.* Kansas City, Mo.: Kansas City Star Books, 2001.

Worley, William S. *J. C. Nichols and the Shaping of Kansas City: Innovation in Planned Residential Communities.* Columbia: University of Missouri Press, 1990.

———. *Development of Industrial Districts in the Kansas City Region: From the Close of the Civil War to World War II.* Kansas City, Mo.: Midwest Research Institute, 1993.

———. *The Plaza: First and Always.* Lenexa, Kans.: Addax Publishing, 1997.

———. *Kansas City: Rise of a Regional Metropolis.* Carlsbad, Calif.: Heritage Media, 2002.

Wright, Herbert P. "Kansas City as an Investment Center." *Harper's Weekly* 57 (June 14, 1913): 23.

Wyman, Walker D. "Kansas City, Mo.: A Famous Freighter Capital." *Kansas Historical Quarterly* 6 (1937): 3–13.

Young, William H., and Nathan B. Young, Jr. *Your Kansas City and Mine* 1950. Reprint, Kansas City, Mo.: Midwest Afro-American Genealogy Interest Coalition, 1997.

Ziegesar, Peter von. "Art in the Heartland." *Art in America* 83 (June 1995): 51–55.

Index